DISCOURSES ON SOCIETY

Sociology of the Sciences

A YEARBOOK – VOLUME XV – 1991

DISCOURSES ON SOCIETY

THE SHAPING OF THE

SOCIAL SCIENCE DISCIPLINES

Edited by

PETER WAGNER

Wissenschaftszentrum Berlin für Sozialforschung

BJÖRN WITTROCK

*Swedish Collegium for Advanced Study in the Social Sciences, Uppsala, and
University of Stockholm*

and

RICHARD WHITLEY

University of Manchester

KLUWER ACADEMIC PUBLISHERS

DORDRECHT / BOSTON / LONDON

ISBN 0-7923-1001-2

Published by Kluwer Academic Publishers,
P.O. Box 17, 3300 AA Dordrecht, The Netherlands.

Kluwer Academic Publishers incorporates
the publishing programmes of
D. Reidel, Martinus Nijhoff, Dr W. Junk and MTP Press.

Sold and distributed in the U.S.A. and Canada
by Kluwer Academic Publishers,
101 Philip Drive, Norwell, MA 02061, U.S.A.

In all other countries, sold and distributed
by Kluwer Academic Publishers,
P.O. Box 322, 3300 AH Dordrecht, The Netherlands.

Printed on acid-free paper

IN MEMORIAM NORBERT ELIAS

Upon being asked, in one of the last interviews he gave, where he thought university-based research and sociology were going, Norbert Elias replied: "The drawback of sociological research – and not only of it alone – is that it marches towards an increasingly pronounced form of specialisation. It is indispensable to give life to a sociology which operates in an interdisciplinary sense, taking account of the other sciences and to base itself upon a conceptualisation of knowledge which does not rest exclusively upon the economy. The shrinking of the horizon of knowledge, the obtuse and obstinate specialisation, is a response which is completely inadequate to the situation in which we find ourselves" ("Marx e Weber, ovvero gli opposti estremismi", di Klaus Davl, *Corriere della sera*, 18 ottobre 1990). Norbert Elias' life-long work and the contributions he made to the Yearbook series as a member of the Editorial Board are in complete agreement with this statement. He saw the sociology of the sciences as an important challenge because it implied that a profound re-thinking of our theory of knowledge was being called for. Knowledge for Norbert Elias, was human-made and consisted of powerful, ever-changing symbols which were used as a means of communication and as a means of orientation. Knowledge was thus interdependently linked with societal processes and the ability for expanded synthesis. It also was an integral part of the civilising process, since scientific knowledge especially entailed a high degree of self-distanciation. But to look for society in social studies of science also meant to render visible the social configurations which impinge upon the development of scientific knowledge. Norbert Elias' interest therefore turned to what for him was their most visible manifestations; scientific hierarchies and what he called scientific establishments. Most scientific work, he maintainded, took place in hierarchical settings, both within an between disciplines, within and between scientific elites and other groups in society. The more or less authoritative nature of scientific establishments shaped the development of scientific knowledge in decisive ways and yet, seen in a long-term perspective, the sciences had succeeded in forming their own relative autonomy, both with regard to older scientific establishments and to other establishments in society. This concern with scientific establishments led to the publication of *Scientific Establishments and Hierarchies* as volume 6 of the Yearbook in 1982.

Norbert Elias was a founding member of the Editorial Board of the Yearbook in the Sociology of the Sciences and played a crucial role in its establishment and development. This commitment was one of the few "professional" functions of this kind which he held in his delayed career and belated recognition. He brought to our meetings his enormous capacity for re-thinking the obvious and the breadth as well as the historical depth of his sociological vision. He also contributed his specific curiosity of approaching science and scientific knowledge via society and social theory, because he was convinced that one would otherwise fall into the trap of being under the hegemonic claims of other scientific disciplines. He excelled in his obstinate way of asking seemingly simple questions and in his tremendous personal warmth and support for our endeavour. The collective style of work adopted by the Editorial Board appealed to him, since he saw in it an expression of the way how scientific knowledge is and ought to be developed.

A great sociologist has gone from us. He professed no academic specialisation in the conventional sense, but his life was his work. We dedicate this volume to his memory.

Helga Nowotny and Richard Whitley
for the Editorial Board

TABLE OF CONTENTS

PART III

The Discourse on Politics between Philosophy, Science, and Profession

PART IV

The Constitution of a Science of Society

PART V

The Institutionalization of Economics: Educational Practices, State Policies, and Academic Recognition

PART VI

Western Social Sciences in Space and Time

ACKNOWLEDGEMENTS

The editors would like to thank the Swedish Collegium for Advanced Study in the Social Sciences and the Wissenschaftszentrum Berlin für Sozialforschung for jointly sponsoring the organisation of the conference at which the contributions to this book originated, held in Berlin, November 9–11, 1989.

PREFACE

This book, which represents probably the most comprehensive discussion of the emergence of modern social science yet produced, is of far more than merely historical interest. The contributors set out to rewrite the history of the social sciences and to show the limitations of conventional conceptions of their development. These tasks they accomplish with great success and much distinction. Yet in so doing they contribute in a direct way to our understanding of the relation between social analysis and the nature of human societies today. The brilliant and distinctive perspective of the papers in this collection is to demonstrate, with many specific examples, that social science and modern institutions have helped shape each other in mutual interplay. Modern systems are in some part constituted through the reflexive incorporation of developing social science knowledge; on the other hand, the social sciences organise themselves in terms of a continuing reflection upon the evolution of those systems. Such a perspective, as Wagner and Wittrock in particular make clear, does not in any way either impugn the status of knowledge claims made within social science or destroy the independent reality of social institutions.

The book questions the notion that the institutionalising of the social sciences can be understood as a process of their increasing autonomy from external social connections. 'Autonomy' forms a mode of legitimation and a basis of power rather than a distinctive phenomenon as such. Moreover, it is a mistake to identify the institutionalising of social science only with the formal recognition of the social science disciplines within the academy. The forging and reforging of links between emerging academic modes of discourse and more practical involvements with other social settings, particularly within the sphere of the state, were, and have remained, of fundamental importance. If political science was most immediately involved in these connections, in some degree they affected

P. Wagner, B. Wittrock, and R. Whitley (eds.), Discourses on Society: Volume XV, 1990, xiii–xv.

the whole of the social sciences. A consequence of this new picture of the formation of modern social science is that much more emphasis than before is placed upon variety and differentiation. The social sciences develop divergently in different countries, and different core conceptions – up to and including systematic variations in what is understood as 'science' – are found. These processes involve contradictory elements, both within and between different countries and disciplines; and the institutionalising of social science is not a simple one-way process, but one which is discontinuous and in which there are sometimes marked reversals.

The essays in this book sound a death-knell for those who hold that social science progressively accumulates knowledge as a result of continuous empirical investigation and more and more sound 'theory building'. The decisive advances in social science as a whole, and in each of the separate social sciences, derive much more from the attempts of thinkers to come to grips with crisis situations in society at large and in the arena of the state. This is a situation, as it were, of mutual appropriation and distancing. New ideas are appropriated by policy-makers and put in the service of attempts at social control or transformation; at the same time, crisis situations serve to energise social reflection. These processes do not, however, bring about a collapse of academic enquiry into practical activity, or the evaporation of practice in favour of analytical knowledge. Rather, processes of mutual appropriation often serve to consolidate both the status of social science disciplines within the academic field and institutional forms within the broader social world. One instance of this, discussed in various places in this book, is to be found in the connections between certain transitions in social science development and the emergence of modern welfare states. The circumstances which originally prompted the emergence of welfare systems were thoroughly permeated by, yet also provided a basic prompting to, innovative developments in social science.

The papers contained in this book not only link up with recent developments in social theory, which in some part inform them, they also help illuminate some of the tasks the social sciences face in the present day. Social science is actively bound up with its 'subject matter', which in some part it helps reflexively to constitute. As all the authors in the book agree, recognition of this phenomenon does not lead us towards an unhappy relativism, in which all truth claims are in some sense contextual. On the contrary, we are led to look for a reconstruction of social science which is both adequate to its own historical development and relevant to the problems which confront us in the contemporary social world. Facing up to these problems may demand as substantial a reorientation of the social sciences as anything documented in these pages for previous periods. We live today in an era of stunning social change, marked by transformations radically discrepant from those of previous periods. The collapse of Soviet-style socialism, the waning of the bi-polar global distribution of power, the formation of intensified global communication systems, the apparent world-wide triumph of capitalism at a time at which global divisions are becoming acute and ecological problems looming more and more large − all these and other issues confront social science and have to be confronted by social science. As the papers in the book demonstrate, we can no longer hold to the view that increasing knowledge about the social and material worlds allows us thereby rationally to control them. The socialisation of nature and the reflexive constitution of social systems are both expressions of intensified human intervention into processes once determined by 'given' conditions. Yet this self-same intervention creates an erratic, runaway world and sets up new types of individual and collective risk which we must face. The social sciences must recognise that they will not consistently be able to generate accurate predictions of global futures, if only because whatever predictions are made enter into the shaping of those very futures.

The conference at which these papers originated was held in Berlin at the exact time at which the Wall was breached, in November 1989. All of us present at the meeting were deeply affected by the feelings of euphoria and release which these events provoked, as well as by the high historical drama that they represented. A world which has shaken free from the freezing dogmas of Cold War is naturally one full of hope. Yet, as with all the main parameters of modernity, opportunity and potential catastrophe intermingle against a backdrop of an uncertain future. The social sciences today, like all forms of human knowledge, participate in that uncertainty and in some degree contribute to its very origins. Understanding how this should be so forms an essential component of any attempt to rethink their concerns and prospects. As the various contributions to this book make clear, grasping their constitutive role in social organisation and transformation is integral to our own self-awareness as social scientists today.

ANTHONY GIDDENS

PART I

THE POLITICS AND EPISTEME OF DISCOURSES ON SOCIETY

CHAPTER ONE

ANALYZING SOCIAL SCIENCE: ON THE POSSIBILITY OF A SOCIOLOGY OF THE SOCIAL SCIENCES

PETER WAGNER AND BJÖRN WITTROCK

Towards a Sociology of the Social Sciences

The historical development of the social sciences is often seen in terms of a gradual liberation from traditional bonds which prevented them from realizing their full potential as producers of true, undistorted knowledge of society. The emancipation of social science is then regarded as a process of institutional autonomization to be accompanied by, and enhancing, scientific maturation in epistemological and methodological terms. In constrast, the contributors to this volume argue that the nature of institutionalization and its alleged consequences have to be questioned on a number of grounds.

First, institutionalization cannot be easily equated with *autonomization* but rather can be seen as a redefinition of the relation of the (social) sciences to various parts of society (1). It is indeed significant that this redefinition occurred largely in terms of the creation of a separate sphere for scientific activity. This was one of the key concerns of the Humboldtian university reforms in the early nineteenth century, and the theme was taken up in other countries later, mostly towards the end of the century (2).

It would, however, be grossly misleading to take the ideology of the scholars and university reformers of the time as a basis for assessing the outcome of these transformations. Pierangelo Schiera focuses explicitly on the institutional and cognitive relation between "science and politics" in Germany and Italy. He clearly brings out the degree of difference between the two constellations and the impact this had on the social sciences. He also shows that the notion of autonomy hardly applies to either of the two cases. The two essays focussing on American social

P. Wagner, B. Wittrock, and R. Whitley (eds.), Discourses on Society: Volume XV, 1990, 3–22.
© 1990 *Kluwer Academic Publishers. Printed in the Netherlands.*

science, by Peter T. Manicas and John G. Gunnell respectively, identify the idea of autonomy of expertise as a social means to validate certain forms of knowledge and to enhance the social status of the knowledge producers (3). In France, as Johan Heilbron shows, different approaches to social science differ dramatically in their degree of autonomy from the power centres of society. These differences are not least related to institutional structures.

Secondly, the institutionalization of the social sciences did not necessarily occur in *academic* forms. The link between social knowledge and social reform that can be identified almost everywhere in Western societies by the mid-nineteenth century did not neatly dissolve into the academic project of a science of society, nor into a functional differentiation of tasks as part of modern society's division of labour (see Helga Nowotny, in this volume). In contrast, the organizational unity of research and teaching in the reformed university, and the continued linkage of this university to political institutions, at least in the state-centered continental European societies, provided the emerging discourses on society with other orientations beyond that to scientific advance. Political profession, educational practice, and state policy were among those other objectives which often proved difficult to reconcile with academic goals.

French political science provides an excellent example of a case in which an intellectual project has subsided when its proponents had to give in to strong societal demands for professional training. To save his institution, the founder of the *Ecole libre des sciences politiques,* Emile Boutmy, in fact largely abandoned his ideas for a political science as a scholarly project. The institutional success of his school had a lasting impact on the shape and image of French political science (4). Among the social science disciplines, political science was most pronouncedly shaped by its orientation towards becoming the administrative profession of the modern nation state. The debates among would-be political scientists about the intellectual profile of their discipline had an extraordinarily wide range – and often a concomitantly low depth – as shown by both John G. Gunnell and Malcolm Vout.

But other disciplinary projects were certainly not free from the vicissitudes of a multiplicity of intellectual and institutional orientations either. Keith Tribe analyses educational practices at English universities and their impact on the cognitive structure of economics around the turn of the century. One important conclusion is that the dominance of neoclassical theory appears to have been less pronounced than later disciplinary historians would like to have it. Once one starts to look beyond one or two major scholars at the overall field and its curricula, the picture changes significantly. Italian economics, as Gabriella Gioli points out, has to be analyzed in terms of the relations between universities and commercial schools, on the one hand, and between university discourse and state policy, on the other. For some periods of social science development, one can even speak of cases in which social science identified with policy objectives. This holds both for late-nineteenth-century German social science and Bismarckian social policy (see Pierangelo Schiera, in this volume) and for post-Second World War Swedish sociology and the model of the welfare state (see Katrin Fridjonsdottir, in this volume).

Thirdly, institutionalization did not always, or even often, occur on the basis of an unequivocal understanding of how a *science* of society should proceed in theoretical or methodological terms. Alain Desrosières analyzes the development of statistics in its relation to sociology and identifies intimate linkages between methodological developments, changes in the notion of the constitutive features of a scientific study of society, and transformations of the state. Peter T. Manicas describes the struggles over the formation of social science associations, and subsequently disciplines, as being waged over different conceptions of social science itself. He brings out the contingent nature of social science conceptions which later came to be taken for granted and to be seen as the very epitomes of scientificity in social science. To a considerable extent, the modern *disciplines* – in particular the "mainstream" approaches in economics, sociology, and psychology – embody different conceptions of science in their organizational distinctions.

It was, however, *fourthly,* not at all predetermined that social science should emerge from the academic and political transformations of the outgoing nineteenth century in a disciplinarily segmented structure. Peter Manicas shows that approaches to a comprehensive, historically oriented social science only gradually gave way to formalized, ahistorical disciplines. And Peter Wagner argues that those intellectual projects commonly labelled, and often praised as, "classical sociology" were in fact the last great attempts for a long time to propose and promote such a comprehensive science of society. They were certainly not ideas suggesting the creation of a narrowly conceived discipline, lacking interest in historical, economic, and political matters, as some of their current sociological successors would like to see it, who are, in fact, often less considerably anchored in the tradition of Durkheim and Weber than the appropriation of these names would seem to suggest.

Finally, though institutionalization meant in fact consolidation, it should not be mistaken to entail complete *stability* over time. As mentioned above, Peter Wagner gives some indications of discontinuities discussing the lost heritage of some important approaches in present sociology. Katrin Fridjonsdottir develops this theme in her analysis of the regional creation of a sociological field after the Second World War. This occurred in intellectual terms which were markedly different from what had seemingly consolidated at the turn of the century. Similarly, Malcolm Vout discusses the two postwar decades as a period of a major transformation of the idea of a political science in England.

Thus, social science in the twentieth century is not well characterized by the notion of smooth intellectual progress after successful institutionalization of the disciplines. Rather, it should be looked at in terms of regionally and intellectually varying continuities and transformations. The period between approximately 1920 and 1960, i.e. between the end of the "formative years" of institutionalized social science and the heyday of a globalized, universal, "modern" social science, stands out as a long transitional phase. While the most recent developments are not in the centre of interest in this volume, the last contribution, by Peter Wagner and Björn Wittrock, adresses key elements of a long-term perspective in the sociology of the social sciences.

In the remaining part of this first chapter, we shall give an overview of the much-needed rethinking of the development of the social sciences as it is reflected in the various contributions in this volume. This theme will be pursued both in terms of national profiles of the structures of intellectual fields and in terms of more specific analyses of how segments of the field were demarcated in institutional and disciplinary terms. In the final two sections, we shall return to the fundamental questions raised at the beginning. We shall ask what the analytical paths taken in this volume entail for the possibility of a sociology and philosophy of the social sciences.

Varieties of National Profiles

The structure of the intellectual field of the social sciences varies considerably across nations. There is no reason to assume that these varieties are deviations from a standard, or delays in reaching that standard. Instead, long-term analyses reveal that national profiles have their roots in the specific intellectual, institutional, and political constellations under which "social scientists" have tried to develop discursive understandings of their societies.

The American case is particularly interesting because it comes closest to the prevalent view on the structure of the social sciences. The argument implicitly made here, in Peter Manicas' analysis, is that the American disciplinary structure has come to be seen as a model, because it could be relatively successfully diffused over the western world, rather than that it became hegemonic worldwide, because it had demonstrated its superior, model-like character in intellectual terms. Thus he rejects the argument that disciplines somehow represent "natural kinds". Instead Manicas develops an historical perspective on the American social sciences which tries to show why they emerged in their particular organizational and cognitive structure under the specific politicoinstitutional conditions of the United States of the late nineteenth century.

Whereas American social science was widely regarded as the norm against which the developments in other countries could and should be assessed, the cognitive orientations of French social science are often seen as odd from the nowadays dominant point of view. One can cite dozens of studies – sometimes sympathetic, sometimes just exhibiting curiosity and bewilderment – which have demonstrated the literary, apolitical character of sociology in France (5), the administration-oriented, professional character of political science (6), and the mixture of neoclassical and engineering thinking in economics (7). All these features have well been observed, but they seem difficult to understand unless an open and long-term historical perspective is taken. Johan Heilbron invokes institutional cleavage lines dating back into the seventeenth and eighteenth centuries to explain the present tri-partite structure of French social science. In the processes of institutional restructurings, transformations of the French state turn out to have had a decisive impact on the cognitive identity of the social sciences.

Such an observation holds similarly for the German and the Italian cases, though the outcomes were different given the specific historical constellations. During the long formative period of the modern social sciences, throughout the nineteenth century, these two societies were culturally and intellectually dominated by the national question, i.e. the debate about the formation of unified nation-states along lines of cultural identities. The completion of these political processes between 1860 and 1870 was followed by increasing industrialization and urbanization towards the end of the century, and by the emergence of the so-called social question. The social sciences, often significantly labelled "state sciences" in Germany, developed in this context essentially as contributions to efforts at solving these questions. They were, in fact, intellectually constituted in terms of their state-orientation, as shown by Pierangelo Schiera.

Juxtaposing the American development of the social sciences, as portrayed by Manicas, with the three examples of Continental European experiences, analyzed by Heilbron and Schiera, the relevance of political structures stands out. In the "state-centred" societies of Europe, the social sciences formed in institutions which were defined by their relation to the state, a state which, to a greater or lesser extent, controlled and supervised them. In the United States, in contrast, the modern universities – often with a tradition of strong presidential leadership (8) – were oriented to cater to the educational needs of diverse groupings. In the leading institutions this certainly occurred with a view to help underpin the further development of the institutions through the support of key sections of societal elites. Early American social science largely grew out of the efforts of parts of some of the traditional elites to assert their positions and, in that process, redefine the political institutions in a period of rapid change.

Being clearly beyond the scope of "unitary, universalistic accounts of scientific knowledge" (9), this feature has mostly escaped studies of social science developments. Interest in such issues can be found in early studies in intellectual history and in socioinstitutional histories of academia. However, only recently have accounts of the social sciences focused on their relation to political institutions (10). We shall not deal with this question in detail in this introduction, but rather return to it at some length in the concluding chapter of the volume.

The variety and persistence of national intellectual profiles, as portrayed here, undermines the assumption of a linear and progressive evolution of the social sciences. But the analysis can be made much more refined by looking at specific transformations of social science discourses, transformations which involved the very understanding of what the social sciences should be about and how they should proceed. The analyses which follow the study of national profiles in this volume are centred around problems of, and struggles over, definition and demarcation of institutionalized social sciences. They involve the very problems that are cognitively constitutive for the social sciences: the nature of "the things political", the possibility of a science of "society", and the understanding of the "economy" and its workings in relation to state and society. The transformations that are analyzed and their outcomes show clearly that the nature and the internal structure of the social science field were, and remain, contested.

Between Philosophy, Science, and Profession: The Discourses on Politics

Disciplinary historians of economics and of sociology had an easy task in constructing a unilinear developmental path compared to those who attempted a similar endeavour for political science. The former could point to Adam Smith and Auguste Comte as founding fathers of, at least, modern understandings of the sciences of the economy and of society. No similar intellectual event can be singled out for political science. Accounts of the roots of the discipline consequently tend to go back to Aristotle and Plato or, with reference to modern thought, to Machiavelli and Hobbes, but they hardly convince their readers that there are direct lines from these political writers to the present discipline.

In part, the problem stems from the very fact that economics and sociology have sprung up – or severed themselves – from the earlier discourses and, by way of their separation, have destroyed that degree of continuity that might have existed (11). Thus, "political economy" was originally the science of governance and no specialized discourse of one sphere of society (12). Adam Smith was a political philosopher who came to diagnose the political relevance of contemporary transformations in economic organization. When it developed momentum in the latter part of the nineteenth century, sociology, in turn, was a reaction to reductions in economic thought, both in methodological and political terms (13).

By the end of the nineteenth century, then, in the midst of the struggles over disciplinary formation, not much was left of "that noble science of politics" (14) that had had a prominent place in intellectual discourse a hundred years before. That earlier science had had very different cognitive orientations from those turn-of-the-century discourses striving for scientific legitimacy. It had either been political philosophy searching for the terms of "good governance", or it had been the systematic study and ordering of the sphere of administrative activities in the tradition of the so-called policy and cameral sciences. Though well established at academic institutions both approaches proved unable to be transformed into a formalized scientific discipline or otherwise enhance their institutional legitimacy in this period of major social and political change.

The debates about a "political science" to be created took different turns in the second half of the nineteenth century. To a large extent, they were geared to providing professional training for increasing numbers of bureaucrats and diplomats in the expanding state institutions, sometimes then labelled "political and administrative sciences". These attempts met with little success in England where a more informal understanding of elite training prevailed (see Tribe in this volume), and in Central Europe where the legal conception of the state predominated and the systematic, scientific study of the state emerged in highly formalized form from the law faculties, as the legal theory of the state (15). Only in France, as mentioned above, did "political science" gain full institutional recognition as a profession without a cognitive core.

In the "stateless" society of the United States (16), the quest for a political science was phrased differently than in Europe. The proponents of such a discipline saw themselves as dealing with the development of some new understanding of governance in this new type of society, namely one without firm, well-entrenched elites and traditional conceptions of the state which could easily be rephrased. As John G. Gunnell shows, the academic discourses on politics in this context developed around the attempt to propose a concept of state – as adapted from the European, in particular German, tradition – as a cognitive means to give historico-institutional meaning to the American notion of "people" and to secure the latter's political coherence.

Both the professional and the scientific understanding of political science of French and American origin, respectively, had an impact on institutional developments in the twentieth century. In interwar Germany, the objective of creating a democratically oriented corps of administrators and party politicians dominated in the early years of the Weimar Republic's College for Politics, founded in Berlin in 1920. The institute developed a research orientation only for a brief period in 1931–33 (17). In England, political philosophy had predominated at the elite institutions in Oxford and Cambridge throughout the first half of the twentieth century. Transformations of the discourse, or "idiom", of political science, as those proposed by Mackenzie, can exactly be understood as the reactions to the passing predominance of traditional elite governance, a mode of governance which had worked without a formal constitution, and to the turn towards more systematic, organized politics under changed political conditions – without losing the ethical bases though, of Oxbridge education (see Malcolm Vout, in this volume).

A number of highly varying, even contradictory objectives entered into the attempts to create an institutionally legitimized discipline of politics. The early "political sciences" held an ambiguous position between traditional political philosophy, empirical-analytical social science, and the core component of an administration-oriented profession.

The Possibility of a Science of Society

In contrast to "political science", attempts to develop a science of society – often but not always labelled "sociology" in the late nineteenth century period – were less defined by a political objective (though such motivations were clearly not absent, see Wagner, in this volume). Their constitutive moment, i.e. their common interest and defining element, is the search for their object, "society".

That something like this actually existed was far from clear. Johan Heilbron shows how such a notion came into being in French discourses, how it was, first, distinct from the church and politics and, second, from the economy. In Germany, in contrast, such a conceptual liberation of society from the state was much more precarious, and in the early twentieth century a sociologist could still be denied a professorship on the grounds that it was both inappropriate and dangerous to establish a concept of society besides those well-understood and appreciated ones of church and state.

The first contested question, thus, for would-be sociologists was the ontological one of developing key concepts for an analysis of the social world. The second and related one was epistemological and methodological, how and with what means to acquire knowledge of the elements of this world. The three essays devoted to these questions, while focusing on different aspects of them at different times in different places, build on one another when inquiring on historical projects for a science of society.

Alain Desrosières links the ontological to the methodological question in his analysis of the relation of the social sciences to statistics. He goes back to, and radically rephrases, Durkheim's statement on the need to see social phenomena as "things" – as social facts, to be precise, i.e., as "things made". He considers statistics, both as a political and as a scientific activity, as the work of making social facts, and relates the development of statistical tools and their application to different phases of state development. The social sciences are, thus, constantly involved in producing the society which they study. A major element of their work, if truly understood as analytic and emancipatory, therefore, has to be the critical questioning of the existing social facts and the mode of their production.

Where Desrosières portrays the activities of sociologists as essentially interrelated with the society of their time, Wagner's analysis focuses on one specific, and significant, period of highly contested sociological work, namely the so-called "classical" one, regularly associated with the constitution of sociology as an academic discipline. It shows the specific interrelation of a society in transformation with the transformation of the discourses about this society, not as a one-to-one reflection, but as the action of the intellectuals involved mediated through the intellectual traditions in which they grew up and the academic institutions in which their discourses were to be placed. "Classical sociology", i.e. the work of scholars such as Max Weber, Emile Durkheim, and Vilfredo Pareto, is characterized by a high degree of awareness of the political crises of their nations and a high sensibility to the epistemological problems of acquiring reliable knowledge about these societies. This awareness and sensibility distinguishes them from the plain and optimistic positivists, who were their predecessors or contemporaries. But their insistence on the possibility of an adequately complex social science also distinguishes them from many of the succeeding generations of intellectuals who either abandoned the project altogether or reduced it to a neopositivist sociology wedded to the organized society of the modern welfare state.

This latter project is dealt with by Katrin Fridjonsdottir in her analysis of the archetypical example of the democratic, capitalist, interventionist welfare state, Sweden, and its sociology. She describes the transformation of sociology from its philosophical origins to an empirical, even empiricist, and service-oriented organized research endeavour (18). It is significant that the latter development was accompanied by the rapid insertion of sociology in the state universities. This parallel of institutional achievement and intellectual transformation occurred during a period in which the harmoniously functioning welfare state, known as "the Swedish model" and founded on basic agreements between employers' and workers' associations under the hegemony of the social democratic party, came to full bloom. From being a practical philosophy trying to understand the condition of humankind, sociology had turned into a "policy science" in search of solutions to social policy problems.

From these observations, which hold in modified ways for a number of other countries as well, one can conclude that sociology experienced its academic "take-off" more than half a century after its initial inception in academic institutions, and that it did so only after an epistemic alliance had been struck with policy interests. Sociologists in the 1950s and 1960s untiringly claimed that their discipline had made decisive advances in terms of methodology and theory. The main references were to the sophisticated quantitative research techniques in the vein of Paul F. Lazarsfeld's work, Talcott Parsons' functionalist theorizing, and the elegant synthesis of both in Robert K. Merton's emphasis on middle-range theory-building. While many practitioners doubtlessly believed in these advances, it is hard to imagine that the institutional breakthrough would have been achieved without the political concomitant of placing sociology in the service of the modern welfare state (19).

Educational Practices, State Policies, and Academic Recognition: Towards the Institutionalization of Economics

During the period in which sociologists were struggling for the recognition of their discipline, economics seemed institutionally well established and intellectually highly "consolidated." In standard histories of economics, no major problems arise after the emergence of the neoclassical approach, apparently solving the theoretical problems of classical political economy. The two contributions to this volume focusing on the economic sciences show, however, that the institutionalization of economics cannot be considered as the inevitable result of the rise in scientific standing due to the "marginalist revolution." The institutional development of economics between its so-called classical and neoclassical eras exhibits striking analogies to the one of sociology between its "first" and "second breakthrough" (20).

Without reference to political circumstances, there are basically two ways of describing intellectual progress in economics in the nineteenth century. Both raise serious problems of interpretation.

One way would be to see in Adam Smith's 1776 volume on "The Wealth of Nations" the cornerstone of the science of political economy. With Smith and his followers, like Ricardo, the discourse was intellectually established; and one could even add that it was so, as might be expected, in the most advanced industrial-capitalist society. But if this argument held, one would still lack an explanation as to why this thinking and teaching was institutionalized only towards the end of the nineteenth century, i.e., a hundred years later and rather parallel to similar moves in other countries. This is how Keith Tribe, in this volume, describes the starting-point of his analysis.

The other standard way of interpretation, which apparently solves this problem, is to see in the move from "classical political economy" to "neoclassical economics", i.e. the thinking introduced by Marshall, Jevons, Menger, and Walras, the decisive step towards a real science. In that case, the timing of the institutionalization of economics would roughly correspond to this achievement, and the working of the rationale of scientific-institutional progress were empirically established. However, any closer look, like those by both Keith Tribe and Gabriella Gioli, in this volume, at the actual processes of institutionalization in England and Italy respectively (21) reveals that it was exactly not the neo-classical discourse which found an institutional basis originally.

Educational practices, oriented to an improved commercial training of the entrepreneurial as well as the working class, and state policies for the promotion of national economic development had a decisive impact on the teaching of economics, as it was introduced in broader scale in the universities towards the end of the nineteenth century. For those reasons, approaches like Historical Economics of the "German" type, public finance and Listian economic theory as well as more technical economic subjects like accounting and banking were often rather preferred to, or at least existed alongside, the rigid deductive thinking of marginalist economic theory.

It was only later, after the broad establishment of these institutional practices, that the image of the economic sciences was seen from the perspective of representatives of the neoclassical approach. Often, however, this view was far from being accurate in institutional terms. While Marshall, in fact, dominated the Cambridge approach, other institutions continued along the established lines (Tribe). Pareto and Pantaleoni, the lauded spokespersons of Italian turn-of-the-century economics, had, in fact, quite a difficult institutional stand (Gioli).

Following these analyses, which distinguish between institutional representation and cognitive orientation, the hypothesis is very plausible that "the teaching of economics in a recognizably modern form is a postwar phenomenon" (Tribe). Economics is marked by cleavages between theoretical work and orientations to the education of professional practitioners and, more recently, to empirical research (22). Economic research is often completely unrelated to the theoretical concerns of the field's core, and is in identifiably lower esteem (23).

In sum, thus, this book strongly argues that conventional assertions of intellectual progress in the history of the social sciences being enhanced through institutional autonomization, scientization, and professionalization do not hold. It does not argue, though (what could be inferred *ex negativo*), that there has been no intellectual progress in the social sciences, or that there can be no way to sensibly talk about it. Even in contrast, it does obviously hold that social science statements can be made about the social sciences. These questions lead to the two final points to be made.

Between Contextualism and Discourse Analysis: The Possibility of a Sociology of the Social Sciences

Over the last two decades, newly emerging currents in the sociology of science have issued theoretical challenges to earlier approaches in the same field and to sociological theorizing in general. In laboratory studies or in the so-called ethnomethodological approach, it has been stressed that earlier sociology of science was based on misconceptions of science. It was claimed that only the direct observation of scientists' activities could reveal "how it really is." In approaches like the "strong programme" the specific character of scientific knowledge as distinct from other types of knowledge has been questioned and the principles of "impartiality" and "symmetry" with regard to knowledge claims have been advanced (24).

These strands of theorizing can be understood as a critical reaction to structural-functionalist and functionalist theorizing, which was reproached of neglecting individual human action in favour of preconceived, coherent macro-theories of society, and as a response to traditional philosophies of science, in which the superiority of scientific knowledge was grounded in specific rationales of research and theoretical activity.

In our view, such critique of the theory and philosophy of sociology was overdue. Convincing challenges to traditional conceptions have been advanced, and many of the critical claims made justify well that any work in sociology of science places itself in relation to these arguments. However, most of the strong positive statements made can hardly be upheld: First, sociology of science should not be methodologically reduced to direct behavioural observation, a reduction which implies theoretical asceticism as well. And, second, it should not give in to fashionable epistemological asceticism, not refuse attempts to give priority of certain discourses over others. The remaining two sections of this introductory chapter will be devoted to discussing these two key questions, which are crucial to any sociology of the social sciences.

Debates about the status of social knowledge, whether scientific or not, have been meandering between two extremes. On the one hand, intellectual activity has often been seen as a mere reflection of social interests, responding immediately and directly to changes in the structure of interest in society. In terms of an implicit functionalism, which can still frequently be found in social science, knowledge transformations are then basically responses to efforts at maintaining and reproducing the structure of society. On the other hand, scientific activities and discourses are often regarded as being endowed with their own logics. Social structures are then absent in this conception. Actors are seen to create their own spheres of action according to their motivations and the material arbitrarily at hand in their immediate environment (25). Or, in a slightly different "text-driven" type of analysis, discourses move without subjects and in accordance with their internal structural properties.

The deficiencies of these extreme modes of conceptualizing should be only too obvious to merit further consideration. But often, scholars are inclined to take their stand-points with regard to the relative deficiencies of earlier work efforts at their own field. Thus, John Gunnell reacts against overly rapid derivations of the development of American political science from the demands of state-building and insists on emphasizing the structure of the actual discourses led by the early American political scientists. What he proposes, however, is far from a study of texts decoupled from the societal contexts they were written in; it is, in this sense, a textually sensitive contextualism. In contrast, Pierangelo Schiera's approach is a response against ways of theorizing implicit in intellectual history, where theories seem to move by their own force or are exclusively carried by extremely gifted, ahistorical individuals. His attempt at putting things right in the analysis of German and Italian social science, therefore, moves into a direction opposite to the one Gunnell takes. The contradiction between their different approaches is, however, more apparent than real; Schiera's analysis of macropolitical constellations is as firmly based on knowledge of the social and political theories of the time as Gunnell's discourse analysis is grounded in an understanding of state developments in nineteenth-century America. The different emphases made in the individual contributions to this volume, of which we have just portrayed the relative extremes, therefore, do not add up to a dissensus. What is exactly needed is that over the full range of such emphases social phenomena are analyzed in terms of human action without losing out of sight the, in part, very durable and very extended constellations in which action takes place and to which it, by necessity, refers. In very broad terms, this is the programme of "structuration theory" whether explicitly proposed under this label in the works of Anthony Giddens or, under the name of "theory of practice," by Pierre Bourdieu. At the present stage, it is the advantage of the former to have developed a truly historical theorizing in his works on the nation-state, for instance, and at the same time the advantage of the latter, for this case, of having contributed to science studies through his analyses of the structure of French science and higher education (26).

The Relativist Critique and Beyond: Towards Critical Realism

Pierre Bourdieu has distinguished himself from many of the recent contributors to the sociology of the sciences by insisting that the conditions for the "progress of reason" are of interest to him (27). The debate on relativism with regard to knowledge claims, aroused by some of the strong statements in science studies, should definitely be taken seriously as an indicator of the general status of the sciences in contemporary society, a status marked by widespread doubts and skepticism, which the sciences, given many of their practices, surely deserve.

But the findings of science studies are often not as directly related to issues in the philosophy of the sciences as their producers tend to think. Shaking the grotesque assumption, still prevalent in the 1960s, that the functional working of the mechanisms of scientific communities is identical to securing the growth of valid knowledge, is one thing; debating the possibility for valid statements at all, another. This difference seems to become increasingly recognized by alleged adherents of the relativist movement themselves. Thus Trevor Pinch, for instance, writes, commenting on the positions of his colleagues: "In order for any claim to be made, some areas of discourse must be privileged.... Bloor in effect privileges his own discourse, Collins privileges social science discourse, and Mulkay, Woolgar, and Ashmore claim to privilege nothing at all, and thereby as far as I can see claim nothing at all" (28).

To avoid being caught in such a reflexivity trap, the only way is to continue the deconstruction of knowledge claims by a move towards reconstruction. One of the contributors to this volume, Peter Manicas, has, in fact, tried to get the sociology of scientific knowledge "straight" by showing that these arguments can be reconciled with and actually only sensibly understood in the context of a transcendental realist philosophy of the social sciences (29).

We shall not go deeper into this debate here but shall conclude the argument by pointing to that contribution which tackles it most explicitly. Alain Desrosières's paper is a good example to show that a realist interpretation of the "strong programme" is feasible. Against a first intuition, Desrosières does not embark on a free-floating constructivism of "making things," but a socially situated constructivism of making "things which hold together." Thus, he poses exactly the question of the social conditions for the possibility of knowledge claims to be made. Pursuing this argument, he comes up with a fairly strong sociological concept of the state, as being constructed and reconstructed over long periods of time, and, at a given point in time, rather stable, really existing, and capable of "holding things together."

Such a statement is grounded in a "structuration theory" of society, and based on a "critically realist" epistemology. This seems to be the direction to pursue further, in the sociology of the social sciences, and in social theory at large.

Notes

1. For a comparative account of the increasing distance of academic institutions to other societal institutions see Rolf Torstendahl, "The Transformation of Professional Education in the 19th Century", in: Sheldon Rothblatt and Björn Wittrock, eds., *The Three Missions. Universities in the Western World,* forthcoming.
2. See for Germany, McClelland, *State, Society and University in Germany, 1700–1914,* Cambridge, Cambridge University Press, 1980; for France, George Weisz, *The Emergence of Modern Universities in France, 1861–1914,* Princeton, Princeton University Press, 1983; for the U.S., Alexandra Oleson and John Voss, eds., *The Organization of Knowledge in Modern America, 1860–1920,* Baltimore, Johns Hopkins University Press, 1979; for Italy, Antonio la Penna, "Università e istruzione pubblica", in: *Storia d'Italia,* Vol. V.2, Torino, Einaudi, 1973.
3. Both authors go, thus, considerably beyond the standard accounts of "professionalization" of the social sciences (see, e.g., Thomas S. Haskell, *The Emergence of Professional Science,* Urbana, University of Illinois Press, 1977;

Mary O. Furner, *Advocacy and Objectivity: A Crisis in the Professionalization of American Social Science 1865–1905*, Lexington, University Press of Kentucky, 1975; Dorothy Ross, "The Development of the Social Sciences", in: Alexandra Oleson and John Voss, eds., *The Organization of Knowledge in Modern America, 1860–1920*, Baltimore, Johns Hopkins University Press, 1979) and relate social strategies of intellectuals to institutional possibilities and cognitive contents. For a related perspective, in English-American comparison, see Libby Schweber, "Social Policy-Making and the Institutionalization of Social Science in Britain and the United States", in: Dietrich Rueschemeyer and Theda Skocpol, eds., *Social Knowledge and the Origins of Modern Social Policies*, forthcoming.

4. See Pierre Favre, "Les Sciences de l'Etat entre déterminisme et libéralisme", in: *Revue Française de Sociologie*, **22**, No. 3, 1981, and Johan Heilbron, in this volume.

5. A well-informed example of this species is Charles C. Lemert, "Reading French Sociology", in: Charles C. Lemert, ed., *French Sociology, Rupture and Renewal Since 1968*, Columbia University Press, New York, 1981, and "Literary Politics and the Champ of French Sociology" in: *Theory and Society*, **10**, No. 5, 1981.

6. Besides the works of Favre, already mentioned, one should name Jean Leca, "La science politique dans le champs intellectual français", in: *Revue Française de Science Politique*, **32**, No. 4–5, 1982, for instance.

7. Joseph A. Schumpeter, a keen observer of developments in the economic sciences in the first half of this century, already noted this peculiarity: *History of Economic Analysis*, London, 1955. See otherwise Lucette LeVan-Lemesle, "L'économie politique à la conquête d'une légitimité", in: *Actes de la recherche en sciences sociales*, No. 47/48, 1983, and Pierre Rosanvallon, "Histoire des idées keynésiennes en France", in: *Revue Française d'Economie*, **2**, No. 4, 1987.

8. Martin Trow, "Leadership and Organization: The Case of Biology at Berkeley", in: Rune Premfors, ed., *Higher Education Organization: Conditions for Policy Implementation*, Stockholm, Almqvist and Wiksell, 1984, pp. 148–178.

9. Richard Whitley, "The Structure and Context of Economics as a Scientific Field", in: *Research in the History of Economic Thought and Methodology*, **4**, 1986; p. 186.

10. Examples of the former kind are Hans Maier, *Die ältere deutsche Staats- und Verwaltungslehre*, Munich, Beck, 1980 (first 1966); Norberto Bobbio, "Profilo ideologico del novecento", in *Storia della letteratura*, Vol. 9, Milan, Garzanti, 1969; and Fritz K. Ringer, *The Decline of the German Mandarins*, Boston, Harvard University Press, 1969; for the latter, Pierangelo Schiera, *Il laboratorio borghese. Scienza e politica nella Germania dell'Ottocento*, Bologna, Il Mulino, 1987; Peter Wagner, *Sozialwissenschaften und Staat*, Frankfurt/M. Campus, 1990; and to some extent Giorgio Sola, "Sviluppi e scenari della sociologia italiana, 1861–1890", in: Giorgio Sola and Filippo Barbano, *Sociologia e scienze sociali in Italia, 1861–1890*, Milan, Angeli, 1985.

11. This observation points to the very impossibility to give an historical-sociological account of the development of "political science" as a disciplinary discourse on its own. Even more than the other current disciplines, the discourses on politics were an inseparable part of the intellectual field of the social sciences at large.

12. The notion goes back to the mercantilist type of state regulation of the economy; see James E. King, "The Origin of the Term 'Political Economy'", in: *The Journal of Modern History*, **20**, 1948. Its connotations prevailed until far into the nineteenth century; see the respective remarks by Gioli and Tribe in this volume. It was only Marshall who in his 1890 volume on the "Principles of Economics" explicitly tried to rid the subject of its political character.
13. See Göran Therborn, *Science, Class and Society*, Göteborg, Revopress, 1974; Geoffrey Hawthorn, *Enlightenment and Despair. A History of Sociology*, Cambridge, Cambridge University Press, 1976; and Wagner in this volume.
14. Stephan Collini *et al.*, *That Noble Science of Politics. A Study in 19th Century Intellectual History*, Cambridge, Cambridge University Press, 1983.
15. See Pierangelo Schiera in this volume, as well as Kenneth H.F. Dyson, *The State Tradition in Western Europe*, Oxford, Robertson, 1980; Peter von Oertzen, *Die soziale Funktion des staatsrechtlichen Positivismus*, Frankfurt/M. Suhrkamp, 1974; Cesare Mozzarelli and Stefano Nespor, *Giuristi e scienze sociali nell'Italia liberale*, Venice, Marsilio, 1981, and Peter Wagner *op. cit.*
16. To use the problematic term introduced by J.P. Nettl, "The State as a Conceptual Variable", in: *World Politics*, **20**, 1968, pp. 559–592; for a discussion of the more-or-less state-oriented character of societies see Bertrand Badie and Pierre Birnbaum, *The Sociology of the State*, Chicago, University of Chicago Press, 1983 (French original 1979); Dieter Grimm, "The Modern State: Continental Traditions", in: Franz-Xaver Kaufmann, Giandomenico Majone, Vincent Ostrom, eds., *Guidance, Control and Evaluation in the Public Sector*, Berlin, De Gruyter, 1986.
17. On the College see Ernst Jaeckh, *Die "alte" Hochschule für Politik*, Berlin, Büxenstein, 1952; Detlef Lehnert, "'Politik als Wissenschaft': Beiträge zur Institutionalisierung einer Fachdisziplin", in: *Politische Vierteljahresschrift*, **30**, No. 3, 1989, pp. 443–465, for example.
18. For ways of characterizing similar transformations in other countries see Jean Stoetzel, "Sociology in France: An Empiricist View", in: Howard Becker and Alvin Boskoff, eds., *Modern Sociological Theory in Continuity and Change*, New York, Holt Rinehart and Winston, 1956; and Theodor W. Adorno, "Zum gegenwärtigen Stand der deutschen Soziologie", in: *Kölner Zeitschrift für Soziologie und Sozialpsychologie*, **11**, 1959, on Germany and France, with different, almost opposite evaluations.
19. For a development of this argument with reference to Continental European experiences see Peter Wagner, "The Place of the Discourse on Politics among the Social Sciences", in: Kari Palonen, ed., *Politics: Texts, Concepts, Languages*, Helsinki, Finnish Political Science Association, 1990.
20. For these notions, referring to the 1890s and the 1960s and developed for the case of French sociology, see Johan Heilbron, *Sociologie in Frankrijk*, Amsterdam, SISWO, 1983.
21. For other countries see William Barber, ed., *Breaking the Academic Mould: Economists and American Higher Education in the 19th Century*, Middletown, Wesleyan University Press, 1988; Lucette LeVan-Lemesle, *op. cit.*; Norbert Waszek, ed., *Die Institutionalisierung der Nationalökonomie an deutschen Universitäten*, St. Katherinen, Scripta Mercuriae, 1988.

22. Professional orientation marks the field of sociology to a considerable extent only in the U.S. and the Netherlands, to a minor extent in Sweden and Germany, where, however, orientations to research and theory prevail. In Sweden, new professional disciplines like social welfare emerge outside sociology proper. Such development is reminiscent of social administration occupying the space for an absent sociology in interwar England.

23. For an analysis of post-Second World War economics in these terms see Richard Whitley, *op. cit.*

24. This is not the place to give a detailed analysis of recent sociology of science. We have made such an attempt ourselves in Peter Wagner and Björn Wittrock, *Social Sciences and Societal Developments*, Berlin, Wissenschaftszentrum für Sozialforschung, Paper P 87–4, 1987; other critical overviews are Richard Whitley, "From the Sociology of Scientific Communities to the Study of Scientists' Negotiations and Beyond", in: *Social Science Information*, **22**, No. 4/5, 1983, pp. 681–720; Steven Shapin, "History of Science and Its Sociological Reconstruction", in: *History of Science*, **20**, 1982, pp. 157–211; Karin Knorr-Cetina and Michael Mulkay, "Introduction: Emerging Principles in Social Studies of Science", in: Karin Knorr-Cetina and Michael Mulkay, eds, *Science Observed*, London, Sage, 1983, pp. 1–17; with special regard to social science, Wolfgang Bonsz and Heinz Hartmann, "Konstruierte Gesellschaft, rationale Deutung. Zum Wirklichkeitscharakter soziologischer Diskurse", in: Wolfgang Bonsz and Heinz Hartmann, eds., *Entzauberte Wissenschaft, Sonderband 3 der Sozialen Welt*, Göttingen, Schwartz, 1985.

25. It should be clear that our critique does not amount to saying that such studies should not be continued. While ethnomethodology in science studies at large has in fact been running empty, in our view, we would find it useful to extend this research to social scientists' activities; observing how they code their data, write their texts, listening to what they talk about. In this volume, Alain Desrosières's contribution is clearly most informed by this research orientation, though he does not develop it himself.

26. On other occasions we have tried to sketch how a theory of "discourse structuration" in the social sciences would look like; see Björn Wittrock, Peter Wagner and Hellmut Wollmann, "Social Sciences and Modern States", in Peter Wagner, Carol H. Weiss, Björn Wittrock and Hellmut Wollmann, eds. *Social Sciences and Modern States*, Cambridge, Cambridge University Press, 1990; Björn Wittrock and Peter Wagner, "Social Sciences and State Developments", in Stephen Brooks and Alain G. Gagnon, eds., *Social Science, Policy and the State*, New York, Praeger, 1990; and Peter Wagner, "Social Science and the State in Continental Western Europe", *International Social Science Journal*, **36**, No. 4, 1989, pp. 509–528; and Wagner, *Sozialwissenschaften, op. cit.* See also Chapter 13 in this volume.

27. Pierre Bourdieu, "The Specificity of the Scientific Field and the Social Conditions of the Progress of Reason", in: *Social Science Information*, **14**, No. 6, 1975, pp. 19–47.

28. Trevor Pinch and Trevor Pinch, "Reservations about Reflexivity and New Literary Forms: Or Why Let the Devil Have All the Good Tunes", in: Steve Woolgar, ed., *Knowledge and Reflexivity*, London, Sage, 1987.

29. Peter T. Manicas and Alan Rosenberg, "Naturalism, Epistemological In-
dividualism and the 'Strong Programme' in the Sociology of Knowledge", in:
Journal for the Theory of Social Behavior, **15**, 1985, and Peter T. Manicas and
Alan Rosenberg, "The Sociology of Scientific Knowledge: Can We Ever Get It
Straight", in: *Journal for the Theory of Social Behavior*, **18**, No. 1, 1988, pp.
51–76; as well as his *History and Philosophy of the Social Sciences*, Oxford,
Blackwell, 1987. See also Roy Bhaskar, *The Possibility of Naturalism*, Brighton,
Harvester, 1979, and *Reclaiming Reality*, London, Verso, 1989.

CHAPTER TWO

KNOWLEDGE FOR CERTAINTY:
POVERTY, WELFARE INSTITUTIONS AND
THE INSTITUTIONALIZATION OF SOCIAL SCIENCE

HELGA NOWOTNY

Social Science as Discourse Systems: Knowledge Formed and Transformed with the Help of Institutions

The emergence of the modern, secularized nation-state and the firm installment of capitalism in the wake of massive industrialization were extremely powerful forces in shaping Western societies. It is now widely recognized that the social sciences were intimately linked with these developments, especially from the later part of the nineteenth century onwards. They not only provided searching interpretations for the far-ranging transformations witnessed by contemporaries, but also offered advice and various 'solutions' for the social ills which accompanied the processes of industrialization and urbanization. Social scientists were engaged in a lively and passionately conducted debate either by pressing for reforms and new kinds of collective schemes, by lobbying, polemicizing or as political activists in the name of those who suffered most. Once, however, new collective arrangements of social protection had been set up more or less efficiently to help people cope with the deficiencies and adversities which afflicted them on a massive scale, once the emergent welfare state began to take shape with its service bureaucracies, social security and other transfer-payment schemes, collective health care and education, expert knowledge was needed to administer, monitor, expand and readjust these arrangements.

In the course of the past century, as de Swaan and others have shown, teaching, healing and helping have become almost exclusively the province of highly organized groups within the state and at its periphery.

P. Wagner, B. Wittrock, and R. Whitley (eds.), Discourses on Society: Volume XV, 1990, 23–41.
© 1990 Kluwer Academic Publishers. Printed in the Netherlands.

The avenue into their ranks was through formal education, by means of cultural capital accumulated during the long march through the teaching institutions which originated in an earlier wave of collectivization and state regulation. The resources of these experts consist in formally recognized knowledge, made certifiable and interchangeable through diplomas (1). For a large part, the kind of expert knowledge underlying the professionalization of welfare services and buttressing the expert regime was social science knowledge. Moreover, the emergence of expert regimes affected the basic stances and concepts with which people handled their day-to-day interaction and experience: it led to what de Swaan calls protoprofessionalization, to ways in which patients, clients, schoolchildren but also the public at large "learned" in a simplified and censored version professional expert knowledge which was transmitted to them in a continuous formative and informative practice (2).

Such a widely cast view of the interconnections between social science knowledge, state formation, the rise of expert regimes and their knowledge base as well as its effects on general social awareness and knowledge in turn, provides the historical backcloth against which a more narrowly defined interlinkage is to be analyzed here: the process of institutionalization of the social sciences as professionalized discourse systems owes as much to the "solutions" which finally emerged through the process of collectivization of protection and care and which it had helped to put into place, as to the public discourse with its social knowledge base which preceded it and which it superseded. The rise of the social sciences as academic disciplines has been a highly uneven process, both when compared among countries and across various disciplines. There can be no question, however, that this rise was linked to the collective administrative arrangements which came to culminate in the welfare state (both, in its "earlier" form with the installation of a quasi-universal social security system and in the fullblown version in which it emerged after the Second World War). Rather than solely inquire about institutional arrangements and how they came to be implemented, the social discourse which preceded, accompanied and continued to shape these arrangements and institutions allows one to interpret the social sciences as a discursive concomitant to the vast increase in administrative and communicative capacities which characterize the new type of state formation in the late nineteenth and early twentieth centuries (3).

The analysis of social discourse presupposes producers and carriers of discourse, but equally themes of discourse. They emerge from underlying conflicts and problems and are defined and shaped by those who engage in discourse. A long-term historical view backwards should therefore allow for a better understanding as to how certain key "themes" in society gradually took shape – by being named, recognized, interpreted; by providing possible guides for collective action to be fought about by competing elites, but also themes for the worker's movement struggle against the established powers of industry and the state. The social sciences partook on these long-term concomitant processes in two, quite different roles: *first* by helping to shape the societal discourse, to name and interpret the overriding theme that deeply unsettled society, by tracing it back to forces and processes that were seen as causing the "tourbillion social", out of which only gradually measures of intervention and effective control arose. It was a mode of discourse which authorized and legitimated a world shaken by the Great Transformation. When attempting to make this discourse intelligible to other collective actors, social scientists were equally drawn into helping to shape the collective arrangements which eventually were to become society's answers to the profound uncertainties which had beset it. The *second* role, assumed only at a later stage, was that of giving expert advice, of acting and enacting qua their professionalized expertise how the institutions which had been set up in the meantime were to be managed and to monitor the effects they would have on wider society.

The emergence of the modern social sciences clearly reflected wide-spread concerns about the enormous social problems to which the processes of industrialization and urbanization as well as the emergence of the market had given rise. These new forms of knowledge dealt with possible new institutional arrangements of social security and care. Such arrangements were only gradually and unevenly installed in different political settings after decades of political conflicts. Generally, they tended to lead to considerable increases in the power of state administrations. The social sciences can be seen to assume different functions in subsequent phases of historical development, as briefly described above. They also oscillate between phases of relative certainty within society about societal directions and phases of deeply unsettling insecurities with regard to society's future, goals and ways of achieving them, as will be described below. In their origins, however, and in recurrent periods of relative uncertainty, they reveal themselves as organized systems of discourse in close vicinity to quite different carriers of other modes of discourse and action. Out of these vicinities *three different* kinds of discourse systems *within* the social sciences have emerged which are still actively being pursued today, although content and style have changed considerably.

One is the mode of discourse which accepts as its leading concepts and categories those which are most useful in the daily routine of administration and politics. It is a mode of discourse which is apt to use a quantitative approach, culminating in an elaborate system of social statistics. Counting, weighing and measuring whatever the state deems important, laying the foundations for making it possible, aggregating and disaggregating figures and indices in order to make them useful inputs for the political discourse and rhetoric as well as fitting them into administrative decision-making frameworks – this mode of largely quantitative statistical discourse remains attractive as well as indispensible in all policy arenas in which the state was able to install itself as administrator and regulator. Its origins can be traced to the period which will be described below, when counting and measuring the poor, providing empirical and quantitative evidence for the degree, kinds and areas of depravation of the population, became one way of attempting to cope – by initiating reforms with the help of quantitative arguements – with the social ills unleashed by the dire consequences of industrialization. The *other* mode of social science discourse still actively pursued to this very day is located in close vicinity to discourse as it runs through social movements. It is a discourse highly committed to letting the poor speak for themselves or to speaking in their name; to unmasking hypocrisy and illusion, to demystifying the official reality of social phenomena and to renaming them by recurring to another, allegedly more authentic version thereof; to producing counterexpertise, opposed to the "disciplinary" expertise of professional groups and the control exerted by state and state administration. The *third* mode of social science discourse is the academically "purified" and systematized version, with social scientific knowledge moving as far as it could into the vicinity of knowledge as it is produced by the natural sciences. Whether it takes the form of "theory" or of mathematical modelling, it is committed "not to making the world a better place to live in", but to pursuing the discoveries, if not of scientific laws, at least of generalizations of social phenomena (4). This mode of discourse too has its roots in early social sciences, when emulating the discovery of the equivalent of natural laws in society provided a strong incentive and temptation as to how the transformations which were witnessed could be adequately described, named and interpreted in the name of science. While one can clearly recognize institutionalized and semi-institutionalized forms of these modes of social science discourse today, whereby institutionalization takes place both within and at the periphery of academic institutions, they were all intermingled in the founding stage. Social science discourse only gradually succeeded in superimposing itself upon general public discourse by becoming professionalized and institutionalized. It did so concomitantly with the rise of those institutions which were built as part of the expansion of the modern state and as response to the unsettling effects which had created deep uncertainty within all segments of society. The institutionalization of a proper and systematized social science discourse system, whether fully incorporated into the academic system or remaining at its periphery, can therefore also be interpreted as a kind of channelling or "disciplining" of an ultimately too free-ranging social discourse system. By bringing it under control, by transforming it, partly at least, into an academic "discipline" and into expert knowledge certified and controlled through professional bodies, it was made "useful" for and by the institutions it had helped to create in the first place. It was also made "useful" – although to a lesser degree and in a different sense – for those, who were to become clients and patients and – especially after World War II – the employees of these institutions.

The Debate on Poverty:
The Loss of Certainty and the Search for New Reassurance (5)

When reconstructing the main debates as they had been conducted in Germany and England during and especially in the last part of the nineteenth century as well as following the social policy attempts with which these societies were searching to cope with the consequences of the expansion of the market and the industrial system, one is struck by one dominant theme: it is the pervasive sense of loss of certainty and the groping atempts to find new forms of reassurance. It is manifest in public debates, in theoretical as well as empirical writings, but equally present in the general social consciousness of the time as well as in the search for finding new institutional arrangements. The early poverty debate is overshadowed by the question as to the future development of society as a whole; in the attitudes towards the poor attitudes about the survival of society increasingly became reflected (6). The social effects of the technical and industrial development of the time – leading to widespread poverty, unemployment, urbanization and the concomitant uprooting of

people, their loss of social identities as well as the acute threat they were
seen to embody for the established classes – were felt as profound loss of
certainty and of security. They underscore why certain approaches to the
very problems from which social science as an organized discourse
system originated were undertaken and how they were transformed into
"solutions" to which the century-long construction of the welfare state
was devoted. Seen from a long-term perspective a prolonged social
learning process of coping with uncertainty can be discerned: a constant
oscillation between the temptation to cling to meta-social and meta-
historical guarantees of social order and of establishing new notions of
social reassurance, which would help people to regain security, their
social identities and social competence. Ultimately, it would transform
them into becoming citizens, equipped with political and social rights.
The poverty debate served to crystallize and highlight a key theme and
problem which was the strategic axis around which both early social
science developed its understanding of society and the working of societal
mechanisms and around which state administration and professional
bodies developed their competence and expertise for intervening and
shaping society.

Looking backwards upon this tormented period of social history and
societal development two main questions stand out. One seeks to answer
the nature of the collectivizing process: how and why did people come to
develop collective, nationwide and compulsory arrangements to cope with
deficiencies and adversities that appeared to affect them separately and, at
least initially, to call for individual remedies? (7) The second question
deals with the conditions under which the process of collectivizing social
protective and care arrangements arose: the conditions of uncertainty (8).
How did people overcome the profound uncertainties which threatened to
affect them with all their negative consequences for which poverty had
become the epitomizing condition? How was it possible to turn dangers
and threats – sudden loss of work and income, of health and life, of social
identity and one's feeling of belonging – into what were to become
socially defined, regulated and subsequently partially "normalized
dangers" – namely calculable (social) risks? The dangers were of two
kinds: primarily they threatened and afflicted the "poor", who later came
to be divided into the "workers" and the "residual poor". But in turn, the
mere existence of the poor under conditions of severe deprivation came to
be seen as a major threat also to that minority which was seen to govern
and to exploit them. The "morally depraved poor" could no longer be

trusted to remain in their position of subservience. Hence, the entire fabric of social order was in grave danger.

A macrosociological perspective thus suggests a viable approach to historical problems relating to the interaction of both social sciences and societal development. For the question of *what* becomes a *problem* in society and *how,* and *how* social science reacts by naming it, and taking it up as a problem, constitutes the framework for the more technical and empirical approaches and eventual "solutions" offered by the social sciences. Only through the wider process of problem awareness, the identification and interpretation of events and processes thought to be problematic and to have brought old certainties and securities to the breaking point, is the way made for new scientific and socio-technical problem-solving models. Only if the way of looking at the problem eventually succeeds in requiring a political answer, by being experienced collectively, and by stirring public sentiment as well as by leading to new coalitions among competing elites, are avenues opened up for the introduction and application of common approaches to the problem in question. The concept of "applied sciences" presupposes that there already exists a consensus for which kind of research is needed, as well as for its intended direction and expectations of results. If application is successful, it clarifies the point of orientation from which solutions and practical modalities of action begin to emerge. Yet, history clearly shows that even the most ingenious constructions of reality are limited. Therefore the framework of certainty wherein applied science can function has to be seen as one which is a reversible condition: certainties can be eroded again, breaks occur and new certainties will then have to be reconstructed. This is a result of the real power balances as well as of the nature of the constructions themselves. The central concept of "poverty", the transformation of its meaning as a scientific and political construct by putting it up against the other competing central concept of "work", portrays an instructive example for a process, where various actors, coping with their uncertainty through the utilization of different concepts of "poverty" or "work", rebuild the framework of certainties through which applied science gets its meaning.

When searching through the enormous amount of literature on the topic of poverty which accumulated first in England and later in Germany from the early nineteenth century onwards, one has to bear in mind that an institutionalized social science discourse system did not yet exist. Therefore, the boundaries between autodidacts, like Malthus, whose controversial writings brought him sudden fame and continued to influence public opinion, and well-installed German professors like Mohl, whose publications led to his ungracious dismissal, remained fluid. They ranged over a wide field of philosophy, political economy, the craftman-ship of collecting and classifying statistical data and information; they encompassed social engineering approaches like those professed by factory inspectors, medical doctors, municipal civil servants and others just as much as moral treatises. The core of a social science discourse on poverty and pauperism can perhaps be located within the categories of political economy. Yet there were important contributions coming from medicine and hygiene. Statistics and empirical surveys documenting in detail the living and working conditions of the poor helped to complete the picture. In all these writings and data collections, the knowledge base was rather broad, and it is hardly possible at this stage to distinguish a specific social scientific knowledge from other kinds. Yet, social scientific knowledge was to emerge, from its semi-literal form, as practised in pamphlets and political reformist tracts, and from its semi-statistical form, as collected and put together from detailed descriptions as well as the early fore-runners of social surveys. It was also to emerge from the social knowledge base existing within the working-class movements and their forerunners. Almost by default, it had to remain open in its categories and visions, in its empirical roots and observational tools, towards all other forms of discourse, including the social knowledge generated by and reproduced through social movements and reform-minded state administrators. The categories of social science and their observational tools were therefore in competition with and had to remain open towards other forms of discourse and observations rooted both in the everyday experience of those who were themselves affected by the conditions described, and the knowledge and experience of those who wished to set up new institutional arrangements (9). It was not only the lack of institutionalized academic boundaries in the period under consideration which made for such openness. Rather, it was the specific state in which societal arrangements found themselves in a phase of profound uncertainty, when old guaranteeing concepts of orders and institutional arrangements had begun to crumble, making way for something which initially did not even have a name.

Loss of Certainty: The Impact on Social Science Discourse

Social science discourse systems, whether already professionalized and "academized" or not, rely to a great deal on rhetoric, on conceptual definitions and interpretations (10). To name certain aspects of social reality and to define them means to grasp them – the first step in order to make social reality disposed towards political and social intervention, to impose administrative rules on it, policies and in more modern terminology, management strategies. Yet whenever social reality, as it has become familiar and taken for granted, is subject to abrupt changes, to breaks in continuity, uncertainty sets in. Social science knowledge begins to lose its conceptual grip and while the technical handles of administration and routine management still may continue to turn, there is a widespread feeling of lost motion, of waste and loss of purpose as well as of direction. The poverty debate illustrates vividly such a period, in which social reality was overturned and seen to dismantle with new structures arising and with consequences that no one had foreseen. Pauperism or destitution, as it became known, was the most immanent, tangible and threatening of them. It undermined the social identities of the vast majority of the population with "moral degradation" setting in, and it threatened to undermine the very basis of societal order when the poor propertyless came to be seen as an imminent danger for those with property. For the contempory observers the connection with the rise of the market and the speedily proceeding process of industrialization were clear – but where would it all lead to? Was it merely a transitory phase through which society was passing, or were the newly prevalent disorders the necessary conditions for a newly created social and economic order, an admittedly high price which had to be paid?

In such periods of profound uncertainty, social science concepts and discourse systems also loose the ascertaining legitimizing function which they hold in periods of "normal" stability and under reasonable conditions of overall material and social security. They can no longer provide the basic, consensus-building "orientation knowledge" which assures society and its members that they have indeed embarked on the road towards further societal progress. Uncertainty also befalls the social sciences. It is in such periods of search for new orientations that social science discourse systems are relatively open for other kinds of knowledge and discourse systems. The everyday knowledge and experience of those who are attempting to regain certainty by self-assurance, as it occurs in social movements which also provide an instrument for the construction of new social identities, may well be ahead of the more systematic discourse systems in periods of upheaval and accelerated change. This is precisely what happened with the key conceptual distinction which was to emerge out of the mass of the poor: "workers" came to claim their own special status and indentity, they were eventually able to gain new rights and to have diffuse dangers turned into calculable risks against which they were protected through a collective and compulsory social security system. The concept of "work" became a leading concept also within the social sciences, as well as the linch-pin of the entire social security system. Yet it is important to see that the legitimatory and reassuring function of the social sciences is heavily dependent on a societal context which retains a validating control over any social scientific discourse. If the societal context changes in unexpected, bewildering and threatening ways, social science discourse is also in a period of searching for reassurance and ways to regain both its own certainties of knowledge and its reassuring function with regard to the social order.

It is one of the characteristics of social science as discourse system, already apparent in its incipient stage in the nineteenth century, that it cannot escape to take a stand *vis-à-vis* the transformations that are at work in society. To the degree that the basic certainties of the old cultural and orientating framework of attitudes, values and standards of behaviour have been shaken, if not lost, the preconditions of social science discourse are also rapidly eroding. Where to go next, what order is to be restored or newly constructed? Either the continuous validity of traditional values, norms and behaviour had to be legitimized and hence defended or the necessity of the already existing validity of a new order had to be proven. Hence different value and policy-orientations were to emerge and the poverty debate was phrased within these cultural orientations: lack of basic consensus, of a common framework of understanding, is translated into divergent paths of action which are advocated accordingly.

In Germay especially, an agrarian romanticism was strongly represented (11). Its analysis of poverty and degradation was linked to the belief that an option to return to previous stabilities and the stable balances of rural economic and social life existed. The industrial system itself was characterized as a "reversible, historical error" (12). But there were also strong voices, especially in the intermediate realm of social surveys and reporting, of reform attempts and political activism with scientific means, who did no longer believe that the new industrial system could be abolished. They sought ways to reconcile forms of rural life-styles, with their protective care arrangements, with the new industrial culture. They thought it feasible that small producers could and should survive under the new conditions, just as in some large cities attempts were made for re-implanting housing schemes which sought to imitate rural life-styles (13). But there were also the optimists, who full-heartedly agreed and supported the new industrial system. They, like the British economists of the eighteenth century, believed that either poverty would vanish once the market system reigned supreme or that progress and poverty went hand in hand, with poverty being an integral part of increasing the wealth of nations (14). There were, however, also attempts to explain poverty with the help of approaches taken from biology and in particular eugenics. Demoralization, alcoholism, ignorance and laziness were "explained" as consequences of the biological laws of inheritance. These approaches, which began in the middle of the nineteenth century and were to reach a first climax towards its end, represent an extreme case of regaining certainty by "scientific means": they issued a certified "good consciousness" for society, for it was the poor's fault if they reproduced, but also other, more repressive practices against certain categories of the poor could now be justified in the name of "science" (15).

From Deterministic Social Laws to the Discovery of the Shapeability of Society (16)

Which type of order is to be newly established? An order that will contrive to succesfully combat poverty, or an order that causes the opposite to emerge, namely large-scale poverty? In view of the establishment of a new social order the social sciences assured themselves that the newly structured reality is one that can hardly be changed and that is in accord with deterministic social laws. The given economic system enforced the existence of poverty as the other side of wealth by seemingly equating it with fate. This is the notion of poverty that prevailed until the end of the 1860s both in science and politics. As regards poverty, the institutional systems and regulators have the function of establishing secured demarcation lines between "good citizens" and "paupers" rather than of opening up ways out of misery for the poor. Throughout the early history of social scientific discourse, be it on the level of enlightened reporting or of social critical reasoning, the same question posed itself in view of the challenges of pauperism: how was it associated with the

process of development of the free market and large-scale industrialization? Did the "most ruthless form of poverty", i.e. pauperism, develop
merely as a transitory event? Was it a necessary feature of a new social
and economic order, or only a leftover from the previous one? It was
possible to count and measure the poor – but there was a lot of uncertainty about the message of such empirical findings. In the historical
interim between the decline of an old society and the formation of a new
"industrial society", also in terms of what is called the "culture of the
industrial age", new points of orientation had to be created during the
debate with disintegrating old cultural patterns. The social science
discussion moved between forms of agrarian production and those of
large-scale industry, between the closed-in markets in village communities and industrial mass-production schemes, between the geographical concentration of the community and the mobilization of individuals,
above all lacking a basic point of orientation. The specific uncertainty in
the phrase of transition was a product of the erosion of old structures and
the still-uncertain structuring of new assumptions within social scientific
thought. Repeatedly, it was felt necessary to proffer reasons for enduring
validity of traditional values, standards and views, to stop the erosion of
the traditional social knowledge orientations, or to prove the validity of
new norms. In this sense the discussion around the "value change" and
the change of orientations became an integral part also of the poverty
debates of that time.

The views on the interlinkage between economic and societal development, between economy and poverty that finally emerged from the
sustained search for common denominators and orientations were based
on the attempt to use the concepts developed within political economy for
clarification of the apparant connection between poverty and market
order. Political economy and its Marxist critique viewed poverty and
pauperism in the context of economic laws which – as was thought –
operated on society with the precision and infallibility of natural laws.
Thus, there resulted two contrary yet, at the same time, complementary
"application offers", which – in minimizing the possibilities and necessities of a socio-political reform – encountered each other in the capitalist
market system. Poverty, according to assumptions of the liberal school of
thought, ought to be a gradually disappearing phenomenon which is to be
overcome with an increasing recognition of and adjustment to the laws of
the market. Or, according to Marxist theory, poverty was perceived as an
irreversible consequence of these laws so that it had to be accepted as the

natural flip side of the new wealth. However, possibilities for escaping out of mass poverty would emerge, which in many but by no means all cases were seen to involve the destruction of the capitalist order and its economic laws.

Although such theories may hardly be considered useful for combatting practically and immediately the dangers of poverty, they were, on the other hand, most helpful in restoring a sense of security and certainty for both society and politicians in the face of mass poverty and pauperism.

Amongst explanations of poverty which coped with uncertainty by defending the natural and/or peripheral character of the phenomenon. Manchester Liberalism offered reassurance, stating that poverty could be regulated without collective or, in particular, state intervention. Sieferle writes, "if the nightmare of modernized poverty within pauperism has initially been a valid argument against capitalism and the industrial system, now the economists started turning the tables. Especially pauperism now required a techno-industrial expansion as a way out of legitimizing the scandal of the industrial system" (17). In coping with the extensive uncertainties of that time, the attempt to normalize them offered security in the hope that one would trust the fact that behind the destruction of traditional social orders the development of a secure new order was concealed. This new order of the market economy did not have to be artificially generated by the state. All that was necessary for its creation in terms of political intervention was something like "midwifery" and "promotion".

Completely different were the pledges of reassurance the political economy of the revolutionary Marxist theory offered to the fledging workers' movements: the progress of industrialization itself would show the limits of the exploiting capitalist system; and the working class would therefore find itself in harmony with the rules of history and industrial progress. If, in the name of a more equal distribution of the fruits of progress, it questioned the market laws which signified the perpetuation of the working classes' insecurity and misery in the middle of wealth.

Certainly not all of the offered applications and explanatory schemata from the social sciences fell under the guidance of political economy. The writings of Engels on the situation of the working classes represent the transition to a second, different discourse culture concerned with poverty: efforts were undertaken in the fields of statistics and hygienics/medicine with a view to more lucidly explaining the characteristics of poverty and to making them more perceptible. Counting the poor – this meant directing attention to the wealth of data on the specific outward living conditions of the poor, whose social situation accounted for a markedly high incidence of diseases, epidemics and a particularly high mortality rate. The private local "Statistical Societies" that came into being in England from the end of the 1830s and from which in 1857 originated the "National Association for the Promotion of Social Science" played no less important a role than did the various initiatives of state institutions, such as factory inspections, parliamentary commissions and committees with their techniques of empirical "taking of evidence". To a great extent the state emerges as a direct originator of empirical social science in instances requiring policy making to combat poverty and employment problems. During the consideration of many problems and legal regulations in England, "commissions" were set up whose main tasks consisted in collecting available knowledge, additional "facts", and in drawing up proposals to be submitted to policy makers.

The developmental stages of defining and discussing poverty were also closely connected with the process of further development of social movements. This was part of the unfolding and transforming of further "social knowledge" on poverty and its social circumstances: research findings furnished by those who were themselves affected by poverty. The development of a workers' movement in which a part of those once termed "the poor" now gained identity as a social class formulating its demands can be seen at the same time as a long process of struggle for and acquiring knowledge of its own. In addition to the knowledge *about* the poor there now also existed knowledge *of* the poor about themselves. It was articulated in attempts at defining their identity and at alternatively interpreting the social environment. In the process of the "making of the working class" (Thompson), which was also a powerful social learning process, the critique and stimulation of social science through social knowledge was portrayed.

A consequential upheaval was in the offing. It affected not only the way in which poverty was chosen as a theme in society and in social science and the way selfassurance was gained from the various social actors in an established and acknowledged industrial system, it also led to the search for new social reforms and controls which became the common credo of both bourgeois and socialist theorists and practitioners. The result, which from that time onward decidedly influenced also the utilization context of social science research, is as simple as that: poverty was no longer perceived as a fateful (be it permanent or already fading) product of economic principles and/or individual fault, but as a "social evil" which required and was open to collective societal interventions and collectivized protective arrangements.

In the wake of expanding positive knowledge, of counting and measuring and of attempts made by those affected by poverty to articulate themselves as "poor *workers*", as well as of incremental public security and reform practices, the competing bourgeois and Marxist schools of thought altered their ideologies and systems of interpretation. The economic principle was no longer seen as a dogma: in bourgeois political economy this conviction increasingly gained ground in the last third of the past century, be it in the English policies of economic reform or in Germany, where social scientists in the "Verein für Sozialpolitik" tried to forge a comprehensive conception of social development and poverty and the development of reform-oriented institutions and policies. By postulating that economic laws gave leeway for reforms and remedies within the poverty dilemma and that collective efforts by social policy-makers no longer had to conflict with economic laws, a utility-oriented context of science, which stressed the formation and support of social reform policies, was strenghtened.

The Institutionalization of the Social Sciences

Two modes of discourse which provided the basis for the institutionalization of the social sciences have already been discussed. One was political economy. The concepts and methods developed within its framework were mainly directed to answer questions about economic causes and consequences, how to evaluate them and assess the likely effects of interventions and policy measures. Methodologically, a deductive system of inference was followed, rather than a mode of inquiry resorting to empirical quantification. This field in turn provided for the other flowering branch of institutionalized social science research to come into existence. From the early landmarks onwards, such as John Philipp Kay's "The Moral and Physical Condition of the Working Classes", published in 1832, to Engels' well-known survey or Edwin Chadwick's "Sanitary Report", published in 1842, a long line of development can be traced, in which local statistical societies as well as national ones, like the "National Association for the Promotion of Social Science" in England, factory inspectorates, parliamentary commissions and other reform-minded institutions played an important role in generating ever new "findings" as well as techniques of gathering empirical "evidence". A similar development can be observed in Germany, where a long-standing tradition of statistical data-collecting methods came eventually to be merged with enquêtes like those initiated in 1848 in Prussia regarding the living and working conditions of rural workers in Prussia, which was to be repeated in 1874 and 1891, followed by similar inquiries about factory workers and other deprived groups (18). The production of empirical, instrumental and technical knowledge about the effects and scope of poverty was linked to a search for an increase in certainty. It was no longer solely the prevailing "spirit" or attitude which counted, nor only public opinion which had to be influenced one way or the other, but the organization and utilization of factual knowledge was produced within a framework of commonly shared orientations. The rise of a welfare state administration was preceded by parliamentary or royal reform-minded commissions, by factory inspectorates and other professional bodies which set up and thereby generated the continuous production of empirical social research. These commissions, as well as findings and factual knowledge provided by empirical social science, came to play an important role in helping to shape public opinion, in sensitizing the middle classes not to relegate, forget or marginalize the poor strata of society. Although these empirical investigations neither had the intention nor the possibility of contradicting the political economists, they nevertheless provided important basic orientations for a reformist state incrementalism. There was no grand luster of scientific legitimacy which flowed from these empirical investigations, but they provided nevertheless a bit of scientific reassurance which came from having surveyed and measured new societal territory. It was territory which was to provide new policy arenas for a welfare state which expanded and continued to grow in its interventionist claims as well as in the effectiveness of its policy measures. It was a territory, upon which collectivized, universal and compulsory social security and care arrangements were to be installed and where new expert knowledge would hence be in demand, in order to run, improve and manage the expanding welfare system.

The third strand of social science discourse, the one closest to social knowledge of the poor and deprived, or to the more articulated discourse of social movements, undoubtedly played a temporary avant-garde role, but its institutionalization remained frail, if it came about at all. Since it was a discourse bound to the ups and downs of social movements, it shared their fate. With the success of the workers' movement, it partly became superfluous or was turned over into the official discourse system of welfare bureaucracies and their demand for expert knowledge. Moreover, through the societal transformation which brought about entirely new, nation-wide and universal systems of care and security – the health system, an educational system and welfare services as well as a social security system which was to cover most of the risks connected with working life – the poor with some exceptions had largely vanished as well. They had been transformed into "workers" and later into "employees". They became citizens, with not only political rights, but also social rights. They became patients, entitled to health care services, and clients, entitled to welfare services in case of need. Only the residual poor were left, those who had failed to gain their entitlements through a place acquired in the labour market. Even the rise of unemployment, although periodically causing concern, became a "manageable problem" and the more recent debate about the "new poverty" has remained within the circle of social policy analysts.

Although there were repeatedly interruptions and breakdowns in the course of its history, the collectivization process which culminated in the welfare state can be looked upon as a remarkable achievement. It peaked once more, in the three golden decades after the Second World War, as a true "hyperbole of expansion" (19). The state apparatus which had, as a result of mobilization for total warfare, increased enormously in capacity, prepared government bureaucracies for the administrative challenges of a much-enlarged welfare system. In these efforts and achievements it was aided by the expert knowledge of social scientists who joined in the expansionist efforts by entering the "reform coalitions" offered to them (20). In these frameworks, they continued the tracks of institutionalized and orderly discourse of inquiry which had been devised much earlier in history. They went on consulting and giving policy advice. They continued to furnish empirical data about the state of society and its members. A minority continued, on a precarious and barely institutionalized ground, to challenge all official versions while claiming to speak in the name of "the people" or setting up research schemes, designed to teach them to "help themselves".

All this could well have continued, if the road to progress (or its opposition to it) had not become blocked and suddenly been interrupted. New limits to growth became visible on a horizon which no longer seemed open-ended and destined to lead to an ever better future. New kinds of dangers and risks appeared – associated with large-scale technologies at first, now all pervasive with their potential effects on an environment which has become a highly precious and scarce resource. Profound uncertainties befell industrialized societies in the last decades of this century about the future course to be taken. And as before, with vanishing certainties consensus about the basic directions and interpretation of the the world also began to vanish. Social sciences – and this time to some degree also natural sciences – lost their reassuring function. New social movements sprung up, offering new concepts and notions with which to grasp a world which could no longer be taken for granted. And the social sciences as institutionalized discourse systems began to respond...

But that is another story.

Notes

1. de Swaan, A, (1988): *In Care of the State. Health Care, Education and Welfare in Europe and the USA in the Modern Era,* Cambridge: Polity Press, p. 233.
2. *Ibid.,* p. 244.
3. Wittrock, B. (1989): "Social science and state development: transformations of the discourse of modernity," *International Social Science Journal,* November 1989, p. 497.
4. Österberg, D. (1989): "The challenge of contemporary knowledge. Social statistics, social research and sociology," *Studies of Higher Education and Research,* 4: 10–17.
5. The arguments contained in what follows have first been developed in Evers, A., Nowotny, H. (1987): *Über den Umgang mit Unsicherheit. Die Entdeckung der Gestaltbarkeit der Gesellschaft* (Coping with uncertainty: discovering the shapeability of society). Frankfurt a.M.: Suhrkamp.
6. Polanyi, K. (1978): *The Great Transformation.* Frankfurt a.M.: Suhrkamp.
7. de Swaan, *op.cit.*
8. This is the leading question followed by Evers, A., Nowotny, H. (1987): *Über den Umgang mit Unsicherheit. Die Entdeckung der Gestaltbarkeit der Gesellschaft* (Coping with uncertainty: discovering the shapeability of society), *op.cit.*
9. For example, see also Weir, M., Skocpol, T. (1985): "State structures and the possibilites for 'Keynesian Responses' to the great depression in Sweden, Britain and the United States," in *Bringing the State Back In.* Evans, P., Rüschemeyer, D., Skocpol, T. (eds.). Cambridge: Cambridge University Press.
10. This is where new approaches from science studies meet similar ones from political science: see, for example Majone, G. (1987): *Public deliberation and the policy sciences,* Workshop on Social Sciences and Societal Development, Berlin, January 29 – February 1, 1987 (Manuscript).
11. Sieferle, R. (1984): *Fortschrittsfeinde? Opposition gegen Technik und Industrie von der Romantik bis zur Gegenwart.* Munich: Beck.

12. See also Preußer, N. (1982): *Armut und Sozialstaat, Band 2*. München, p. 23; and Tennstedt, R. (1981): *Sozialgeschichte der Sozialpolitik in Deutschland*. Göttingen, p. 83.

13. See also Vester, M. (1970): *Die Entstehung des Proletariats als Lernprozeß*. Frankfurt a.M.

14. One example here would be Townsend, P. (1979): *Poverty in the United Kingdom. A survey of household resources and standards of living*. New York.

15. Webster, C. (ed.) (1981): *Biology, medicine and society 1840–1940*. Cambridge; and Stepan, N. (1982): *The idea of race in science: Great Britain 1800–1960*. St. Anthony's College, Oxford.

16. The following argument has been dealt with more extensively in Evers, A., Nowotny, H. (1989): "Über den Umgang mit Unsicherheit. Anmerkungen zur Verwendung sozialwissenschaftlichen Wissens," in: *Weder Sozialtechnologie noch Aufklärung?* Beck, U., Bonß, W. (eds.) Frankfurt a.M.: Suhrkamp, pp. 355–383.

17. Sieferle, R., *op.cit.*

18. Jonas, G. (1968): *Geschichte der Soziologie II, Sozialismus, Positivismus, Historismus*. Reinbek.

19. de Swaan, *op.cit.*

20. Wagner, P. (1987): "*Social sciences and political projects: reform coalitions between social scientists and policy-makers in France, Italy and West-Germany*," in: *The Social Direction of the Public Sciences*, Stuart S. Blume *et al.* (eds.). Dordrecht: Reidel, pp. 277–306.

PART II

NATIONAL PROFILES IN
A LONG-TERM PERSPECTIVE

CHAPTER THREE

THE SOCIAL SCIENCE DISCIPLINES:
THE AMERICAN MODEL

PETER T. MANICAS

Introduction

A persistent assumption of disciplinary histories of the social sciences is
the idea that each of the main branches of today's social sciences reflects
at least reasonably firm strata of the social world. There is, thus, a
'natural' division of labor which was finally realized with the maturation
of the distinct social sciences. Explaining the emergence of the disciplines, then, takes the form of showing how pathfinders, interested in
constituting analogues to the successful modern natural sciences, broke
from the prescientific past and established restricted domains for controlled inquiry. Each story is different, of course, and some are stormier
than others. Some, for example psychology, are even less settled than
others (1).

This altogether Whiggish view of the history of social sciences must, I
think, be rejected – along with the assumptions on which it is founded.
This is not the place to give arguments against these assumptions, but
especially the assumption that the disciplines constitute, like tigers and
tangerines, 'natural kinds.' What follows takes an alternative tack. I
assume that the very idea of a social science was (and is) a contested idea,
that there were (and are) alternatives to the practices which we now call
social science. But more than this, I assume that the branches of what we
think of as the modern social sciences were creations from materials at
hand by persons at particular times and places in history. Put in other
terms, practices in social science could have been different. What needs
explaining, then, is not how the disciplines escaped from a prescientific
past, but how and why they were constituted as they are. My argument

P. Wagner, B. Wittrock, and R. Whitley (eds.), Discourses on Society: Volume XV, 1990, 45–71.
© 1990 *Kluwer Academic Publishers. Printed in the Netherlands.*

presupposes, of course, a theory of history and society. But this will be displayed rather than argued (Manicas, 1987).

My task in this chapter is to give a sketch of what seems to me to be the most critical juncture in this constitution, in the United States from approximately the mid-1880's to the period immediately following World War I. The critical players saw two deeply related problems: First, could social scientists in America have authority without having some specialized 'discipline'? As Becker put it, was 'a science without an identifiable central problem ... a science at all?' (Becker, 1971: 82). Second, how was social science to be 'objective' and yet have political impact in a rapidly changing America? These problems were incompletely resolved by the first generation. But as the American students of their German-trained professoriate came to occupy places in a very rapidly expanding university system, they defined their newly articulated 'disciplines' in the empiricist terms which have since characterized modern disciplinary social science. As I have noted elsewhere, were we, as social scientists, to transport ourselves to Oxford, the Sorbonne, Harvard or even Berlin, in say, 1890, we would find practices unfamiliar. There would be no 'departments' of sociology or psychology, the research practices would be for us a hodgepodge of philosophy, social theory, history and hard science methods. There would be no undergraduate 'introduction,' no textbooks which set out the domain of inquiry, its central problems or the 'history' of the discipline. The Ph.D. (or Dr. phil.) degree would be just that, a doctorate in Philosophy. But if we were to make a similar visit to any prominent American university in 1925, we would find very little which is not familiar. To be sure, there would be some 'traditionalists' in these departments – there still are – but they could not be said to define the discipline. The chapter gives but a sketch of the period; any sort of adequate account would not only have more to say about it, but would, of necessity, need to begin much earlier and elsewhere, at least in the seventeenth century in Western Europe.

Speaking abstractly, there were, I believe, four sets of materials from which the disciplines were constituted: First and fundamental, post-Civil War America experienced an explosive *capitalist development*. This generated a host of new problems – 'the social question': immigration, urbanization, and class war. Second, the US had an extremely *weak state*. Federalism, the lack of a significant state bureaucracy, and a middle-class political culture which de-emphasized politics, had marginalized governments in Washington, in the several states, and in the counties and cities.

In the period under study, these were to grow, especially with World War I. Still, the institutions and capacities of government, relative to other modern states of the period, were (and are!) minimal. But if the conjunction of explosive development and the weak state made some responses less possible, it made others more possible. As I think is by now well acknowledged, the leaders of America's largest corporations and financial institutions, all 'progressives,' brought together 'thoughtful men of all classes' into a new corporate liberal order (Kolko, 1967; Weinstein, 1968). This was the fundamental fact. But by itself it cannot explain what happened in American social science. We need to add at least two more dimensions.

Most critically, a new breed of 'educational managers' in cooperation with these 'thoughtful men' reconstituted *higher education* in America. In some twenty-five years, a host of new private universities came into existence, among them Cornell, Johns Hopkins, Chicago, Clark and Stanford. Meanwhile, the 'traditional' colleges of the East reluctantly but rapidly transformed themselves into modern universities. Along with these came dozens of new land-grant institutions spawned by the Morrill Act of 1862. Originally conceived as agricultural and mechanical colleges, some of these were transformed into full-fledged university centers. Undergraduate enrollments escalated, from 154,300 in 1890 to 582,000 in 1920, and graduate degrees, unknown in the United States before the 1860's, went from 2,400 in 1890 to 15,600 in 1920 (McClelland, 1980). In 1890, some 315 institutions of higher learning had productive funds of 74 million dollars; ten years later 488 institutions distributed 166 million dollars and by 1928, 1.15 billion dollars went to 1,076 institutions (Mills, 1954: 45).

There was nothing inevitable about this. Nor do I believe that the leaders of this movement had any sort of clear idea of the consequences, consequences which far outrun those of immediate concern in this essay. Although, as one writer notes, 'it is a commonplace to describe the emergence of the modern university in post-Civil War America as a phenomena of revolutionary proportions,' it is usually not emphasized that this development was not merely the indispensable material condition for what John Dewey called 'the new body of studies' that emerged out of the traditional curriculum of 'moral philosophy,' but given the conditions of this development it was, as well, a fundamental constraint on what this new body of studies was to become.

Here we can distinguish two features. First, as Veblen saw, the rule of higher education was taken out of the hands of clerics and put in the hands of businessmen – and this in a double-barrelled sense. The fortunes of the Carnegies, Rockefellers, Cornells, Hopkins, Clarks, Vanderbilts, Stanfords, etc., would be used to build the new universities. But just as important, both these, the public institutions which mimicked them, and the older traditional 'colleges,' Yale, Harvard and Columbia, which now found themselves competing for students and status, would be led by educational entrepreneurs whose values and goals were closely aligned with the leaders of the emerging corporate liberal order (2). Although it cannot be developed here, the earlier institutionalization of 'higher learning' in England and France, in conditions which were vastly different, had issued in different outcomes. In Germany, too, 'modernizers,' leading a revolution from above, faced different problems (McClelland, 1980; Schiera, and Heilbron, in this volume).

There was a critical fourth factor, the *conceptual materials* which were available to those who would constitute the social sciences in America. While difficult to characterize briefly, it can be said, I believe, that there were three main sets of notions.

First, there was *a distinctly German, historical and holistic conception of society*. Of course there was considerable disagreement and difference over the precise content of this conception, from Ranke to Droysen to Schmoller, to Dilthey, Simmel and Max Weber. Nonetheless, we are entitled to follow Iggers (1983) and think of this tradition of thought as both distinct and distinctly German. That this body of thought figures critically in our story is not surprising if we remember that the majority of the 9,000 Americans who studied in Germany between 1820 and 1920 did their studies in the 'social sciences' in the last decades of the nineteenth century (Herbst, 1965). These included not only many of the men who were leading architects of the new universities in America, Andrew Dickson White and Jacob Gould Schurmann (Cornell), C.K. Adams (Cornell and Wisconsin), Daniel Coit Gilman (Johns Hopkins and California), G. Stanley Hall (Clark), Edmund J. James (Northwestern and Illinois), Arthur T. Hadley (Yale) and Benjamin Ide Wheeler (California), to name but a few, but it included nearly all the leading first-generation academics in the social sciences in America. Even a partial list is stunning: Herbert B. Adams, John W. Burgess, Richard Ely, John Bates Clark, Frank Goodnow, Simon E. Patten, E.R.A. Seligman, Munroe Smith, Richmond Mayo Smith, Albion Small, Henry Farnum, Frank Taussig, James Mark Baldwin, Edward S. Tichener and James McKeen

Cattell. William Graham Sumner's degree was in theology; William James studied medicine. Nor ought we to exclude Franz Boas, Herman W. von Holtz and Hugo Münsterberg, Germans who played large roles in the earliest years in the process of the development of American social science (see also Gunnell, in this volume).

Yet – and this needs explaining – this distinctly German conception of social science could not take root in the soil of America. As I argue, political and institutional pressures – as Veblen rightly diagnosed – provided resistance which its most adamant advocates were unwilling to challenge. It is tempting to argue that what emerged was a unique synthesis, for example, an American pragmatic version. I believe that this was tried by some, John Dewey and Albion Small come quickly to mind, but as I shall argue, Small succumbed and Dewey was misunderstood where he had impact and otherwise ignored. This is, I believe, a most important dead-end in the mainstream history of the social sciences.

Of course, it is easier to be clear now about what was at stake than it was then and, in addition, these ideas had to compete with other ideas, including the individualistic, naturalistic and evolutionary ideas which owed to Herbert Spencer and to British political economy. Sumner, and in different ways, Franklin Giddings, are associated with this strand. It is important to notice that Lester Ward should not be. It is true that, like Sumner and Giddings, he is properly thought of an evolutionary naturalist, but Ward's debt was to Comte, not Spencer. Ward had a more holistic conception of the social along with a 'statist' orientation which put him much closer to Ely or to Small. As I suggest, Ward was never a force in the professionalization of American sociology.

Of far more significance to our problem, second, was *an optimistic variation of 'old' laissez-faire political economy.* America had a version of the *Methodenstreit,* between Richard Ely, inspired by the *Verein für Sozialpolitik,* and Simon Newcombe, an able and articulate spokesman for the abstract deductivist conception of political economy which Ricardo had inspired and which J.S. Mill had tried to restrict. John Bates Clark's original integration of the new marginalism effectively 'answered' the socialists and single-taxers and was an important part of the ideological battle which had to be fought. A consequence of the American battle over the nature of political economy, impelled by wholly independent institutional factors, was the opportunity provided to the 'political scientists' to establish 'government' as their domain and to Small, Giddings and E.A. Ross, one of the first of Ely's Wisconsin Ph.D.'s, to capture the residue under the heading of an autonomous sociology. In the course of this, of course, all three disciplines had to be separated from history.

But if I am correct, the ideas of science which were held, if but vaguely, by the first generation insufficiently distinguished their work (or the promise of their work) from the work done by men of the previous generation. These earlier efforts were seen to be moralistic and metaphysical, a priorist and undisciplined. A clearer articulation of social science as *science* was a desideratum which was mucht sought. With the advance of chemistry and the culmination of classical physics, the precise nature of a genuine science was just then being debated by an eminent group of philosopher/physicists in Germany, France and England. Kirchhoff's *Principles of Mechanics* (1874), Mach's *Science of Mechanics* (1883), and Ostwald's *General Chemistry* (1888) were among the first blasts toward establishing *a stringently anti-metaphysical empiricist philosophy of science* (Passmore, 1957: ch. 14), the third conceptual source early American social scientists drew on. These writers were joined by Boltzmann and Hertz in Germany, by Duhem and Poincaré in France, and in England by W.K. Clifford and, following the path of Mach, by Karl Pearson. Much of this new philosophy was not new (3). What was new, however, was that with the industrializing of the physical sciences and with the manifest practical applications which attended it, these men could command an authority which would have made Bacon envious. Most critical was the much older idea that scientific explanation was not metaphysical, requiring, as Mach put it, the elimination of superfluous assumptions which cannot be controlled by experience, and above all, assumptions that are metaphysical in Kant's sense (Mach, 1959: xl). Americans of the period were very much aware of this program, and from C.S. Peirce and William James, Giddings and Veblen, it quickly drew responses (Manicas, 1988). Plainly, these ideas had application to social science, and after 1900, they increasingly became part of the explicit rationale for a social science which was self-consciously aimed at prediction and control.

Writing near the end of this transition, Veblen clearly grasped the links between the 'new' empiricist philosophy of science and the constraints and opportunities presented to social scientists. In his brilliant 1906 essay, 'The Place of Science in Modern Civilization,' Veblen defended an old-fashioned view of science in which 'idle curiosity' motivated the search for causal explanations. And he explicitly attacked Pearson and the new school of anti-metaphysicians: 'Those eminent authorities who speak for a colorless mathematical formulation invariably and necessarily fall back on the (essentially metaphysical) preconception of causation as soon as they go into the actual work of scientific inquiry' (Veblen, 1961: 15). The German-influenced social science of the first generation of American professionals, like the evolutionary naturalist conception which was articulated by Lester Ward, had insisted that empirical outcomes, e.g., poverty, had complex 'underlying' causal determinants. But the search for these causes could be dangerous. As Veblen put it, even if this sort of inquiry 'should bear no colour of iconoclasm,' its outcome will 'disturb the habitual convictions and preconceptions on which they rest' (Veblen, 1957: 136). Given 'the exigencies of competitive academic expertise in America,' with 'businessmen' as executives of the new universities, there was little choice but to domesticate and de-fang this style of holistic social science. Accordingly, he continued, 'the putative leaders of science' 'enlarge the commonplace,' put aside questions of causes in favor of questions of use, 'on what ought to be done to improve conditions and to conserve those usages and conventions that have by habit become imbedded in the received scheme of use and wont, and so have been found to be good and right.' The result was 'a "science" of complaisant interpretations, apologies, and projected remedies' (*ibid.*). As it turned out, the new defense of empirical philosophy could not have been better suited for the new professionals.

On my view, World War I was decisive in the victory of positivism. In a stunning consensus, American social scientists enthusiastically encouraged American entry into the war and then enthusiastically cooperated with the government in realizing America's self-defined mission 'to make the world safe for democracy' – even when this meant putting into abeyance both their democratic and their scientific principles (Gruber, 1975; Manicas, 1989). For Anglo-Americans, the defeat of Germany represented, as well, the defeat of 'metaphysical,' 'statist,' historical and holistic German social science. Long suspicious of it in any case, the war proved to them that older British and French empirical philosophies, continuously represented in the 'old' political economy and in British utilitarian theories of government, had been right all along.

The ASSA and Society

We must here pass discussion of both the explosion in capitalistic development after the Civil War and the character of the American state. With these assumed as key features structuring choices, we can give some institutional flesh to the account by providing some details about the American Social Science Associaton. Its creation, in 1865, marks the first self-conscious organizational effort by educated Americans

to aid the development of Social Science, and to guide the public mind to the best practical means of promoting the Amendment of Laws, the Advancement of Education, the Prevention and Repression of Crime, the Reformation of Criminals, and the progress of Public Morality, the adoption of Sanitary Regulations, and the diffusion of sound principles on Questions of Economy, Trade and Finance. (ASSA Statement of Purpose, quoted from Silva and Slaughter, 1984: 40–41).

The immediate precedent for this was the British Association for the Promotion of Social Science, organized in 1857. A comparison of its goals and composition is here apt. Most of the leadership of the ASSA 'pursued careers as elite cultural workers': college presidents and faculty members, clerics, lawyers, doctors and editors. Some 17.5% were in commerce or manufacturing and only 5% were public officials (Silva and Slaughter, 1984). This contrasted sharply with its British inspiration, whose council included thirty-one peers, forty-eight MPs, nineteen Doctors of Law, fourteen Fellows of the Royal Society and 'numerous' baronets, knights, ministers of the Church of England, professors and Fellows of the London Statistical Society (Abrams, 1968). In middle-class America, this contrast might be expected, but it also exposed a basic flaw in the American association. This comes out if we look at the assumptions and goals of the two organizations.

As the ASSA statement of purpose shows, it followed an older British 'ameliorist' tradition in which the social science which people had in mind was British political economy. More important, it suggested that 'the social problem' could conveniently be defined as a *moral* problem. It is surely the case that such a view, *ceteris paribus*, is ideally suited to a capitalist social order: If you're so smart, why ain't you rich? And it is true also that this has been a continuing feature of social 'analysis' – as more recent strategies of 'blaming the victim' confirm. Still, in the naked form in which it first emerged, it seems to have been *too* simple-minded. After all, if laissez-faire capitalism worked so well and the social problem *was* a moral problem, then, presumably, all that is required is less state and more effective preachers and moralists. But even with the recent (and quite stunning!) resurgence of these ideas, especially in the US and Britain, there were many who recognized that more and better preaching would not suffice, especially since, in an increasingly secularized world, preachers had an increasingly difficult time sustaining their claims to authority.

It is hard to judge the impact of the efforts of the ASSA, but surely the members helped fuel a growing recognition that the problems needed the attention of persons with 'sound opinions.' They published the *Journal of Social Science,* were important in the creation of the National Civil Service Reform League, involved in the planning of the Ninth US Census, and perhaps more important, they came before numerous legislative committees, town meetings and public forums in their efforts to provide their 'sound opinions' on 'the great social problems of the day' (Silva and Slaughter, 1984: 42–50). Nevertheless, they had little support from either business or government – and after all, they were 'amateurs.'

An 1874 editorial in *Popular Science Monthly* could not have been more blunt:

Recognizing that the aim of this organization is excellent, and much of its work highly commendable ... we are of the opinion that it falls short of what should be its chief duty... So far from promoting social science, we should rather say that social science is just the subject which it particularly avoids. It might be considered as a general reform convention. It is an organization for public action, and most of its members, hot with impulses of philanthrophy, are full of projects of social relief, amelioration, and improvement. Of pure investigation, of the strict and passionless study of society from a scientific point of view, we hear but very little. (Quoted from Furner, 1975: 31).

Silva and Slaughter write that the ASSA leadership became increasingly sensitive to the uses and claims of expertise, and in the late 1870's, they opened their ranks, meetings and publications to the new 'Doctors' returning from Germany. Henry Carter Adams, Henry W. Farnum and Edmund J. James became officials of ASSA. In 1878 the ASSA offered to merge with the newly created first graduate center in America, the Johns Hopkins University; but Daniel Coit Gilman, then president of both the ASSA and Hopkins, declined the offer (Haskell, 1977: 144–167). In his 1880 presidential address, he affirmed the goals of ASSA, but argued that ASSA needed more specialization if it was to generate the needed facts and opinions. He proposed as well that another department be added. Inspired by the *Verein für Sozialpolitik,* it would specialize in 'historical sociology.' Indeed, the sort of investigation Gilman seems to have envisioned called not only for specialization, but for resources which he saw could be provided by the new university, working hand in glove with

both business and government. Gilman knew, of course, that the
University of Berlin had established an organizational model for the
industrializing of natural science. And he knew full well that this was
becoming the cutting edge of Germany's rapid modernization. The new
university in America could assemble the resources, money, and people to
industrialize social science. Indeed, as early as 1875, contemplating the
future Hopkins, Gilman had written:

I incline more and more to the belief that what is wanted in Baltimore is not a
scientific school, nor a classical college, nor both combined; but a faculty of medicine,
and [following the German model] a faculty of philosophy ... that each head of a
great department ... shall be as far as possible free from the interference of other
departments ... that advanced special students be first provided for.... (Quoted from
Vesey, 1965: 160).

Gilman was not alone in this conception. It was shared by other leaders,
for example, Andrew White of Cornell (founded in 1868) and Samuel
Eliot of Harvard, as well as by Michigan's Angell and, after its creation
with Rockefeller money in 1892, by Chicago's William R. Harper.
'Departments' with 'head professors' won autonomy at Cornell and
Hopkins in the 1880's, at Harvard after 1891 and at Chicago at its
inception. No doubt this vision of the university was shared by many both
in and out of the university.

At the heart of these educational manager's vision was specialization. Systematically
organized, specialized knowledge would place university-based experts in a position
of advantage in answering the full array of technical and social questions facing
industrial America. Legitimate monopoly would follow successful solution of
problems and the university – not regional culture, traditional religion or corrupt party
politics – would develop "scientific" criteria for national decision making. (Silva and
Slaughter, 1984: 71).

Up to this time the idea of specialized social sciences had not been
institutionalized; but as suggested, it seems likely that the Americans got
the idea from German 'institutes' in the natural sciences, and especially
the medical specialties. In America, propelled by the American ideology
of 'freedom,' Lernfreiheit was early on transformed into the elective
system, first at Eliot's Harvard in 1869. The idea that students should be
free to choose in the academic 'marketplace' was easily joined to the new
demand to specialize.

The success of this project required that 'progressive' leaders in big business and national politics see that it was an idea which could easily serve their interests. And, of course, it required the cooperation, perhaps leadership, of the Doctors of *Staatswissenschaften* returning from Germany. But before turning directly to them, three further developments should be noted. They help us to see how converging interests outside the university structured an outcome which professors cooperated in producing and how, looking back, the outcome had all the feeling of the inevitable.

The NCF, the NML and American Empire

Leaders in business, labor, government and education had sensed that the problems being generated needed some creative and imaginative response. The National Civic Federation (NCF) was remarkably successful in this regard. Organized in 1900, its founding statement compares with that of ASSA. The NCF aimed

to organize the best brains of the nation in an educational movement towards the solution of some of the great problems related to industrial and social progress: to provide for the study and discussion of questions of national import, to aid thus in the crystalization of the most enlightened public opinion; and when desirable, to promote legislation therewith. (Quoted from Silva and Slaughter, 1984: 186).

But the membership of the NCF stands in stunning contrast to the membership of the old ASSA. From business came Marcus A. Hanna (its first president), Andrew Carnegie, Cyrus McCormick (tractors), George Perkins (J.P. Morgan) and George B. Corteyou (Consolidated Gas), to name but a few. By 1903, there were representatives in the NCF from one-third of the 367 corporations with capitalization of more than $10 million. Organized labor was also represented in its council. Seated were Samuel Gompers (the First Vice President) and John Mitchell of the United Mine Workers, along with heads of the major railroad unions and the American Federation of Labor. The executive committee included future and former presidents of the US: Grover Cleveland, William Howard Taft and Woodrow Wilson. Not forgetting its mission, of course, it included prominently in its leadership the new educational managers, including Nicholas Murray Butler (Columbia) and serving as president from 1908, Seth Low, the man who had transformed Columbia College into Columbia University, Benjamin Ide Wheeler (California) and Harvard's Eliot.

Weinstein judges that the NCF was 'the most important single organization of the socially conscious big business men and their academic and political theorists' (1968: 6). Indeed, the NCF Review reported some twenty NCF projects ranging from mediating agreements between unions and employers, to stimulating welfare programs in factories, to investigations aimed at influencing legislation regarding trusts, public utilities, regulation, immigration, currency reform, workmen's compensation and child labor. Remarkably, thirty-six university and college presidents played roles, along with some twenty-one additional 'educational managers,' some forty-five leaders of the very recently organized disciplinary associations and another forty-four academics from the new social sciences (Silva and Slaughter, 1984: 188–192). The direction of these activities, both substantive and ideological, is clear enough. The NCF 'stood in opposition to what it considered its twin enemies: the socialists and radicals among workers and middle class reformers and the "anarchists" among the businessmen (as it characterized the NAM)' (Weinstein, 1968: 6).

The members of the NCF, of course, were 'progressives,' and they were not wrong in their recognition of their 'twin enemies.' On the right were the small businessmen, the ruling class base of traditional urban America, along with their ideologists: the clerics, lawyers, schoolteachers and physicians – the people who promoted the 'old economics' and the idea that the social problem was fundamentally a moral problem. On the left was a very broad and largely disorganized range of 'radicals,' from genuine socialists, e.g., Eugene Debs, to single taxers, Bellamyites and anarchists, to genuine progressives, e.g., Senator Robert La Follette of Wisconsin, to 'middle class reformers,' including the most progressive elements of the new academics.

The men of the NCF shared with the 'radicals' and 'reformers' in seeing the relation between capital and labor as the central problem for the emerging order. An active member of the Massachusetts Civic Federation, Louis Brandeis, remembered for his critical judicial role in progressivism, identified the issue in terms of the most pressing policy problem. Collective bargaining, he insisted, was essential if capitalism was to survive and prosper. Indeed, unions were 'a bulwark against the great wave of socialism' (quoted from Weinstein, 1968: 17). The problem was to absorb the right, squash the radicals, and domesticate the reformers. As suggested, the university played a critical role, defining itself in terms which satisfied its sponsors, beautifully represented by NCF.

Central to this was realization of the idea which Gilman and the other educational managers had so clearly articulated, an industrialized social science of specialists.

There was a second related development which also helps us in grasping the outcome. With the largest immigration in the history of the world in full force and with infra-structural demands on cities accelerating monumentally: housing, harbors, streets and railways, water supply, electricity, sanitation, and fire control, city politics in the US was creating opportunities for both new possibilities for graft and corruption and, even less agreeable to the older oligarchy, grass roots ethnic politics. On this, the businessmen, journalists, and reformers of WASP America could join hands; but as above, the solutions were not all equally agreeable to the older oligarchy or to the new corporate liberals.

German-educated Frank Goodnow put the problem: 'It has been felt that city government must, to be efficient, be emancipated from the tyranny of the national and state parties, and from that of the legislature – the tool of the party... [But] to avoid tyranny and preserve control is not easy' (quoted from Silva and Slaughter, 1984: 219). The ideal solution had been articulated earlier by John H. Patterson, the founder and president of Dayton's National Cash Register Company. For him, 'a city is a great business enterprise whose stockholders are the people.' Ideally, 'municipal affairs would be placed on a strict business basis.' They would, accordingly, be directed 'not by partisans, either Republican or Democratic, but by men who are skilled in business management and social science' (quoted from Weinstein, 1968: 93). Commission and council manager government was the 'natural' solution. This development goes very far in explaining the assertion of autonomy by political scientists in the American university. 'Public administration' could be a 'scientific' subdiscipline of the new 'political science.'

There was one final development. America had also begun a quest for empire. But in contrast to Great Britain and even to Germany, it lacked an imperial civil service. Here then was another developing structural place for academic expertise. This opportunity was exploited in Panama, Nicaragua, Puerto Rico, the Philippines, and Mexico. Indeed, at its 1898 annual meeting, 'the AEA [American Economic Association] ratified the expansion of American capitalism by appointing a blue ribbon committee under the chairmanship of [J.W.] Jenks, with the assistance of [E.R.A.] Seligman and [C.H.] Hull to work out the best means of administering colonies' (Furner, 1975: 276). Jenks 'guided the reorganization of

Philippine finances,' Hopkins' economics professor Jacob Hollander became nothing less than treasurer of Puerto Rico, and Samuel Lindsay of Pennsylvania's Wharton school, 'organized and administered the Puerto Rican school system from 1898–1902' (*ibid.*: 286). Most interesting perhaps was the role social scientists played in the US's first response to 'democratic' China. Following the revolution of 1910, Harvard's president Eliot, touring China on behalf of the Carnegie Endowment for International Peace (CEIP) – by no means a party lacking distinct and not always benign global interests – agreed to petition the CEIP for a list of experts to be sent to assist Chinese political reform. As a consequence, Frank Goodnow sailed to China to become constitutional advisor to the new regime. He was replaced, in 1916, by W.F. and W.W. Willoughby, both Doctors of *Staatswissenschaften* and leaders in the American Political Science Association. Woodrow Wilson, himself, of course, a 1886 Hopkins's Ph.D., appointed Ely-trained Paul Reinsch as ambassador. Goodnow, interestingly, embarrassed Wilson when he advised the regime that China was not ready for sophisticated democratic forms. President Yuan Shai-Kai was pleased to act on his advice. He reconstituted the monarchy with himself as emperor (Silva and Slaughter, 1984: 231)!

The Development of the 'Disciplines'

The materials for a reconstituted disciplinary social science were thus at hand, but the final outcome depended upon what key players within the academy would do with these materials. The new Doctors, employing these structured resources, conceptual and institutional, did not engage in a conspiracy. They did not need to. Like actors anywhere, they acted with a variety of purposes. And, as anywhere, their cumulative activities had consequences which outran their intentions. Given their specific structured situations, sketched in the foregoing, the outcome was a set of new social science disciplines, each shorn of German metaphysics and the 'heat' of philanthropic impulse; each committed to the 'strict and passionless study of society from a scientific point of view.'

The process was to take two generations, beginning with creation of graduate programs in the social sciences. Columbia's School of Political Science, established under John Burgess in 1880, compared with Herbert B. Adams's Graduate Program in Historical Studies at Hopkins. While the names of the two programs differed, there was no appreciable difference in their offerings. These included courses in history, politics, economics and geography. Educated willy nilly in all, the first generation of American social scientists moved easily from one topic to another. The process of abandoning a German-inspired, comprehensive conception of social-scientific inquiry in favor of pragmatically and professionally defined, narrowly disciplinary discourses may be highlighted by way of a brief account of intellectual and institutional developments in two key disciplines, namely economics and sociology.

Economics

The relation of political economy – or since Marshall's *Principles of Economics* (1890) simply 'economics' – to history and political science is complicated. Political economy had been taught as part of the curriculum in 'moral philosophy' in America's schools. Its teachers had included Francis Wayland, a Baptist minister and later president of Brown, Henry Carey, a business man with extensive Pennsylvania mining and manufacturing interests, and clerics, Francis Bowen, John Bascom and Arthur Latham Perry, to name but a few. In the 1870's, this tradition, representing a melding of laissez-faire British economy and Puritanism, had a firm grip on the posts in political economy in the older college curriculum in America (O'Connor, 1944; Dorfman, 1949). Although this is usually not much noticed, the problem in America was that the new doctors returning from Germany had deeply imbibed German historical economics (4). It was by no means guaranteed that in challenging the older tradition, the German brand would lose out. It was not merely that these men had the authority of their decrees, but that they were reformers in a period when reform was very much in the air.

The theoretical issue was joined when in 1884 Richard Ely published 'Past and Present Political Economy,' in Adams' *Johns Hopkins University Studies in History and Political Science* (Furner, 1975: 60). There was nothing surprising about what he said. The 'old' political economy was deductivist, hypothetical, abstract; it glorified the baser emotions and selfishness and made it seem that competition was divinely ordained. The 'new' political economy, anchored in concrete history, had a firm grip on reality and it could show how the state could be used to advance the interests of people in society. Ely's attack earned a response. It came from Simon Newcombe, author of *Principles of Political Economy* (1885), also a professional on the Hopkins faculty, but not all that surprisingly, a mathematician and an astronomer! Newcombe confidently and ably defended the apriorism of British political economy, and while Schumpeter (1984: 866) asserts that his book is 'the outstanding performance of American general economics in the pre-Clark-Fisher-Taussig epoch,' he did it, unsurprisingly, without any of the qualifications or restrictions which J.S. Mill's evidently ignored 'Unsettled Questions' had tried to make clear.

Mill, it may be remembered, defended political economy as an 'essentially abstract science'; but he went on to argue that its conclusions, 'like those of geometry, are only true, as the common phrase is, in the abstract' (Mill, 1974: 144). Accordingly, 'it does not treat the whole of man's nature as modified by the social state, nor of the whole conduct of man in society. It is concerned with him solely as a being who desires to possess wealth...' (1974: 137) – just as Ely had charged. Mill had concluded that the problem for practice was how to go from 'abstract truths' to the 'facts of the concrete, clothed in all the complexity with which nature has surrounded them' (1974: 148). That Mill did not settle the 'unsettled questions,' of course, is exactly why there was a *Methodenstreit* in Germany, why Durkheim rose to challenge French political economy, and why, in America, Ely and Newcombe were at war. The critics shared in believing that the real world did not answer to the abstractions of the classical school and thus that they could not be used to grasp concrete social life (5).

Nearly coincident with the opening shots, Edmund J. James and Simon N. Patten had begun planning for an organization, modeled on Schmoller's *Verein für Sozialpolitik*. It would

combat the widespread view that our economic problems would solve themselves, and that our laws and institutions which at present favor industrial instead of collective action can promote the best utilization of our material resources and secure to each individual the highest development of all his faculties. (Quoted from Dorfman, 1949, Vol. 3: 205)

Ely grabbed at the chance to professionalize political economy along lines that he and his German-influenced colleagues had set out. Since the enemy camp had established chairs in universities, this complicated matters considerably. The original statement of principles had been blunt, asserting that 'the conflict between labor and capital has brought to prominence a vast number of problems, whose solution requires the united efforts, each in its own sphere, of the church, of the state, and of science' (quoted by Wesley C. Mitchell, 1969: 233). But to secure enough members to get the organization going, the group found it necessary to qualify this, adding that 'this statement ... was not be regarded as binding upon individual members' (*ibid.*). The American Economic Association came into existence in 1885. Within three years the constitution was disemboweled and only the first objective was left standing: the encouragement of economic research. E.R.A. Seligman subsequently insisted that the changes were not made 'in deference to a coterie.' Even if so, the fact remains that the organizing group was asking some of their colleagues to bite off more than they could chew.

The problem, plainly, was the implicit and explicit socialism which these men endorsed (6). When in 1885, Ely had published an essay, 'Recent American Socialism,' and a book, *The Labor Movement,* Sumner was led to call Ely a 'charlatan.' In an unsigned review, Simon described the book as 'the ravings of an anarchist and the dreams of a socialist.' He concluded that 'Dr. Ely seems ... to be seriously out of place in a university chair' (quoted by Dorfman, III, 1949: 163).

The assessment was wildly unfair. Still, it surely served the wider purpose for which it must have been intended. The events of the period, including the boycott by Yale and Harvard of the AEA, but more importantly, 'unprecedented labor violence and vicious capitalist retaliation,' and then, in 1886, the Haymarket affair, led to a break in the ranks. In a critical essay in *Science,* Henry C. Adams, himself in difficulty with his split appointment at Cornell and Michigan, capitulated. As Furner puts the matter: 'Professional economists were not going to be permitted to make ethical judgments that challenged basic values or threatened entrenched interests. To avoid catastrophe for his emerging profession, Adams proposed giving up any claim to moral authority' (1975: 101). From the other side, Charles F. Dunbar, head of economics at Harvard, was prepared to offer concessions. In the first issue of the *Quarterly Journal of Economics,* which he edited, Dunbar offered that 'revisionist' political economy was 'no revolution, but a natural reaction, probably salutary, and destined to promote ultimately a rapid but still orderly development of the science, upon the lines laid down by the great masters of what is called the deductive school' (quoted by Furner, 1975: 110). This was so much nonsense, but because it was a hand eagerly taken by the 'revisionists,' the fundamental differences in the two conceptions of political economy have since been obscured (7).

Ely surely had a conception of his science which differed from
Dunbar's; but he had never been a radical in any useful sense of the word.
Two years previously he had himself denounced 'rebels against society'
who stood for 'common property, socialist production and distribution;
the grossest materialism,... free love ... and ...anarchy' (quoted by
Herbst, 1965: 9). Ely called himself 'a progressive conservative.' But red-
baiting was already a potent weapon in America. In 1892, Ely was forced
to resign from his long-held position as secretary of the AEA. The year of
the Pullman strike (1894), he was charged with speaking and writing 'in
favor of socialism and social violence' (Silva and Slaughter, 1984: 89).
He disavowed any such sympathies and eventually was acquitted. By the
time that he was elected President of the AEA in 1900, he had changed
his mind sufficiently to endorse almost everything he had once opposed.
In his presidential address, he offered that competition was both natural
and beneficient. On his more considered view, what was needed was a
balance between 'the socialist extension of government activity ... and
that of conservative demand' (quoted by Silva and Slaughter, 1984: 147).

It is of considerable significance to note that the 'orderly development'
to which Dunbar had referred included John Bates Clark's enduring
answer to the moral implications of the idea of surplus value. Summarizing Clark, Silva and Slaughter write, 'if socialists could prove that
capitalist society defrauded workers of their product, then all good men
would join them.' Accordingly, said Clark: 'I wish to test the power of
recent economic theory to give an exact answer to this question' (quoted
by Silva and Slaughter: 111). Marginalism, of course, exactly did this.
Schumpeter notes that Clark must be given credit for 'subjective
originality,' in that while Thünen, Jevons, Menger and Walras preceded
him in arriving at marginalism, Clark quite independently had arrived at
similar conclusions. Schumpeter offers that American economists took
slowly to the marginalist message. Perhaps in America, the rout of the
challengers could have been accomplished even without it? The outcome,
in any case, is clear. Rid of its Germanisms and formally fitted with
differential equations, economics was securely in the hands of descendents of 'the great masters of the deductive school.' As for the others who
stayed, they were, like Veblen, derisively termed 'sociologists,' or
perhaps more kindly, as with Commons, Wesley Mitchell and his
descendents, 'institutional economists.'

Sociology

A fallout from the debate over the character of economics was the emergence of the first department of sociology in the world, in the new University of Chicago. Chicago had institutionalized *de nova*, with separate departments in the social sciences. Political economy was the largest. It was led by J. Lawrence Laughlin and included Veblen. History, led by J. Franklin Jameson and German-born von Holtz, was next. Political science was the smallest, with Harry Pratt Judson as its head. It included E.J. James, professor of public adminstration, who left in 1902 to become president of Northwestern, and Ernst Freund, associate professor of jurisprudence and public law. Charles E. Merriam, joined the department in 1900. Significantly, his was the only appointment designated as 'political science' (Karl, 1974: 44–45). John Dewey headed the department of philosophy, psychology and pedagogy, which included G.H. Mead.

Albion Small's sociology department numbered four. It included Vincent and W.I. Thomas. Thomas's year in Germany had been spent studying Wundtian 'folk psychology,' and like Vincent, he taught while he earned his Ph.D. Karl writes that Small's department 'dominated in spirit.' At that time, he perceptively writes that sociology could be viewed 'as a modernization of the reform sciences' (*ibid.*). Speaking generally, by this time, courses in 'social science' were residual in the colleges and universities of the US and included a host of subjects which were not covered in the standard offerings in history, politics and economics. Indeed, along with courses called 'municipal sociology,' even up-to-date Hopkins offered a course entitled simply 'Charities and Corrections,' taught by Jeffrey R. Brackett, the Chair of the Board of Charities and Corrections of the city of Baltimore (Bernard and Bernard, 1943: 643).

The conventional wisdom has it that the conceptual framework of American sociology is rooted in Comte, mediated by Lester Ward, and in Herbert Spencer. Though it was plainly self-serving for Small to argue that Ward 'improvised an entirely mistaken interpretation of cause and effect when he led Americans to believe that they owe sociology to Comte,' he was not wrong in insisting that there was an 'efficient cross-fertilization' which had come 'from the German tradition' (Small, 1924: 315). This was, of course, a tradition, which along with so many others, he had represented. It included a host of scholars who had identified themselves as political economists, including E.A. Ross, author of the influential 1901 *Social Control*. Perhaps, Ross's professional trajectory speaks volumes about the emerging discipline of sociology. In 1897, Ross wrote to Ward that the president of Stanford, David Starr Jordan,'took occasion after the horror excited in the East by my free silver advocacy to remove me as far as possible from all connections with Finance by making me Prof. of Sociology' (quoted by Faris, 1967: 6).

There were, then, at least three streams in these early years: the Comtean, through Ward, the Spencerian, developed, as Small says, by Sumner and Franklin H. Giddings, and the German. Ward was quickly marginalized within the academy. Not only was he an imperializing sociologist, but his style of technocracy must surely have frightened the corporate liberals. For almost opposite reasons Sumner too was marginalized. His individualism was too ragged for the emerging mainstream. Because it was a hybrid of Greek and Latin, Sumner evidently disliked the word 'sociology.' He died (in 1910) as Professor of the Science of Society.

The German roots of so many of the reformers help us to explain how the force of Small's presence at Chicago critically impelled the particular professionalization of sociology in America. Not only was Chicago a model, but Small was editor of *The American Journal of Sociology* (founded in 1894), the only professional journal of sociology until 1921. He was senior author of the first textbook in sociology (written with George E. Vincent), a book which had wide use in America. Finally, along with Ward, Giddings and Ross, already leaders in AEA, he was one of the organizers of the American Sociological Society which, in 1905, broke off from the AEA (Silva and Slaughter, 1984: 162).

In his 1907 *Adam Smith and Modern Sociology: A Study in the Methodology of the Social Sciences,* Small articulated the main point: 'Modern sociology,' he wrote, 'is virtually an attempt to take up the larger program of social analysis and interpretation which was implicit in Adam Smith's moral philosophy, but which was suppressed for a century by prevailing interest in the technique of the production of wealth' (quoted by Becker, 1971: 12). This was an accurate description of the way Smith was read *after* Ricardo isolated what Schumpeter and others identified as the 'analytic core' of economics. And it suggested, as Small knew, the substance of the 'Menger-Schmoller debate,' which Small treated extensively in his *Origins of Sociology*.

There was, however, a serious flaw in his original conception. It was a flaw which he shared with Ward and which he came quickly to acknowledge: If the social process was the outcome of many concurrently operating causes, nothing was irrelevant to understanding what was going on. But if so, didn't that make sociology an imperialist inquiry, subsuming all the others? As Becker writes: 'Who would transact with such a monster: Who would welcome its meetings? Who would be comfortable with its aims and findings, if these aims and findings were in explicit defiance of what one was doing oneself?' (Becker, 1971: 18).

There were some alternative possibilities. One had been realized by Richmond Mayo Smith, who at Columbia had aligned 'social science' with demography and vital statistics, The titles of his two main books are significant: *Statistics and Sociology* (1895) and *Statistics and Economics* (1899). Not irrelevantly, Giddings had been invited to replace Mayo Smith while he was on leave, and in 1894, president Seth Low created a chair in sociology which Giddings filled. Giddings seems to have been deeply method conscious, getting from Lewe's *Problems of Life and Mind* the positivist's idea that laws were but relations of 'antecedents and consequences.' He adopted Mill's methods, and in the late nineties, he discovered Mach, and Pearson's new 'correlation coefficient,' little *r*. These influences were developed in his *Inductive Sociology* (1901), which called for a rigorous quantitative sociology. This found little favor with Small, not surprisingly. On his view, and perceptively, Giddings vacillated between a method which was 'essentially Baconian' and one with stressed 'first principles,' 'a picturesque yoking together of the scientific ox and the speculative ass' (quoted by Bannister, 1978: 73). (8).

Gradually, perhaps without conscious design, Small retreated from his original vision. Later, he explained his imperialist enthusiasm as the 'sin' of 'amateurish ambition.' By 1924 he had arrived at the following quite agreeable position: 'A sociologist, properly speaking, is a man [sic] whose professional procedure consists in the discovery or analysis of categories of human group composition or reaction and behavior, or in use of such categories as means of interpreting or controlling group situations' (Small, 1924: 348).

Professional sociology was, first of all, method. This allowed that sociology could be thought of as disciplined social research, the qualitative and quantitative description of society. Second, sociology concerned 'groups,' all sorts of groups: families, criminals, ethnic groups, peasants, etc. This gave sociology a critical role to play in the new division of labor and allowed it to exclude all those important social questions which had so annoyed the patrons of the educational managers. Indeed, without notice, it made sociology consistent with the dominating methodological individualism of political science and economics. How many today think of 'groups' in identifying 'the social?' Third, sociology would have a particular 'theoretical' component – very much in keeping with the later *mis*reading of Weber's 'sociology': 'the discovery and analysis of categories' (Manicas, 1987: 127–140). Gone and quite forgotten was the original causal thrust of Small's earlier vision. The construction of typologies would replace this. Finally, and not unimportantly, sociology had a practical role: As Ross had urged, it was 'a means of interpreting *and* controlling group situations.' Professional sociologists were neither charlatans nor muck-rakers. Nor were they professionalizing social workers or untrained reformers. But in identifying a domain consistent with the recently articulated domains of history, political science and economics, they could still participate in the reformist liberal corporate order. As Silva and Slaughter conclude, 'in 1904, sociology was beginning to establish its monopoly of knowledge from reformist European social theory and the ASSA's leftovers' (1984: 174).

The Great War was decisive. Led by Small until his death in 1926, Thomas, and journalist-turned-sociologist Robert E. Park, the Chicago department of sociology had fostered a rich qualitative if psychologistic approach in their studies. But in the terms of the 20's and later, it was dubiously 'science' (9). We can, perhaps, use 1929 to date the maturation of empirical sociology in the US. That year, funded by the Rockefeller foundation with support from the SSRC and the Encyclopedia of the Social Sciences, Herbert Hoover assembled a distinguished group of social scientists 'to examine into the feasibility of a national survey of social trends ... to undertake the researches and make ... a complete impartial examination of the facts' (quoted from Gerstein, 1986). The report, known informally as 'the Ogburn Report,' after sociologist William F. Ogburn, contained over 1600 pages of quantitative research. Perhaps it was fitting that in 1930, Ogburn, a spiritual descendent of Giddings, left Columbia to go to Chicago.

Conclusion

This chapter has made the effort to give an explanation of the particular institutionalization of the social sciences in America, a model which, I believe, is now dominant in the world. One would like to think that this is because the disciplines represent natural kinds and because reigning empiricist methodologies are the surest way to truth. The argument here suggests otherwise. Briefly, as anything in the social world, the social sciences are social constructions. Thus they were constituted by specific, often nameable persons operating in concrete situations with specific resources at hand. I have tried to argue that the political and economic conditions of late-nineteenth-century America structured possibilities for institutional changes in higher education, that these were exploited by educational managers and then by academics well placed in the new universities. I have argued, as well, that particular outcomes depended critically on the conceptual materials at hand, materials which themselves have a social history. All of this could have been otherwise. Most important, perhaps, by understanding this, we may be clearer about what, as social scientists, we should be doing.

Notes

1. I have in mind here most especially those characteristic perfunctory 'histories' which form the introduction of all modern textbooks in the social sciences. The pattern is the same, however, even when the history is given a full-dress treatment, especially if the author is a competent professional of the discipline. Indeed, this is the case even where the result is a *very* useful study. Outstanding examples are Boring's classic, *History of Experimental Psychology* (1929) and Schumpeter's monumental *History of Economic Analysis* (1954).
2. See Bledstein, 1976, Silva and Slaughter, 1984, and Mills, 1964. Vesey writes that Santa Fe tycoon Leland Stanford selected David Starr Jordan as president 'because he admired firm-minded executive ability and wanted someone who could manage things "like the president of a railroad"' (1965: 398).

   Public institutions, excepting Michigan and Wisconsin, played very small roles in establishing the pattern of the American university. Vesey comments, 'by 1900 only a handful of states had provided outstanding public universities, fit to be compared with the leading private establishments' (p. 15). Ezra Cornell, whose Western Union Telegraph boomed during the Civil War, generously endowed Cornell, but his machinations with the legislature set back public higher education in New York State for many decades. See Bishop, 1962. There are good histories of the leading institutions which each provide valuable detail.

   Vesey remarks that it is false to assume that the competitive style of American development spurred innovation and fluidity (pp. 330–331). This was likely true initially, but once institutions collectively discovered that the now-familiar pattern suited the new environment, it became suicidal to risk innovation. Clark, for example, began in 1889 as an all-graduate institution, dedicated to 'pure science', e.g. natural science, mathematics and psychology. Clark quickly became disillusioned and president G. Stanley Hall failed to secure ancillary funds. For decades, the institution languished until the 'experiment' was abandoned. More recently, Vesey's own University of California at Santa Cruz is a good example.

3. The empiricist philosophy of science of these writers should be contrasted not to neo-Kantian philosophies, e.g., the philosophy of Hertz, which also restricted science to the empirical, but to 'realist' philosophies, rightly associated with the 'English' physicists Thomson and Maxwell, with Helmholtz and then later with Planck and Einstein (Manicas, 1987). It is important to notice that Vienna positivism, surely impelled by the War, owed much to these earlier views. The use of *Principia* logic enabled the Vienna positivists to generate a powerful – and incredibly influential – view. Vienna positivism would powerfully influence the generation of the late 30's and thereafter. It would do so, however, because the basic orientation had already been established.

4. I recognize differences, of course, between the so-called 'first generation' of historical economists, Roscher and Knies, e.g., the second, Schmoller, and the third, Weber, but for present purposes, I do not here try to separate influences of these. I believe that most Americans were most influenced by the Schmoller school. Weber made no impact – until Americans got Talcott Parsons's imaginative version.

5. These critics were to include Veblen, who joined the argument somewhat later. Veblen was not trained in Germany. Indeed, he was a 'philosopher,' who encountered C.S. Peirce at Hopkins and wrote a dissertation on Kant at Yale! Veblen thoroughly controlled classical and neo-classical economics and wrote still-valuable critiques of these. For him, they were 'taxonomic.' He believed that while 'the Historical School' did attempt 'an account of developmental sequence,' they followed 'the lines of pre-Darwinian speculations,' 'They have given a narrative survey of phenomena, not a genetic account of an unfolding process' ("Why is Economics Not an Evolutionary Science?" (1987), reprinted in Veblen, 1961).

6. As American 'socialists of the chair,' of course, even those who endorsed socialism were in no sense radicals, still less revolutionary socialists. Ely was a Christian Socialist. The ideas of socialists like Daniel De Leon were out of the realm of academic debate. De Leon, who could not be promoted at Columbia after he supported Henry George in the New York mayoral race (1889), left the academy to become a leader in the American Socialist Party (formed in 1903).

7. Characteristically, Furner (1975) does not appreciate this. She offers that both sides exaggerated differences and that the motivations of Ely and Simon, the original contestants, were more personal than theoretical. Accordingly, 'moderates' came to prevail. To see what was at issue one needs only to consider the list of figures discussed by Schumpeter as worthy of discussion and to see who is omitted (1954: 865–873). Included are Dunbar, Hadley, Newcomb, Sumner, Clark, Taussig and Fisher. 'Exemplifing' those who 'neither contributed to the development of our apparatus of analysis nor proved themselves masters in its use' are Ely, Henry C. Adams and Seligman. The 'institutionalists,' Veblen and Commons, are but mentioned.

8. Nor did this version of 'science' find favor with philosopher of science C.S. Peirce. As Bannister cites him: 'Giddings, like Gabriel Tarde, copied "the phraseology of mathematics, as if that possesses, in itself, a secret virtue of

rending vague ideas precise"' (Bannister, 1987: 76–77). Is it unfair to say that the 'yoking together of the scientific ox and the speculative ass' remains a key feature of mainstream sociology?

9. The dilemma is beautifully expressed in the 1937 SSRC assessment of *The Polish Peasant*, Thomas and Znaniecki's five-volume work. It was named by an SSRC poll of leading sociologists for a conference as 'the most significant piece of research in American sociology' (Faris, 1976: 17). Herbert Blumer, also of the Chicago Department, led off the assessment. Blumer concluded that 'the massive materials on the Poles did not, and could not, constitute a test of any of the propositions of the Methodological Note' (*ibid.*: 18). Faris summarizes: 'Although it was never put this bluntly, it would seem that *The Polish Peasant* consists of two little-related parts. Concrete data [four volumes] on the peasants themselves were but slightly used by the authors and perhaps not at all by other sociologists; the contribution of this part perhaps was to inspire successors to undertake labor of data gathering on a massive scale. The Methodological Note, on the other hand, which stood apart from the rest of the study, launched an important and enduring discussion of the attitudes and values, contributed to the weakening of the instinct theory by the formulation of wishes, and helped to give sociologists the courage, in defiance of the growing vogue of behavioristic psychology, to find a place for subjective aspects of human life' (*ibid*). Of course, Ogburn, Chapin, Lundberg and the methodologists found little, if any, science in this. What remained, then, was a disconnected 'social psychology' and the 'labor of data gathering on a massive scale."

References

Abrams, P. 1968. *The Origins of British Sociology: 1834–1914*. Chicago: University of Chicago Press.

Allen, Gay Wilson. 1967. *William James: A Biography*. New York: Viking.

Bannister, Robert C. 1987. *Sociology and Scientism: The Quest for Objectivity, 1880–1940*. Chapel Hill and London: University of North Carolina Press.

Becker, Ernest. 1971. *The Lost Science of Man*. New York: Braziller.

Bernard, L.L., and Bernard, Jessie. 1943. *Origins of American Sociology: The Social Science Movement in the United States*. New York: Crowell.

Bishop, Morris. 1962. *A History of Cornell*. Ithaca: Cornell University Press.

Bledstein, Burton. 1976. *The Culture of Professionalism: The Middle Class and the Development of Higher Education in America*. New York: Norton.

Boring, E.G. 1929. *A History of Experimental Psychology*. 2nd Edition. 1950. New York: Appleton-Century-Crofts.

Danziger, Kurt. 1979. "The Positivists Repudiation of Wundt," *Journal of the History of the Behavioral Sciences*, **15**.

Darnell, Regna. 1970. "The Professionalization of American Anthropology: A Case Study in the Sociology of Knowledge." Microfiche of typescript, Brooklyn, N.Y.

Diamond, S. 1980. "Wundt Before Leipzig." In R.E. Reiber (ed.)., *Wilhelm Wundt and the Making of a Scientific Psychology*. New York: Plenum.

Dorfman, Joseph. 1949. *The Economic Mind in American Civilization: 1865–1918*, 3 Vols. New York: Viking.

Faris, Robert E.L. 1967. *Chicago Sociology, 1920–1932*. San Francisco: Chandler.

Furner, Mary O. 1975. *Advocacy and Objectivity: A Crisis of Professionalization of American Social Science, 1905–1965*. Lexington: University Press of Kentucky.

Gruber, Carol S. 1975. *Mars and Minerva: World War I and the Uses of the Higher Learning in America*. Baton Rouge: Louisiana State University Press.

Hale, Matthew Jr. 1980. *Human Science and Social Order: Hugo Munsterberg and the Origins of Applied Psychology*. Philadelphia: Temple University Press.

Haskell, Thomas L. 1977. *The Emergence of Professional Social Science: The American Social Science Association and the Nineteenth Century Crisis of Authority*. Urbana: University of Illinois Press.

Helmholtz, Hermann. 1971. *Selected Writings*, Russell Kahn (ed.). Middleton: Wesleyan University.

Herbst, Jurgen. 1965. *The German Historical School in American Scholarship*. Ithaca: Cornell University Press.

Higham, John, Krieger, L., and Gilbert, F. 1965. *History*. Princeton: Princeton University Press.

Hilgard, Ernest R. (ed.). 1978. *American Psychology in Historical Perspective*. Washington, D.C.: American Psychological Association.

Iggers, George G. 1983. *The German Conception of History: The National Tradition of Historical Thought from Herder to the Present*. Middleton: Wesleyan University Press.

James, William. 1950. *The Principles of Psychology*, 2 Vols. New York: Dover. First published in 1890.

Karl, Barry D. 1974. *Charles E. Merriam and the Study of Politics*. Chicago: University of Chicago Press.

Kolko, Gabriel. 1967. *The Triumph of Conservatism*. Chicago: Quadrangle.

Leary, D. 1979. "Wundt and After: Psychology's Shifting Relations with the Natural Sciences, Social Sciences and Philosophy," *Journal of the History of the Behavioral Sciences*, **13**.

Lowie, Robert H. 1937. *The History of Ethnological Theory*. New York: Holt, Rinehart and Winston.

Mach, Ernst. 1959. *The Analysis of Sensations*. New York: Dover. First published in 1883.

Manicas, Peter T. 1987. *A History and Philosophy of the Social Sciences*. New York and Oxford: Basil Blackwell.

Manicas, Peter T. 1988. "Pragmatic Philosophy of Science and the Charge of Scientism," *Transactions of the Charles S. Peirce Society*, Vol. **XXIV**, No. 4.

Manicas, Peter T. 1989. "Explanation and Quantification." In Barry Glassner and Jonathan Moreno (eds.), *The Qualitative-Quantitative Distinction in the Social Sciences*. Dordrecht: Reidel.

Manicas, Peter T. 1989. *War and Democracy*. Oxford and New York: Basil Blackwell.

Manicas, Peter T. 1990. "Modest Realism, Experience and Evolution." In Roy Bhaskar (ed.), *Realism and Social Being*. Oxford: Basil Blackwell.

Margolis, J. Manicas, P.T., Harre, R., and Secord, P.F. *Psychology: Designing the*

Discipline. New York and Oxford: Basil Blackwell.
Matthews, Fred H. 1977. *Quest for an American Sociology: Robert E. Park and the Chicago School*. Montreal and London: McGill-Queen's University Press.
McClelland, Charles E. 1980. *State, Society and the University in Germany, 1700–1914*. Cambridge: Cambridge University Press.
Mill, John Stuart. 1974. *Essays on Some Unsettled Questions of Political Economy*. 2nd. Edition. Clifton, N.J.: Augustus Kelly. First published in 1844.
Mills, C. Wright. 1959. *The Sociological Imagination*. Harmondsworth: Penguin.
Mills, C. Wright. 1964. *Sociology and Pragmatism: The Higher Learning in America*. New York: Oxford.
Mitchell, Wesley Clair. 1969. *Types of Economic Theory: From Mercantilism to Institutionalism*, Joseph Dorfman (ed.). Reprint. New York: Augustus Kelly.
O'Connor, Michael J.L. 1944. *Origins of Academic Economics in the United States*. New York: Columbia University Press.
Passmore, John. 1966. *A Hundred Years of Philosophy*. Rev. ed. New York: Basic Books.
Perry, Ralph Barton. 1935. *The Thought and Character of William James*. Boston: Little Brown.
Ringer, Fritz. 1969. *The Decline of the German Mandarins: The German Academic Community, 1890–1933*. Cambridge, Mass.: Harvard University Press.
Robinson, James Harvey. 1912. *The New History*. New York: Macmillan.
Samelson, Franz. 1979. "Putting Psychology on the Map: Ideology and Intelligence Testing." In A.R. Buss (ed.), *Psychology in a Social Context*. New York: Irvington.
Schumpeter, J.A. 1954. *History of Economic Analysis*. New York: Oxford University Press.
Sarason, Seymour B. 1981. *Psychology Misdirected*. New York: Free Press.
Saveth, Edward N. 1974. *American History and Social Science*. New York: The Free Press.
Silva, Edward T., and Slaughter, Sheila A. 1984. *Serving Power: The Making of the Academic Social Science Expert*. Westport, Conn.: Greenwood Press.
Small, Albion. 1924. *Origins of Sociology*. New York: Russell and Russell.
Somit, Albert, and Tanenhaus, Joseph. 1967. *The Development of American Political Science: From Burgess to Behavioralism*. Boston: Allyn and Bacon.
Veblen, Thorstein. 1957. *The Higher Learning in America: A Memorandum on the Conduct of Universities by Businessmen*. New York: Sagamore. First published in 1918.
Veblen, Thorstein. 1961. *The Place of Science in Modern Civilization and Other Essays*. New York: Russell and Russell.
Veysey, Lawrence R. 1965. *The Emergence of the American University*. Chicago: University of Chicago Press.
Weinstein, James. 1968. *The Corporate Ideal in the Liberal State, 1900–1918*. Boston: Beacon.
Woodward, William. 1984. "William James's Psychology of Will: Its Revolutionary Impact on American Psychology." In Brozek, Josef (ed.). 1984. *Explorations in the History of Psychology in the United States*. Lewisburg: Bucknell University Press.

CHAPTER FOUR

THE TRIPARTITE DIVISION OF FRENCH SOCIAL SCIENCE:
A LONG-TERM PERSPECTIVE

JOHAN HEILBRON

If even the most autonomous disciplines owe some of their characteristics
to the context in which they develop, and if this context is characterized at
least partly by relations with other disciplines, the question arises as to
how one could define the set of interdisciplinary relationships that has
been most pertinent to the development of the social sciences.

On a general level, one can argue that the "intellectual field", as Pierre
Bourdieu has called it, represents the most important setting. Here
different groups and individuals compete for intellectual authority. And
everyone engaged in intellectual pursuits will have to respond to the
issues that are at stake here, whether this response takes a positive or
negative form, whether it results in the recognition of a "challenge" or in
the attitude of "refusal". Wolf Lepenies has shown that the tensions
between "science" and "literature" form a crucial dimension of the
modern intellectual field, and that this accounts for many different aspects
of the development of sociology (1).

On a somewhat lower level of generality, one can take the social
sciences themselves as forming a constellation that is of great importance
for each of these disciplines. Although it is well known that these
relationships differ in different countries, it is not at all clear what these
constellations precisely look like. Certain aspects are known, such as the
importance of the *Staatswissenschaften* in Germany, but more systematic
analyses do not seem to exist. Scholars have generally concentrated on
one particular discipline, usually their own. They have paid attention to
rivalry with neighbouring disciplines, but they seem to have ignored the
more general question of what type of structure the social sciences have
come to form in different national contexts.

P. Wagner, B. Wittrock, and R. Whitley (eds.), Discourses on Society: Volume XV, 1990, 73–92.
© 1990 *Kluwer Academic Publishers. Printed in the Netherlands.*

Pursuing this question I would like to present three arguments about the social sciences in France. The first is that the French social sciences form a specific and relatively stable constellation, which can be described as a *tripartite structure*. Social science in France is practised either as "political science", "economic science" or "human science", These three disciplinary groups do not form a relatively unified and subtly differentiated set of disciplines, but, on the contrary, a constellation that is marked by structural differences.

The second argument is that this division can be understood only by analysing the genesis of this constellation. To do so, however, implies returning to what can be called the *predisciplinary history* of social sciences. This area of inquiry is largely neglected. The history of the social sciences is still very much disciplinary history, closely interwoven with disciplinary demands and divisions, and the predisciplinary past is either taken for granted or considered to be merely prehistory. That neglect, as I will try to show, is one of the reasons why certain characteristics of the social sciences are not well understood. Many notions and assumptions of the modern social sciences have predisciplinary origins. This applies, for example, to the modern notions of the "state", "economy" and "society", just as to the modern conceptions of human action.

The third argument is that this tripartite constellation was not just an administrative or organizational arrangement, but a true division of labour that profoundly affected the *cognitive identity* of these three disciplinary groups.

The fact that the social sciences in France have clustered around three poles, the "political sciences", the "economic sciences" and a third, somewhat larger and more diffuse group, the "human sciences", is best illustrated at the institutional level. The political sciences were very long deprived of autonomous possibilities for teaching and research. When finally institutional arrangements emerged, they took the form of a professional school, that was separated from the universities and that primarily trained upper-level civil servants. This occurred only after the Franco-Prussian war of 1870, that is during the period when the social sciences experienced their first breakthrough as disciplines, endowed with special chairs and journals.

For the humanities or human sciences the first modern institutional arrangements were academies like the *Académie française* (1635) and the *Académie des inscriptions et des belles lettres* (1662). During the eighteenth century, the human sciences came to include different forms of social theory, and this extension was institutionalized during the nineteenth century. The human sciences now included disciplines like philosophy, psychology and sociology and were integrated in a separate faculty of letters. The faculty of letters prepared people mainly for intellectual careers (teaching, research). In the same period that psychology and sociology officially entered the faculty of letters, economics was incorporated in the faculty of law and developed in an institutional setting that was clearly distinct both from the "political" and the "human" sciences.

This mode of differentiation has remained a basic feature of these disciplines up to this day. With the second breakthrough, which occurred after 1945, the social sciences became full-fledged disciplines, but this happened without great changes in the basic division. There is in France, for example, no separate faculty for the social sciences (despite attempts undertaken in that direction during the 1960's), and the postwar expansion took place largely within the existing arrangements. The *Ecole libre des sciences politiques* (1871) was transformed into the *Fondation nationale des sciences politiques* and an *Institut d'études politiques*. A professional organisation emerged, the *Association française de science politique* (1949), and a new journal was established, the *Revue française de science politique* (1951) (2).

Similar developments occurred in the other disciplinary groups. In 1958, for example, a *licence* degree was created for economics. Economics now became a university discipline in its own right, and in the same year the faculty of law was rebaptised "faculty of law and the economic sciences". As to the faculty of letters, a *licence* degree in psychology was created in 1947; in 1958 the same happened for sociology, and the "faculty of letters" was renamed "faculty of letters and human sciences" in the same year.

With the rapid expansion of the social sciences after 1945 new tendencies occurred. Within each of the three disciplinary groups changes occurred, sometimes very fundamental changes, but a tripartite division is still clearly recognizable.

To understand this structure and its significance, it is necessary to take a closer look at its genesis. The question of how and why this division occurred, however, can be properly answered only by going back a little further than is commonly done.

Jurists and the Decline of Political Thought

Before the rise of modern concepts of the social world, there was an essential unity in the dominant conception of human matters. In the Aristotelian tradition, these questions were part of "practical philosophy", a branch of learning that consisted of ethics, politics and matters of household management. As such, these disciplines were taught in the universities, and in countries where the universities remained the dominant centres of learning, Aristotelian schemes continued to be a basic reference until well in the eighteenth century. In Germany, for example, the new forms of political theory (Machiavelli, Bodin, Hobbes) were introduced very late (3), and someone like Pufendorf, the leading representative of modern natural law, formulated his ideas within the formal framework of practical philosophy (4).

In France, the universities did not remain important centres of learning. Their decline is well known and is illustrated by the fact that the curriculum of "practical philosophy" remained virtually unchanged all through the seventeenth and eighteenth centuries (5). French universities had close ties with the church, but they were increasingly overshadowed by new institutions, founded and supported by the state. The *Collège de France* (1530) was the first example, later came the *Jardin du roi* (1635), and with the founding of national academies in the seventeenth century, a whole new cultural regime emerged. Under the patronage of the state, a rapid secularization took place, and for the new intellectuals that gathered around these academies, new forms of political and moral philosophy were of much greater importance than the classical heritage.

The new intellectual regime offered a great deal of independence from the church and the universities, but since this was possible only by support from the state and the court, the new intelligentsia was particularly dependent on these circles, and on what they did and did not appreciate. These new forms of social constraint explain much of the curious development of moral and political theory.

During the French Renaissance, jurists formed a leading intellectual group. It was in their work that for the first time a modern notion of the state emerged (6), and they made important contributions to other fields of scholarship as well (7). But their predominant role in intellectual life came to an end during the seventeenth century. With the rise of absolutism, the jurists lost much of their political and intellectual functions. In a way they were defeated with their own weapons (8). Under Richelieu and Louis XIV the notion of "sovereignty" that had been developed by Bodin and others was of strategic importance in depriving the parliaments of their political power and transforming the French monarchy into an absolutist state. The conditions for more-or-less autonomous work on political questions rapidly deteriorated, and in the seventeenth and eighteenth centuries French jurists largely restricted their work to the elaboration of existing forms of law. With few exceptions, they no longer produced original political studies, and they ignored or rejected the theories of natural law that developed mainly in Protestant countries. Amont the great names of seventeenth-century political thought there are Englishmen (Hobbes, Locke), Dutchmen (Grotius, Spinoza) and Germans (Althusius, Pufendorf), but there were no longer any Frenchmen.

The expansion of the French state had given juridically trained members of the bourgeoisie the opportunity to enter the ranks of the ruling classes. For a long time, jurists operated as an extremely important ally of the king against the church and the powers of the local aristocracy. They thus played a vital role in the establishment of a centralized state, a service for which the king honoured them with aristocratic titles (9). Gradually, and especially during the eighteenth century, the differences between the old nobility and the *noblesse de robe* diminished. But while they had become part of the ruling elite, they had at the same time lost their intellectual significance. Not only Jean Bodin had been a jurist; Montaigne and others belonged to the same group. In the seventeenth and eighteenth centuries there were no longer jurists with a similar position. The *philosophes*, for instance, expressed contempt for them. In a letter to Voltaire, Condorcet remarked that ever since the seventeenth century, the *robe* had produced only one man whose work was worthy of attention: Montesquieu. "One remains in parlement only if one is incapable of anything more reasonable. Montesquieu left parlement immediately after he discovered his talents" (10).

With the rise of absolutism and intellectual decline of the group of political specialists, political theory more or less disappeared. Everything that touched upon matters of state was reserved for official bodies; what could be written and defended publicly were basically only variations on the orthodox doctrines. Nothing illustrates the fate of political theory in absolutist France more clearly than the failure to establish an academy for law or political science. Since academies had been founded for literature, art, music, architecture and the natural sciences, these institutions had become the most dynamic and most prestigious cultural institutions (11).

Teaching remained an affair of the *collèges* and universities, but for
research and scholarship the academies were the leading institutions.
They were the centres of intellectual and cultural life, and were officially
charged with the task of setting new standards. But precisely because
these academies were bound to the state, the one domain for which no
academic rights were granted was that of politics, law and administration.
From at least 1692, when *abbé* Choisy formed a small group to discuss
political and social matters (12), until the Revolution, every attempt to
create something like a political or juridical academy failed. The *Club de
l'Entresol* (1724–31) probably came closest to a realization, but after
some years of tacit permission the gatherings were again forbidden. Half
a century later, in 1774, the intelecual debate had changed so much that
the "Academy for public law" that was now proposed would primarily
serve to counter the "subversive literature" that had become a threat to the
authorities (13). Quite typically, even this proposal was rejected.

What holds for the academies as bodies of learning and scholarship
also holds for the teaching of the political sciences. Here the pattern was
the same: despite numerous initiatives, at least from the beginning of the
eighteenth century (14), a school for the political or administrative
sciences was not founded until almost a century after the Revolution. The
political sciences were not only granted no academic rights; the training
of civil servants equally remained under the immediate control of the
authorities. The creation of a "school", even a purely professional school,
would have meant the recognition of a certain autonomy. For political
matters that minimum of independence from state control was too much.
Politics and administration were not matters that could be left to scholars
and teachers. It was only after the Franco-Prussian War and the Commune that an *Ecole libre des sciences politiques* (1871) was founded, but
– quite typically – that was the result of a "private" initiative.

Political theory and law were not flourishing disciplines in the early
modern period in France. They lacked a minimum of autonomy, and as
far as they formally existed, they were in a position comparable only to
theology. They were taught at the universities, but as such, they were
much more dependent on the orthodox doctrines than all the fields for
which academies had been founded. One might even say that – just like
theology – political and juridical theories came to be more or less
excluded from the intellectual universe that arose around academies and
salons. In absolutist France, politics was a state monopoly and was not
recognized as being a legitimate subject for intellectual consideration. So

intellectuals tended to avoid it or, as happened in the eighteenth century, tried to discuss political questions from a non-political point of view, for instance from an economic or a moral perspective.

The Language of Morals

Although the regulations of the academies mentioned that "moral and political questions" could only be treated in accordance with the authority of the king, the government and the laws of the monarchy (15), a fundamental difference had arisen between what was considered to be "moral" and what was "political". In fact, from at least the beginning of the seventeenth century, moral theory and political theory developed in opposite senses. Whereas there had been a sharp decline of political thought, there was a simultaneous rise of moral theory. This phenomenon, although widely neglected (16), was one of the main characteristics of social theory in early modern France.

Morals was a subject much closer to literary culture than to politics or law. As such it was of importance to the group that had gained a dominant position within the new intelligentsia: the writers. Contrary to philosophical specialties such as logic and metaphysics, morals belonged to the humanities, and was part of the curriculum of the *studia humanitatis* (17). Following the ancient moralists, it covered a broad range of questions about human existence and human action. A central theme was the role of the passions. In the doctrines of the church, the passions were objects of prohibition and served to encourage penance and willingness for sacrifice. In the secular tradition, the passions were not so much seen in a more positive as in a more neutral way. They were not so much considered as sinful affections, but rather as motives or driving forces of human action. However unworthy *amour-propre* and ambition might be, it was sensible to reckon with its importance, and it was reasonable to try to get a better understanding of its role.

Because the passions were seen as the true motives of human action, they also formed the starting point for considerations of life-style and the art of *savoir vivre*. That was the reason why in aristocratic circles there was a strong interest in these matters. Although knowledge and learning were considered to be too "pedantic" for the nobility, morals represented an important exception. Around the court new codes of behaviour had emerged, and parallel to that a demand had arisen for a secular discourse about the nature of human conduct that would be of use for a new understanding of the question of manners and morality. To maintain oneself at court was possible only if one paid close attention to the behaviour of others and to possible changes that might occur (18). Because of the high level of self-constraint and the rich variety of polite manners, it was very dificult to understand the "true" feelings of a courtier. Attention and a certain "psychological" insight were required to understand what the reason was for a certain act; the same attention and insight were required for acting in an effective manner oneself. A certain finesse was also imperative in the treatment of rivals and opponents. In that case too, remarks and allusions were all the more effective as they were "striking" and "to the point". A compliment is most effective when it actually "touches" the one who is complimented; the same goes for insults. *Plaire* and *toucher* were both referred to as rules of conduct to which court nobles had to conform. But to actually do so insight was a prerequisite, and to acquire that insight effort and study were necessary. It was by no means sufficient to know how to behave. At least intuitively, one also had to know why to behave in a certain fashion, in other words why certain actions were more effective than others. That was the reason why in aristocratic circles one spoke and thought a lot about these passions that in social intercourse were so carefully hidden. In the salons impulses, passions and temperaments were favourite topics of conversation, and both literary and more reflective writings prospered as never before. The *Maximes* (1665) of La Rochefoucauld, Pascal's *Pensées* (1670), the *Essais de morale* (1671) of Nicole, the *Caractères* (1688) of La Bruyère, all were widely read and imitated. The enormous growth of publications about morals, as this genre was called, was in the latter half of the seventeeth century equalled by no other genre (19).

Observation and close scrutiny of the behaviour of the people with whom one interacted was part of the aristocratic lifestyle that had developed around the court and the salons. In Germany, Madame de Staël remarked, one studies books, in France one studies people. Court life and salon culture are hard to imagine without special attention to the psychology of human behaviour. And in classical French literature this preoccupation is very much present. Portraits and character sketches became prominent literary genres, the depiction of manners and morality became a familiar part of literary work, and the dissection of human conduct was raised to a special art in the work of the *moralistes*. La Rochefoucauld, to mention only the most important and probably most imitated author, showed that it is not out of courage that people are courageous, and rarely out of virtuousness that people are virtuous. Human actions are seldom noble and disinterested. *Amour-propre* is the most common and most powerful drive, even when disinterestedness seems to rule. From La Rochefoucauld to Chamfort, these moralists again and again stressed that even the most sublime acts were motivated by human, and often all too human, motives. For Nietzsche this moralist tradition was the main reason for the vitality of French culture. Nowhere else, he wrote, is there an equivalent for the psychological sensitivity and curiosity, that in France one even finds in the newspapers and the boulevard theater (20).

In this moralist tradition, the objective was not to give moral lessons. What *moralistes* understood as "moral" was morality in the sense of *mores, moeurs*, and ethics in the sense of *ethos*. They described, considered and analysed human behaviour, but without formulating any ethical doctrines or moral commandments. Their central question was "why do people behave as they do?", and that question was linked to the one "what would in this respect be a sensible thing for me to do?" In this tradition human conduct was no longer treated in relationship with duties and ideals, but in terms of motives and effects. The more-or-less practical theories of action that emerged in this way were of crucial importance for the rise of the social sciences. Gradually the idea took shape that of all the passions that dominated men, *amour-propre* was the most powerful and stable one (21). The result was that human beings were no longer seen as an unpredictable prey to the passions, but as beings that in a fairly coherent way strive for their own profit. Human conduct therefore seemed more stable and orderly than had been supposed in the Christian doctrines. Human actions were less accidental and arbitrary, they were oriented towards gain and avoidance of loss. The anarchy of the passions that, so to speak, had to be tamed from "outside" and "above", namely by enforcing political and religious duties, gave way to a new conception. The originality of this new conception was not the predominant role of *amour-propre*. That was a very old theme in both theological writings and political theories. What La Rochefoucauld and especially Nicole introduced was the *positive* role of self-interest. In their work self-interest was for the first time systematically upgraded. Self-interest and self-love were not only considered to be "natural" and legitimate motives; these motives could also be used as a basis of social order. Their argument concerning the positive effects of self-love was later taken up by Mandeville. That "private vices" could lead to "public benefits" was one way to formulate the transition to a more positive evaluation of self-interest.

In the French moralist tradition, two themes developed that were crucial for the rise of the social sciences. First, a new and secular conception of human action emerged. This new anthropology would serve as a foundation for the economic and social theories that emerged in the eighteenth century. One of the most important conclusions that could be drawn from the writings of the moralists was the idea that people could be left to themselves. That may well be described as one of the most important theoretical innovations of the early modern era. Contrary to the teachings of the church and to Hobbesian political thought, a strict observance of religious and political duties was not a necessary condition for social order. There existed an order different from the realm of the state and the church: civil society, as it came to be called, and this order was not based on official regulations and duties, but merely on man's capacity to act according to his self-interest. It was on this anthropological foundation that "economic" and "social" theories arose. On that basis a break became possible with the theocentrism of the church and the state-centrism of political theory. In the eighteenth century theories emerged in which "civil society" was the focus of attention; its functioning was conceived as a more-or-less self-regulating mechanism, solely based on the assumption that people would act according to their interests.

The second and closely connected theme that developed in the moralist tradition was the particular significance of *moeurs et manières*, as Montesquieu called it. Human action was primarily based on *amour-propre*, but because of great differences in morals and manners, human conduct was immensely varied. Even if *amour-propre* provided an invariant anthropology there was no uniformity of actual conduct. In their analysis of *amour-propre* moralists therefore carefully studied and specified the context of the actions they sought to understand. Their concrete and contextual analyses would later serve as an example for more historical and comparative work.

The moralist tradition that emerged in France during the seventeenth century was a distinctive and quite original intellectual tradition. It was close to literary culture and salon life, and had clearly diverged from the politico-juridical tradition. By the end of the seventeenth century it represented a separate *intellectual genre* that had acquired a much greater cultural prestige than political theory and law. So in France, it was in and through the works of moralists that a shift emerged from the "civic to the civil" (Pocock). It was this shift that was taken up and more systematically elaborated by the *philosophes*.

The Moral Sciences in the Eighteenth and Nineteenth Centuries

It was the moralist tradition that provided the starting point for most of the historical and theoretical work of the *philosophes*. There is no doubt that the *philosophes* went beyond this tradition. But it can be shown that they did so mostly by extending and redefining it. Morals and morality covered a broad area that allowed for a reasonable amount of liberty with respect to orthodox doctrines. In the language of morality the *philosophes* could express themselves on almost any subject, also on controversial issues that related to the church and the state. In the language of morals, it was possible to appropriate controversial topics, to gain some intellectual authority and to confront the spokesmen of the orthodox doctrines. Moral philosophy or moral science (in a non-technical sense) became the point of departure for considerations not only about human conduct in smaller groups, but also about state and politics, culture and history, law and society. To understand human communities, the *philosophes* argued, it was not sufficient to see human beings as "subjects" and "citizens". Human beings had to be viewed as moral (and physical) beings in the widest sense of the word. Moral science was the most encompassing and, as Voltaire remarked, the first of the sciences (22).

For the *philosophes* morals was nothing else than the science of man, and the human sciences were moral sciences. In his preliminary discourse to the *encyclopédie*, d'Alembert distinguished three grand domains of science: the science of God, the science of nature and the science of man. In the science of man, he distinguished between logic and morals. Logic referred to a certain number of formal capacities, morals were divided into a general and a specific part. The *morale générale* was concerned with general and universally valid notions (happiness, virtue, etc.), the *morale particulière* referred to the duties of man as an individual (law), the duties of man in the family (economics) and the duties of man in society (politics). Morality was the general denomination of human reality, that is as far as it differed from nature, in other words, as far as there was some degree of civilization. Theology and duties toward God were not part of the moral sciences, and political and juridical questions were considered to be part of this moral universe.

This classification was, of course, not very original, but the *philosophes* used it in a particularly striking and strategic manner. "Morals" became a critical substitute for political and theological vocabularies. Morals and manners were increasingly referred to as a range of phenomena that was of much greater importance than political regimes. And in some cases it was explicitly used against political and juridical modes of speech (23). Whereas seventeenth-century moralists had avoided political issues altogether, some of the *philosophes* tended to derive political conclusions from their moral considerations. Descartes had written a *Traité des passions* (1649), but contrary to Hobbes or Spinoza not one single conclusion followed for the organization of the state. In that respect, Holbach and Helvétius represented a radical change. Their "moralization" of politics and their dream of an "ethocracy", as Holbach called it, represented a particularly radical conclusion (24). But the tendency to treat political questions from a moral point of view was found among many authors. When Duclos remarked that "les moeurs, plus que les lois, font et caractérisent une nation", he might have intended to paraphrase *De l'esprit des lois*, but what he said was not at all foreign, neither to French aristocrats nor to French writers.

Even if it would be misleading to reduce the contributions of the *philosophes* to an extension or a generalization of moral philosophy, it is nonetheless true that they conceived their work as belonging to the moral sciences. The *sciences morales* or *sciences humaines* gradually became more encompassing, and during the nineteenth century they came to include disciplines like philosophy, psychology and sociology. The new disciplines often remained in the tradition of the moral sciences. Questions of morality, for instance, were crucial to French sociology. Durkheim's sociology was very much centred on the study of moral practices and representations, and he conceived the social function of his work as a contribution to a modern and secular morality. The link between sociology and morals later even became institutionalized. When in 1920 sociology became an official part of the philosophy curriculum, the subject in question was called *morale et sociologie*. The courses that were given for this certificate were for forty years the only official courses in sociology.

The Distance to Political Science

While the moral sciences during the eighteenth and nineteenth centuries gradually extended to include both philosophy and disciplines such as psychology and sociology, they did not extend to the knowledge of the state. Political science was something different and remained so. The *Ecole libre des sciences politiques* (1871) was not linked to the universities, and the distance to the humanities and other social sciences did not disappear after 1945. The political sciences were from the beginning onwards much more practical disciplines. The *Ecole libre des sciences politiques* trained many generations of upper-level civil servants, but the intellectual ambitions of its founder, Emile Boutmy, were never realized (25). Representatives of the political sciences rarely transcended the limits of an administrative science, and in a way, the political sciences remained more or less outside the boundaries of the intellectual field proper.

The fact that the political sciences were just as marginal to the intellectual field as they were close to the political field is confirmed by data about the backgrounds of political science students (26). In comparison with other institutions during the 1960's, political science students were of high social backgrounds but had comparatively low school achievements. Among a very great number of disciplines and institutions that were analysed, they were closest to the students of a business school, the *Ecole des hautes études commerciales* (HEC), and of the *Ecole normale d'administration* (ENA). Their social backgrounds were much higher than the students of the faculty of letters, whereas their school results compared unfavourably with the students of the more intellectual *grandes écoles* such as the *Ecole normale supérieure* (ENS).

The specific position of the "political sciences" with respect to the "human sciences" remained also in another way of more structural importance. It corresponds namely to the division between "experts" and "intellectuals". The human sciences, from the seventeenth century onwards, were practised by a different group of people than the political sciences. Both groups of disciplines fulfilled different social functions, and these differences were embodied in distinctive social roles. This can be seen quite clearly in the terms employed to designate both groups. The expressions *gens de lettres, moralistes, philosophes,* and somewhat later again *intellectuels*, all implied a principal distance to the specialist who invests his competence in obtaining positions in the state administration. The practitioners of the political sciences had no clear name of their own. But they were seen more as administrators or experts than as "intellectuals". Just as men of letters and intellectuals tended to be excluded from political and administrative responsibilities, the political science specialists tended to be excluded from the intellectual field. This contrast, which had been commented upon by Voltaire in his letters on England or by Tocqueville in his analysis of prerevolutionary France, has often led to a political science that is merely a form of practical learning, and forms a human science in which the state is non-existent. The political sciences tended to avoid a whole range of questions concerning their status as intellectual or scientific endeavours, just as in the tradition of the moral sciences there has been a tendency to avoid questions about the state. The moral sciences initially acquired their autonomy by avoiding everything that directly touched upon matters of the state. In the seventeenth century that was quite literally the orientation of the *moralistes*. It is remarkable, however, that the human sciences have very much remained in this tradition.

Two examples can illustrate this: Durkheimian sociology and the *Annales* school. Both represented central paradigms in the social sciences. Sociologists in principle have no reason at all to exclude the state from their object. But from Comte to Durkheim, French sociologists were often concerned with social relations in which the state was absent. For an elaborate sociology of the state, one has to turn to Max Weber or to the Italian theorists, but for Durkheim the level of politics had lost much of its social significance. And political sociology was absent even from the different classifications the durkheimians proposed for their discipline (27).

The same phenomenon can be observed for the period after 1945. For the historians of the *Annales* school, which became the most central group in the human sciences, the political level was categorized as the most superficial level of history. A history of the state was not part of the long-term history Braudel proposed. As in the case of Durkheim, Braudel's proposals had a place for many disciplines, from demography and geography to sociology and anthropology, but he deliberately ruled out the "political sciences". In 1969, for example, he wrote that they had not yet become properly scientific disciplines (28). The political sciences had no place in the *sixième section* of the *Ecole pratique des hautes études*. That in itself was a significant example of the *longue durée*.

Economics as a Third Domain

The only social science that gradually broke away from the division in "moral" and "political" sciences was economics. The notion of economics in a modern sense started to emerge in the seventeenth century. The *Traité d'économie politique* (1615) of Antoine de Montchrestien was one of the very first publications in which the term "political economy" appeared. The management of wealth was no longer confined to private households, but was defined as a public affair that formed the object of a new speciality (29). Because this new speciality was conceived as a "political science", these forms of knowledge remained closely linked to state functions and state institutions and tended to remain confidential. Contrary to England, political economy was in France not really a subject. The French state gathered all kinds of statistical and other data, but they remained secret. The political sciences in France were practised by state officials who published little, so that there is no literature comparable either to German Cameralism or to English political arithmetic. But for political economy this situation started to change around 1750 (30). The number of economic writings rapidly began to increase, and even specialized journals were founded such as the *Journal économique* (1751–72). In approximately the same period, the first schemes emerged in which the "economy" was conceived as a specific and autonomous order, independent from the state (Cantillon, Quesnay). In the work of the physiocrates, knowledge of the "laws" of this "natural order" was seen as a preconditon for state intervention, and in most cases *laissez-faire* was considered to be the best maxim the state could adopt. The "economy" was a complicated, self-regulating system, and the first task of the state was not to prescribe regulations and rules, but to understand the "laws" of this "natural" order (31).

With the claim to autonomy, based on the elaboration of the schemes Cantillon and Quesnay had provided, "political economy" could be transformed into "classical economics". The "mercantilist" orientation was replaced by the economics of markets and the invisible hand, an orientation that in France was codified by Jean-Baptiste Say. Economics became closely linked to liberal ideology and the politics of the *laissez-faire*. That alliance furnished the social conditions for a further distance to the state and the "political sciences" in the traditional sense. Economics then was not a "human science", developed mainly by philosophers in the faculty of letters, and was no longer a "political science", developed by civil servants in relation to problems of state administration.

But economics was not a theoretical discipline either. Theoretical innovations were either very rare or ignored (Cournot), and it was not until economics was institutionalized in the faculty of law that a more scholarly type of economic analysis emerged, for which the *Revue d'économie politique* (1887) served as an outlet (32). At the end of the nineteenth century, economics came to occupy a position in between the political and the human sciences. It was a university discipline, somewhat more scholarly than the political sciences, yet clearly separated from the human sciences.

The separation of economics from the moral and political sciences is presently all too clear in the conceptual development of the discipline. Based on the assumptions of *homo economicus*, economists have constructed models which allowed them to ignore the non-economic dimensions of economic processes. But while this general outcome has not been specific for France, there have no doubt been other aspects (the relationship with law or with engineering) that can account for more specific features of economic theory in France

The Specificity of the French Constellation

What has been most typical of the French development was the separation and subsequent divergence of the moral and political sciences. The decline of political theory in the seventeenth century and the simultaneous rise of the moral sciences eventually led to a configuration in which most social sciences were included in the human sciences and were institutionalized in the faculty of letters. That resulted in the formation of disciplines that theoretically depended a great deal on philosophy, but for which the literary disciplines also had a particular importance. Many of the most creative French social scientists were trained in philosophy and had a critical attitude towards the lack of rigour they observed in literary studies (Durkheim, Lévi-Strauss, Bourdieu). Most distant for this group of human sciences were the questions and concepts associated with the politico-administrative sciences. These disciplines have occupied a position at the periphery of the intellectual field. This split between the political and the moral sciences seems to be fairly specific for France, especially in its far-reaching consequences.

As in most other countries, economics became a fairly independent endeavour in the nineteenth century. At first practised mainly by advocates of *laissez-faire* liberalism, it was institutionalized in the faculty of law. The practical involvements and the connections with the study of law both turned out to be major obstacles for the mathematization of the discipline. Whereas Cournot had been ignored, Walras had to go to Switzerland to get a chair. It was only after the economic crisis of 1929 that economics started to attract mathematically trained *polytechniciens*. They gained leading positions in institutions such as the INSEE and eventually replaced the professors of law as leading economists. Although that very much changed the discipline, it did not fundamentally alter the relationships with the political and human sciences.

The decisive factor in the formation of this tripartite structure seems to have been the process of state formation. That process sealed the fate of the political sciences in France, and some would say that they have never recovered. With the rise of absolutism the political sciences developed largely as practical disciplines under immediate control of the official authorities. As a result political theory and scholarship, which had flourished during the Renaissance, declined.

The development of absolutism, on the other hand, was also central in the emergence of the modern intellectual field, which gained a high degree of independence from the church and the universities. Institutions such as the academies were royal institutions, located in Paris. They rapidly acquired great prestige in almost all fields, from literature and art to architecture and natural sciences, with the notable exception of the political and juridical sciences. In this intellectual field, the moral sciences occupied an important position. This was due partly to the links with literary culture, partly to the specific interest in these matters among aristocrats. The moral sciences thus became a particularly important and prestigious branch of intellectual activity. They gradually extended to different forms of social theory, and this tradition has very much remained a "tacit dimension" (Polanyi) of the human sciences in France. It would be interesting in this respect to compare the French moralist tradition with the German tradition of the *Geisteswissenschaften*. Whereas the German tradition was more strongly linked to the university, the French moralist tradition emerged outside the universities, was linked to salon encounters, and has remained alive in French literature.

The transition from "political economy" to a more independent economic science was less specific for France than the divergence of the moral and political sciences. Contrary to the other forms of political science, economics was linked to powerful groups outside the state. Economists could therefore achieve a degree of autonomy from the political authorities that other "political sciences" (statistics, demography) have never reached or reached only very much later.

If this analysis makes any sense, it should help to clarify a few general characteristics of the social sciences in France. As such it can also lead to a better understanding of the "exceptions". If this tripartite structure was indeed a relatively stable division, then the attempts to build more general models probably resulted from the intention to transcend these boundaries.

Another effect of this analysis is that it can be used for a better understanding of national differences. Comparisons between political theory in France and Germany or between sociology in England and France should take into account that these disciplines form part of constellations that have a very different structuration. It would therefore be useful to pay more attention to the question of what type of structure the social sciences form in different national contexts.

Notes

1. W. Lepenies, *Die drei Kulturen. Soziologie zwischen Literatur und Wissenschaft*, München, Carl Hanser Verlag, 1985.
2. For a general overview of political science, see P. Favre, "Histoire de la science politique", in M. Grawitz & J. Leca (eds.), *Traité de science politique*, Paris, Presses Universitaires de France, 1985, vol. I, pp. 3–45. I have furthermore relied on J. Heilbron, *Sociologie in Frankrijk. Een historische schets*, Amsterdam, SISWO, 1983, and *id.*, *Over het ontstaan van de Franse sociologie (1750–1850)*, Amsterdam, 1990 (forthcoming).
3. H. Maier, *Die ältere deutsche Staats- und Verwaltungslehre*, München, Deutscher Taschenbuch Verlag, 1980, pp. 281–288.
4. H. Denzer, *Moralphilosophie und Naturrecht bei Samuel Pufendorf*, München, C.H. Beck, 1972, pp. 296–300.
5. L.W.B. Brockliss, *French higher education in the seventeenth and eighteenth centuries*, Oxford, Clarendon Press, 1987, pp. 331–333.
6. Q. Skinner, *Foundations of modern political thought*, Cambridge, Cambridge University Press, 1978.
7. D.R. Kelley, *Foundations of modern historical scholarship. Language, law and history in the French Renaissance*, New York, Columbia University Press, 1970.
8. W.F. Church, "The decline of the French jurists as political theorists, 1660–1789", *French historical studies*, 5, 1967, pp. 1–40.
9. On the process of state formation see N. Elias, *Über den Prozess der Zivilisation. Soziogenetische und psychogenetische Untersuchungen* (1939), Frankfurt am Main, Suhrkamp, 1981. On the role of the jurists see P. Bourdieu, *La noblesse d'Etat. Grandes écoles et esprit de corps*, Paris, Editions de Minuit, 1989, pp. 533–559.
10. Quoted by W.F. Church, "The decline of the French jurists as political theorists" (note 8).
11. On these academies see A. Viala, *Naissance de l'écrivain. Sociologie de la littérature à l'âge classique*, Paris, Editions de Minuit, 1985, pp. 15–50.

12. P. Janet, *Histoire de la science politique dans ses rapports avec la morale* (1858), Paris, Alcan, 1913, Volume II, p. 307.
13. J. Portemer, "Recherches sur l'enseignement du droit public au XVIIIe siècle", *Revue historique du droit français et étranger*, **37**, 1959, pp. 341–397.
14. See G. Thuillier, *L'ENA avant l'ENA*, Paris, Presses Universitaires de France, 1983.
15. D. Roche, *Le siècle des lumières en province. Académies et académiciens provinciaux, 1680–1789*, Paris, Mouton & Cie., 1978, volume I, p. 102.
16. See for example N.O. Keohane, *Philosophy and the state in France. From the Renaissance to the Enlightenment*, Princeton, Princeton University Press, 1980.
17. P.O. Kristeller, *Renaissance thought II*, New York, Harper & Row, 1965, pp. 20–68.
18. See the remarks in N. Elias, *Die höfische Gesellschaft*, Frankfurt am Main, Suhrkamp, 1983, pp. 159–168.
19. H.-J. Martin, *Livre, pouvoirs et société à Paris au XVIIe siècle (1598–1701)*, Genève, Droz, 1969, pp. 826–830 and 1074. On the moralists see A. Levi, *French moralists. The theory of the passions, 1585 to 1649*, Oxford, Clarendon Press, 1964; L. van Delft, *Le moraliste classique. Essai de définition et de typologie*, Genève, Droz, 1982.
20. F. Nietzsche, "Jenseits von Gut und Böse" (par. 254), in *Werke*. Herausgegeben von K. Schlechta, Frankfurt am Main, Ullstein, 1979, volume II, pp. 721–23. Similar remarks in "Menschliches, Allzumenschliches" (par. 35 and 214), in *ibid.*, volume I.
21. A.O. Hirschman, *The passions and the interests*, Princeton, Princeton University Press, 1977. For a detailed study of the notion of *amour-propre* see H.-J. Fuchs, *Entfremdung und Narzissmus. Semantische Untersuchungen zur Geschichte der "Selbstbezogenheit" als Vorgeschichte von französisch "amour-propre"*, Stuttgart, J.B. Metzler, 1977.
22. Voltaire, "Essai sur les moeurs" (1756), in *Oeuvres complètes*, Paris, Hachette, 1876, volume X, p. 43.
23. For this theme see R. Koselleck, *Kritik und Krise. Eine Studie zur Pathogenese der bürgerlichen Welt*, Frankfurt am Main, Suhrkamp, 1973.
24. On this tendency see E.C. Ladd, "Helvétius and Holbach: 'la moralisation de la politique'", *Journal of the history of ideas*, **23**, 1962, pp. 221–238. For the context see A.C. Kors, *d'Holbach's coterie. An Englightenment in Paris*, Princeton, Princeton University Press, 1976.
25. See P. Favre, "Les sciences de l'Etat entre déterminisme et libéralisme, Emile Boutmy (1835–1906) et la création de l'Ecole libre des sciences politiques", *Revue française de sociologie*, **22**, 1981, pp. 429–465; D. Damamme, "Genèse sociale d'une institution scolaire: l'Ecole libre des sciences politiques", *Actes de la recherche en sciences sociales*, **70**, 1987, pp. 31–46.
26. P. Bourdieu, *La noblesse d'Etat. Grandes écoles et esprit de corps*, Paris, Editions de Minuit, 1989, esp. pp. 183–264.
27. See P. Favre, "L'absence de la sociologie politique dans les classifications durkheimiennes des sciences sociales", *Revue française de science politique*, **32**, 1982, pp. 5–31. On the strategic aspects of durkheimian sociology see V.

Karady, "Stratégies de réussite et mode de faire-valoir de la sociologie chez les durkheimiens", *Revue française de sociologie*, **20**, 1979, pp. 49–82.

28. F. Braudel, *Ecrits sur l'histoire*, Paris, Flammarion, 1969, p. 7.
29. On the traditional notion of economics see O. Brunner, "Das 'ganze Haus' und die alteuropäische Ökonomik", in *Neue Wege der Sozialgeschichte*, Göttingen, Vandenhoeck & Ruprecht, 1956, pp. 33–61.
30. J.-Cl. Perrot, "Economie politique", in *Handbuch politisch-sozialer Grunbegriffe in Frankreich, 1680–1810*, München, Oldenbourg, 1988, Heft 8, pp. 51–104; *id.*, "Nouveautés: l'économie politique et ses livres", in H.-J. Martin & R. Chartier, *Histoire de l'édition française*, Paris, Promodis, 1984, volume II, pp. 240–257.
31. On the physiocrates see E. Fox-Genovese, *The origins of physiocracy. Economic revolution and social order in eighteenth-century France*, Ithaca, Cornell University Press, 1976.
32. On economics in the nineteenth century see L. Le Van-Lemesle, "La promotion de l'économie politique en France au XIXe siècle jusqu' à son introduction dans les facultés (1815–1881)", *Revue d'histoire moderne et contemporaine*, **27**, 1980, pp. 270–294; C. Bidard, *L'autonomisation du champ de la théorie économique*, Thèse de 3e cycle, Université de Paris VIII, 1978; H. Dumez, *Walras ou l'émergence de l'économie mathématique*, Thèse de 3e cycle, Université de Paris IV, 1983.

CHAPTER FIVE

"SCIENCE AND POLITICS" AS A POLITICAL FACTOR:
GERMAN AND ITALIAN SOCIAL SCIENCES
IN THE NINETEENTH CENTURY

PIERANGELO SCHIERA

Reasons for a Comparison

Studies on the history of political science have often focused on the development of the scientific discipline in so-called "internal" terms as opposed to an analysis of the impact of "external" phenomena such as political constellations, institutional arrangements, or state transformations. Epistemological and methodological considerations have tended to be at the center of interest – leading to classifying schemes which, while not without value, are certainly incapable of providing any type of more comprehensive understanding of the development of political analysis. Often, the main question has been that of the "scientific" status of early political science, "scientificity" being understood as the adherence to the "method of the generalizing sciences", i.e. to a procedure which is supposed to have been successfully applied in the natural sciences. The social sciences are, thus, regarded and assessed from a perspective of the progress of scientific knowledge according to a more or less positivistic conception (1).

My point of view is quite different. The working assumption that I shall follow here, as I did in earlier writings, is that the development of the German and Italian social and state sciences around the turn of the century can be fruitfully analyzed in terms of the relation between academic and political institutions. In the German context the social sciences have been crucially shaped, and themselves contributed to shaping, the relation between the general German intellectual discourse in post-Enlightenment history – and in particular German scientific dis-

P. Wagner, B. Wittrock, and R. Whitley (eds.), Discourses on Society: Volume XV, 1990, 93–120.
© 1990 *Kluwer Academic Publishers. Printed in the Netherlands.*

course ("*deutsche Wissenschaft*") – and the formation of a new ruling class. This class emerged from groups with different social origins but increasingly came to define itself through its common "professional" orientation (2). The Italian debates about developing social science have to a considerable extent related to the German experience, often considered a successful model, but their specific character is revealed when set in the context of the institutional features of Italian politics and academia.

That part of the development of the social and state sciences which I am dealing with here took place in a context of profound political transformation, both in Germany and Italy, during the second half of the nineteenth and the first decades of the twentieth century, i.e. the period of the emergence of unified nation-states and modern industrial societies. This commonality of political transformations is the background to the following comparative analysis, a commonality, however, which should not lose sight of the very different courses of development both societies went through. Nevertheless, important comparative conclusions can be drawn about the contribution of scientific production to the respective modernization processes (3).

The key social and political subjects involved, commonly labelled bourgeoisie, and the state apparatuses of power and intervention constantly redefined their relationship during this process. To many actors, science as a cultural and political phenomenon promised answers to the dominant themes of the time, offering avenues to help improve the running of the state machinery both by means of technical training of the increasing number of state officials and of in-depth analysis of social reality and effects of government intervention. Social science, however, also held the promise of providing the new classes aspiring to leadership with instruments for the comprehension and control of reality. In this context, the social and state sciences underwent a process of progressive professionalization which corresponded to an internal disciplinary diversification (4).

My basic objective is to propose and develop a common interpretive model for the meaning and role given to science, the social and state sciences in particular, at the turn of the century. The key argument is that the social and state sciences were constitutive factors in the transformation towards more modern social and political systems in both countries during this period.

The political processes that characterized German and Italian societies throughout the nineteenth century have many things in common. What mainly distinguishes them, though, is the role played by the state. This difference is due both to general historical traditions and to the specific politico-constitutional paths to national unification in the two countries. Paradoxically, the seemingly weaker German one, i.e. the federal-imperial constitution, turned out to be much stronger statewise than the Italian one, unitarian and centralizing as it was. While in Germany during the second half of the nineteenth century the state was one of the leading factors of modernization, to many Italians a working unified state was one of the objectives to be obtained through that process. The evolution of the social sciences and the different relationships established between them and politics in the two countries bear testimony to this difference (5).

Another commonality of both nations is their slow response to processes of political unification, of economic development, and of social homogenization that in countries like Great Britain, France, but also Belgium, had advanced or already been completed. There are, however, important differences behind this commonality. If Germany has often been called a belated nation, the "lag" of Italy was much more pronounced and was to remain so for a long time.

A number of indicators can just summarizingly be introduced to illustrate the "great transformation" we are talking about: the ever-closer and more direct ties between the state constitution and public administration; the rise of social groups, the working class, with political leanings antagonistic to the aspiring political elites; as a consequence the political dominance of "the social question"; the increasingly pronounced reference to conscious and planned reform as an instrument to ward off the spectre of popular insurrection and revolution; the elaboration and implementation of social policies (often technically rather than politically well designed); secularization of politics through the definite and irreversible detachment of the state from the church (*Kulturkampf*, with different connotations in Italy and Germany), not least in the name of science and through state presence in education and social assistance. Science (or better: the sciences), understood as technologies, and politics (or better: policies), understood as administration, are the key notions for characterizing the instruments of transformation in these late-nineteenth-century modernizing societies. This will be shown first with regard to the German situation (6).

The Institutional Position of the Social Sciences in Germany

The relation between science and politics in late-nineteenth-century Germany can best be captured by the juxtaposition of the two notions, widely used at the time, of German Science and *Realpolitik*, realistic politics. The former denoted the key role academic institutions were to play in the rebuilding of the nation after the Napoleonic wars, with the Humboldtian university reform as the starting-point. The latter is the expression of the moderate liberal forces' desire to recuperate the "territory of facts"; it became widespread in the 1850s and 1860s, after the defeat of the liberal revolution of 1848, when many liberals redefined their political objectives in terms of heading for the possible instead of striving for an ideal. After the founding of the Empire in 1871, this orientation was reinforced and had its material basis in the politics of the new nation-state (7).

Realpolitik has often exclusively been understood as the Bismarckian political strategy aiming at a management of power completely lacking ideal orientations. In contrast to such a view, I hold that *Realpolitik* has to be seen as a definition of the field of action and political intervention of German liberalism after the crisis of 1848. As liberal, post-revolutionary – and, if viewed from the perspective of the socialists, also anti-revolutionary – politics, *Realpolitik* is a crucial conception to understanding the political activities of the German professoriate during the second Empire, creating the specific constellation of science and politics that characterized the social sciences.

The work of Lorenz von Stein can be considered as emblematic for such an orientation. Therein, the accurate description of the accumulation of power in the hands of the proletariat is accompanied by lucid indications of political solutions that might bend such a force to the dominant interests of the bourgeois class, political solutions that would draw in modern ways on the particular German tradition of social monarchy and state mediation in social conflicts (8).

Von Stein's "realpolitical" analysis is often set against the work of Karl Marx. It must be noted, however, that the seemingly antithetical approaches of the two interpretations of the contemporary political situation had one important point in common: the identification of society as a sphere, endowed with laws of its own, for the emergence and resolution of conflicts between individuals and groups (9). This cognitive step is the precondition for the emergence of, first, a science of society and, second, of social groups who see their political task in the "scientific" solution of social problems.

German science, the particular relation between science and politics in nineteenth-century Germany, develops in this cognitive and institutional context. German science can in fact be defined as the characterization of that new scientific approach to politics. It is pursued at the Humboldtian university, an institution grounded on teaching and research, inspired by the principle of education through science, by professors and scientists whose positive attitude to politics goes back to the old direct political commitment during the *Vormärz* and the Revolution of 1848. In the five decades I am interested in, the state and social sciences occupied the preeminent position in this cultural and academic panorama.

The relationship between German science and *Realpolitik* can then be more specifically defined by a look at the historical constellation during this period, one which was overwhelmingly dominated by the national question. Three main elements can be singled out for an understanding of this problem (10). First, and most commonly known, a historical need of the German people was perceived to construct a legislative and administrative unity, national political institutions, fitting the degree of autonomous and unified historical and cultural conscience already attained. Second, in social terms, German political society was characterized over centuries by a particular "corporate" organization and had preserved such a self-understanding into the nineteenth century. Third, as in other European countries, the spreading of politics, both active and passive, to larger parts of the population stood on the agenda. The comparative lateness of Germany with respect to democratization had important consequences at the political level, if one bears in mind the internal multifariousness, or lack of homogeneity, typical of Imperial Germany and, in consequence, the greater challenges the unitary state had to meet.

German science devoted its attention to all these main aspects of the national question; those of politicoadministrative institutions, societal organization, and political participation. This was the case even though the field of science and education policy, and in particular the organization of higher education, was the area of competence most jealously guarded by the single states against intervention by the Empire. The ever more widespread and commonly accepted appeal to a German science mitigated and almost erased such institutional differences at the cognitive level, the actual level of scholarly production. This appeal expressed the positivistic trust in the advance of knowledge and transferred the notion of a unifying function of such knowledge to the problems of constructing German unity.

In effect, however, this unifying function was less a result of positivism as a universal concept of knowledge generation than of the activities and orientations of the professoriate. The *Gelehrtentum*, the community of socially well-positioned scholars and professors, spokespersons of a national, social, and political project, expressed the coherence of the corporate society of which it formed a constitutive part (11). Conceptually and normatively, the social sciences contributed to defining and understanding the mass phenomena related to the new state and the new society. The preeminent interest in public law, for instance, was in the capacity and capability of the state to provide for social welfare. Research in political economy and sociology, organized in the Association for Social Policy (*Verein für Socialpolitik*), was thematically equally dominated by the interest in solving the social question (12).

This proximity between political problems and research developments was much more than just thematic affinity. During the second half of the nineteenth century, the double incentive of coping with belated industrialization and social transformations on the one hand, and with the political-constitutional about-face towards a federal-imperial structure on the other, brought about an extreme intensity of reform activity. The resulting institutional transformations did not just have indirect or superficial ties with the course of academic production, but affected profoundly its rhythm and direction. I shall try to demonstrate these links by portraying the "modernizations" of German society, in theoretical understanding and actual occurrence, in terms of new and different, namely scientific, "systems of allocation"; allocation of competences, control, resources, and legitimacy, each related to specific aspects of the state and social sciences.

As far as competences are concerned, the most important reform movement was the one related to internal administration. The objective of the reforms, pursued under the leading role of the Prussian state, was the rationalization of administration both in territorial and functional terms. With regard to the latter aspect, a basic concept was the consolidation of administration as an autonomous field of exercise, to which the upcoming discipline of administrative law would devote itself (13). The development and application of administrative rules occurred under two complementary, though distinct, scientific perspectives that maintained close ties for a long time: the science of administration (*Verwaltungslehre*) as represented by Lorenz von Stein on the one side, and administrative law proper (*Verwaltungsrecht*), as a special branch of public law on the other, which had Otto Mayer as its most representative founder.

The origins and achievements of administrative law as an autonomous science also provide clues to the second aspect of modernization mentioned above, the allocation of control. This can be seen by looking at the introduction of administrative jurisdiction. Following the example given by Baden in 1863, administrative jurisdiction was introduced in Prussia in 1875 and successively in all other German states, using the Prussian model. Just like in the case of administrative reform, the objective and effects of the move were the strengthening of the constitutional state and the tendencies towards a working institutional unification.

These effects were attained not least owing to the debate on administrative justice led by experts and scholars in a rather compact and homogeneous manner. Theoretical principles were developed, historical and comparative references were established and discussed, and different contexts of application of administrative jurisdiction were analyzed. The debate centered on the search for the "juridic method", the corner-stone on which simultaneously the science of public law and the institutions of administrative jurisdiction would be erected (14).

The proximity of legal reform and legal science was further enhanced through the role of the universities in higher education. The need to train administrative judges required an accentuation of the formational differences between law students going into civil service and those aspiring to become members of the bench. This problem was the topic of a discussion over juridic principles which involved the contemporary chairholders in law as well as parliament, at the level of the states and even the Empire. In this debate, the organization of academic subjects at the university was directly related to the concrete demands for knowledge and abilities in the institutional structures of the state apparatus (15).

Reform of administration and reform of jurisdiction, thus, can be regarded as two sides of the same coin; the inscription on this coin, however, was *Sozialpolitik* (social policy). *Sozialpolitik* refers to the third aspect of modernization, the allocation of resources.

According to a recent historiographic definition, the complex of Bismarckian social policies which goes under the name of *Sozialpolitik* is nothing less than the sum of those interventions in economic life and political ordering of society that were deemed necessary for the protection and the elevation of wage-earning workers and for the just inclusion of

the working class into the established *status quo*. Another definition
presents *Sozialpolitik* as "a systematically instrumentalized aspect of a
territorial state's comprehensive politics," more precisely as "the whole of
the state measures necessary for – or at least aiming at – the protection,
the socioeconomic elevation and the social and political integration of the
working class after its rapid expansion due to industrialization." Social
policies had to be carefully linked to economic policy, both in the passive
sense of fiscal measures necessary to provide resources and in the active
sense of definition of addressees and distribution to the subordinate
classes (16).

The role of the newly emerging social and state sciences could be
nothing but central in such a compact system of interests and interventions – for the design of concepts and planning of social policies, for the
technical elaboration of the measures to be taken, and for their implementation. Such has been the case, and the political success of *Socialpolitik*
brought with it a transformation of academic organization. It codified the
insertion of the social and state sciences into the scientific and academic
world, both in the cognitive terms of new special disciplines taking shape
in connection with the rising government intervention in society, such as
political economy (*Nationalökonomie*), public finance (*Finanzwissenschaft*), public law, especially administrative law, and sociology, and in
the social terms of the new professors, representatives of these disciplines, who merged political with academic motivation and achieved
recognition for their accomplishments.

In summary, one has spoken about a new "political constellation"
which was formed in Germany, oriented simultaneously at four primary
objectives; external security, internal order, economic growth, and
welfare (17). For Germany on the way to modernization, these four
objectives constitute the connective tissue of the political legitimacy of
the imperial state. As was shown, all the social and state sciences I have
been concerned with up to now played an important part in achieving at
least the latter three of these objectives. The German professors were,
thus, a key social group in enhancing the legitimacy of the newly built
nation-state.

As a result of this analysis of the interlacement of the powerful thrusts
towards integration that shaped Germany's constitutional history in the
second half of the nineteenth century, the strong presence of German
science as an important instrument in these processes becomes clear. The
development of the social and state sciences during this period is

testimony to the swiftness with which the new political topics became topics of study and teaching. Similarly, the state's increasingly sophisticated political answers to the population's social needs are indicators of the scientific basis that the new mass politics drew upon: from the technical point of view of concrete legislative and administrative actions to be taken as well as from the more general point of view of legitimation and consent. The result was politics with a scientific basis on the one hand and science that made politics a more and more direct object of its research and teaching on the other.

Two qualification, however, have to be added to this picture, qualifications on aspects which have escaped the attention of many observers. First, the development of German science must be seen as its growth to a disciplinary complex on the way to increasing specialization and organization, and not in terms of epistemological unity and unitarian results of research. Second, emphasis on the wide range and key position of German science in the overall structuring of that extremely potent and yet, as we know, in the end so fragile apparatus that was the second Empire should not make us overlook that science was itself a structure of that apparatus, of which it also acquired the contradictory aspects of power and fragility during this period, according to a dynamics strongly endowed with political-constitutional meaning.

This latter aspect once again raises the question of *Realpolitik* and, therewith, the criteria regulating the relationship between science and politics in Imperial Germany. The active subjects of this relationship, i.e. the professors, occupied a different position during this period compared with both the preceding and the succeeding one. They were neither the *political professors* dating back to before 1848 nor the *unpolitical person*, aptly described in this formula by Thomas Mann, but lived through a relation to the political sphere which can best be characterized as one of controlled separation.

The seeming continuity, or better, renewal of an active and aggressive fighting position, conceals an important change relative to the "political " period, a change towards realistic politics. The call for realism by professors like Rochau, Treitschke, or Baumgarten must be understood as a realignment of the liberal topics to the new economic, social, and political needs that marked the founding years of the Empire *(Gründerjahre)* and their aftermath (18). And it is exactly through this change in orientation that science comes to play a central role with respect to both the new governments techniques, more or less constitutional, and to the subjects, active and passive, involved in the political processes. This political orientation goes in line with the intellectual one, already indicated as well, of the discovery of society as the real seat of conflicts between individuals and groups, and therefore also as the seat of conflict resolution.

In the "complicated game of equilibria" installed by Bismarck, "without which Germany would not have been able to accomplish the cyclopean act of which it was capable in only seven years," as the Italian Ferrero noted at the time, German science did not only play an important role. It was one of the lasting structures, growing at a dizzy speed, even when the equilibrium was lost and the "political conflicts between the classes, (which) are not only of an economic but also of an intellectual and moral nature," erupted. The importance of science policy, interpreted by Director Althoff at the respective Prussian ministry, and of which William II was well aware, constituted one of the few fixed points in the zig-zag path that characterized German political life after Bismarck's retirement.

Scientific specialization turned out to be a means for the exponents of the liberal bourgeoisie who were the German scholars and professors to "objectively" do research and "politically" collaborate. Within his disciplinary sector, institute, and chair, every researcher was free and autonomous. But to make such an institutional arrangement possible, a unified and comprehensive system, articulated and well organized, was required that supplied the single services of each researcher with general political relevance. Such a system was German science, and it was so long before Althoff became associated with it. According to Werner Sombert, in his article *Althoff*, which appeared in Vienna's *Neue Freie Presse* in 1907, "the *Althoff system* is not a cause, but an effect". Sombart's observations were very negative with respect to the "progressive" academic world in Germany (Max Weber, for instance), which seemed incapable of grasping the general causes for the intellectual crisis in which it found itself, and sought only to blame the "director of the system": "It is infantile to maintain that universities today are such because Althoff made them so" (19).

The ills of German universities were older than the wicked Althoff; they had their roots in the universities' peculiar relationship to politics, which was a controlled separation of the two fields of science and politics. In this sense, the world of science and of the university reflected the problems of the specific type of Bismarckian liberalism. It fully expressed the ideal of *Realpolitik*, an ideal that for the case of science consisted in the particular relation of internal objectives of research, i.e., its alleged objectivity and consequent detachment from politics, to the constitutive characters of the Bismarckian political system, i.e. management of the "game of equilibria" on behalf of a centre in which decision-making power was concentrated.

The Main Differences between the German and the Italian Contexts

As in Germany, politicians and scholars in Italy worried about a unified vision, and possibly a unified management, for the enormous problems which the new times brought with them. From the beginning of the nineteenth century, such a need was perceived, at first more in terms of an encyclopaedic vision or, as it was said, in a "large and complex" manner. From the 1850s onwards, the demand for "special analysis" grew in Italy, opening the door to the emergence and recognition of the new social sciences. However, even though many recent studies have analyzed the development of these sciences – mostly in disciplinary terms and with an internalist perspective –, no overall view of a hypothetical "Italian science" has been advanced, relating intellectual and institutional to historic-constitutional developments (20).

It is much more difficult to reconstruct a process of modernization for Italy; a similar operation holds less interest and entails more difficulties than for the German case. The institutional position of science was markedly different from the German one, and remained rather undeveloped throughout the nineteenth century. The development of the nation-state, though apparently parallel, took a quite different path.

The formation of the Italian state came about in a hurriedly unifying and centralizing way. The laws on administrative unification, on a Piedmontese model drastically stretched to fit the whole country, were passed by 1865. At this time, the full importance of political unification – which was not even completed in territorial terms – was hardly grasped, and discussion of the best possible steps to take in order to wind up the difficult process was just about to begin (21).

Insofar as this acceleration led to the illusion of having the most important problems solved, it tended to aggravate their relevance for the future. After technical solutions to these political problems had been imposed from above without any serious discussion, it seemed natural that social scientists tended to take political stands rather than develop

technical expertise. Their relation to politics was one of direct interference between scientific reflection and political action, as it had been in
the German *Vormärz* but diminished thereafter.

The integration of Italy faced several deep-seated problems. *First*, the
different political traditions of the pre-unification states were no less
important in terms of complexity and richness than they were in
Germany. Apart from Piedmont and the Church State, one need only
think of states such as Lombardo-Veneto and Tuscany or the Kingdom of
the Two Sicilies. In the process of unification, attempts were often made
to forcefully remove the diversity instead of integrating differences, as for
Lombardo-Veneto, for the Kingdom of the Two Sicilies or for the Church
State. In the German case plurality and attention to the different components had more weight, and these differences were reflected in the
federal-imperial constitution of the new state. In Italy, a kind of Piedmontese imperialism came about which turned out to be much more direct and
heavy-handed than the Prussian one in Germany.

Second, notwithstanding the presence of popular heroes of the
Risorgimento, the national-liberal movement, the national spirit was much
less pronounced in Italian academic and cultural circles than in Germany.
In the absence of anything similar to German Science and its role in
German unification from the end of the eighteenth century onwards, the
political unification process always lacked a spiritual counterpart in Italy.
After the completion of unification with the conquest of Rome in 1870,
Theodor Mommsen, the leading German historian of the time, is said to
have turned to Quintino Sella, the Italian Prime Minister, to ask what the
cosmopolitan destiny of this city would be. Sella, who in fact was to earn
many merits for his support of scientific organization later, answered that
its destiny would lie in science, a response that even today sounds
ridiculously unrelated to the situation of Italian academia (22).

These differences to the German situation might have been of little
relevance had they not been accompanied, *third*, by the fundamental
problem of the economic lag of Italy. Italy continued to present serious
delays in industrialization long after unification. Not only did the
prevailing themes in economic debate remain agrarian, but also the very
characteristics of immobility and passivity, of conservatism and opaque-
ness typical of a predominantly agrarian society reverberated on the entire
political structure in the process of its formation, not even sparing the new
social and state sciences (23).

The country's basic lack of social homogeneity was repeatedly pointed out, relating not least to such persistence of orientations which were deemed inadequate for a modern, industrial society. As a consequence, *fourth*, intense preoccupation was voiced about the formation of public opinion, a preoccupation that had been a major theme of debate much earlier elsewhere, for example in Germany, and had subsided in the wake of the immense attraction and mediative role of education.

Owing to all these factors, "Italian Science," as we may label the relation of Italian political and social sciences to politics, played a different contextual role than German Science. This difference is the higher ambition of Italian scientists to directly influence Italian politics corresponding to a much lower effective capacity to exert such influence. Simultaneously there was a much lower inclination towards *Realpolitik* in Italian liberalism and in the bourgeoisie, the sociopolitical class which advocated it. Consequently, such an orientation was lacking in the governments formed by this class and in the relationship between them and the exponents of the world of research and science.

Nonetheless Italy probably witnessed more discourse activity in the social sciences, and their relation to politics, than Germany did. In fact, such discourses were particularly welcome in a parliament where many scientists were also politicians. It is to these discourses that I now turn.

The Educational Role of the Social Sciences in Italy

In Italy, the discourse on politics oscillated among art, technique, routine, studying, theory, and science. Meanwhile some of the more fundamental contents were lost, contents which a nineteenth century author still assigned to political thinking, namely to be a "doctrine of profitable means to a particular society, deducible from the formation and the context of the passions and the interests," or to become a "discipline determining the state's duties within the society it represents,... and the means for the proper fulfillment of those duties," or even a "science of the state, of its forms, of its government, of its periods of unwinding, of its necessities" (24).

When the development of political science was proposed in the second half of the nineteenth century, some mentioned a "science of political constitution" at an intermediate position between politics and constitutional law (Vincenzo Miceli 1885), while others spoke of a "sociological theory of the economic constitution of society and power" (Achille Loria) or more simply of an "economic theory of political constitution" (the title of an 1886 book by Loria) (25). An interpretation of social reality was proposed in these Italian debates which joined jurists, economists, and other social scientists together and was obviously not in the least disturbed by the unquestionable rupture introduced by Gaetano Mosca in 1886 with the publication of his *Elementi di scienza politica*, an attempt to give a specific foundation for the study of things political.

Mosca proposed a positive method for political science, to be accompanied by a historical-comparative one in which history is seen as the "laboratory" from which the "materials" serving for political science reasoning are taken. He tried to introduce a basic distinction between formal and substantial aspects of politics. History, its subordinate role notwithstanding, should be intensively studied, with particular attention paid to institutions, culture, and ideas, to organizations and arrangements.

The most interesting aspect of the political reflections succeeding unification is probably the persistence of the separation and juxtaposition of rulers and ruled, i.e. of the political class proper and the politically active classes in society in general, namely "proprietors, employees and professionals." Such a separation assumes the existence of two realms of discourse and basically corresponds to a distinction between instrumentally effective knowledge and public opinion. Exchanges between the two realms are frequent and necessary: the typically Italian phenomenon of "transformism," for instance, can be understood as a translation process between the two spheres enacted to find politically acceptable solutions to policy problems (26).

In this separation, however, we also find condensed the unresolved contradiction of Italian political science, a lacking of clarification of the relation between science and public opinion which impedes the academic political discourses from becoming truly scientific because they tend to be a substitute for political education which otherwise would not exist. Even according to Mosca, political science, defined as the macrophysics of power, has two main complementary objectives: to "steer clear of violent blows and sudden revolutions" and to perform a "political education"(27). It was not least the absence of task clarification which impeded systematization and focalization of the scientific discourses on politics. This can be shown by a glance at the variety of concerns of early Italian political science.

The understanding of political science need not be limited to the study of the political class or the "political formula", an Italian term for power constellations. It may also include the analysis of the institutional framework for power acquisition and the relationship between political forces and forms. Then, however, the common reference to Gaetano Mosca as the founder of the discipline is not quite correct. One needs to go back to authors active in the 1860s and to the stream of political science literature, broadly understood, which indeed constitutes the main stream of Italian social science to the end of the century.

One of the topics upon which that pre-scientific discussion dwelt was that of the "political party," a concept which can be seen as preceding and preparing the one of "political class" with which Mosca essentially completed the passage to scientific formalization. With the help of the latter concept the composition, formation, and organization of the ruling elite was to be analyzed as well as its legitimation in society, the relationship between the governing and the governed, and between minority and majority, between organized and unorganized groups, and between aristocracy and the people (28).

The theorizing on political parties was pursued as part of an empirically larger and conceptually broader perspective, that of a theorizing on associations, merging historical, juridical, and economic considerations with political ones. In this area a substratum also formed from which proposals for a sociology as the science of minor human groups emerged. In this broad range of political thinking, analyses of the ideal and constitutional character of institutions, i.e. the traditional area of politics, met with others of a more technical and juridical character as well as with those of a more sociological nature referring to pressure groups in politics (political factions, cliques, and gangs, as Mosca often phrased it). Mostly, these discourses exhibited a blending of scholarly reasoning and ideology and interest-led considerations, hardly ever disentangled, which profoundly characterized the attempts at formalization of both political science and sociology as independent disciplines towards the end of the nineteenth century (29).

Such a wide range of rather undifferentiated questions that absorbed bourgeois public opinion reflected the real state of the political process. It may suffice just to recall a series of problems to set a frame of reference for the Italian situation during the period following unification: the definition of the role of national parliament and the electoral system; the role of parties in society and in the state (the question of a multiple- or two-party system); the relation between centre and periphery; the relation between politics and administration; political transformism, corruption, and the patronage system; governmental instability and fragility of the institutional framework. One may add a series of data on important crises and turning-points during these years: the fall of the Right and the transfer of political power to the Left in 1876; the turn towards protectionism in 1878; the extension of the franchise in 1882; the founding of the Italian Socialist Party in 1892; and the culmination of the debate over political corruption in association with bank scandals in the same year.

These phenomena are mirrored, and most often not systematically, in the political reflection of the times, whose authors find it convenient to move halfway between official scientific production and opinionative essay-writing. The case is slightly different though for the two major institutionalized disciplinary branches of the intellectual field of the social sciences, namely law and economics. I shall turn to the latter first.

The pretence of economics to offer a complete picture of the fundamental political problems goes back in Italy to the period immediately following the Enlightenment. The series *Scrittori classici italiani di economia politica* (Classical Italian writers in political economy) was started by Custodi in 1803 with the intent to prepare for Italy, "first among all nations,... the codex for the true science of governments and of the teaching of the people," already showing, by the way, the double orientation to science and education. Only a few years later, in 1815, Melchiore Gioia compiled the *Nuovo prospetto delle scienze economiche ossia somma totale delle idee teoriche e pratiche in ogni ramo d'amministrazione privata e pubblica* (New prospectus of the economic sciences or the sum total of theoretical and practical ideas for all branches of private and public administration). In 1852, Giuseppe Ferrara inaugurated the *Biblioteca dell'economia* with an open polemic on the wide encyclopaedic approach of the preceding works and with the programme of advancing a rigorous scientific method, advancing, that is, disciplinary formation and liberal economic thought (30).

The *Biblioteca* is of interest for two reasons. The first one concerns the relation of "economics" to "political science." The start of the publication series preceded by thirty years the one of the *Biblioteca di scienze politiche. Scelta collezione delle più importanti opere moderne italiane e straniere di scienze politiche* (Library of political sciences. Selected collection of the most important modern Italian and foreign works in the political sciences), directed by Attilio Brunialti from 1883 onwards (31). The second reason, more related to the internal understanding of the economics discipline, is that Ferrara presented himself as the proud opponent of the theoretical movement in the field of economics that reproposed the position of German *Kathedersozialismus*, historical, state-oriented economics, in Italy and that was to play a quite important part in the consolidation of the science of economics, in particular with respect to politics and the role of the state. The development and crisis of liberal ideology in Italy during the second half of the nineteenth century can be focused on the opposition of these two schools of economics, an opposition which represented the contradictory interlacement of the inalienable principles of the individual and the appearance of the first social reforms around 1885.

The Italian historical school of economics, against which Ferrara polemicized, emerged from a conjunction of intellectual developments in the field, including questions of method, on the one hand, and of the crisis of liberalism, related to constitutional debates and demands for sociopolitical reforms, on the other. This conjunction was so intricate that one should consider the theoretical position of Gustav Schmoller's *Kathedersozialismus*, as it appeared in Italy, rather as an ideological legitimation of political solutions adopted in terms of its scientific ambitions (32).

For reasons of these different contexts, then, it is not possible to speak of a direct dependency of Italian economists on the German model, though they drew many inspirations from the German Historical School. If one looks beyond intellectual history at the discourses on society in terms of their contribution to the reflexive monitoring and legitimation of political action, however, multiple orientations and greater discrepancies to the German situation emerge. While Germany was looked at with great interest in terms of economic policy, in particular after the protectionist turnabout, and of sociopolitical development, the English parliamentary model remained the preferred one in terms of ideology and political theory, and interest in French political developments increased towards the end of the century. In the Italian "school" of economics, to which, to name but a few, Scialoja, Cossa, Messedaglia, Luzzatti, Lampertico, Boccardo, and Ricca-Salerno should be counted, questions of economic science, social development, and political constitution mingled to an extent that made the components almost indistinguishable. Debates on method and contents of economics often seemed confused and accidental for this reason, favouring a "pragmatic" mentality which often became the common denominator for scholars whose opinions diverged otherwise (33).

Italian economics, then, was characterized by a triple commitment, a methodological one to the empirical study of reality, to the "experimental" method as it was called; a politico-ideological one to pragmatic state policies, including protectionism; and a scientific one to the search for the "economic law." This triple commitment, inconsistencies pragmatically overlooked, also determined the economists' contribution, as liberal reformers, to the elaboration of the ideology of the modern welfare state. It was based on the assumption that state intervention should be seen as complementary to the actions of individuals and social forces, whereas in Schmoller and his school's more coherent German model the state was the exclusive bearer of all initiatives to social reform. Thus, an idea of "sociality" received particular attention by the Italian historical school of economics. The subjects are not just the state or the individuals, but additionally that multitude of "institutions and bodies to whom the individual itself attributes life and persona through law" (34).

A broadly similar orientation can be found in public law as the other of the two core disciplines of the social sciences at this point. The representatives of the juridic sciences reacted to the public debates on the development of the Italian nation, and they did so in a similarly double, or undecided, mode as did the economists, namely with regard to the legal understandings of state and society. On the one hand, the theory of the juridic personality of the state was developed and put to the service of the constitutional state. On the other hand, a theory of consociate pluralism was perfected. Both types of theorizing were guided by the formal methodological criterion of scientific purity. For models of reference, one initially looked to the developing legal theory of the state in German science (1860–1880), while efforts were put into the construction of an Italian juridic science later (1880–1890). This held true both for private law, especially with Rocco, and for public law, which saw Vittorio Emanuele Orlando in a leading role (35).

These were the answers jurists were trying to give to the crisis of the bourgeoisie, to the difficulties in steering the social transformations underway in the magic climate of the *fin de siècle*. A steady discursive specialization and separation, topped with formalism, went along with extreme eclecticism trying to build conceptual bridges between these specialties in order to keep up with the growing social complexity. Despite its proclamations and aspirations the science of public law was not self-sufficient. Interferences with economics were frequent. Conceptually ambiguous and multivalent approaches such as so-called juridic socialism, private social law, and even many areas of administrative law asserted themselves and gained importance, even if they did not acquire full disciplinary status themselves. In particular in criminal law and labour law, interferences with other sectors of social-knowledge production developed increasingly, types of interferences that juridic formalism had wanted to avoid at all cost (36).

This cautious, intermediate, and slightly ambiguous attitude of Italian reformers reflected conservative intentions, apparently well-suited to a society and country which up to 1895 did not experience a strong trend towards industrialization. Most authoritative critics of Italian liberalism around the turn of the century define its condition in markedly critical terms. Those who speak of a "defective theoretical foundation and courageous intentionality" seem to join those who stress the inclination to "research for compromises" with, as a consequence, the eternal dissatisfaction with the incapacity to come up with definitive solutions. While one could, thus, be inclined to judge this situation as compared to the German one in terms of underdevelopment and inferiority, it is more important to identify clearly the differences and their causes (37).

At this point, I shall return to the problem of transformism, already briefly introduced. As continuous infiltration between administrative and parliamentary, peripheral and central, social and political levels, it operates in petty politics as well as in the formation and change of governments. As a pervasive feature of sociopolitical interaction in Italy, it serves to characterize the relationship between science and politics in an analogous way. Marco Minghetti was a good representative of this attitude, both in theory and in practice. In 1883, for example, he portrayed transformism as the "general law of living things," as science continuously reshaping itself "according to public demand, different as time and place require."

The result of transformism in the area of social science was a "middlecourse between speculation and experience, theory and practice, the general and the particular" (38). In the Italian context, the dominance of soft methodology and theorizing seemed appropriate to confront the magical "social question," the dominant theme of public opinion and reform strivings. The Italian version of the *Methodenstreit* reduces essentially to this.

The linkage to the German matrix which the notion of *Methodenstreit* captures was not purely methodological though. The political reference point in the Italian debate, translated into scientific approaches, was the

stability of Bismarckian Germany, which was as desired as the frailness
of the French framework was feared, one which had produced the
spectres of the *Commune* and continued to show risks of an overthrow of
the social order. In the view of many liberal intellectuals, Italy was not
free of the French dangers but at the same time incapable of reaching
German stability. It had to cope with double notions of state and society,
could centre neither on the one nor on the other. The main underlying
theme of liberal thought was to mediate interests between state and social
groups, where possible with the technical expertise of economics and law
to be applied in finance and administration.

In this sense, the contents of the social sciences developing in Italy in
the 1870s and 1880s can politically be understood in terms of attempted
"neutralization." Liberal ideology boiled down to efforts thwarting any
social conflict and above all that synthesis of political conflictuality
which could lead to socialism. Bourgeois science operated against the
latter and for scientifically founded politics. As Minghetti, for instance,
stressed, it was a science that aspired to furnish practical directives for
politics. "Italian Science" was, therefore, much more directly and openly
engaged in political reasoning and struggle than German Science, in
which the mediating role was performed much more subtly and passed
through the demands of an inalienable statute of science, apparently
separating science clearly from politics (39). In Italy, politics and science
could be portrayed on a continuum that did not allow for a neat separation
of roles and responsibilities. In consequence, science could often not be
science, and politics could not manage to be politics.

For some time, especially after the taking of Rome, the political class
was well aware that science was a dynamic factor of state development.
Numerous attempts at reform – or better, efforts to create a national
university system – pointed in this direction. One example was the so-
called Bonghi Act of 1875, the experience with which led to the insight
that the pretention to reproduce the German university model was
misleading and dangerous: "... such an argument, gentlemen, does not
seem any more serious than the argument of someone who, seeing an old
chestnut tree extending its branches far out, sets out to create a similar
one. But that chestnut tree cannot be imitated; you may admire it if you
like it, but if you were to propose to yourself or others to create a similar
one, the chestnut, if it had the gift of speech, would laugh at you" (40).

Germany is Germany, "a country of professors, and it has the advantages and disadvantages deriving from this"; and one of its features, for

better or worse, was science for science, not giving any importance "to the practical application of the doctrines." This statement by Gianturco, in a speech given as a member to the Chamber of Deputies, expressed the profound difference between Germany and Italy. In Germany, the two fields of science and politics were divided, but the support in terms of technical expertise and legitimation that science gave to politics was decisive. In Italy, there was no clear separation; the middle course triumphed as in all fields. As a consequence, science became much more directly political without politics becoming much more scientific in return.

The argument has been laid out and needs to be wound up at this point. Before doing this, it needs to be noted that the comparison is imbalanced insofar as studies on the "development of the complex relationship between state and society, politics and administration, institutions and bourgeois capitalist modernization, power and masses" are still in their beginnings for the Italian case (41). Even less frequent are works that place the observation and analysis of developments in the field of the social sciences in the centre of their interest. Still missing, for example, is a complete study of Brunialti's above-mentioned *Biblioteca*, which accompanied the debate about sciences of state and society relating the reflections on the Italian state under construction to a broader European development of social knowledge.

To draw the conclusion from this example, it is a typical trait of the Italian situation that the specialization of the social sciences rarely qualified in terms of cognitive-scientific criteria, in terms of, say, methodological peculiarity and a subsequent separation from other approaches. In contrast, new concepts were often advocated in terms of "practicability of the reform proposals aiming at modifying the existing socioeconomic order" (42).

Science and Politics in Germany and Italy Compared

My comparative conclusions on the relationship between science and politics in Germany and Italy are provisional and need further elaboration in future work. A first result is that this relationship did not only take its long-term characteristic shape during the period under study, but that it had, in turn, a notable impact on the foundation and building of the respective systems of political institutions.

Since approximately the beginning of the nineteenth century, scientific reflection on social, economic, and political reality no longer served exclusively to provide technical solutions to problems defined by the sovereign and his chamber, as it had done before, in particular during the Enlightenment. Throughout the nineteenth century, the sciences of society voiced the claim to compete in determining the very goals of government and of politics, beyond merely giving support in searching for the means to reach these goals.

The new claim was probably more closely related to a renewal of political thought in liberal and democratic terms than to the intrinsic development of scientific method and concepts – though the connection between these two aspects is worth further exploration. It is nevertheless not an exaggeration to state that the nineteenth century truly became the one of the sciences of society, just as the seventeenth century had been the one of physics, and the eighteenth the century of biology.

The perspectives of observation broadened from those of the "sciences of the state" to "social sciences" (43). It is worth emphasizing that this was an enlargement, not a substitution of scientific points of view. The revolutionary events did not do away with the absolutist dimension of the state, but reformed it. Efficiency and organization of the state administration moved to the centre of interest; devoting themselves to the functioning of the state machinery was a constitutive task of the new political sciences. In addition to this focus on the state, the second reference of the social sciences were the problems emerging from the historical development of that bourgeois society which had sprung up from the revolutions and had acquired its own dynamics.

These orientations are perfectly reflected in the German case, where one often spoke of the social and state sciences. On the level of denominations, it is less evident for Italy, where the expression *scienze dello Stato* was much less frequently used. This difference is not just a lexical one, but corresponds to a distinction that has emerged from the analytical reconstruction.

Due to a number of socioeconomic features of the Italian situation, as described above, the social groups aspiring to leadership, usually labelled bourgeoisie, had considerable difficulties in organizing themselves and asserting their claims to power. Intending to make up for these deficiencies, the liberal intellectuals who were the protagonists of the social sciences in Italy assumed a formative and pedagogic function in the political field. Fluctuating between scientific goals and the intention to give supportive legitimacy to political action, Italian social scientists often opted for the latter objective, considerably sacrificing their scientific potential. Seemingly paradoxically, the failure to achieve the controlled separation of science and politics that characterized the German constellation decreased the effectiveness of the social scientists to influence the political processes.

The reference to the formative role of the social sciences leads me to my concluding observation. As is well known, the organization of the university was a key concern in nineteenth century German politics. The extraordinary development of the sciences, in particular, but also more generally the very high degree of integration reached by German society and the rapid rise of Germany to the status of an economic and political super-power, can hardly be explained without reference to the "Humboldtian" university system (44). Thanks to the reformed organization of the university, often described as a *Grossbetrieb* (large-scale company), German science was able to play its double role in promoting science in favour of the state and civil formation in favour of society.

The German university model enjoyed worldwide renown. German universities were the frequent destination of visiting students but also of official commissions from foreign countries hoping to discover the secret of the dual concept of scientific research and higher education united in one institution. The visitors included many Italians, who were never able, though, to put into policy practice their long-standing admiration for the "German professors" (45). Lacking stable organizational and politicocultural support, Italian scientific research was left on its own. For the social sciences, this meant that they found their most fertile ground in political polemics, a live broadcast, as it were, of the internal problems of society and of groups and forces fighting in it.

It would be erroneous, though, to conclude that Italian scientific production as such was inferior to the German one as a result of this constellation. Examples could be given to argue strongly against such a conclusion. The important conclusion is that academic orientations and activities can be decisively shaped by the politicoinstitutional setting in which scholars work. And Italian political institutions developed along quite different lines than the German ones, though some starting-points at the time of national unification were similar, including analogous motivations among political elites.

The preceding analysis has devoted itself to these different paths. Beyond trying to explain the different positions of the social sciences in both societies in terms of institutional relationships, an analysis of academic discourses on societies, in turn, also sheds light on the varying ways in which the two essential notions of the liberal political system were understood in Germany and Italy.

The relation between science and politics remains relevant in the contemporary context. These two realms of social activity are no less decoupled today than they were a century ago. A renewed reflection on their interrelation seems urgent given their equally far-reaching and incompatible claims. Scientific discourse is today just as frequently portrayed as existing for its own sake and as manifesting the triumphs of an inarrestable process of conceptual conquest and cumulative growth as was the case a century ago. These claims, furthermore, are advanced amidst a process of ever-growing diversification of the disciplines and their ultimate technicalization and mutual incommunicability, on the one hand, and a complementary reduction of politics to a purely practical element, necessarily arbitrary and utilitarian, with the ultimate prevailing of administrative and technical logics devoid of any value connotation, on the other.

Notes

1. These considerations were critically suggested by the reconstruction of Italian political science in the nineteenth century (to which I am indebted) made in the introductory essay by G. Sola, in D. Fiorot and G. Sola, "Positivismo e politica tra '800 e '900. Terza parte. Bibliografia sulla scienza politica in Italia (1861–1900)". In *Schema* **8** (1986), Appendice al n. 2, pp. 11–85.
2. P. Schiera, *Il laboratorio borghese. Scienza e politica nella Germania dell'Ottocento*. Bologna: il Mulino, 1987.
3. G. Gozzi, *Modelli politici e questione sociale in Italia e Germania fra Otto e Novecento*. Bologna: il Mulino, 1988.
4. On this problem, for the USA, see the essay by Peter Manicas in this volume.
5. The "Istituto storico italo-germanico" in Trento has in the past few years dedicated many efforts to the reconstruction of modern ideologies in Germany and Italy in the nineteenth and twentieth centuries. See various volumes on Socialism, Liberalism, Catholic Thought, Nationalism (all published in Bologna: il Mulino). See also the more recent series devoted to the historiographic element of the nineteenth century "ideology": scientific discovery and reconstruction of antiquity, Middle Ages, Renaissance, Modernity (published in Bologna and Berlin: il Mulino and Duncker & Humblot). In the Istituto a German-Italian group is also working on the theme of professionalization and scientific specialization around the turn of the century. Law and economics were till now the major field of investigation. Many results of this work will be cited throughout my paper.
6. Different ways of presentation have been used in analyzing the two countries,

more "literary" for Italy, more "constitutional" for Germany. The German case is better known to me, whereas concerning the Italian case I have limited myself to second-hand information. One must also consider than undoubtedly the German situation at the turn of the century was far more structured than the Italian one: it was much easier to make out a series of constitutive elements in this case.

7. A.G. Manca, "Prassi politica e questione organizzativa nel liberalismo politico prussiano negli anni della Nuova Era (1858–1862)". In *Annali dell'Istituto storico italo-germanico in Trento* **14** (1988): 341–388. I. Cervelli, *Liberalismo e conservatorismo in Prussia.* 1850–1858. Bologna: il Mulino, 1983.

8. On Lorenz von Stein, see above all *Staat und Gesellschaft. Studien über Lorenz von Stein.* Herausgegeben und eingeleitet von Roman Schnur, mit einer Bibliographie von Max Munding. Berlin: Duncker & Humblot, 1978.

9. See the old but still-valid reconstructions by S. Landshut, *Kritik der Soziologie. Freiheit und Gleichheit als Ursprungsproblem der Soziologie* (1929), now in *Kritik der Soziologie und andere Schriften zur Politik.* Neuwied and Berlin: Luchterhand, 1969, and H. Freyer, *Soziologie als Wirklichkeitswissenschaft. Logische Grundlegung des Systems der Soziologie.* Leipzig and Berlin, 1930.

10. See above all T. Nipperday, *Deutsche Geschichte 1800–1866. Bürgerwelt und starker Staat.* München: Beck, 1984.

11. At the same time the *Gelehrtentum* provided for mobility and mediation between the different classes of which it was composed. Here my analysis *Il laboratorio borghese.* Ch. III, deviates from the account given by F.K. Ringer, *The Decline of German Mandarins. The German Academic Community 1890–1933.* Cambridge (Mass.): Harvard University Press, 1969.

12. See I. Gorges, *Sozialforschung in Deutschland 1872–1914. Gesellschaftliche Einflüsse auf Themen- und Methodenwahl des Vereins für Socialpolitik.* Königstein/Ts.: Hain, 1980; and in this volume the essay by Alain Desrosières.

13. The first step of the reform was the *Kreisordnung* for the eastern provinces dated December 13, 1872. It was followed by the *Provinzialordnung* on June 29, 1875, by the *Dotationsgesetz* on July 8, 1875 and lastly by the *Zuständigkeitsgesetz* dated July 26, 1876. The reform was wound up with the law on *allgemeine Landesverwaltung* dated July 26, 1880, bringing about the correspondence of administration in all of its parts with the reform introduced in the meantime. Later, the administrative reform was extended to the new provinces and to the western ones, starting from Hannover in 1884 and going as far as Posen in 1889.

14. W. Wilhelm, *Zur juristischen Methodenlehre in 19. Jahrhundert. Die Herkunft der Methode Paul Labands aus der Privatrechtswissenschaft.* Frankfurt: Klostermann, 1958. M. Fioravanti, *Giuristi e costituzione politica nell'ottocento tedesco.* Milano: Giuffré, 1979.

15. A major role in this direction was played by the introduction of new "social and State disciplines" into syllabi and exam programs: above all the new specializations of public and administrative law but also of *Nationalökonomie* and *Finanzwissenschaft.* Also this complex matter underwent a profound rationalization and reform that once again saw its cornerstone in Prussia, but affected all of Germany as well. Its first institutional moment was the law on juridic exams and on the preparation of higher juridic service, dated May 6, 1869. From that moment on, the attention placed on the capacity of higher civil servants grew and

the problem expanded from administrative jurisdiction to the entire civil service. For the most general implications of this process see W. Bleek, *Von der Kameralausbildung zum Juristenprivileg. Studium, Prüfung und Ausbildung der Höheren Beamten des allgemeinen Verwaltungsdienstes in Deutschland im 18. und 19. Jahrhundert.* Berlin: Colloquium Verlag, 1972. On the theme of professionalization see Ch. E. McClelland, "Zur Professionalisierung der akademischen Berufe in Deutschland". In W. Conze and J. Kocka (eds.). *Bildungsbürgertum im 19. Jahrhundert; Teil I: Bildungssystem und Professionalisierung in internationalen Vergleichen.* Stuttgart: Klett-Cotta, 1985, which is also the reference work on the general argument.

16. P. Schiera, *Il laboratorio borghese*, Ch. IV. Not only the fiscal reforms undertaken in Prussia by Miquel in 1891 and 1893 are relevant for this. It can be very useful to consider the system of social security (wherein next to the scholastic system, the effort of legislature and social politics was concentrated) as resulting from the more-or-less balanced crossing of two factors: a country's economic power on the one hand, and the population's politically affirmed social pretences on the other.

17. P. Flora, "Krisenbewältigung oder Krisenerzeugung? Der Wohlfahrtsstaat in historischer Perspektive". In W. J. Mommsen & W. Mock (eds.) *Die Entstehung des Wohlfahrtsstaates in Großbritannien und Deutschland 1859–1950.* Stuttgart: Klett-Cotta, 1982.

18. I. Cervelli, "Realismo politico e liberalismo moderato in Prussia negli anni dell decollo". In Lill R. & N. Matteucci (eds.) *Il liberalismo in Italia e in Germania dalla rivoluzione del '48 alla prima guerra mondiale.* Bologna: il Mulino, 1980, pp. 77–290.

19. B. vom Brocke, "Hochschul- und Wissenschaftspolitik in Preussen und im Deutschen Kaiserreich 1882–1907: das System Althoff." In P. Baumgart (ed.), *Bildungspolitik in Preussen zur Zeit des Kaiserreichs.* Stuttgart: Klett-Cotta, 1980. E. Shils (ed.), *Max Weber. On Universities. The Power of the State and the Dignity of the Academic Calling in Imperial Germany.* Translated, edited and with an introductory note by E. Shils. Chicago and London: 1973.

20. See the essays in P. Schiera & F. Tenbruck (eds.), *Gustav Schmoller e il suo tempo: la nascita delle scienze sociali in Germania e in Italia – Gustav Schmoller in seiner Zeit: die Entstehung der Sozialwissenschaften in Deutschland und Italien.* Bologna and Berlin: il Mulino and Duncker & Humblot, 1989.

21. U. Allegretti, *Profilo di storia costituzionale italiana. Individualismo e assolutismo nello stato liberale.* Bologna: il Mulino, 1989. See also A. Berselli, *La Destra storica dopo l'Unità, II: Italia legale e Italia reale.* Bologna: il Mulino, 1965.

22. The best presentation of the problem is, by far, still that offered by F. Chabod, *Storia della politica estera italiana dal 1870 al 1896.* Bari: Laterza, 1962, Ch. II.

23. R. Romeo, *Risorgimento e capitalismo.* Bari: Laterza, 1959. G. Are, *Il problema dello sviluppo industriale nell'età della Destra.* Pisa: Nistri-Lischi, 1965, and *Alle origini dell'Italia industriale.* Bologna: il Mulino, 1974. A. Cardini, *Stato liberale e protezionismo in Italia (1890–1900).* Bologna: il Mulino, 1981. On the Italian economic thought of the period see: R. Faucci, "La cultura economica

dopo l'Unità". In M. Finoia (ed.) *Il pensiero economico italiano*. Bologna: il Mulino, 1980, and *La Scienza economica in Italia (1850–1943): da Francesco Ferrara a Luigi Einaudi*, 1981; P. Barucci (ed.), *Le cattedre di economia in Italia*. Firenze, 1988. See also the essay by G. Gioli in this volume.

24. For the reconstruction of Italian political science at the end of the nineteenth century I have followed G. Sola, "La scienza politica italiana" (note 1). The three quotations are respectively by Saverio Scolari, Biagio Brugi, and Emilio Morpurgo.

25. G. Sola, "La scienza politica italiana", pp. 31, 45, 57.

26. The best book on the argument is still that by A. Caracciolo, *Stato e società civile in Italia. Problemi dell' unificazione italiana*. Torino: Einaudi, 1968.

27. See. G. Sola, "La scienza politica italiana", p. 23.

28. G. Sola, "La scienza politica italiana", pp. 38, 42.

29. For a discussion on the possibility of a "definitive" formalization of such sciences in the period, see the essay by P. Wagner in this volume.

30. P. Schiera, "Amministrazione e costituzione: verso la nascita della scienza politica". In *Il pensiero politico*, **15** (1982), pp. 74–91.

31. I. Porciani, "Attilio Brunialti e la 'Biblioteca di Scienze politiche'. Per una ricerca su intellettuali e Stato dal trasformismo all'età giolittiana". In A. Mazzacane (ed.), *I giuristi e la crisi dello Stato liberale in Italia fra Otto e Novecento*. Napoli: Liguori, 1986, pp. 191–229.

32. G. Gozzi, "Ideologia liberale e politica sociale: il socialismo della cattedra in Italia". In P. Schiera & F. Tenbruck, *Gustav Schmoller e il suo tempo*, pp. 181–216. See also Gabriella Gioli in this volume.

33. L. Mangoni, *Una crisi fine secolo. La cultura italiana e la Francia fra Otto e Novecento*. Torino: Einaudi, 1985.

34. F. Lampertico, *Economia dei Popoli e degli Stati*, Milano, 1874, as quoted by G. Gozzi, "Ideologia liberale e politica sociale", p. 202, in reference to Adam Schäffle and Adolph Wagner.

35. On this point see above all the already-quoted reading by A. Mazzacane (ed.), *I giuristi e la crisi dello Stato liberale in Italia*. See also F. Tessitore, *Crisi e trasformazioni dello Stato. Richerche sul pensiero giuspubblicistico italiano tra Otto e Novecento*. Milano: Giuffré, 1963, and G. Cianferotti, *Il pensiero di V. E. Orlando e la giuspubblicistica italiana fra Ottocento e Novecento*. Milano: Giuffré, 1980.

36. C. Vano, "Riflessione giuridica e relazioni industriali: alle origini del contratto collettivo di lavoro", and M. Fioravanti, "Stato di diritto e Stato amministrativo nell'opera giuridica di Santi Romano", both in A. Mazzacane (ed.), *I giuristi e la crisi dello Stato liberale*. On juridic socialism see P. Grossi, '*Un altro modo di possedere'. L'emersione di forme alternative di proprietà alla coscienza giuridica postunitaria*. Milano: Giuffré, 1977.

37. R. Gherardi, "L'Italia dei compromessi. Politica e scienza nell'età della Sinistra". In P. Schiera & F. Tenbruck (ed.), *Gustav Schmoller e il suo tempo*, p. 217, who quotes the already-cited Allegretti and R. Ruffilli, "Lo Stato liberale in Italia". In R. Lill & N. Matteucci (eds.), *Il liberalismo in Italia e in Germania*, pp. 217–219.

38. R. Gherardi, "L'Italia dei compromessi", p. 226.

39. This is the main thesis of P. Schiera, *Il laboratorio borghese*, in partial opposition to F.K. Ringer, *The Decline of German Mandarins*. See also the review of the German translation of the latter by B. vom Brocke. "'Die Gelehrten'. Auf dem Weg zu einer vergleichenden Sozialgeschichte europäischer Bildungssysteme und Bildungseliten im Industriezeitalter". In *Annali dell'Istituto storico italo-germanico in Trento*, **10** (1984), pp. 389–401.

40. R. Gherardi, "L'Italia dei compromessi", p. 247.

41. I. Porciani, "Attilio Brunialti", p. 199, who quotes R. Ruffilli, "Lo Stato liberale in Italia", p. 485.

42. I. Porciani, "Attilio Brunialti", who quotes Giuseppe Ricca Salerno. On the problem of social reform in Italy see V. Sellin, *Die Anfänge staatlicher Sozialreform im Liberalen Italien*. Stuttgart: Klett-Cotta, 1971.

43. O. Brunner, "Das Zeitalter der Ideologien". In *Neue Wege der Verfassungs- und Sozialgeschichte*. Zweite vermehrte Auflage. Göttingen: Vandenhoeck & Ruprecht, 1968, and in this volume the essay by J. Heilbron on the French situation.

44. The best work on the subject is, notwithstanding my critical position to it, Ch. E. McClelland, *State, Society and University in Germany, 1770–1914*. Cambridge: Cambridge University Press, 1980.

45. See, for a particular case, G. Cianferotti, "Germanesimo e università in Italia alla fine del'800. Il caso di Cemerino". In *Studi senesi*, **100** (1988), pp. 328ff.

PART III

THE DISCOURSE ON POLITICS BETWEEN
PHILOSOPHY, SCIENCE, AND PROFESSION

CHAPTER SIX

IN SEARCH OF THE STATE: POLITICAL SCIENCE AS
AN EMERGING DISCIPLINE IN THE U.S.*

JOHN G. GUNNELL

> I am, indeed, not one of those who believe
> that every institution here is incomprehen-
> sible to all human beings except the
> natives of this country. The institutions of
> the United States are the work of man, and
> can be understood by men.
>
> Francis Lieber

Introduction

Although the study of the history of political science may not be as fully
developed as that of some of the other social sciences, this area of
research in the United States has now reached a point where it is difficult
any longer to contemplate writing a single general treatment. Although
there are reasons to be dissatisfied with existing work, particularly
because of the tendency toward polemical and apologetic genres, the
general contours of the development of the discipline and profession are
quite accessible (1). However, in the way of corrective and specialized
endeavors, there is still much to be accomplished. One of the subjects that
has remained somewhat fallow is a careful consideration of the concept of
the state. Although for a long period, in the early years of the field, this
concept was virtually constitutive of political inquiry, it seemed by the
beginning of the behavioral era in American political science, by the mid-
1950s, that it was at best a vestigial notion. During the last decade,
however, many social scientists have been "bringing the state back in,"
even though others are still uneasy about such tendencies and worry about

P. Wagner, B. Wittrock, and R. Whitley (eds.), Discourses on Society: Volume XV, 1990, 123–161.
© 1990 Kluwer Academic Publishers. Printed in the Netherlands.

the "return of the state" and about the concept of the "political system besieged by the state" (2).

On the whole, the "state" remains a significant element in the vocabulary of social and political science, and the history of the "state" tells us a great deal not only about the evolution of political science but about the discipline's relationship (actual, wishful, and perceived) to politics. This essay is devoted to an exploration of how the "state" became the subject of political science as the discipline evolved during the nineteenth century. This account also reflects a definite methodological perspective.

Intellectual history, particularly in the case of the social sciences, has been dominated by a variety of "externalist" approaches which seek to explain the emergence and evolution of ideas and concepts in terms of contexts. Although, in principle, I have no quarrel with this strategy, and sympathize with the spirit of "contextualism" in historical research, simply locating discourse in a context does not explain it. More attention to the internal dynamics of intellectual change is necessary, and more is required in the way of concrete connections between text and context.

Putative contexts are seldom persuasively linked to the phenomena that they purport to explain. They tend more to be juxtaposed than connected. Furthermore, the proffered context is often less a logically comparable account of an intellectual matrix than, at best, a general historio-sociological reconstruction from secondary sources which is taken as a given datum or, at worst, some highly abstract summary characterization of a situation to which the ideas in question are supposedly a functional response.

It is tempting, and common, to suggest that the emphasis on the state in the discourse of political science, particularly during and subsequent to the Civil War, was a response to, and a catalyst in, the process of state-building in American politics. Stephen Skowronek has, for example, pursued this argument. He argues that "professional social science has traditionally played the part of a protagonist in the expansion of American national government" and that political science with its emphasis on the state was part of "an emergent intelligentsia," a group of professionals who rejected conventional politics and sought political reform from the top by acting as a "vanguard" and taking up "the challenge of building a new kind of state in America" (3).

This kind of argument obscures the fact that the vision of social science required the state more than the state needed it. But while there is no doubt that public policy and the development of governmental institutions during the last quarter of the nineteenth century, aided by strong nationalist sentiments, provided a congenial ambience for the proliferation of academic discourse about the state, noting this fact is not a substitute for a disciplinary archaeology of the "state." My concern is to reconstruct the genealogy of the concept through an internal, but contextually sensitive, examination of the evolution of the discourse of political science.

The principal arguments that I wish to advance are, *first*, that the evolution of the concept of the state must be understood not only in terms of political science's attempt to come to grips with politics as a subject matter but with its practical relationship to politics – the relationship between public and academic discourse. *Second*, although there were certainly some concrete connections between political science and the political practice involved in American "state-building," the particular conception of the state that was adopted, and the very fact of its adoption, was most essentially a function of the Germanization and disciplinization of political studies. This is not, in its most general terms, a novel claim, but it is also a claim that has not been carefully explicated and documented. It is also not an uncontested claim.

James Farr has set out to qualify, at least, the assumption that talk about the state in the mid-nineteenth century was in some fundamental way an anomaly in American political discourse.

We may see that Americans had a sense of the state going back to the earliest years of the Republic. The language of the 'state' was a broadly European and, then, American one which had dominated political discussion well before the Civil War, and certainly before a number of professional academics went off to Germany in the latter decades of the century in pursuit of *Staatswissenschaft*. (4)

This point is well-taken as a response to those who would suggest that the concept of the state and the idea of a science of the state were bizarre intrusions into the life and language of American politics. It is possible, as Farr demonstrates, to find uses of the word "state" and references "to the science of politics" in political discourse and commentary such as the *Federalist*, the work of Nathaniel Chipman (*Sketches of the Principles of Government*, 1793), and the analyses of Tocqueville. Nevertheless, Farr's claim that "the 'state' was a term which came naturally to these American republicans" (5) requires considerable qualification.

Although the word was sedimented in discourse about politics, the

concept of the state had little significant place in the early literature, and it
was never an object of theoretical reflection. Similarly, the notion of a
science of politics, or as John Adams put it, the "divine science of
government," was quite consistently understood as cumulative wisdom
that might inform a practical science of institution-building rather than as
a theoretical or academic science.

Although it is necessary to take into account the extent to which the
authors of the *Federalist* reserved the word "state" for talking about the
American state governments and the United States, and tended to avoid
its more generic use, what came most naturally to their language were
terms such as "government," "civil polity," "civil society," and "nation."
Chipman's use of the term "state" had little pointed theoretical meaning,
and even a European writer such as Tocqueville used it primarily in
talking about "sovereign power in Europe" except when discussing the
American state governments. Anna Haddow's exhaustive account of the
literature and curriculae of political science prior to 1900 reveals only
scarce and circumscribed references to the "State" before the last part of
the nineteenth century (6).

The lack of emphasis on the concept of the state in the later part of the
eighteenth century and early part of the nineteenth was, however, not an
American idiosyncrasy. The theory of the state in continental literature,
which would be so influential in the United States, had not yet emerged.
When it did emerge, it found an audience in the American search for an
academic vocabulary for talking about politics. But it is important to be
cautious about precipitous conclusions about political science professionalism and the use of the concept of state.

Bernard Crick described the nineteenth-century concern with the state
as essentially a flirtation with German ideas that belonged to the prehistory of American political science. He argued that the concepts of state
and sovereignty in this literature were "almost meaningless for *American*
politics" and that it was "so alien to American experience and institutions,
that it shows the failure of the German-trained scholars ... to establish
any roots in the American tradition." According to Crick, a distinctive
American political science really began with the Progressivist and
pragmatist influences after the turn of the century, and he argued that
"none of those things that predisposed it towards the 'scientific method'
arose from within itself." (7). This is indeed an inaccurate assessment of
the situation. And Crick's claim that John Burgess, whose work
represented the apotheosis of the state in nineteenth-century American

political science, "left no intellectual disciples at all" and "contributed little to what became its dominate techniques and concerns" (8) is an even greater exaggeration.

Although Daniel Rodgers is considerably more sensitive, and properly so, to the strategic dimension of discourse about the state, his treatment evokes an almost conspiratorial image of conservative political scientists jettisoning republican ideas and engaging in self-serving tactics to enhance their professional status and "wrest the language of political legitimacy away from the people." The "State," Rodgers claims, was an abstraction designed to give authority to a new kind of priesthood by "formalizing the amateur talk about politics" and providing a professional identity for political scientists. It gave political science a domain that distinguished it from, and claimed precedence over, other social sciences, but most of all "the State was the antonym of the People" and served the conservative function of providing "a formidable barrier to popular claims to rights" (9).

Rodgers maintains that the notion of "the all-sovereign state ... was nothing but a gigantic verbal riddle." It was frought, in the works of ardent nationalists like Burgess, who was the principal "architect of the idea of the absolute, unlimited state," with impossible contradictions spawned by their conflicting goals and their attempt to transpose German ideas to an American context (10). But most of all, he claims, the idea of the state was a "tool" that was invented to come to grips with the Civil War and the Union and give coherence both to politics and to the emerging discipline of political science. The hope was that it would do what religion had failed to do and that it would provide the kind of mystical entity of professional authority and identity that sociologists had found in the notion of society.

There is no doubt that the evolution of the concept of the state was closely tied up with political science's search for identity and with its attempt to come to grips with its relationship to politics as well as to understand the politics of the age, but there are significant substantive and methodological problems with Rodgers's analysis.

First of all, like Crick, Rodgers suggests that the concept of the state "evaporated as a word of consequence" with the advent of the Progressive era (11). This was simply not the case. Although the new generation of political scientists were palpably uneasy with, if not in revolt against, much that individuals such as Burgess had promulgated, they also worked within the structure of ideas, including the idea of the state, that he had contributed to constituting. Second, the claim that the state was largely an instrumental construct for advancing various professional and political interests is not evidentially sustained. For example, far from being an antonym for the "people," it was, I will suggest later, in large measure a synonym. But the difficulty with these claims is closely tied to the historiographical assumptions represented in this kind of research.

Rodgers's argument draws heavily upon the growing body of secondary literature of nineteenth-century professionalism, and it reflects the kind of methodological problem alluded to at the beginning of this essay. There is a distinct tendency in this literature to rationalize history and to present phenomena not only as functional responses to concrete events such as the Civil War but to much more retrospectively constructed contexts such as "social fragmentation." And, at least in the case of Rodgers, there is a tendency to go beyond functional explanation to the attribution or a kind of intentionality that makes history appear as the outcome of instrumental reason. This dramaturgical approach may provide insights, but it also obscures how things happened and banishes accident from the world of conceptual change.

Politics and the State

Although by the early years of the twentieth century the statist language of politics was being somewhat undermined by more recent trends in political science, it was to a great extent in the response to the First World War that a frontal attack on the idea of the state appeared. In England, pluralist theory was already hostile to the theory of the state, and Sir Ernest Barker not only condemned German philosophy and the "worship of power" in the work of individuals such as Nietzsche and Treitschke but criticized Austin's theory of sovereignty as never having fitted English "polyarchism" (12). In the United States, John Dewey attacked German idealism as "an a priori and an absolutist philosophy gone bankrupt," and he rejected its evolutionary philosophy of history in favor of a critical and "experimental philosophy", which, he believed, undercut the kind of nationalism which led to the war (13).

The State was hardly rejected as the subject of political science by individuals such as W.W. Willoughby, who had done so much to make it coincidental with the domain of political science, but the association with German philosophy precipitated a reevaluation. Willoughby argued there had been a conspiracy between political authority and German professors of political philosophy in propagating Prussian ideals in the form of the myth of the state and a philosophy of history celebrating the evolution of the Teutonic people (14). Franklin Giddings, a sociologist who had been much involved with the discipline of political science, stated the case most dramatically.

The thoughts of sober-minded men have turned anew to theories of political life because a Teutonic philosophy of authority has incited, has directed, and sought to justify the most diabolical collective conduct that the human race, in all its career since the Heidelberg jaw was clothed in flesh, has infamously committed. This theory has seized upon a creation of the demoniac imagination and called it The State, spelled with a large "T" and a capital "S" (15).

Even Giddings, however, did not reject the state, which he maintained was the "noblest expression of human purpose," but only the idea, of the "Treitschkes and Kaisers," that it was "absolute" rather than "finite and relative" (16). But by the last decade of the nineteenth century, the organic theory of the state to which Giddings was reacting, had come to inform political science and American education. It is not surprising, given the theological background of many of the early social scientists, that they would transfer to the state the redemptive attributes of religion.

One popular textbook of the period, written by a student of Julius Seelye (Amherst College) and John Burgess (Columbia), spoke of the State as representing the two "great truths" of the "individuality of man and the organic unity of the race" and accorded to it attributes worthy of deity "one and universal," "manifold," and "supreme." The "true State" was nothing less than the sovereign people in their "organic capacity" and the source of all rights. As such it was "the greatest of all earthy institutions", and, as it expanded "its sway over the earth," it ushered in a world of "righteousness and peace" (17). It is the evolution of this image that I wish to explore.

The paradox of American social science in the nineteenth century has been well-documented (18). Social science in many of its basic dimensions began as a reform movement. Lacking political authority, it sought purchase in the authority of knowledge which in turn led to specialization, differentiation, and a gravitation toward the university to ensure its claim to science. Once it was academically institutionalized, professionalization created demands that not only competed with political commitment but contradicted it, and protecting academic status from political encroachment and defilement became a continuing problem.

Among the emerging social science disciplines of the nineteenth century, political science was relatively conservative, both ideologically and with respect to attempts to engage in political activity. Few of the major cases of academic freedom involved political scientists. The history of political science, from the end of the nineteenth century, could be read as a story of how the discipline, once successfully insulating itself from politics, sought to devise safe strategies for reengagement. The problem of the articulation of public and academic discourse remained a constitutive issue.

When political scientists were seeking disciplinary autonomy, "politics" was, both internally and externally, far from the most congenial subject matter. The case of Frank Blackmar at the University of Kansas is representative and instructive (19). Like so many of those who established the early departments of history and political sciences, he was trained (1889) at The Johns Hopkins University. Recruited by the Kansas Regents, he proposed to found a department of "History and Politics," but was told that "the people of Kansas would not tolerate a Department of Politics within the University, as they had enough politics within the state already." His second proposal for a department of "History and Political Science" was also rejected, and he settled for "History and Sociology."

Fear of politics was, however, more deeply rooted. George Beard, one of the founders of psychoanalysis in the United States, attributed the ubiquity of "neurasthenia" or "American nervousness" to politics and religion (20). And, many years earlier, Francis Lieber, when still a "stranger in America," asked "how does ... our system of politics affect the mind?

Are the frequent excitements, which penetrate into the smallest arteries of our whole political system, not productive of much evil in this very particular? Aristotle, even in his time, observed the great problem of insanity among politicians ... Do then our politics not lead, with many individuals, to an alienation of the mind? (21)

In the end, Lieber concluded that, at least as a "final cause," elections and other aspects of democratic politics and its "disappointments" in the United States were less responsible for the "appalling frequency of alienation of the mind" than "religious excitement" and "a diseased anxiety to be equal to the wealthiest" (22). But from his perspective there was no doubt that politics was an unsettling business, and both conceptually and existentially, Lieber's approach to politics, like those who succeeded him, was circumspect.

Francis Lieber and the Idea of the State

In addition to his prominence in general histories of political science, a great deal has been written about Lieber's life and work (23). It was generally recognized by Lieber's successors, and it has been characteristically affirmed by historians of American political science and by Lieber's biographers, that he was the founder of systematic political studies in the United States. He was the first to employ the concept of the state as something more than a synonym for nation or government and to make it an object of theoretical analysis. And for a period of nearly three decades Lieber's work was the principal matrix for the conversation about political inquiry. It moved along, and contributed to defining, the boundary between public and academic discourse. Lieber was continuously sensitive to the dangers of politics, while attracted by it, as both an activity and object of analysis, but what is most striking is that he, the first American theorist of the state, was the last to be intimately, or maybe successfully, involved in public life. After Lieber, the issue of articulating politics and the academy became distinctly different.

Lieber thought of himself as both a political philosopher and a "publicist", and, for a person of this time, his professional life as an academician began at a relatively late age, at 35. His early years were deeply involved in patriotic causes. His family was dedicated to Prussian nationalism and revered Frederick the Great, and these attitudes were reinforced on a more intellectual basis at the University of Berlin by his exposure to Wilhelm von Humboldt, Johann Gottlieb Fichte, and Frederick Schleiermacher. His relatives had fought in the war of liberation (1813–14), and he himself was wounded at Waterloo. After his army service, his nationalism was transformed into radicalism in response to the weakness and repressiveness of Frederick William III and Metternich. His deep involvement in the nationalistic *Turner* movement led to his arrest and denial of entrance into the university. Although he eventually matriculated at Jena and gained a doctorate in 1820, he was banned from teaching and further study because of his continued agitation.

After going off to fight for the liberation of Greece, Lieber's views were moderated by disillusionment and by his subsequent association with Niebuhr in Rome. Upon returning to Germany in 1823, first to Berlin and then Bonn, he was still under surveillance as a subversive and imprisoned for a time before escaping to England in 1826. Utilitarian friends aided him in securing a position as a gymnasium instructor and swimming coach in the United States, and he emigrated in 1827, settling in Boston. He became a correspondent for a German newspaper, but for the next five years, he dedicated himself principally to translating portions of a German encyclopedia and creating an American version (thirteen volumes) which became an authoritative publication and gave him a measure of financial security.

It was in the *Encyclopedia Americana* that the state, as the organizing concept of political inquiry, was first introduced in the United States. "As the idea of *politics* depends on that of the *state*, a definition of the latter will easily mark out the whole province of the political sciences ... This idea of the state is the basis of a class of sciences, and gives them a distinct character as belongs to the various classes of history, philosophy, theological, medical &c., sciences" (24). The state, it was claimed, was the "natural condition of man, because essential to the full development of his faculties," and it was postulated as something quite distinct from "the form of government" which was "merely a means of obtaining the great objects of the state" (25).

Lieber also presented the distinction, so basic to the German curriculum and eventually to American categories, between the "*abstract*, or purely philosophical, and the *historical* and *practical*," study of politics. And he suggested twelve more specific divisions: natural law; abstract or theoretical consideration of the state and literature on this subject from Plato to the present; political economy; police science; practical politics (administration); history of politics; history of the European and American states; statistics; public (constitutional) law; international law; diplomacy; and political practice (26).

Lieber, naturalized in 1832, was actively seeking more regular employment, either in government or academia, during the years that he worked on the *Encyclopedia*. Although his efforts were frustrated, he made influential friends and persisted in the task of applying European concepts to the analysis of American institutions. His association with Tocqueville, initially through a common interest in prison reform, was important in this respect, but there are also strong indications that Tocqueville took much from both the *Encyclopedia* and his discussions with Lieber. He moved easily between academic and governmental circles while seeking a position and dealing with various reform issues. His political views and associations were, in American terms, basically conservative. He was, for example, certainly against slavery but avoided the abolitionist movement. And arguments for feminist rights were an anathema.

He eventually secured a position as professor of history and political economy at South Carolina College. Although it was here that he wrote his major treatises, he never failed to view the twenty years he spent at this institution as a form of cultural and political "exile." He was initially considered for the college presidency, but he was deemed too young and foreign and found himself continually forced to be politically and socially wary with respect to matters such as slavery, religion, and states' rights.

The two volumes of Lieber's *Manual of Political Ethics* (1838–39) are difficult to characterize. He later described political ethics as a kind of enlightened patriotism, and he saw it much along the lines of the public aspects of moral philosophy taught in American colleges. But despite its practical purpose of political education, and tempering political "excitement," it was the first example in American literature of a systematic treatment of government, politics, and law. It was specifically designed to compete with, or supersede, classic texts such as that of William Paley (27) and other works in moral and political philosophy written from the English/Scottish perspective and to apply European concepts to the analysis of American politics. Above all, *it was the first study of the state in America and the first study of America as a state.*

A stylistically ponderous and exhaustingly comprehensive work (although touchy subjects such as slavery were conspicuously missing), it was a studied attempt, following the path of German scholars of the period, to meld theory and fact or philosophy and history, dealing with everything from the metaphysics of the state to smuggling. Foremost among its goals was to distinguish the state from the family, the church, and other social entities and to establish its primacy – and by implication that of the field devoted to studying it.

Lieber presented and extended theoretical discussion of the state as a *"jural* society" which referred to a moral relationship founded on right and justice yet prior to positive law. The state was natural, or "aboriginal with man," and existed by necessity. While yet a means, and not supersed-ing the individual, it was the highest form of society, "the glory of man," and its purpose was to obtain the highest ends of mankind (28). Central to his position was, again, the notion that the state was prior to government. The truly legitimate state, the "hamarchy," was a sovereign organism, exemplified in the United States and England and the historical evolutionary path leading to their appearance (through Christianity, the rise of the Teutonic world, and the advent of representative government and capitalism). An "autarchy" referred to a regime where power was vested in a monarch or some particular class (29).

Lieber emphasized the reciprocity of rights and duties, but for the purpose of stressing the latter. He put a premium on the state as a sovereign patriotic community and totally rejected contractarian theories, yet he held on to a notion of natural rights and the priority of individual liberty. He attacked socialism, and defended the sanctity of property as an extension of the individual. The Gallic disease that he feared was democratic absolutism, which, he believed, always manifested an element of communism. The answer was "institutional liberty" created through representative government and the system of checks and balances characteristic of the *Federalist* with its image of decentered and limited governmental power.

Lieber resigned from Carolina in 1855 and finally, in 1857, was appointed to a chair at Columbia that he asked to be designated as History and Political Science. Although his *Civil Liberty and Self-Government* (1853) had been silent on the issues of slavery and the Union, Lieber's repressed concerns became manifest in a militant nationalism and republicanism. Through the period of the Civil War and its aftermath, he was consistently involved in affairs in Washington and wrote tracts on guerrilla warfare, international law, and the governance of armies in the field. In the classroom, he approached the issue by attacking contract theory as an intellectual basis of the South's position and by defending the North in terms of the organic image of the State as the "proper destiny" of man as a "political being" (30).

In his inaugural address at Columbia (1858), on the necessity of studying history and political science in "free countries," Lieber argued for the "need of a national university." This would not be a governmental institution but would function in "spirit" and "effect" like the Prussian university that had contributed to "quickening and raising German nationality" and, within a short time, making the state a great power. Although there was constant danger of governmental centralization, the United States also required a greater sense of nationality and patriotism, since only nations could represent the "great commonwealth of our race which extends over Europe and America" (31). In this address, Lieber also presented the most systematic exposition of his image of political science or "political philosophy."

He argued that people are born into society, an organic entity which was not the product of artifice but grounded in "love and instinct of association." "History" and "Statistik" were but respective modes for studying the past and contemporary, continuous and static, dimensions of social relations. And in approach, he stressed a middle road between the "so-called historical school," which valorized the past, and the "philosophical school," which postulated necessary laws of social evolution. But primarily Lieber wished to identify the domain of political science with the state. Political science, he claimed, "treats man in his most important earthly phase; the state is the institution which has to protect or to check all his endeavors, and, in turn, reflects them." And, in the end, the history of the state was nothing less than the history of civilization from primitive society in Africa to "Anglican self-government and liberty" (32).

By the advent of the Civil War, Lieber pursued the theory of the state in support of the union and argued that the American state, with its population of European immigrants, represented the latest stage in the history of the Teutonic state and "in the history of the cis-Caucasian spreading over the globe" (33). With respect to the Constitution, he claimed that

It is the political organism permeating our entire nation that answers the modern political necessities, and it alone can perform, as faithful hand-maid, the high demands of our civilization. The highest type, its choicest development, is the organic union of national and local self-government, not, however, national centralism, or a national unity without local vitality. (34)

Lieber spent his last years at Columbia in the law school after President Barnard, who had come from Mississippi, attempted to have him dismissed altogether (on the avowed basis that his approach was not needed in an undergraduate college). He continued to be involved in public affairs at the national, state, and city level and in circles of higher education until he died in 1872. Not only did he set the stage for the development of the graduate program at Columbia, but he had a profound effect on individuals such as Daniel Coit Gilman, the first president of The Johns Hopkins University and sponsor of political studies at that institution, and on Theodore Woolsey at Yale. But there was another important connection which was central to the development of the ideas introduced by Lieber.

The State as Organism

In a posthumous tribute to Lieber, Bluntschli noted that "from 1860 to 1870, Francis Lieber, in New York, Edward Laboulaye, in Paris, and I in Heidelberg, formed what Lieber used to call a 'scientific clover-leaf,' in which three men, devoting themselves especially to political science, and at the same time uniting the historical and philosophical methods, combining theory with practical politics," maintained close intellectual contact (35). It was probably in large measure from Bluntschli that Lieber derived his methodological ideas as well as his organic image of the state. Although Bluntschli's work would not be available in translation until 1885, when it became a popular text, many of the Americans who studied in Germany during the previous decade were influenced by his ideas. The great impact of Bluntschli's work, in both Germany and the United States, has not been sufficiently recognized. Herbert B. Adams, the principal organizer of studies in history and political science at The Johns Hopkins University, studied with Bluntschli (as well as Johann Droysen, Heinrich von Treitschke, and Karl Knies) in 1876 and secured his academic appointment on the basis of Bluntschli's recommendation.

The state, as conceived by Bluntschli, was a "moral and spiritual organism," masculine in personality, as distinguished from the feminine church (he had earlier written a work on *Psychological Studies of the Church and State*), and something whose history began with the "appearance of the white races, the children of light, who are the bearers of the history of the world." He conceded that, like the evolution of human beings, there was a bodily history represented by the inferior races which was the material cause and preceded "proper history" like the "pigments and brushes" do "the work of the artist" (36).

He rejected both what he called the idea of the legal state, which was limited to the protection of rights, as well as the police state. It was necessary to take account of both justice and public welfare, and this is what he saw as happening in an age in which national states were being formed. He had no doubt that communism was in conflict "with the nature of man as created by God" and that even though socialism was "more temperate and humane," it was "equally absurd." The state had "no absolute power over private property" which lay "outside the range of public law" even though it was necessary to recognize the limits of private property and the need for *res publicae* (37).

In his view, the idea of a social contract, however, was as unhistorical, illogical, and dangerous as the idea of divine right or of might making right. There were glimmers of truth in all such doctrines, but the state arose from the social impulse of human nature and passed from unconscious to conscious stages of development. Bluntschli saw himself, and individuals such as Lieber as reflecting, and even adumbrating, in theory what was being realized in practice in the modern age, and he believed that representative democracy, originating in America, pointed toward the historical completion of the state.

Herbert Adams claimed that "the great northern and the great southern tributaries to American political science were brought together when Theodore Woolsey edited, in 1874, a revision of Lieber's *Civil Liberty and Self-Government*" (38). Woolsey was the first of the major native American theorists of the state and political science to be educated abroad (at Bonn and Paris), and he reinforced the general pattern of analysis by Lieber and Bluntschli.

After graduating from Yale in 1820, Woolsey studied law and theology (training as a Presbyterian minister). He returned to the University as a professor of Greek in 1830 and served as president from 1846–70. Writing on subjects as diverse as international relations and divorce, he was much influenced by Lieber. He taught "Political Philosophy", which at Yale, as well as elsewhere (and, for example, in Lieber's work), tended to be a rather generic designation encompassing political science, the constitution, economics, and related subjects. And he later specialized in teaching international law. In addition to publishing a collection of his sermons on religion delivered at Yale, his work on political science and the state appeared in 1878 and became an influential text (39).

Derived from his lectures at Yale from 1846–71, the work considered the Doctrine of Rights as the Foundation of a Just State, Theory of the State, and the State – Practical Politics (which basically followed the German classification of *Naturrecht, Staatslehre*, and *Politik*). He rejected the classic idea of natural rights and contract theory in favor of rights connected with the ends of humanity and given by God. He stressed the extent to which the state was a natural entity which was not merely a protector but creator of rights, and he warned against the extremes of communism and socialism and the conditions of modernity that gave rise to them. Most of the work, however, was devoted to an encyclopedic discussion of various aspects of the history and current practice of politics and political ethics.

By the time that the major graduate programs in political science began to appear at institutions such as Colombia and Hopkins in the 1880s, the theory of the state, as advanced by Lieber, Bluntschli, and Woolsey, constituted, both substantively and methodologically, a distinct and influential paradigm. And it would be further sedimented by the new generation of scholars who were trained in Germany and France and who were most influential in institutionalizing graduate education in political science during the last quarter of the century.

The State and the University

A School of Political Science was established at Yale in 1886, and Andrew D. White, who grafted systematic political studies on the base of moral science at Michigan, and later at Cornell where he was the first president, was a student of Woolsey. White also studied at the Sorbonne and Collège de France, where he worked under Laboulaye, and at Berlin with Ranke. Charles K. Adams was White's student and succeeded him at Michigan, where he introduced the German model of studies, which he had observed at Bonn, Berlin, and Leipzig. He then followed White as president of Cornell (and later became president of Wisconsin).

Herbert Adams and John Burgess, however, were certainly the most crucial figures in this development, but one other individual and institution deserves particular mention. Adams and Burgess, as well as many of the colleagues and students they recruited, came from Amherst College under the tutelege of Seelye, who was professor of "mental and moral philosophy" and later president.

Although not a principal author himself, Seelye used, and revised (1880), Laurens Hickok's popular textbook on moral philosophy (40). Such works, which had been at the core of the traditional college and university curriculum, had characteristically dealt with public or practical ethics and discussed classic texts in the history of political thought. And there is reason to suggest that in large measure the social sciences, or at least important elements of these fields as academic disciplines, developed out of the specialization and differentiation of elements of moral philosophy (41). Seelye's interests were eclectic, but in his revision of Hickok he extended the discussion of the state and particular aspects of state authority, law, and politics. Government (divine, civil, and parental) was already a principal focus of the book, which emphasized the continuity of moral and public duty, obedience to government, natural law, the organic character of the state as a body of citizens, and the notion of government as an agent of the sovereign state.

Gilman, who did so much to further the professionalization of the social sciences, and who was an ardent admirer of Lieber, strongly supported Adams' program and his department of history, politics, and economics (beginning in the late 1870s) at Hopkins. He had also studied abroad and was committed to the creation of graduate research universities based on the European model. He taught at Yale (geography) before becoming president of the University of California. When his notion of graduate education was resisted at Berkeley, he accepted the first presidency at Hopkins on the basis of the trustee's strong commitment to allow the implementation of his plan.

Although for Adams the dominant category was history, it was, in his view, as for those who preceded him, virtually indistinguishable from political science. Edward Freeman's aphorism "History is past Politics and Politics present History" appeared frequently in his work and even as a sign in his seminar room. The method, it might be said, was historical no matter what the diverse subject matter taught in the extensive interdisciplinary, or predisciplinary, curriculum and discussed in the series of *Studies in Political and Historical Science.* Adams's own specialty was local history and government (42). He believed that the study of this subject would serve to connect a student's own community "not only with the origin and growth of the State and Nation, but with the mother-country, with the German Fatherland, with villages and communities throughout the Aryan world" (43).

The Teutonic theory of the State was central to the course of study, but it was an extensive and diverse curriculum which included such advanced subjects as studies in socialism (Marx, nihilism, etc.) as part of the program in political economy. The graduate seminar began in 1881 and included not only resident faculty but visitors from abroad such as James Bryce. Adams maintained that it was neither "slavishly following foreign methods" nor "establishing in this country a German university," but even though it may have been in many ways "pre-eminently American" (44), the form and content unmistakably reflected Adams's image of German education in historical and political science. The Historical and Political Science Association, created in 1877 by Henry Carter Adams as an extension of the seminary and designed to draw in lawyers and others from the community, was described by Herbert Adams as "a kind of

Staatswissenschaftlicher Verein ... like that in Heidelberg University" (45).

An impressive group of students were trained at Hopkins and many did seminal research and institutional work in the emerging, yet often not clearly defined, social scientific disciplines at major graduate institutions: Albion Small (sociology, Chicago); E.A. Ross (sociology, Stanford and Wisconsin); John Commons (economics, Syracuse and Wisconsin); Edward Bemis (economics and sociology, Chicago and Kansas); Henry Carter Adams (political economy, Cornell and Michigan); John Dewey (philosophy and education at Michigan, Chicago, and Columbia); Frederick Turner (history, Wisconsin); Thomas Woodrow Wilson (history, political economy, jurisprudence at Wesleyan, Bryn Mawr, and Princeton).

A group of these students, including Ross, Commons, H.C. Adams, and Bemis, were also the principles in some of the most notorious cases of the late nineteenth century involving academic freedom. What in part was manifest in these cases were the problems of reconciling academic and political commitment and of defining the relationship between the university and politics. While Adams and Burgess were relatively secure, but maybe less than realistic, in their vision of the university and political studies vis-à-vis politics, their students were forced to deal more directly with the practical dimensions of the problem.

For individuals such as Herbert Adams, Germany offered not only a model for the structure of university education but an image of the relationship between the university and the state. The idea of the university as a place for political education and as a voice of social authority was already present in the American tradition – and in the ideas and activity of Lieber. For Adams, Burgess, White, and C.K. Adams, as well as others who led the institutionalization of political science in American colleges and universities after the Civil War, it was clear that the principal purpose of history and political science was political education – to foster citizenship and leadership. Yet the highly professionalized research university such as that which developed at Hopkins and Columbia raised new issues about the articulation of academic and public discourse – and the tensions between them. Burgess, for example, was not able to find a compromise between the goals of scholarship and traditional moral education at Amherst. And at Columbia, the practical dimension of political science tended to give way to the demands of scholarship.

For Adams, Burgess, and others who studied in Germany, it was not merely the concept of the state which they adopted but images of the relationship between theory and practice, between the university and politics, which they believed were applicable to the United States. These images may have been partial, or less than accurate, representations of the actual, and complex, situation in Germany, but there were general features of the relationship between the state and university that were attractive to American scholars.

No matter what the particular perspective, the German intellectuals of the period were united in their attachment to some form of an idealist vision of history and the evolution of the state. Nationalism overrode particular political differences, and in various ways individuals as diverse in some respects as Otto von Gierke and Treitschke were united in their sanctification of national power and their organic and communal vision of political life which entailed a rejection of natural rights and contract theory.

They were committed to German unification and found justification for this position in the work of Humboldt, Fichte, Schleiermacher, and Hegel and the idea of the state as an organic metaphysical world-historical entity reconciling authority and freedom or power and right. They believed that liberal values were to be realized within the framework of a *Rechtsstaat* which they conceived as embodied in Bismarck's reformed Prussian nation. Although someone such as Droysen, like Lieber and Burgess, emphasized the limited sphere of state competence internally, he stressed the state as representing the ethical community of the nation, giving identity to the individual, and as serving as the vehicle of historical progress exemplifying God's providence and the spirit of reason.

The German professoriate, the "mandarins" (46), were a special class which not only legitimized the state theoretically but traditionally accepted its authority and conceived of their role as organically tied to the sphere of state action. They were a distinctive elite who were held in high esteem and deeply tied to various forms of state power through the system of examinations that provided entrance into the bureaucracy and other privileged ranks of state service. Academic values had public and official recognition, and the professors in turn spoke for dominant values in society. The professional autonomy of the university faculty and its attachment to the value of *Lernfreiheit* and independent scholarly research were mitigated by the assumption that it was in very large measure a functionary of the state and a social class deeply integrated into the structure of state power. These scholars were employees of the state and represented the establishment on matters of culture and education.

It would be a mistake to assume that the "mandarins" were a monolithic group or that their situation did not undergo considerable change during the last quarter of the century. There were important generational and professional differences. The legal theorists were, for example, the most influential. But, on the whole, their influence was largely a function of their conformity and their subservience to Bismarck (cf. Schiera, in this volume).

What is important is less whether Americans such as Adams and Burgess accurately construed the situation in Germany than how they interpreted that situation. But, furthermore, the models that they generated did not easily apply to the American context, where the role of the emerging university and its relationship to politics was far from settled. While they believed that it was possible in some fundamental respect to emulate the role of the university that they perceived in Germany, one of the things that most distinguished the American academy was the lack of any definite institutional tie to political elites and political authority.

While the work of Adams and Burgess reflected one perspective on the German context, and the one that most clearly came to inform the discipline of political science, other notions about the relationship between academic professionalism and public life were derived from the experience of those who studied in Germany. And to understand political science, it is necessary in part to understand the path that the discipline, as a whole, did not take.

There were two complementary and converging dimensions to the development of social science in the United States. One involved the differentiation and specialization of the traditional nineteenth-century university curriculum, while the other involved the institutionalization, and eventual academization, of social reform movements. In an important respect, the schools of history and political science founded at Hopkins and Columbia, as well as the American Historical Association (1884) and the American Political Science Association (1903), were defections from the American Social Science Association and its program for social change, but there were other paths exiting from the Association.

The story of the rise and demise of the ASSA has been told as both tragedy and progress (47). Whatever the perspective, however, the growth of academic professionalism and the fact that the ideals of reform and pure science "did not dwell in peace" has been a common theme (48). What has not been sufficiently recognized is the extent to which this development was tied up with the Germanization of social theory and the idea of the state, which in various ways drew social scientists away from the Anglo-American roots of the ASSA. But within the latter trend, it is important to recognize how the development of political science, and the work of individuals like Burgess, both resembled and diverged from the vision initially represented by the American Economic Association, which was the second professional organization to break away (1885) from the parent association.

Although the American social science movement was, through its membership and its concerns, consistently tied to the world of higher education, its roots were more practical than academic. It was born of a concern with political and economic reform and was initially inspired by the British Social Science Association which had been devoted to the amelioration of the conditions of the working class. It would be too simple to suggest that social science succeeded religion in this respect, but many of the founders of American social science, both those, such as Richard Ely, committed to the state-sponsored control of capitalism and political corruption, and his *laissez-faire bête-noire*, William Graham Sumner, came from evangelical backgrounds and viewed their efforts as a continuation of their religious goals.

It was, however, in many respects quite consciously, the search for legitimacy and authority that propelled the social science enterprise into the university. Lacking political authority, it sought the authority of knowledge. Ironically, however, once situated within the academic world, reformism tended to founder on shoals of academic professionalism and political conservatism. Even the search for academic freedom ultimately became largely a defense of professional security that tended to depoliticize the enterprise of social science. Its entrance into the university, then, institutionalized social science – in every sense of that word (cf. Manicas, in this volume).

John Burgess and the Foundation of Modern Political Science

Few individuals have described their intellectual position as succinctly as Lieber's successor at Columbia in the course of characterizing his magnum opus on *Political Science and Comparative Constitutional Law*.

... I would say that the book represents the Teutonic nations – the English, French, Lombards, Scandinavians, Germans and North Americans – as the great modern nation builders, that it represents the national State, that is, the self-conscious democracy, as the ultima Thule of political history; that it justifies the temporary imposition of Teutonic order on unorganized, disorganized, or savage people for the sake of their own civilization and their incorporation in the world society; that it, therefore justifies the colonial system of the British Empire especially; that it favors federal government, and finally, that it extols above everything the system of individual immunity against governmental power formulated in the Constitution of the United States and upheld and protected by the independent judiciary (49).

Burgess, born in Tennessee in 1844, was on the scene of American political science until 1931. He had served with the Union army and was a passionate American nationalist, but if Sanborn was a supporter of John Brown, Burgess, despite his view that the Civil War was the objective manifestation of the human spirit working toward the perfection of the union and the modern state (50), saw Brown's raid as a precipitous crime of passion that violated the plan of providence and reason.

Burgess had been an undergraduate at Amherst, from 1863 to 1867, but he had been dissatisfied with the curriculum in history and political science. Attracted by Lieber, he attended Columbia law school for a time, but, after contracting typhoid, finished his studies as an apprentice in Springfield, Massachusetts. Rather than practicing law, however, he took a post teaching history and political economy at Knox College. After two years, he went, in 1871 on the advice of the American (Hegelian) historian George Bancroft, to Germany. He studied, until 1873, at Göttingen, Berlin, and Leipzig.

In this post-Hegelian and post-Rankean atmosphere, he worked under figures such as Theodor Mommsen, Roscher, Droysen, and Treitschke (51). He became firmly attached to both the philosophy and practice of the German state and to, at least his image of, German education and its relationship to politics. His favorite teacher was Roscher, but he was less ideologically attuned to his work, since "whether conscious of it or not, he was laying the groundwork for state socialism." He expressed "reverence for Mommsen" who "was Nietzsche's conception of a superman" and who was dedicated to the collaboration of Germany, England, and the United States (52). But he noted that "the teacher, however, who led me in the line of the work to which my subsequent professional life was devoted was Rudolph von Gneist, the chief professor of public law and the counsel to Bismarck on all legal matters." Burgess believed that while studying in Germany, he "practically saw the German Empire constituted" (53).

It was this vision of the unity of academic study and public policy that

Burgess brought back to the United States – a vision that was reinforced by his memory of the career of his predecessor at Columbia. But Burgess's efforts, much more than those of Lieber, were single-mindedly directed toward the goal of creating a systematic science of politics and a curriculum to support it.

Burgess wished to develop a program of graduate education based on various European designs. Although the German model was consistently paramount, he had in mind the Sorbonne, Collège de France, and particularly the Ecole Libre, which through its independence of government control he believed had exercised a sane and conservative influence on France. His goal was to establish a private institution with a public purpose. Through vehicles such as the *Political Science Quarterly* (a journal founded in 1885 and devoted both to the promotion of science and to practical political issues) and a professional science association, he hoped "to create a school of American political philosophy and distinct American literature" that would reflect the "progressive development of truth through free research" (54).

Burgess came to Colombia in 1876 with a dual appointment in the School of Arts (history and political science) and the School of Law. He had failed, during the previous two years, despite the encouragement and aid of Seelye, to create a program of graduate education on the German model at Amherst College. More specifically, he noted that "the conscious object of my work at Amherst was to establish a school of political thought" (55). But the idea of a scientific study of politics did not appeal to an Amherst establishment that still saw higher education as primarily theological training.

In 1880, the trustees invited him to formulate a plan. His proposal called for a faculty of political science, composed of individuals in a variety of fields from both the School of Arts and the School of Law, that would offer graduate instruction in history, political economy, public law, and political philosophy. The proposal was accepted, and the trustees resolved to create "a school designed to prepare young men for the duties of public life, to be entitled a School of Political Science" and to offer a curriculum "embracing the History of Philosophy; the History of the Literature of the Political Sciences" and a number of other areas touching upon comparative public law and political institutions. The "purpose" was "to give a complete general view of all the subjects both of internal and external public polity, from the threefold standpoint of History, Law, and Philosophy," and the "prime aim," announced in the college catalogue of the academic year 1880, was "the development of all the branches of the political sciences" with the "secondary aim" of preparing "young men for all the political branches of public service" (56).

There is little basis for quarreling with Burgess's own assessment that, during the decade between 1890 and 1900, the school became the leading graduate faculty in political science in the country (57). But in this endeavor, the "primary aim" of creating professional political science increasingly overshadowed the "secondary aim" of preparation for public service. And as it did so, the question that became more pressing was how the purpose of a practical science, in the Aristotelian sense of having an end in action, was to be realized.

Burgess's claim, however, was that the primary aim was essential to the secondary one, a thesis which would persist among those who followed him during the next century. The development of political science was the way to a better public policy. He argued that "unless a sounder political wisdom and a better political practice be attained, the republican system may become but a form, and republican institutions but a deception." This required "a higher political education" that would provide "the elements of the political sciences with their literature and with the methods of a sound political logic" (58).

By 1891, the school was divided into departments which included a department of history and political philosophy. The key to the entire program was the "historical method" and the teaching of substantive history which Burgess maintained was the foundation of "a true and valuable public law and political science. Theory and speculation in politics must be regulated by historic fact." There was an undergraduate department of history and political science which employed the "gymnastic method" of drill and recitation and which brought students by the end of the third year to the beginning level of the School of Political Science, which included courses in "history, philosophy, economy, public law, jurisprudence, diplomacy, and sociology" and which moved the student in the direction of independent scholarly research involving primary courses (59).

The method of graduate study continued to be one that in Burgess's view, much like that of Bluntschli, was designed "to escape the dangers of a barren empiricism on the one side, and of a baseless speculation." Here the curriculum was organized around the "history of *institutions*, the origin and development of the State through its several phases of *political organization* down to the modern constitutional form," and this included "the history of the philosophic theories of the state." The next phase was a study of "the existing actual and legal relations of the State," and the culmination was to "seek finally through comprehensive comparison to generalize the ultimate principles of our political philosophy" (60). The general structure of the program leading to the Ph.D., including the form of examinations, became a model that significantly informed subsequent graduate education in political science in the United States.

Burgess understood his endeavor in the most comprehensive sense as founding "a School of Political Thought," and part of this institution, along with the *Political Science Quarterly* and the library, was the Academy of Political Sciences. This was an association of scholars drawn from the faculties and graduates of the Schools of Law and Political Science. Burgess considered this as the "central point of our whole system" and as designed to provide continuity through "a permanent body of growing scholars" devoted to original research and publication in political science (61). It may be worthwhile to note that Burgess had little to say about how the scholarly organization of the school of political science would concretely relate to the world of public affairs. This problem he ultimately bequeathed to his students.

Herbert Adams praised the "alliance of History and Political Science" that began with Lieber and which was building under Burgess during the 1880s. "Political science is the application of this historical experience to the existing problems of an ever progressive society. History and politics are as inseparable as past and present. This view is justified by the best historical and political opinion of our time: Ranke, Droysen, Bluntschli, Knies, Roscher, Nietzsche, Freeman, Seeley" (62). And he praised the special library, which was another example of the "best of German training," as well as the new general library administration under Melvil Dewey which, "like the School of Political Science, has been grafted from young Amherst college upon the sturdy trunk of old Columbia." Here, he noted, resources "can be massed upon any given point with the precision and certainty of a Prussian army corps, in the execution of a military manoeuvre" (63).

To suggest that Burgess was a racist and a reactionary may evoke images that detract from a historically situated understanding of his position, but it is difficult to find other categories. He was persistent in his attachment to the idea of the superiority of "the three great branches of the Teutonic stock" represented in Germany, Great Britain, and the United States (64), and he could never reconcile himself to the American entrance into World War I and the estrangement from Germany. Western imperialism, manifest destiny as a basis for the expansion of the United States, anti-Catholicism, and bans on immigration were all essential elements of his position.

Although he conceived the state as the locus of unlimited sovereignty and the ultimate source of law, Burgess, like Lieber, was intent on distinguishing it from government and particularly from the legislative branch which, like the *Federalist*, he saw as a source of caprice and a danger, particularly in the form of economic regulation, to the liberty and property of the people and nation. Constitution and government were creations, delegates, and agents of the state. He was not, however, an advocate of natural rights or contract theory. Rights were created by the state in the course of its evolution and protected by the Supreme Court from politicians and mass majorities represented in institutions such as labor unions which might extend government in a socialist direction. It was in part his distrust of government that led him to conclude that "the American university must therefore be a private institution" (65).

No one propagated the Teutonic theory of state and the Hegelian image of history as long and as assiduously as Burgess, and no one did more to make the state the object of political science (66). History was the objective record of "the progressive revelations of the human reason" and "spirit" and "its advance toward its own perfection" (67). Thus political science was a historical science focusing on the evolution of the state, and the development of liberty and sovereignty, from classical democracy through modern representative governments and projected toward an eventual world state wherein politics and political science would be complete. What Burgess designated as "the doctrines of political science" were understood as objectively embodied in constitutional law, but although consciousness of "the political idea" and the state first arose in "post-Roman Europe," it was not until modern times that "philosophical reflection" attained a level that allowed the formulation of propositions that could be "arranged into a body of science" (68).

Burgess understood himself as applying the methods of natural science to politics and law (69). Political science, he argued, was not merely history, or the compilation and recounting of facts, but the selective ordering of facts "in the forms and conclusions of science" which raises history to "a higher plane" (70). And in an important way it also went beyond the facts altogether. Following Bluntschli, Burgess distinguished between the "concept" of the state, which was a product of empirical science and the historical examination of actual states, and the "idea" of the state, which was an ideal construct which pointed toward perfection.

Inquiry involved "philosophical speculation" which was the "forerunner of history" and awakened "ideals" which in "the form of propositions" were, like generalizations from facts, also "principles of political science" which could inform political practice. Such speculation should not go unregulated and depart from a "constant, truthful and vital connection with the historical component," but "it lights the way of progress, and directs human experience toward its ultimate purpose" (71). Although history and political science, as modes of inquiry, were not identical

the two spheres so lap over one another and interpenetrate each other that they cannot be distinctly separated. Political science must be studied historically and history must be studied politically ... Separate them, and the one becomes a cripple, if not a corpse, the other a will-o'-wisp. (72).

The Transformation of the "State"

There were a number of English works that were influential in American political science and which reinforced notions about the identity of political science and history as well as, often, some version of an evolutionary theory of the state and an emphasis on the practical utility of political studies. These included Walter Bagehot's *Physics and Politics* (1873); James Bryce's *American Commonwealth* (1888); Frederick Pollock's *An Introduction to Political Science* (1890); and J.R. Seeley's *Introduction to Political Science* (1896). But the theory of the state was largely an American enterprise, and, apart from Bryce, who spoke more extensively about American institutions than any previous writer, these individuals had little impact on the structure of the discipline.

Woodrow Wilson, who had been a student of Ely's, wrote his famous work on *Congressional Government* (1885) while still at Hopkins. Although in retrospect it may seem to have signaled a greater concern with the actual practice of government, Wilson remained tied to the paradigm of the state and the historical comparative method. Although he claimed that there was no "model" for his 1889 study of the state (73), it still reflected the basic idea of Aryan development as it traced the history of government (authorized organized force) from earliest times to the present and particularly to American institutions.

The last "grand" theorist of the state in American political science, however, was Westel W. Willoughby, who had also studied at Hopkins and published his *An Examination of the State; a Study in Political Philosophy* in 1896 (74). There are two distinct trends that are apparent in Willoughby's work. One is the demystification of the state and its equation with the institutions of government, and the other is an increased emphasis on distinguishing political science and politics. In both respects, Willoughby was pointedly critical of Burgess – a position which few individuals of the period were willing to take.

Willoughby argued that the domain of political science was constituted by the state, which was to be studied descriptively and historically in its various forms. He believed in undivided total sovereignty located in the state, which meant basically the authorized organization of government, and that the extent of its actions and the establishment of rights was a matter belonging to "politics or the Art of Government, and not within the domain of political theory" (75). He stressed a division between the "scientific and analytical" dimension, which dealt with the state as it "is," and the "ideal or teleological" dimension, which was concerned with the ends of the state. It was the former that he believed should be emphasized – both to establish the subject of political science and to distinguish it from disciplines such as history, sociology, and economics.

Willoughby criticized Burgess's image of science as flawed – long before he attacked the more general German influence. Burgess, he claimed, had first of all accepted a racist, absolutist, chauvinistic, Teutonic theory, drawn from individuals such as Bluntschli, which postulated the state as a metaphysical entity behind government. This rendered his analysis otiose, but, according to Willoughby, he had also not only blurred the line between the real and ideal but had overstepped the boundaries of science and entered the realm of "politics and statesmanship" (76). Only as objective and independent science, Willoughby argued, could political science be practically relevant.

By the turn of the century, even many of Burgess's students and colleagues were, in various ways, drifting away from his *Weltanschauung*. But there is a danger of overestimating the transformation in political science that took place by the end of the first quarter of the twentieth century.

First of all, the intellectually radical claims of Charles Merriam and others about a new science of politics amounted in many respects more to a transformation in the *idea* than the actual *practice* of the discipline. Second, such features as the changes in ideology, the critique of the

historical method and institutional studies, and the emphasis on behavioral science and its techniques tended to obscure deeper structural
continuities between the ideas of Merriam and individuals such as
William Archibald Dunning and Burgess.

Merriam's early work, prior to World War I, was still largely a
reflection of the Columbia school, and, in many ways, his later behavioral
and psychological approach to politics was an atemporal version of the
idealist history of ideas. And although it is probably safe to conclude that
Merriam in part had Burgess in mind when he spoke of the "intoxicating
effect of the undiluted Hegelian philosophy upon the American mind," he
also noted in his study of the history of the idea of sovereignty, his
doctoral dissertation, that "the results of the American development
finally took scientific form at the hands of J.W. Burgess" (77). As late as
1927, he acknowledged Burgess and Dunning as leading the introduction
of scientific inquiry in social science (78). His vision of a science of
politics that would inform political practice, through citizen education and
an enlightened statesmanship, was surely in part the legacy of Burgess.

Merriam's principal teacher and long-time mentor, however, was
Dunning, whose trilogy on the history of political theories (dedicated to
his teacher, Burgess) would definitively establish that genre within
political science (79). Dunning's academic career took place entirely
within the confines of the Columbia school. He was appointed Lieber
Professor of History and Political Philosophy in 1913 and was elected to
the presidency of both the American Historical Association (1915) and
the American Political Science Association (1922), as well as serving as
editor of the *Political Science Quarterly.*

Dunning continued to stress the identity of history and political science
as well as the idea of historical progress, ideas he attributed to Hegel, but
the concept of the state, although still present, receded as a focus of his
work. It stood for little more than organized authority. He spoke out
rather strongly against American imperialism and excessive nationalism,
and he welcomed Harold Laski's attack on Austin's theory of sovereignty
and the unitary state. Yet at the same time, he never let go of the basic
idea that the history of politics was the progressive history of the
"European Aryan peoples" who were "the only peoples to whom the term
'politics' may be properly applied" (80). Dunning, however, was a
quintessential scholar who vocally shunned contact with public affairs
and rejected the adoption of any systematic or dogmatic political
philosophy.

The ambivalence about the relationship between political science and politics was reflected in the creation of the American Political Science Association. Although initially conceived, at a joint meeting of the AHA and AEA, as a society for the study of comparative legislation, the organizing meeting (1903) gave rise to a separate association. Like all such professional academic associations at this point, it at once took pains to distance itself from politics yet concerned itself with how it might influence public life. And the answer was increasingly through the medium of scientific objectivity.

The Association dedicated itself to "advancing the scientific study of politics," which the first president, Frank Goodnow, still defined as the study of the state and the "various operations necessary to the realization of State will" (81). Its charter stated that it would not "assume a partisan position upon any question of practical politics." Yet, as Henry Jones Ford noted at the time of the creation of the *American Political Science Review* (1906), the goal of political science was to put itself on a truly scientific basis so as to bring it "into a position of authority as regards practical politics" (82). The subsequent history of American political science could well be read as the attempt to cope with this paradox.

For most political scientists during the first two decades of the twentieth century, the state was unequivocally the defining subject of political science. And despite the attacks of pluralist theorists such as Laski on the idea of the state, it remained at the center of the textbook literature. It was still assumed that "the state develops in accord with definite laws and principles" and that "progress comes therefore by purposive modification" of social life "through a governmental policy based on scientific knowledge" (83). For someone such as Ford, as for Lester Frank Ward, it was, however, no longer German idealism that gave meaning to the concept and the story of its "natural history" but rather an examination of the "foundations of political science from the naturalistic point of view established by the publication of Darwin's *Origin of the Species*". But the conclusions were the same: the state was "absolute and unconditioned" – "Man did not make the State; the State made Man" (84).

It would be a long while before there was any clear rejection of the nineteenth-century notion that the study of politics was the study of the state. While institutions represented its "objective" dimension, political theory exemplified its "subjective phase" (85). And it could be plausibly argued that political science and political theory never fully jettisoned this imagery. Even though a residue of the metaphysical aura would remain, the "state" was increasingly becoming "government," but the demystification of the state did not eliminate the concerns that prompted its invention.

The Meaning of the "State"

The image of social science that emerged most strongly in the first quarter of the twentieth century, in political science and sociology particularly, was that of a science of social control. Whether it was the legacy of Ward and his vision of sociocracy, Goodnow's notion of the transformation of politics into administration, or Merriam's ideas about joining science and political power, and later Harold Lasswell's policy science, the vehicle of social and political redemption remained the state, and the state remained something that stood above the irrationality of politics. And there was still a faith that the instrumentality of the state could be an agent of democracy. This suggests that it may be worthwhile returning to the more speculative and global question of what the search for the state had really been all about.

It was surely, either consciously or unconsciously, a matter of establishing the domain of political science as an autonomous field, creating legitimacy and authority for the discipline vis-à-vis politics, finding a secular substitute for the mystery and social bond of religion, and avoiding the danger and baseness of politics. The language of the state may have indeed been arcane and metaphysical, and it may have served, at various times, to mask a conservative ideology regarding domestic policy, justifying a fervent nationalism, and underwrite the Union cause and the process of state-building. But behind it all, behind the convoluted, strained, and ultimately fantastic arguments of someone like Burgess, there were some significant theoretical concerns that did not cease with the retreat of the nineteenth-century theory of the state from the vocabulary of political science.

In an important sense what these theorists were seeking was what had always been required but somehow strangely missing in the theory of American politics, beginning with the *Federalist* – something that would give meaning to the notion that the institutions of government, and even the Constitution itself, emanated from, and were responsible to, a sovereign organic entity called the people that was extended in space and time. Tocqueville, of course, was eloquent in his description of what was missing in American politics and the dangers that the extremes of individualism held for the future of democracy. And someone like Lieber was attuned to this critique. At the time of the American Revolution, the existence of the people, as an organic political community, had been assumed. This was in many respects the essence of traditional republican theory, and it was the belief that the people were no longer virtually and virtuously represented by the British government that justified the Revolution. Between the Declaration of Independence and the Constitution, however, even John Adams, the most traditional republican, lost faith in the existence of such a community – a homogeneous and virtuous people capable of republican government. Although Alexander Hamilton and James Madison clung rhetorically to the idea of the people, and to republican principles, their theory of a society constituted by individuals and factions driven by divisive interest belied the concept and entailed a radical revision of the idea of republican representative government.

One of the principal arguments of the *Federalist* was that the great debate over where sovereignty resided, whether in the national or state governments and in what branches of government, was nugatory, since all government in a representative republic was only the agent of the sovereign people. But while Madison and Hamilton maintained the language of republicanism, they had little direct response to the characteristic anti-Federalist claim that a republican community could not be sustained in so vast a society and territory. Their strategy was to present a new theory of republican government that did not presuppose such a community – and, in fact, presupposed its absence.

They could not find the "people" by classical republican theory – the organic body, with its natural divisions, that should be physically and ideologically manifest. What government governed, and that to which it was responsible, was in the end, for the founders, explicitly the totality of discrete individuals – individuals ultimately aggregated into changing configurations of interest groups (86). And they were forced to devise an institutional and functional substitute for the people as originally conceived. It was, however, both theoretically and practically, a less than satisfactory answer.

In an important sense, what the *Federalist* offered was a vision of a surrogate for traditional republican government, an institutional republic created from a system of governmental levels, countervailing factions, and mechanisms of institutional checks and balances which would substitute for virtuous leaders responsible to a virtuous and organic people. The goal of the founders was unambiguous. It was to create a totally sovereign national government but one that could be rationalized in terms of republican theory, a popular but not democratic form of government. This required retaining the concept of the people, but in this world of "factions and convulsions," of "ambitious, vindicative, and rapacious" individuals, which defined society (87), the people, as something more than an analytical construction, that government was supposed to represent and to which it was to be responsible was no longer an intelligible entity.

The bond between society and government that had been so central to classical republican theory was broken. The separation of powers, while it included the idea of checks and balances within government, had been predicated on a definite separation (the violation of which indicated corruption). It reflected the assumption that the discrete branches of government had a social counterpart and were the medium through which natural, identifiable, and permanent elements of an organic people could virtually participate, or be represented, in governance. In the theory of the American constitution, the separation of powers, which was in fact less a separation than an overlapping arrangement of functions to ensure healthy conflict, was instead conceived entirely as an internal institutional device for achieving an equilibrium. It was contrived to ensure that government would "control itself" as well as "control the governed" (88). Since Madison could not find the "people" as such, it is little wonder that he pointedly rejected the idea that they could or should exercise the primary oversight or government.

Given the absence of the people in the traditional sense, or given the notion that the "people" was largely a synonym for an undefinable universe of self-seeking interests, it is not surprising that what Madison claimed was most novel about the new system, this new form of representative government, was the fact that while it was "a wholly popular" *form* of government, in the sense that it was authorized by, or a delegation from, the individuals who were its subjects and was based on their continual electoral consent, it was one in which there was a "*total exclusion of the people in their collective capacity*" (89). This, he argued, would be, as opposed to earlier and more democratic republics, the source of its stability, but it was also a reflection of his belief that the people had little discernible collective existence.

Madison's idea of a popular government that was not based on a popular majority yet somehow bound by a general consensus regarding the ends and mechanisms of government reflected the same point. In order to "break and control the violence of faction," both in government and society, Madison, in effect, recommended making the infection of faction, rooted in human nature and in the inevitably "different and unequal faculties of acquiring property," acute (90). Control of faction was ultimately beyond the ken and ability of "enlightened statesmen," but it could be achieved by an alchemic science of politics issuing in a constitutional system of institutional virtue that would make up for the "defect of better motives" among leaders and citizens and produce public good from private vice (91). And of course the "faction" that Madison most wished to break and control was that which traditional republican theory had conceived as the precise opposite of faction – a majority will.

It was popular government, then, but one that lacked a people, that assumed little virtue among statesmen, except that achieved by the filtering devices of the electoral process and institutional limitations on power, and that presided over an incoherent social universe. There would, of course, be what might be called a nominal or procedural majoritarianism represented in elections and other aspects of voting for and within government, but the point was that this would be a non-substantive, unarticulatable, ad hoc, and ever-changing majority that would never serve to constitute a definable public interest.

The theoretical and practical dilemmas of what has been called "interest group liberalism" as a theory of popular government (92), dilemmas which are first encountered in the *Federalist* would become increasingly prominent as the somewhat noninterventionist image of American government gave way to notions of a more active centralized authority. As government came to act in a positive manner and intervene in social and economic matters, or as visions emerged of its performing such a role, in the name of the people and the public interest, the questions of exactly what constituency it represented and when it possessed legitimacy and authority became difficult ones.

While individuals such as Lieber and Burgess clung closely to the values and assumptions of the American founders, they also found it necessary to find a state behind the government. In the more complex world that confronted the nineteenth-century theorists of the state, the search for a community that stood behind an expanding and sometimes intrusive government and the conflictual pluralism of region and interest seemed necessary to give substance to the idea of democracy. It was this lack of community and tradition that Tocqeville found most disturbing, and the quest for the state was in an important sense undertaken to secure the faith in the existence of a democratic community. After the turn of century, the search for the state began to abate in American political science, but the search for what it represented continued in other forms.

The increased "realism" of political science in the Progressive era, and the resurgence of the passion for reform with individuals such as Arthur Bentley and Charles Beard, could be construed, at one level, as representing the hope that the science of politics would provide knowledge which would awaken a democratic majority. It was assumed that such a majority lurked behind pluralistic interests and that it could take power back from corrupt politicians and uncontrolled capitalism (93).

With Merriam and Harold Lasswell, and beyond, the faith in the existence of a coherent democratic majority waned, but the older belief that political science could in some way speak truth to power and, through the state, act in the service of the people persisted. The idea of the people, however, the substance of the state, remained an elusive entity, and the concept of the state became a vessel to be filled with various theoretical contents.

Notes

* The final version of this essay has benefited from the comments of Werner Sewing and from James Farr's reading of two earlier drafts.
  1. See John G. Gunnell, "The Historiography of American Political Science," in David Easton and John G. Gunnell, eds., *The Development of Political Science: A Comparative Perspective* (London: Routledge, 1990); John Dryzek and Stephen Leonard, "History and Discipline in Political Science," *American Political Science Review* **82** (1988); Bernard Crick, *The American Science of Politics* (Berkeley: University of Califormia Press, 1959); Albert Lepawsky, "The Politics of Epistemology," *Western Political Quarterly* Supp. (1964); Dwight Waldo, "Political Science: Tradition, Discipline, Profession, Science, Enterprise," in Fred Greenstein and Nelson Polsby, eds., *Handbook of Political Science*, vol. 1 (Reading: Addison-Wesley, 1975); David Ricci, *The Tragedy of Political Science: Politics, Scholarship, and Democracy* (New Haven: Yale University Press, 1984); Raymond Seidelman (with Edward Harpham), *Disenchanted Realists: Political Science and the American Crisis* (Albany: State University of New York Press, 1985).
  2. Peter Evans, Dietrich Rueschemeyer, and Theda Skocpol, eds., *Bringing the State Back In* (New York: Cambridge University Press, 1985); James A. Caporaso, ed., *The Elusive State* (Newbury Park: Sage, 1989); David Easton, "The Political System Besieged by the State," *Political Theory* **9** (1981); Gabriel Almond, "The Return of the State," in *A Discipline Divided: Schools and Sects in Political Science* (Newbury Park: Sage, 1989).

3. Stephen Skowronek, *Building a New American State: The Expansion of National Administrative Capacities, 1877–1920* (New York: Cambridge University Press, 1982), pp. vii, 44.

4. James Farr, "The Estate of Political Knowledge: Political Science and the State," in JoAnne Brown and David van Keuren, eds., *The Estate of Social Knowledge* (Baltimore: The Johns Hopkins University Press, 1990).

5. *Ibid.*

6. Anna Haddow, *Political Science in American Colleges and Universities, 1636–1900* (New York: Appleton-Century, 1939), pp. 101, 155.

7. Crick, *op. cit.*, pp. 30–31, 95–96.

8. *Ibid.*, p. 97.

9. Daniel Rodgers, *Contested Truths: Key Words in American Politics Since Independence* (New York: Basic Books, 1987), pp. 145–6, 163, 165.

10. *Ibid.*, p. 165.

11. *Ibid.*, p. 175.

12. Ernest Barker, *Nietzsche and Treitschke: The Worship of Power* (Oxford: Oxford University Press, 1914); "The Discredited State," *Political Quarterly*, 2 (1915).

13. John Dewey, *German Philosophy and Politics* (New York: Henry Holt & Co., 1915), pp. 123–5.

14. Westel Woodrow Willoughby, *Prussian Political Philosophy* (New York: D. Appleton & Co., 1918).

15. Franklin Giddings *The Responsible State* (Cambridge: The Riverside Press, 1918), p. 48.

16. *Ibid.*, p. 46.

17. Frank Sargent Hoffman, *The Sphere of the State or the People as a Body-Politic* (New York: G.P. Putnam's Sons, 1894), pp. 1–6, 17.

18. Walter P. Metzger, *Academic Freedom in the Age of the University* (Colombia University Press, 1955); Laurence R. Veysey, *The Emergence of the American University* (Chicago: University of Chicago Press, 1965); Mary O. Furner, *Advocacy and Objectivity: A Crisis in the Professionalization of American Social Science* (Lexington: University of Kentucky Press, 1975); Thomas Haskell, *The Emergence of Professional Social Science: The American Social Science Association and the Nineteenth Century Crisis of Authority* (Urbana: University of Illinois Press, 1977); Dorothy J. Ross, "Professionalism and the Transformation of American Social Thought," *Journal of Economic History* 38 (1978) and "The Development of the Social Sciences," in Alexandra Oleson and John Voss, eds., *The Origins of Knowledge in Modern American, 1860–1920* (Baltimore: Johns Hopkins University Press, 1979).

19. See Lepawsky, *op. cit.*, pp. 35–6.

20. George Beard, *American Nervousness: Its Causes and Consequences* [1881] (New York: Arno Press, 1972), p. 122.

21. Francis Lieber, *The Stranger in America* (Philadelphia: Carey, Lea & Blanchard, 1835), p. 197.

22. *Ibid.*

23. Thomas Sergeant Perry, ed., *The Life and Letters of Francis Lieber* (Boston: James R. Osgood & Co., 1882); Lewis R. Harley, *Francis Lieber: His Life and Political Philosophy* (New York: Columbia University Press, 1899); Frank

Freidel, *Francis Lieber: Nineteenth Century Liberal* (Baton Rouge: Louisiana State University Press, 1947); Bernard Edward Brown, *American Conservatives: The Political Thought of Francis Lieber and John W. Burgess* (New York: Columbia University Press, 1951); James Farr, "Francis Lieber and the Interpretation of American Political Science," *Journal of Politics 52* (1990).

24. Francis Lieber, ed., *Encyclopedia Americana* (Philadelphia: Thomas Desilver & Co., 1835), Vol. X.
25. *Ibid.,* Vol. XI, p. 568.
26. *Ibid.,* Vol. X.
27. William Paley, *The Principles of Moral and Political Philosophy* (Philadelphia: Thomas Dobson, 1788).
28. Francis Lieber, *Manual of Political Ethics* (Philadelphia: J.B. Lippincott & Co., 1885), Vol. I, p. 162.
29. *Ibid.,* Ch. XII.
30. Francis Lieber, *Miscellaneous Writings* (Philadelphia: J.B. Lippincott & Co., 1881), Vol. I, p. 217.
31. *Ibid.,* pp. 330–34.
32. *Ibid.,* pp. 367–68.
33. Lieber, *Miscellaneous Writings,* Vol. II, p. 99.
34. *Ibid.,* p. 97.
35. *Ibid.,* p. 13.
36. Johann Kaspar Bluntschli, *The Theory of the State* (Oxford: Clarendon Press, 1885), p. 54.
37. *Ibid.,* p. 235.
38. Herbert B. Adams, *The Study of History in American Colleges and Universities* (Washington: Bureau of Education, 1887), p. 55.
39. Theodore Woolsey, *Political Science or the State Theoretically and Practically Considered* (New York: Scribner, Armstrong & Co., 1878).
40. Laurens Hickok, *A System of Moral Science* (Schenectady: G.Y. Van Debogert, 1853).
41. See Gladys Bryson, "The Emergence of the Social Sciences from Moral Philosophy," *International Journal of Ethics 42* (1932); "The Comparable Interests of the Old Moral Philosophy and the Modern Social Sciences," *Social Forces XI* (1932).
42. See, for example, Herbert B. Adams, *The German Origins of New England Towns* (Baltimore: The Johns Hopkins University Press, 1882).
43. Herbert B. Adams, *Methods of Historical Study,* The Johns Hopkins University Studies in History and Political Science (Baltimore: Freeman, 1884), p. 21.
44. Adams, *The Study of History in American Colleges and Universities,* p. 171.
45. *Ibid.,* p. 194.
46. See Fritz Ringer, *The Decline of the German Mandarins: The German Academic Community, 1890–1933* (Cambridge: Harvard University Press, 1969).
47. Haskell, *op. cit.,* and Furner, *op. cit.*; L.L. and Jessie Bernard, *Origins of American Sociology: The Social Science Movement in the United States* (New York: Russell and Russell, 1943) and "A Century of Progress in the Social Sciences," *Social Forces XI* (1933).
48. Bernard and Bernard, *The Origins of American Sociology,* p. 559.

49. John Burgess, *Reminiscences of an American Scholar* (New York: Columbia University Press, 1934), pp. 254–55. *Political Science and Comparative Constitutional Law*, Vols. 1, 2 (Boston: Ginn and Co., 1890–91).
50. John Burgess, *The Civil and the Constitution, 1859–1865*, vols. 1, 2 (New York: C. Scribner's Sons, 1901).
51. For an analysis of the development of German historical scholarship, see George Iggers, *The German Conception of History* (Middletown: Wesleyan University Press, 1969).
52. John Burgess, *Reminiscences of an American Scholar*, pp. 109, 124.
53. *Ibid.*, p. 131.
54. *Ibid.*, pp. 202–3.
55. *Ibid.*, p. 139.
56. See Haddow, *Political Science in American Colleges and Universities, 1636–1900*, p. 180.
57. Burgess, *Reminiscences of an American Scholar*, p. 244.
58. John Burgess, "The Study of the Political Sciences in Columbia College," *International Review* 12 (1882), p. 346.
59. *Ibid.*, p. 347.
60. *Ibid.*, p. 348.
61. *Ibid.*, p. 350.
62. Herbert Adams, *The Study of History in American Colleges and Universities*, p. 67.
63. *Ibid.*, pp. 83–84.
64. John Burgess, "Germany, Great Britain, and the United States," *Political Science Quarterly 19* (1904), p. 19.
65. John Burgess, *Reminiscences of an American Scholar*, p. 358.
66. John Burgess, *The Reconciliation of Government with Liberty* (New York: Charles Scribner's Sons, 1915) and the *Foundations of Political Science* (New York: Columbia University Press, 1933). The latter was a revised edition of certain basic portions of *Political Science and Comparative Constitutional Law*. For a thorough discussion of Burgess's view of history, see Bert James Loewenberg, "John William Burgess, the Scientific Method, and the Hegelian Philosophy of History," *Mississippi Valley Historical Review 42* (1955).
67. John Burgess, "Political Science and History," *American Historical Review 2* (1897), p. 403.
68. *Ibid.*, p. 404.
69. John W. Burgess, *Political Science and Comparative Constitutional Law*, Vol. 1, p. v.
70. John Burgess, "Political Science and History," p. 407.
71. *Ibid.*, pp. 407–8.
72. *Ibid.*
73. Woodrow Wilson, *The State: Elements of History and Practical Politics* (London: D.C. Heath & Co., 1891).
74. W.W. Willoughby, *An Examination of the Nature of the State* (Norwood: Norwood Press, 1896).
75. *Ibid.*, p. 338.

76. W.W. Willoughby, "The Political Theory of Professor John W. Burgess," *Yale Review* **17** (1908), p. 64.
77. Charles Merriam, *History of the Theory of Sovereignty Since Rousseau* (New York: Columbia University Press, 1900), p. 179; *A History of American Political Theories* (New York: Macmillan Co., 1903), p. 373.
78. Charles Merriam, "William Archibald Dunning," in Howard W. Odum, ed., *American Masters of Social Science* (New York: Henry Holt & Co., 1927) pp. 131–2.
79. William A. Dunning, *A History of Political Theories* (New York: Macmillan, 1902, 1905, 1920).
80. William A. Dunning, *A History of Political Theories, Ancient and Medieval* (New York: Macmillan, 1902), pp. xix, xx.
81. Frank Goodnow, "The Work of the American Political Science Association," *Proceedings of the American Political Science Association* (Lancaster: Wickersham Press, 1905).
82. Henry Jones Ford, "The Scope of Political Science," *Proceedings of the American Political Science Association*, 1906, p. 206.
83. James Quayle Dealy, *The Development of the State* (New York: Silver, Burdett & Co., 1909), p. 3.
84. Henry Jones Ford, *The Natural History of the State* (Princeton: Princeton University Press, 1915) p. 175.
85. See Raymond G. Gettell, *History of Political Thought* (New York: Century, 1924).
86. Jacob E. Cooke, ed., *The Federalist* (New York: Meridian Books, 1961), p. 244.
87. *Ibid.*, p. 28.
88. *Ibid.*, pp. 347–49.
89. *Ibid.*, pp. 84, 428.
90. *Ibid.*, pp. 57–58.
91. *Ibid.*, pp. 60, 51, 349.
92. See Theodore Lowi, *The End of Liberalism* (New York: Norton, 1969).
93. See, e.g., Seidelman, *op. cit.*

CHAPTER SEVEN

OXFORD AND THE EMERGENCE OF
POLITICAL SCIENCE IN ENGLAND 1945–1960

MALCOLM VOUT

Introduction: The Very Idea of Teaching Politics as a Science

During the 1950's a change of direction within the study of politics was
taking place. A new orthodoxy in political studies was evolving and new
directions were being indicated which concerned a shift in focus towards
the social sciences rather than history or philosophy. In sum, expectations
and assumptions were changing in the academic community of politics
lecturers and of course within the wider spheres of culture and political
practice.

Between 1948 and 1957, the study of politics was beginning to
emerge, slowly, outside the 'Thames Valley' (London, Cambridge,
Oxford). Thus, in this period, Manchester, Birmingham, Hull, Leeds,
Sheffield, Nottingham, Liverpool, Leicester and Keele (North Staffordshire) universities, for example, were developing courses in politics.
In all locations there was no single honours course in politics. The
'civilizing' ideals of an Oxford education were being challenged by post-
war 'civic' ideals of social and educational opportunity.

There was a break both in intellectual style and institutional structure
in the political studies community in England. In the post-war setting it
was the ethos of regional development, the emergence of a welfare state,
the attitude in the 'air at the time' that 'we better make plans to ensure we
get it right this time', which directed attention to planning, administration,
policy making and of course the social sciences. Norman Chester
remarked that in the 1930's at Oxford teachers lived rather in an ivory
tower "with little knowledge of and contact with the world of government

P. Wagner, B. Wittrock, and R. Whitley (eds.), Discourses on Society: Volume XV, 1990, 163–191.
© 1990 *Kluwer Academic Publishers. Printed in the Netherlands.*

and industry. The war changed that for a large number of academics became temporary civil servants and some remained permanently in Whitehall. Ministers, Civil Servants, banks and many organisations turned to academics for advice"(1). The war certainly altered attitudes towards the applicability of academic knowledge in the social sciences. Though sceptical of Chester's claim that there was a widespread move to seek academic advice, it is certain that wartime experiences altered perceptions on the direction political education should take.

In an attempt to answer the question, how and why did the study of political science develop in England, the analysis firstly looks at the general features of politics teaching at Oxford university prior to 1950 and secondly, points to Professor W.J.M. Mackenzie's role and attitude as a political educator during the period 1927–60. Mackenzie has been selected because he taught at Oxford in the 1930's and in 1948 became a professor of politics at the University of Manchester, becoming a leading political educator during the 1950's, especially with the establishment of a graduate school at Manchester. It is on record from S.E. Finer, D. Butler and many other participants in the Political Studies Association (2) that Mackenzie was one of the few educators who had read and was later to précis American political science literature (*Politics and Social Science*, 1967). In other words an assessment of Mackenzie illustrates the thesis that a new orthodoxy was evolving in some sectors of the profession and that expectations and assumptions were altering on what constituted the appropriate form for studying and teaching politics.

Thus, a new idiom for political education was struggling to be recognized. By idiom I mean a dialect of a community, a distinct language of a community which provides form to everyday discourse or conversation within that community. Idiom in a sense represents the dialogue of a particular group and as such signifies taken-for-granted values on what constitutes the proper language of that group whether they be atomic physicists, biologists or politics lecturers. The political studies community at Oxford prior to the Second World War could be identified through teachers of politics talking and writing the dialogues, idioms and jargon of history, philosophy and constitutional law. At Manchester a new discourse construction was evolving which adopted in part the language and technical terms of American behavioural science. In sum, the term idiom as opposed to say discourse analysis simply refers to what is considered to be proper conversation within a community or institutional setting. It is a term which is useful in illustrating more forcefully the interplay between content and context, language and institutional setting where discourse is not only constructed in texts but performed in research seminars, lectures and meetings of the academic community. Within the institutional environment of Manchester a different jargon for political inquiry was evolving and a new strategy for what constituted the important principles of political education was being voiced. In other words, a new set of idioms were being constructed in a civic institutional environment.

This analysis of the emergence of political science in England is concerned to elucidate the connections between intellectual developments and changing institutional settings. Mackenzie's activities as political educator, within the institutional setting of a civic university in the immediate post-war period, highlight the shift in direction in the political studies community towards the idioms of sociology, economics and psychology rather than law or constitutional history. The version of political science emerging from the texts or content of Mackenzie's intellectual development *and* the context of a civic university in the 1950's are benchmarks for understanding how political education was reconstituted in England. Mackenzie acted as a filter for American political science literature, placing it within the study of history, languages and philosophy.

While Mackenzie was enthusiastic and a supporter of empirical studies of politics he did not advocate an uncritical replication of American behavioural political science. In Mackenzie's case a middle-ground was struck, a discourse coalition attempted between empirical studies of politics and vigorous historical and philosophical analysis. However, this version of English political science is not just a consequence of Mackenzie's individual intellectual development, it is also a result of his migration from Oxford to a civic institutional environment where interdisciplinarity, graduate research seminars, new research networks and different audiences influenced the direction that political education as political science would take in the 1950's. The civic audience was composed in part of junior clerks from the town hall, local government officers and trade unionists who were undertaking the part-time Diploma in Public Administration or Diploma in Social Studies, and Mackenzie's strategy was to inject a political or political science element into administrative studies. Mackenzie as a professor in a civic university interested in the development and administration of cities continued a tradition of civic commitment developed by philosophers like A.D.

Linsday or trade unionists like Levi Hill of NALGO. At Manchester throughout the 1950's Mackenzie attempted to consolidate political studies as a discipline and a science. He argued that some parts of political science could have a cash value and considered it to the good of the profession that a person trained in public-opinion surveys or public administration could service the needs of the politically powerful.

Such an approach was clearly at odds with the orientations at the London School of Economics (LSE), often regarded as the home of political science in Britain. During the 1950's politics teaching at the LSE was governed in a gentlemanly fashion by Professor Michael Oakeshott, who held the views that firstly there is no such thing as political education and secondly the study of politics was certainly not a science or indeed a discipline. The study of politics was in effect political theory and the history of political ideas, and the rest of the curriculum was public administration or what an Oakeshottian would call the 'plumbing' side of political inquiry. The LSE under the influence of Oakeshott, and certainly in the case of Oxford and Cambridge during the 1930's and beyond, held the view that sociology would lead the study of politics into a 'spurious orthodoxy' and subsequently disrepute. All sociology could offer were descriptive courses in 'Drink, Drainage, and Divorce'.

Because of this split in orientations, to be analyzed in more detail below, the discussion of Mackenzie's leading role in the development of English political science sufficiently characterizes the direction and form political education took prior to the 1960's. There is no doubt that Mackenzie, as a strategist and advocate of the view that politics should be considered a discipline, science and applied field of study, played a key part in changing the perceptions of the political studies community and shifting the idiom or style of political education towards interdis- ciplinarity and the social sciences. The account of this transition aims to identify the particular version of political science adopted in England prior to the expansion of universities, departments of politics and national research councils in the 1960's.

The discussion is organised in two parts. The *first* part of the analysis is a pastiche of inaugural lectures covering the period 1920–50 and is introduced in order to disclose the character and style of an inter-war Oxford education in politics. Inaugural lectures are at times occasions for celebrating and outlining the nature of the discipline or field of study. They are interludes, like a chorus in Greek comedy, when masks are removed and the audience is offered a reassessment of the players and the action. Furthermore, they are an important and very much under-used resource for identifying methodological assumptions and pedagogical values which often remain tacit or taken for granted in educational practice. Oxford had in its educational practice and institutional position acted as a kindergarten for influential members of the state and government. Most political educators who held professorships in this period at Oxford, Cambridge and London were educated at Oxford, and all celebrate their connections to the Oxford Honours Schools, particularly 'Greats', the Honour School of Literae Humaniores.

This first part of the discussion aims to outline the idiom and style of Oxford political education which Mackenzie experienced and to some extent distanced himself from in the post-war period. In order to characterize the transition of an education in politics towards political science it is necessary to provide some identification of the old order which was being challenged. The first part of the analysis, as a pastiche of inaugural lectures, takes the style of a dramatic monologue, a reconstruction of the inaugural lectures in the form of a valediction, which summarizes and gives an overview of the nature and direction of an education in politics at Oxford prior to 1950. The *second* part of the analysis deals specifically with Mackenzie's attitude towards Oxford pedagogy and how in the political and social climate of the 1930's he began to question the value of an Oxford 'gentleman-governor' approach. The discussion proceeds to identify new intellectual allegiances, research interests and the civic institutional setting which characterize and help us understand the emergence of political science in England and the particular version or form English political science took prior to 1960.

Political Studies in Oxford 1920–50 – A Valedictory (3)

Scene – An Oxford College in the Month of June 1950

Imagine a wide panelled corridor with wall lights extending an orange glow and creating shadows over a richly coloured carpet of deep blue and red. On the walls, hung at precise intervals under the lights, are a series of pictures, framed impressions of Oxford life displayed to celebrate the college Valedictory Lecture. The invited audience moves slowly along the corridor. Through large double doors they enter the 'Long Gallery' and scatter themselves on sofas, armchairs and dining chairs placed in the gallery for this special occasion. The person delivering the lecture is an established Oxford teacher and scholar. The audience settle themselves down to what they know will be a short talk, comfortable in the knowledge that they are 'where the action is'.

J.N.S.B. and his goshawk Jezebel

"It was, I remember, bitter winter weather. The Oxford streets, when I arrived late at night from the North, were deep in snow. My lodgings were in Exeter College, and I recall the blazing fires, a particular succulent kind of sausage ... I felt as if I had slipped through some chink in the veil of the past. ... I recollect walking in the late afternoon in Merton Street and Holywell and looking at snow-laden gables which had scarcely altered since the Middle Ages. In that hour Oxford claimed me, and her bonds have never been loosed." (John Buchan *Memory Hold-The-Door,* p. 47).

Valedictory Lecture

I have had the honour to teach political theory and institutions at Oxford, and Cambridge Universities. I was nurtured in the study of politics at Oxford, taking Greats then Modern Greats (P.P.E. – Philosophy, Politics, Economics). I am an Oxford man, who not unhappily travelled to Cambridge immediately after the Second World War. My stay in Cambridge was brief and stimulating but Oxford has always claimed me and tonight I would pay homage to Oxford's traditions, especially her teaching of Greats and Modern Greats.

The valediction this evening is a breaking of silence – I suppose a disclosure of influences and developments in my experience of studying and teaching politics from 1920 to 1950. I have on previous occasions defined the study of political science and its scope and method, but this evening I intend to deliver a reflexive account of some of the more important images and recollections which describe an underlying methodological attitude or what R.G. Collingwood has called 'presuppositions of practical activity' governing the study and teaching of politics at Oxford. It is Oxford's Schools of Modern History and Literae Humaniores (Greats) which capture the glory of urbane, gentlemanly and noble scholarship. It is she who has cultivated the study of political theory, and since Oxford naturally runs to 'Schools' and 'Movements' of thought, we should firstly pay homage to T.H. Green, F.H. Bradley and B. Bosanquet.

In this school of thought she gave to English political science a tradition which, even if we dissent from it, influenced generations of Oxford men, some of whom have been called to steer the political destiny of the country. Those lucky enough to have sat at the feet of their political wisdom were inspired by their revelations on Greek Philosophy and the modern mysteries of German Idealism. It was these Oxford thinkers who, blending Plato with Hegel and Aristotle with Kant, reminded us of what we may still learn from Aristotle and Plato. These great figures nurtured a concern for political philosophy and the theory of the state. In fact the Oxford Honours Schools of Greats, which combines the study of philosophy and ancient history, has been the training ground for many politicians, civil servants and, of course, politics dons in Oxford and has encouraged a close connection between moral and political philosophy. The cultivation of political theory by Oxford philosophers and historians has been a high-water mark in the history of teaching politics in this country. The Oxford tradition of teaching moral and political philosophy as a single subject situates the study of politics closely to ethics. Perhaps I am stating the obvious to an audience aware of the politics and culture of 'Oxford Politics'. Oxford educators hold an underlying methodological attitude which views science in a special sense, a classical sense as the fastidious and virtuous striving for wisdom and truth.

The Oxford tradition of political theory is concerned to elucidate the presuppositions underlying a theory of the State, whether it be in the form of 'Social Contract Theory' or 'Liberal Democratic Theory'. As I see it, political theory is connected to philosophy and particularly to moral philosophy because it talks about human nature and the purposes of man living as a moral being in association with other moral beings. Political theory refers to the values we assume in our efforts to realise certain ends. In fact moral philosophy (or in Cambridge the moral sciences) is the point of interconnection between politics and its sister science economics.

T.H. Marshall has remarked that the consideration between money value and social value 'will be found to underlie nearly all the most serious economic studies'. Moral and political philosophy taught in Oxford as a single subject is the point of interconnection, the intellectual bond, the focus for the teaching of politics. The idea of political theory as moral philosophy applied to the life of the whole community has its intellectual roots in Aristotle and Plato, and this convention is carried on in Henry Sidgwick's *Elements of Politics* and T.H. Green's *Principles of Political Obligation*. Political theory is inexorably linked to moral philosophy by the very nature of its endeavours, namely, to determine the end or ultimate value which governs and determines the life of political society. The study of politics, which would be unthinkable if separated from political theory, is concerned to examine what thinkers in the past have postulated as the human good and aims to discover the agreed and appropriate means for realising a truly liberal society. The realisation of these values are of course never secure in the jumpy world of political practice, *nonetheless*, what endures are questions concerning essence, purpose, value – which transcend the category of time. Philosophy is the study of ultimate value, and that is a necessary criterion for those who pursue the study of social value whether in the field of political life and institutions or in economic life.

Oxford of course was the first to establish a chair in the subject, the Gladstone Professorship of Political Theory and Institutions, established in 1912, and held by W.G.S. Adams (1874–1966), the founder and editor of *Political Quarterly*. The story runs that at Crewe House in London on 23rd July 1912 there was a meeting of the National Memorial to Mr Gladstone where Sir William Anson M.P., Warden of All Souls, proposed that surplus funds should be used for the raising of the readership in politics at Oxford to the status of a professorship to be called the Gladstone Professorship of Political Theory and Institutions. In fact in 1912 Mr Adams was lecturing on representative government for students drawn from both 'Greats and Modern History'.

Politics teaching at Oxford was invigorated with the introduction of 'Modern Greats' (Philosophy, Politics and Economics) in 1920. The introduction of Modern Greats had two general purposes, firstly to consider the important problems of man and society in the modern world and secondly, to provide a degree structure for applicants whose education was not weighted in favour of the 'Classics'. When PPE was first examined in 1923, thirty-one undergraduates sat the examinations. In 1932, 110 candidates presented themselves for examination, and there are currently 800 reading for PPE. One of the obvious consequences of the establishment of the PPE degree structure was the appointment of college fellowships in politics and the propagation of Oxford politics dons. I remember with fondness W.J.M. MacKenzie, K. Wheare, W. Harrison and of course G.D.H. Cole, whom Oxford classified as economics rather than politics or philosophy. There were of course fellows like Fulton, Maud and Franks who are destined to become influential figures in the making of public policy.

In the period between 1918 and 1939 it was still possible to believe that those countries who had not already modelled their institutions upon the British, American or French systems of government would sooner or later do so. The revised PPE syllabus in 1933 aimed toward a study of the structure and functions of modern government, international, national and local with special reference to the constitutional systems of the United Kingdom, United States of America and France. This modernised rubric of the PPE courses, although maintaining a compulsory politics course in British political and constitutional history since 1760, brought the teaching of politics in Oxford into the modern world through the study of the politics of the United States of America and France. However, Oxford's concern with the modern world of politics and economics should not be viewed as an instantaneous acceptance of modern methods of specialisation nor the consideration of politics and economics as a quantitative science. Speaking as an Oxford man, I applaud the courage of those individuals who helped establish 'Modern Greats', particularly A.D. Linsday, who in the face of much criticism steered opinion towards the establishment of PPE. I think Oxford is correct in its opposition to specialisation at the undergraduate stage and we should celebrate its pedagogical heritage that the teaching and study of politics must be understood in terms of a broad humanistic approach where the laboratory of political life is stretched from fifth century B.C. Athens to contemporary studies on the American Political System.

Having been 'cradled' in the Oxford tradition, and no doubt emerging with a particular Oxford 'stamp', it was with some trepidation that I travelled across from Oxford to Cambridge in the 1940's. I was warned against this move by my colleagues at Oxford and informed that at Cambridge the study of politics did not exist outside the history faculty. At the time I did consider this view as another example of a peculiar 'Oxford' prejudice and I found during my time at Cambridge a rich and rewarding series of intellectual challenges, from both history and philosophy. In Cambridge of course we reach the seat of exact knowledge, 'where men walk on the razor edge of acute analysis'. In Cambridge there is one chair of political science endowed by the Rockefeller Foundation and first held by Professor Ernest Barker between 1928 and 1939. The Cambridge ethos was more individualistic than the corporate image of the Oxford 'Schools' and the tradition of political theory. Cambridge had fostered Henry Sidgwick who, writing in the shadow of J.S. Mill, argued for a science of politics, as did Sir John Seeley, Regius Professor of Modern History, and Lord Acton, his successor. The names of Sidgwick and Seeley leap to mind as figures who adopted a position whereby individual liberty, co-operation and consensus became key principles in the discussion of political institutions and the focus for the study of history. Although at times representative of quite diverse analytical positions, this collection of Victorian liberal thinkers of repute framed the study of politics and political theory within the study of history.

Lord Acton in his inaugural lecture comments 'for the science of politics is the one science that is deposited by the stream of history, like grains of gold in the sand of a river; and the knowledge of the past, the records of truths revealed by experience is eminently practical, as an instrument of action and a power that goes to the making of the future ...

History compels us to fasten on abiding issues and rescues us from the transitory and transient. Politics and history are interwoven but not commensurate'. In Oxford the study of politics assumed there existed a vital connection between political philosophy and political theory, whereas in Cambridge the abiding and universal issues and problems of politics could only be elucidated through the study of history. My stay at Cambridge was unfortunately a short one and I must admit, on reflection, a sense of disappointment over the isolation that existed between the study of politics and philosophy. Cambridge philosophy at that time was dominated by linguistic analysis, reflecting the influence of Wittgenstein and his acolytes. The Oxford tradition of teaching politics, through moral and political philosophy, was generally speaking absent. Nonetheless, I found many colleagues and friends in the history faculty and consequently did not feel isolated from the mainstream of Cambridge intellectual life.

Most of us who come to the teaching of politics as philosophers or historians, and as graduates of the Oxford Honours Schools, are not altogether happy about the term 'science' in relation to that study. Science indeed is a subject which has established truths by exact and experimental study of natural phenomena. However the use of the term political science, which is the title of the Cambridge Chair in Politics, reflects a somewhat pretentious and ambiguous image of the study of politics. I think I am correct in saying that the direct connection of science with politics is infrequent. Political education can only be in the most special sense a science. This special sense of the term science I refer to means, perhaps naively, that science refers simply to the systematic study of natural and human phenomena.

We are now witnessing in 1950 the emergence of the professionalisation of the study of politics and it has been agreed to title the group or profession the 'Political Studies' and not the 'Political Science', Association. If we are to use the term science at all in relation to politics, then we should refer simply to the systematic connection of facts according to a general scheme; a scheme which is the result of reasonable speculations about a group of facts in the field of political action. Consequently the term political science is ostentatious and exaggerates the capacity of the study of politics to master the political world as if it were akin to the natural world under the microscope and the razor-sharp analysis of the physical scientist.

My return to Oxford in the late 1940's was a journey of mixed emotions; it was a journey where I reflected on the separation in Cambridge between politics and philosophy and the lack of conversation between historians and modern philosophers.

Nonetheless, I am deeply respectful of the Cambridge historical tradition and its link to the study of politics. In this country Sidgwick, Seeley, Acton, Figgis and Maitland are recognised as Cambridge scholars who devoted themselves to the cause of liberty and the study of history and situated the study of politics firmly within the orbit of historical scholarship. However, as a young and rising historian remarked to me the other day, these figures, representative of a Cambridge 'stamp' on the study of politics, are like 'a collection of heavy awkward, unfashionable pieces of Victorian furniture bequeathed by several remote and slightly dotty aunts of the same name'. Somewhat harsh commentary, but a Cambridge education in politics lacked the vitality of political philosophy or the broad education of 'Modern Greats' that is now so well established at Oxford.

There are many in Oxford who are now nervous about the potential neglect of political theory on the grounds that its subject matter is unsuited to the fine instruments of linguistic analysis. There are current proclamations on the 'Death of Political Theory', and science once considered 'infra-dig' seems to be popular under the influence of Karl Popper and a post-war atmosphere which demands practical programmes for social engineering rather than the fluid insights of individual minds dedicated to understanding the principles underlying the state. However, tonight we celebrate those Oxford-trained political educators A.D.Lindsay, G.D.H. Cole, E. Barker, D. Brogan and of course H.K. Laski who have 'stamped' an Oxford style in and for the study of politics. I am fortunate and consider myself privileged to be part of that liberal, urbane and free-thinking collection of individuals who predominantly viewed the study and the teaching of politics through social and political theory. Hobbes, Locke and Rousseau pervade the study of politics as part of a common stock of ideas which men use only half consciously as their chart in sailing over but a partially known sea to a harbour which ever recedes as they advance.

This evening I acknowledge my association with political educators who have provided a common stock of ideas, which like grains of gold in the sand of the river reveal a promise for the future teaching and study of politics. I celebrate my association with Oxford intellectual figures for the importance they have attached to social and political theory. To be included within their orbit of influence was a revelation. If we were called upon to choose whether to call the study of politics 'Philosophy' or 'Science' we would without hesitation choose 'Philosophy'. However, times change, fashions alter, and fate delivers terrible blows, and it is with regret that I have witnessed since the Second World War an invidious and cunning separation of politics from philosophy. Philosophy has now developed to the point where it requires the mastering of mathematical logic and many of us now feel that modern philosophy is beyond our grasp.

From 1919 to 1939, between the end of one war and the start of another, Oxford remained comparatively stable. A.D. Lindsay and Douglas Cole were radicals who protested against the intellectual conservatism of Oxford but were nonetheless united in the view that a study of politics should demonstrate an allegiance to moral and political philosophy. Politics at Oxford is not taught by discipline specialists but by individuals who have chosen to cultivate skills in Greek and Latin translations, and are happy to dabble in Greek Law and teach British political history or constitutional theory. We are generalists, yet political educators who as 'historically inclined philosophers and theoretically disposed historians' have deep intellectual roots in the Oxford Honours Schools.

W.J.M. Mackenzie's Modernist Attitude to Political Education

The Oxford Years 1927–39

The bitter 1930's was a formative intellectual period when political loyalties were engaged and political attitudes polarized in terms of international and domestic agendas for political action. Mackenzie had won a scholarship to study at Balliol College, Oxford, and in 1927 entered an intellectual and cultural environment which he found to be both puzzling and at times unacceptable given the economic and social crisis at that time.

My own period as a student built up from the General Strike to the National Government coup in the autumn of 1931: and by that time it was obvious that one's loyalties were engaged and one must vote Labour (as indeed I have done ever since, though tending sometimes toward abstention). In that period Marxism at the simplest level seemed the best clue to events. (7)

While a student and subsequently a fellow at Magdalen College, Oxford (1933–48), he began to go against two intellectual traditions which characterised the teaching of politics at Oxford since the mid-nineteenth century, the 'Balliol tradition' and the constitutional textbook tradition associated with Maine, Maitland and Dicey – the 'Knights of the Textbooks'. The Balliol tradition was, according to Mackenzie, an identifiable intellectual motif running from the election of Jowett to a fellowship in 1838 to the death of Lord Lindsay of Birker in 1952, which entailed 'preaching to the best intellectual people in the best intellectual way ... The best students were taught to preach the best sermons, and were fixed up with the best jobs' (5). Mackenzie traced this tradition back to the nature of Scottish philosophy, theology and a liberal impulse since the eighteenth century. It was an attitude which 'spoke large words to a large audience, and prevailed more by oratory than analysis' (6). A tradition in which philosophy, politics and morals were considered to be part of a gentleman's general education, which stressed the maxims that firstly, it was dangerous to act in politics without principles, secondly, it was intellectually indecent to accept political principles without severe scrutiny and thirdly, the most fundamental of these principles is that the next generation should be brought up in the same principles (7).

It was a mould of self-confident liberal and Christian socialist writing, which was broken by 1945 but which operated as an ontological guide for educational aims spanning divergent political outlooks. E. Barker and A.D. Lindsay, to which one could add G.D.H. Cole and H.J. Laski, were figures who influenced a generation of students prior to the Second World War. This was a generation who were told that 'political theory is a branch of moral philosophy, which starts from the discovery or application of moral notions in the sphere of political relations' (8). Politics and philosophy were to the pre-war generation inseparable topics, particularly at the University of Oxford, where politics teaching was largely in the hands of 'generalists', schooled in 'Greats' or 'Modern Greats'. Mackenzie of course was part of this institutional framework for political education but began in the 1930's to consider alternative approaches (12). The modernisms of Marx and philosophical analysis rather than oratory appealed to him in his new role of political educator, when in 1936 he was appointed as fellow in politics at Magdalen College, Oxford.

The 1930's was a period where the 'Knights of the Textbooks' still dominated that self-confident English writing about politics which considered the study of law to be inseparable from social history. The study of politics at this time was influenced by the attention given in the writings of H. Maine and F.W. Maitland to the interaction between law, society and history.

Ernest Barker in his inaugural lecture at Cambridge refers to Maitland in the following manner:

> I can cite no greater name. I can only record the measure of the debt I owe to the man who wrote ... the opening chapters of the *History of English Law*, the introduction to *Political Theories of the Middle Ages* ... How massive was the monument that he erected ... how far-reaching has been the influence which his teaching and particularly his teaching about the character of associations and the nature of their personality, has exerted. (10)

These 'Knights of the Textbooks', who in general believed the study of law and politics to be concerned with the historical process of constitutions and government rather than party-political conflict, gave to the study of politics a particular 'Oxford' stamp. It was an intellectual motif which extended to H.J. Laski and G.D.H. Cole, when pluralist ideas were in the air earlier in the century. E. Barker commented, 'It was Figgis, and Maitland behind Figgis, and Gierke again behind Maitland' (11) who influenced Laski's thought in his New College days.

Mackenzie called this group of historically inclined lawyers, whose texts still dominated the teaching of politics at Oxford in the 1930's, 'the last generation of serious social analysts who had never heard of Marx' (12). It was an intellectual orthodoxy which Mackenzie aimed to confront in his new role as political educator and importantly a role which he considered seriously within the analytical modernisms of Marx and science.

Marxist analysis was attractive to Mackenzie in the atmosphere of Oxford in the 1930's, because 'its prophesies about crisis, imperialism, violence and capitalist decline seemed to be coming out right, partly because an appeal to faith, comradeship and discipline seemed appropriate in a time of weakness, isolation and despair' (13). While being critical of the level of Marx scholarship and Marxist literature, Mackenzie acknowledged the social force and impact of Marxist theory for those interested in injecting an analytical dimension into the study of politics and for those political educators who were interested in the workings of political systems rather than a history and analysis of concepts. From his first appointment in politics Mackenzie considers himself a 'political scientist'. In the 1930's there was a swing of students towards 'Modern Greats' and most of the politics appointments were filled by generalists (14). Mackenzie was one of the few generalists, bringing to political science a broad knowledge of constitutional law, history and political philosophy, who joined the American Political Science Assocation and displayed a general knowledge of American behavioural science.

Mackenzie's modernist attitude to political education, his reaction against both a 'Balliol tradition' and the 'Knights of the Textbooks', signifies one of the early attempts to force a professionalism in the study of politics. Philosophy had to some extent already broken the link with politics, at Cambridge. The modern idioms of linguistic analysis and science were evident in the 'Cambridge books' of Moore, Whitehead, Russell and Wittgenstein, but as Mackenzie argued, there was no one in Oxford to advertise and expound them. However, at Magdalen he entered an interdisciplinary circle which included T.D. (Harry) Weldon, John Austin (Philosophy), P. Medawar (Biology), and A.J.P. Taylor (History). It was a radical group in the atmosphere of Magdalen, which fostered social rather than intellectual distinction.

This intellectual network did shape Mackenzie's views on the possibilities and limitations of scientific knowledge, and its applicability to the social science (15). Unlike many social scientists from the 1930's to the present day, he was not in awe of science; he was suspicious of the view that the social sciences should model themselves upon the natural sciences and was critical of those who would naively demarcate scientific from non-scientific knowledge. In sum, he held an open-ended and pragmatic view on the nature of scientific understanding (16).

The idioms of behaviouralism and the essentially prescriptive and narrow concern with scientific method are not suitable to a political science that 'illuminates by metaphor and analogy' (17). Equally the idioms in a political philosophy, employed to educate by rhetorical effect, are inappropriate for an emergent political science attempting to construct a systematic and communicable knowledge of the workings of political systems. Science has always been entangled with political thought and action. In the case of Mackenzie, the idioms of science were necessary in order to develop some analytical and professional skills for the political educator. Like Weldon, Mackenzie held the view that scientific knowledge helps us to discard some 'metaphysical lumber' which was to Mackenzie all too present in the intellectual atmosphere of Oxford in the late 1920's and early 1930's.

The Emergence of Political Science in Post-War England 1945–60

The Oxford Generalist Approach Lingers On

During the 1950's politics courses were taught at Oxford, Cambridge and London and 'civic' universities in the north, like Leeds, Sheffield, Liverpool and Manchester, and also at the Scottish universities. Following the 'Clapham' provision and the awarding of independent status to Nottingham, Leicester, Hull, Exeter and Southampton (previously colleges of the University of London) politics emerged in an institutional setting outside of 'life on the inner circle line' of Oxford, Cambridge and London. In the early 1950's the membership of the Political Studies Association was around 100, and in 1960 it had reached the figure of 179 (Chester). In comparison, the American Political Science Association was founded in 1904 and in that year membership was around 214, by 1946 4,000 and in 1960 more than 7,000 (Ricci, Crick, Eaulau *et al.* and APSA reports).

In the fifties in Britain there were two pedagogical styles running alongside one another, the humanistic and the civic, the civilizing and the scientific, centred within the institutional contexts of Oxbridge (the civilizing) in contrast with Manchester, Keele and in some respects the LSE (the civic – W.J.M. Mackenzie, S.E. Finer, K. Popper, H. Weldon) (18). They were methodological attitudes which reflected a wider cultural division – the culture of the fifties was a pluralist culture within itself yet an exclusive culture. The 'insideness' of this British elite was a great social machine for creating 'outsiders'. There were in effect two nations within the intellectual class, the nation of Oxford, Cambridge, London, the higher civil service, and the nation of provinces, 'studious, diligent and specialized' (19).

Arblaster in *The Rise and Decline of Western Liberalism* (1984) has described an additional cultural motif operative in the fifties – 'Cold War Liberalism'. This version of liberalism 'claimed to be both non-ideological and anti-ideological and in the late 1950's and early 1960's it even claimed that ideological politics were dying out and that we were entering a new era of rationalist, realistic empirical politics'. It was a liberalism shadowed by arguments on 'End of Ideology', 'Totalitarianism', 'Death of Political Theory', 'Open Society and Its Enemies' – texts and issues which reflected a late Victorian liberalism 'that there is nothing so pernicious in politics than abstract doctrine' (Bryce). Generally speaking it was a perspective which argued for realism, empiricism, in social and political reasoning, while it pictured reality as 'plural, complex and ultimately unintelligible', and at the same time endorsed the value of consensus in political and social life. (20).

'The arguments for "empiricism", "piecemeal social engineering", and the like and against a number of imprecisely defined evils ("positive freedom", "sociological holism" and more) clearly imply that modern Britain is a successful experiment in liberal philosophy' (21) Weldon's *'The Vocabulary of Politics*, Ayer's *'Language Truth and Logic'* and the writings of Karl Popper gave additional intellectual support to this cultural perspective which weaved its way through the intellectual class in the 1950's and in the study of politics provided some intellectual encouragement to reformulate the dominant humanistic tradition which was, and perhaps still is, an important influence in political inquiry (cf. also Fridjonsdottir, in this volume). However, this liberal cultural motif coupled with a linguistic turn in philosophy led many to question the value of traditional political theory and the ethical, utopian and 'political' questions that are characteristic of this area of study. Arblaster remarked that 'The liberal adoption of political empiricism and renunciation of utopianism and ideology brought liberalism into a much closer alliance with conservatism'.

The humanistic, civilizing ideals of Oxford pedagogy lingered on throughout the 1950's. The Political Studies Association had a 'club' atmosphere dominated by Wilfred Harrison (Queen's, Oxford, then Professor at Liverpool), Norman Chester (Nuffield, Oxford) and Kenneth Wheare (University, Oxford) – a visible college of influence and an invisible college of 'gatekeepers' for a style and approach, which kept sociology, psychology and American political science at a distance. It was a small association, an 'in group' projecting an Oxford style which contested the idea that politics could be viewed as a social science. The humanistic framework identified English universities as eclectic in teaching and research, and inclined towards favouring individual initiative rather than major collective enterprises. It was an approach in which the models of Ancient Greece and Rome were 'laboratory studies' for political inquiry. A science of politics would have been considered 'infra-dig' in an atmosphere where 'stinks', 'specialists' (scientists and professions which demanded specialization), were considered too provincial, 'outsiders' in an English civilizing tradition.

In this methodological attitude the cult of the 'generalist' was predominant. It was a view that political inquiry, unlike economics for example, was eclectic, a subject without a core. This viewpoint can be demonstrated by referring to two important UNESCO publications in the fifties dealing with the scope and methods of political science – *Contemporary Political Science* (1950) and *The University Teaching of the Social Sciences: Political Science* (1954) (22).

G.D.H. Cole in the influential UNESCO volume *Contemporary Political Science* (1950) commented that whereas in economics there was a belief in a common body of doctrines which would be "applied" in the specialist branches of economic study, there was in politics *no corresponding central core* that does not evidently involve value-judgements. For Cole, as for many Oxford-trained scholars in the post-war world, politics was not an "applied" science, since it had no core, central body of theory from which specialized studies could emerge.

In the 1954 report W.A. Robson, Professor of Public Administration at the LSE, argued that political science in Britain was taught through history and philosophy and that the historical influence remained strong. In the 'British context' the unifying function of political philosophy or political theory was equally stressed both by Cole and Robson. However, these authors also referred to the LSE as an institution where economics and politics could be learnt together using statistical methods wherever and whenever they could be applied. They acknowledged a debt political education owed to the Webbs for laying the foundations of the institutional approach and method, which argued that reforming society was no light matter and must be undertaken by experts. The contributions by Cole and Robson in these UNESCO publications in the early fifties characterize the ambiguity of political education in post-war Britain. On the one hand they argued that the role of moral and political philosophy was vigorous and on the other they pointed to a more specialized quantitative political science tradition in the context of the LSE prior to the Second World War.

Although some members of the early post-war political studies community were aware of the American literature, few felt inclined to adopt an American disposition that linked political inquiry to the social sciences and none were disposed to adopt uncritically a behavioural persuasion.

In his inaugural lecture at Liverpool (1958) Wilfred Harrison (Appointed Professor at Liverpool, and editor of *Political Studies* throughout the fifties) commented that in a critical examination of political images it is impossible to stop political studies from being eclectic and in fact in order to understand anything so wide as the political sector of human experience we are bound to draw on many standpoints and methods. This call for eclecticism by Wilfred Harrison reflected not only an Oxford 'generalist' stance, but was also indicative of the manner in which American political science literature was received and translated for the growing body of politics lecturers. For example, Harrison in a review article, 'Some Aspects of American Political Science' (23), remarked that the essay '*Game Theory and the Analysis of Political Behaviour*' by Richard C. Snyder was 'particularly worth reading because it appears to indicate pretty clearly the probably very sharply limited applicability of games theory in politics'. Harrison argued that some American and particularly American behavioural literature tended to introduce a degree of rationalism in political thinking which he considered to be cause for alarm. 'In this country our main mentors seem to be historians. Across the Atlantic mentors tend more frequently to come from, or dabble in, "social science"; and some of what they have to say has been repugnant – depressingly narrow, frighteningly naive, frighteningly arrogant or just irritatingly verbose.'

In general, Harrison viewed the clash between 'behaviouralists' and those who argued more traditionally for an 'institutional' analysis as a conflict of 'extreme positions' involving disagreements which no British participant should take seriously. This underlying, taken-for-granted attitude, referred to as a British way of doing things, rooted in an 'inherited framework', a civilizing and eclectic scholarship, accentuated the 'historical' rather than 'social scientific', modes of study.

In another article, also published in 1958, Harrison identified four leading influences on the development of political studies (24), namely
1. The Oxford P.P.E. school – dominated by recent historians.
2. The disengagement of philosophy from political studies.
3. The growth in schools of history in British universities together with a reluctance in those schools to embark on 'recent studies', so that 'recent historians in many cases come to practice under the label of political studies rather than under the label of history'.
4. The slow growth of 'social sciences' in the post-war period, and the reluctance to adopt sociological perspectives.

By the end of the 1950's many acknowledged that the language and approach to politics was altering and the influence of philosophers and historians which had continued almost undisturbed for decades was declining in the shift of the balance of attention towards studies in pressure groups, political parties and political behaviour.

It was the changing image of political theory, the gradual acceptance of sociological perspectives and the growth in 'civic' research networks (Manchester) which challenged the generalist methodological attitude. Throughout the fifties articles appeared on the 'Decline of Political Theory', 'Political Theory: What is it? 'The Case Against Political Theory'; it was an extensive debate which Isaiah Berlin identified as a form of 'systematic parricide'. It was an announcement of the death or decline of political theory as traditionally understood. It was a general disposition which argued for a linguistic analysis of political concepts in order to construct definitions, and usages. This merger of political theory and political analysis signalled a shift of pedagogical style and approach which was more willing to accept social scientific or sociological modes of inquiry within political study, but did not suggest a radical departure from 'historical' modes of analysis or an uncritical acceptance of behavioural methods and techniques. Nonetheless the language and approaches to politics had in some quarters altered by the early 1960's.

Mackenzie at Manchester – Politics as a Social Science

The above themes are important in an appraisal of W.J.M. Mackenzie and the 'Manchester School' which developed a new synthesis for the teaching and study of politics in the fifties. In 1948, Mackenzie was appointed Professor of Government and Administration. It was the first chair of politics at Manchester, although politics/public administration had been taught prior to the war, partly by Norman Chester, who became Warden of Nuffield College, Oxford; in fact Mackenzie considered that the university expected a public administration professor and not a politics don.

Mackenzie stayed at Manchester until 1966, when he moved to the University of Glasgow. In the Introduction to *'Explorations in Government'*, which is a collection of essays and papers, written between 1951 and 1968, covering the Manchester years, Mackenzie gives a short autobiographical account about his experience as a political educator. It is from this account that much can be gleaned about the Manchester experience. Mackenzie as previously noted was acutely aware of the humanistic 'Greats' tradition of Oxford, having been a classics scholar at Balliol College in the 1920's and subsequently a politics don at Mag-

dalen, Oxford, during the 1930's. He had come into close contact with
A.D. Lindsay (Master of Balliol, 1924–49, Vice-Chancellor, University of
Keele, 1949–52) and Weldon (*Vocabulary of Politics*). He commented
that 'Weldon's political philosophy is on record, written in plain language
for all to read. Yet it is continually taken out of context (as was Weldon
himself) as an example of the trivialities of linguistic philosophy. In fact
Weldon was in his profession primarily a Kant scholar, who got involved
in political writing, in a mood of pessimism about wars fought in the
name of ideas ... the deep hatred of cant, of wars said to be fought for
"democracy" and "humanity" when they were fought in fact to gain
power or to defend oneself against it' (25). In Weldon's *Vocabulary of
Politics*, in the rhetoric of 'Cold War Liberalism' and the 'Death of
Political Theory' we sense a post-war cultural climate which was busy
reorganizing the social and political fabric and was opposed to grand
theoretical schemes and utopian discourse – a further dimension of the
incentive in the fifties to adopt empirical techniques and methods.

In 'Political Theory and Political Education' (26) Mackenzie presented
a critique of Michael Oakeshott's views on political education
(Oakeshott's Inaugural Lecture, LSE, 1951) and outlined his perception
of the practice and importance of political science teaching and research.
Mackenzie was prepared to call the study of politics political science, he
was comfortable with the association of politics to the social sciences, and
in Manchester he encouraged links with economics and social anthropology. Mackenzie also believed that political inquiry, although firmly
rooted in the social sciences, entailed more than natural science, since it
involved purposes, aims and values. He in effect occupied a middle
ground which claimed that political science did in fact exist, despite
rumours to the contrary from the 'Oxbridge axis' (Harrison, Oakeshott),
but political science did not owe its existence solely to natural science and
its methods. It was a claim that political science had to develop its own
conceptual schemes and language, and though quantification, model-
building and advances in scientific method could not be ignored, political
science should not be subservient to these developments. Mackenzie
remarked, 'what is relevant is Weldon's encouragement by precept and
example never to be afraid of scientists. Give them beer, bully them a bit
into explaining what they are doing, and take a debatable line about the
perplexities that then emerge'. (27).

Mackenzie put forward a view, which appeared earlier in 'The
Professor as Administrator' and later in 'The Conceptual Framework and

the Cash Basis' (28) that the teaching and research of politics was foremostly a *practical* activity, which involved not only the 'sordid business with syllabuses and local government promotions examinations' but also involved 'incurring a share in responsibility for action', and that it is best to face up to these administrative and practical problems, which Mackenzie viewed as crucial in any serious attempt to develop political science research and teaching. Furthermore, trade union officials, civil servants, local government officers and social workers need a political science which gives information and a reasonably accurate analysis of the structure of the political system.

In the critical discussion on Oakeshott's views on political education, we can sense arguments which were crucial to the *civic* experience of teaching politics in the fifties. *Firstly*, a stress on practical, analytical, theoretical schemes. *Secondly*, the view that political science was an appropriate term for teaching and research. *Thirdly*, a perception that theory and analysis of politics must be linked to current concerns of local government, civil service and trade unions. *Fourthly*, the view that political science must involve itself directly with studies on policy and public administration. These were some of the expressed aims which neither a humanistic 'Greats' tradition nor indeed an Oakeshottian political discourse could accommodate. 'Practically all the big civic universities (and this includes the University of London, in one of its aspects) provided non-graduate Diplomas in Public Administration; Manchester was unique in offering two parallel evening degrees, B.Comm. and B.Admin. In fact, Politics as a subject got into Manchester (the first strong department outside the LSE) as a result of this alliance between philosophy and administration, an alliance with philosophers of A.D. Lindsay's temper who believed in civic commitment, and local pressure' (29).

What new idioms were injected into the study of politics at Manchester in the 1950's? *Firstly*, interest and research was encouraged in 'Public Administration'. Some of the earlier articles by Mackenzie were concerned to assess the 'science of administration'. He, like other members of the Political Studies Association in Britain in the fifties, initially responded to the influence of the American political science literature through public administration rather than political sociology (30). Texts like Dwight Waldo's *The Administrative State* and H.A. Simon's *Administrative Behaviour* figured importantly in Mackenzie's development of public administration studies, but he remarked that 'I learnt political sociology from a social anthropologist not from a sociologist (I did not read Parsons and Co. until I had to, though Dorothy Emmet visited Columbia often, and transmitted to us a good deal from R.K. Merton)' (31). Mackenzie noted that his 'education' in political sociology did not emerge through contact with a post-war interest in Max Weber (32).

The *second* injection of interest in politics at Manchester is the development of studies on 'Pressure Groups'. Birch and Spann commented that soon after Mackenzie's arrival at Manchester he 'quickly established a government seminar with an ambitious programme of its own ... Thus we had a longish series of meetings on the role of pressure groups in British politics, before S.E. Finer's *Anonymous Empire* put this topic on the agenda in most universities (33). S.E. Finer also contributed to this research seminar, and it was an example of the emergence of a *civic research network* in political science in the fifties. In another sense pressure-group study was an example of a more open Anglo-American interchange. S.H. Beer and H. Eckstein were writing enthusiastically on British case studies, especially Eckstein on the British Medical Association, and both Mackenzie and Finer refer to American political science literature (34). Mackenzie was fully conversant with recent and inter-war American literature, and reflecting on teaching politics in the thirties he commented 'The Chicago School led by Charles Merriam was setting new standards in the study of micro-politics, and Lasswell was just beginning to emerge as a conceptual influence, with *Psychopathology and Politics* in 1930, and *Who Gets What When How* in 1936' (35).

The *third* injection of interest in politics at Manchester was in the area of 'Grass Root Politics and Electoral Studies'. During the fifties electoral studies were being established at Nuffield College organized by R.B. McCallum and Herbert Nicholas, and subsequently directed by David Butler and Associates (1951, 1955 and 1959 elections), but Mackenzie realised that there was no literature of 'grass-roots' politics of the type fostered by the Chicago School. Mackenzie remarked that 'nothing was known about constituency politics, or about politics and administration in local government'. He argued that we knew immensely more about grass-roots politics from the age of Elizabeth to the age of Namier than we did about our contemporaries. He found this situation in a scholarly sense 'indecent and undignified' (36). The 'New Elizabethans' went out in the 'field'. In Manchester this new research interest focused on Glossop and the publication of *Small Town Politics* by A.H. Birch in 1959, which was a collaborative research project sponsored by the Department of Government and was a landmark in the new 'civic' pedagogy, which openly referred to Lasswell and P.F. Lazarsfeld, *The Peoples' Choice*. There were articles by A.H. Birch and Peter Campbell on voting behaviour at the constituency level, and parallel studies were conducted at the LSE which focused on Greenwich, which also leant heavily on the techniques described in Paul Lazarsfeld's text. In 1955 the Political Studies Association arranged a joint session with the 'British Sociological Association' on the topic 'Political Behaviour in Contemporary Democratic Countries'. At the end of the decade, essentially through the synthesis of a humanistic and social science pedagogical style, based within a *civic* institutional context, the profile of the teaching and study of politics was beginning to alter.

Mackenzie's migration to Manchester entailed new allegiances and intellectual influences especially in the form of the social science research seminars and the face-to-face encounters with Ely Devons (economics), Max Gluckman (social anthropology), Michael Polanyi (physical chemistry, then social studies), and Dorothy Emmet (philosophy). This new pattern of intellectual interaction was also a mechanism to filter and translate American literature on functionalism, science and methodology. Mackenzie was fundamentally concerned about the professional and applied role of political science and as mentioned wrote extensively on the practical and administrative problem of research in a civic context in the post-war period. Mackenzie's kindergarten was extensive and far reaching; as Birch and Spann attest 'the Manchester Department of Government became the most productive nursery in Britain for professors of politics' (R.N. Spann, A.H. Birch, Brian Chapman, Allen Potter, Richard Rose, Martin Harrison and many others) and so influenced the character and direction of the study of politics in the 1960's at the time of massive expansion in university education (37).

Mackenzie acted as a filter for American political science literature. In 'Idiom in Political Studies', which is a review of two texts by the American political scientist H.A. Simon (one co-authored), he reflected that Simon was attempting to establish a common idiom for political science 'but our idiom plays a very small part in *his* idiom. British political science (including the study of big organisations) is based largely on the study of law, history and languages and is expressed in their idioms: not in the idioms of economics, sociology, psychology' (38).

Mackenzie argued that in the 1950's he was heading in the same area as the behavioural movement but from a very different starting point to that of American political science. He considered himself a disciple of the 'Chicago School' but not an advocate for those who came into political study from psychology, who he considered muddled things for political educators by introducing the term 'political behaviour'.

The emergence of political science in Britain in the period 1945–60 is a complex process. The research strategies and expectations of political educators are heavily influenced by institutional settings. The civic university in a post-war context emphasising the scientific and applied prescribed a different methodological attitude to that of Oxford and its traditions of an urbane and 'generalist' disposition. Evidence shows that two pedagogical styles co-existed in this period. Firstly, a Visible College (Oxbridge and possibly the Oakeshottian wing of the LSE), which considered political philosophy, the history of political thought or constitutional law to be the main topic for analysis. Furthermore, the skills of the philosopher or historian were considered essential and those forming this Visible College would be averse to identifying themselves as political educators and politics as a discipline or a science. I would include in this group those who had passed through the Oxford Honours Schools; who were supportive of a pure PPE ideal of teaching politics, philosophy and economics; who were basically ignorant of American political science literature; who were totally against the inclusion of sociological perspectives in the study of politics and certainly antagonistic to political sociology.

Running alongside this Visible College in the 1950's, within a different institutional context, the civic university, is a political science outlook. This alternative methodological attitude was expressed in the disposition that politics was a discipline; that political science was an appropriate term to describe the study of politics; that we must in a post-war context develop political science so as to inform or enlighten the policy-making process; that we must be aware of American political science literature, but we need to be wary of its pretensions and excesses; that we should encourage both quantitative and sociological dimensions in the study and teaching of political science; that we should never ignore the historical, philosophical and linguistic contours of political inquiry and political education.

These methodological attitudes that have been outlined are expressed within different institutional contexts. They represent very different perceptions of political education but help identify the changing community structure of political education in the 1950's. The attitudes noted are indicative of a process of socialization; a process of constructing mutual knowledge or shared convictions, which became taken-for-granted attitudes, rarely taken into account in current debates o the present and future direction of political science education.

In the 1950's the idea of politics as a science and a discipline emerged with the growth of civic research networks, post-graduate programmes of study, encouragement of interdisciplinarity and the changing image of political theory towards a concern with problems of political analysis and method. These developments were early indicators of the rise of professionalism in the political studies community and map the transition from the 'generalist' to the 'specialist' political educator in English political science. To what extent did this idea of politics as a discipline and a science continue into the 1960's?

Disagreements still remain over whether politics is a science or a discrete discipline. However, since the 1960's with the expansion of universities, politics departments have developed single honours courses, graduate study programmes and specialist areas for teaching and research. Most practitioners in the political studies community would acknowledge important developments in the growth of attitudes of professionalism and specialism which have become perhaps the benchmarks for discussions on the quality and direction of political science education. However, this attitude of "specializing out", that is to say considering scientific approaches purely in terms of detailed specialist study, is far removed from Mackenzie's version of political science.

Mackenzie held a pragmatic and universalist view of science. He argued that we should not take science so seriously that it directs the study of politics into narrow specialisms and that both the natural and social sciences share similar problems in the application of their knowledge. Furthermore, as a political educator and administrator he suggested that the study of politics should develop as a discipline, where there are common problems of analysis and common goals or aims through which political education and research could be viewed as an applied social science. This version of political science was no doubt an early example of the professionalization of the political studies community in England, but it is contestable whether this approach was widely adopted by the academic community coping with the expansion of departments of politics in the 1960's and somewhat removed from the cultural tensions of post-war reconstruction.

Notes and References

1. Chester, N., *Economics, Politics and Social Science at Oxford 1900–85*, Macmillan, 1986, p. 127.
2. Interview with Professor S.E. Finer, February 1986. He suggested Mackenzie was one of the very few British academics who read American literature on politics during the early post-war period.
3. Inaugural lectures collected in Preston King (ed.), *The Study of Politics*, London: Cass, see especially H.J. Laski, 'On The Study of Politics' (LSE, 1926); E. Barker, 'The Study of Political Science' (Cambridge, 1929); D. Brogan, 'The Study of Politics' (Cambridge, 1945); G.D.H. Cole, Scope and Method in Social and Political Theory (Oxford, 1945).
   Interviews with Professor S.E. Finer, D. Butler, Sir I. Berlin, Professor M. Cranston.
   Also Collini, Winch and Burrow, *That Noble Science of Politics*, Cambridge University Press, Cambridge, 1983. Bowra, M., *Memories*, Weidenfeld and Nicholson, London, 1966. Chester, N., *Economics, Politics and Social Studies in Oxford 1900–85*, Macmillan, 1986. Lord Acton, *Lectures in Modern History*.
4. Mackenzie, W.J.M., *Explorations in Government: Collected Papers 1951–68*, Macmillan, London, 1975, Introduction p. xix.
5. Mackenzie, W.J.M., 'Political Theory and Political Education', *Universities Quarterly*, **IX**, No. 4 (August 1955), in *Explorations in Government*, pp. 17–30, 20.
6. Mackenzie, W.J.M., *Explorations in Government, op. cit.*, p. xvi.
7. *Ibid.*, p. 20.
8. Berlin, I., 'Two Concepts of Liberty', Inaugural Lecture, University of Oxford, 1958, in King, P. (ed.), *The Study of Politics*, Frank Cass, London, 1977, p. 121.
9. Mackenzie, W.J.M., 'Knights of the Textbooks', in Frankenberg, R., *Custom and Conflict in British Society*, Manchester U.P., 1982, p. 39.
10. Barker, E., 'The Study of Political Science', Inaugural lecture, University of Cambridge, 1928, in King, P., *op. cit.*, pp. 19–20.
11. Barker, E., *Age and Youth: Memories of Three Universities and Father of the Man*, Oxford, 1953, p. 73.
12. Mackenzie, W.J.M., 'Knights of the Textbooks', *op. cit.*, pp. 43–44.
13. Mackenzie, W.J.M., *Explorations in Government, op. cit.*, p. xxiv.
14. Mackenzie, W.J.M., *Ibid.*, p. xxiii, "In the 1930's in Oxford tutors were generalists, Brogan, John Maud, R.B. MacCallum, K.C. Wheare, Wilfred Harrison, Arthur Slater ... and certainly G.D.H. Cole, the total generalist, whom Oxford classified as economics rather than politics or philosophy."
15. *Explorations in Government*, p. xxii.
16. *Ibid.*, p. 23.
17. *Biological Ideas in Politics*, Penguin, 1978, p. 12.
18. It is not possible in the context of this paper to enter into a discussion of the details of intellectual change at the LSE. References are made to the LSE when appropriate in a discussion which centres on the civic institutional and intellectual climate at the University of Manchester.
19. Shils, E., 'British Intellectuals in the Mid-Twentieth Century', *Intellectuals and*

the Powers and Other Essays, University of Chicago, Chicago, 1972.
20. Arblaster, A., *The Rise and Decline of Western Liberalism*, Blackwell, 1984. See also C.A.R. Crosland, *The Future of Socialism*, Johnathan Cape, 1956.
21. Birnbaum, N., *Toward a Critical Sociology*, 1971.
22. UNESCO working party on developments in political science, contributors included R. Aron, C. Merriams, G.D.H. Cole, *Contemporary Political Science*, UNESCO Pub., 1950. Robson, W.A., *The University Teaching of the Social Sciences: Political Science*, UNESCO pub., 1954.
23. Harrison, W., 'Some Aspects of American Political Science', *Political Studies*, **6**, 1958.
24. Harrison, W., Political Processes', *Political Studies*, **6**, No. 3, 1958.
25. Mackenzie, W.J.M., *Explorations*, *op. cit.*, Commentary on Weldon, Introduction, p. xxi.
26. Mackenzie, W.J.M., 'Political Theory and Political Education', *op. cit.*
27. Mackenzie, W.J.M., *Explorations*, *op. cit.*, Introduction, p. xxii.
28. Mackenzie, W.J.M., *op. cit.*, 'The Professor as administrator: a comment', *Universities Quarterly*, **X**, 1952. 'The Conceptual Framework and the Cash Basis', *Political Studies* **X**, Feb. 1962.
29. Mackenzie, W.J.M., *Explorations*, *op. cit.*, p. xxix.
30. *Political Studies*, 1955. Book review of R.T. McKenzie *British Political Parties*. The development of political sociology was influenced not only by American but also by continental texts (Aron, Duverger).
31. *Explorations, op. cit.*, p. xxix.
32. Mackenzie, W.J.M., 'The Study of Public Administration in the United States', *Public Administration*, 1951; 'Science in the Study of Administration', *Manchester School of Economics and Social Studies*, xx, Jan. 1952.
33. Birch, A.H., and Spann, R.M., 'Mackenzie at Manchester' in Chapman, B., and Potter, A. (eds.), W.J.M. Mackenzie, *Political Questions*, Manchester University Press, 1974, p. 9.
34. References for example to classics A.F. Bentley, *The Process of Government*, 1908; D.B. Truman, *Governmental Process*, 1948.
35. *Explorations, op. cit.*, p. xxx.
36. *Ibid.*, p. xxviii.
37. Birch, A.H., and Spann, R.N., *op. cit.*
38. 'Idiom in Political Studies, review of *Models of Man, Social and Rational*, H.A. Simon', *Political Studies*, **VIII**, 1960.

PART IV

THE CONSTITUTION OF A SCIENCE OF SOCIETY

CHAPTER EIGHT

HOW TO MAKE THINGS WHICH HOLD TOGETHER:
SOCIAL SCIENCE, STATISTICS AND THE STATE

ALAIN DESROSIÈRES

The various parts of this collective book examine the way in which over
the past two centuries the social sciences have acquired more-or-less
stable forms, and have contributed to structuring specific discourses about
society. Everyone agrees on the importance of the *consolidation* of these
sciences – a consolidation that operates in two dimensions, *institutional*
and *cognitive*. To consolidate something means to give it the ability to
endure, to *be transmitted* from hand to hand and to *resist* possible
deformations. According to Durkheim, "social facts" can only be "treated
as things" to the extent that they possess these attributes, which thus
render them comparable to any other scientific object.

Carrying out such a program for the social sciences themselves
necessarily poses the question of the link between the two dimensions –
institutional and cognitive – of this consolidation. It is clear that the
various currents of the sociology of science do not agree on the nature of
this link. Some content themselves with analyzing the institutional
conditions for scientific progress, while according science itself
(sometimes explicitly but more often *de facto*) a great degree of cognitive
autonomy. These writers are not, then, principally interested in the actual
procedures and techniques of the consolidation of knowledge. On the
other hand, others seek to study simultaneously and *in the same way* both
the scientific and the social practices leading to *things that hold together*,
to *facts*. These facts have at the same time *been constructed* (the constructivist viewpoint) and yet once constructed have sufficient *existence* that
none can deny them (the realist viewpoint).

This "strong program" has the advantage of reintegrating all scientific
practices, whatever their nature, into sociological research (Latour, 1987).

P. Wagner, B. Wittrock, and R. Whitley (eds.), Discourses on Society: Volume XV, 1990, 195–218.
© 1990 *Kluwer Academic Publishers. Printed in the Netherlands.*

Further it permits us, by way of a very productive methodological decision rather than by philosophical fiat, to get out of the false opposition between 'constructivism' and 'realism'. Indeed, by deciding to take any social fact as *at the same time* constructed *and* real, one discovers a way of at a stroke transcending the two apparently opposed positions constituting positivist scientism and denunciatory relativism. By taking *all* scientific procedures, technical and social, seriously, we can take science just as seriously as society.

Statistical objectifications have played a key role among the techniques that have contributed to the institutional and cognitive consolidation of the social sciences. Using these, social scientists have forged tools enabling them to transcend individual or conjunctural *contingencies* and to construct *more general things* that characterize for example the social group (for the sociologist) or the long term (for the historian or the economist). However, there are several ways in which statisticians can set about this task. They can draw certain pre-constructed equivalences from society. Equally, they can construct the equivalences themselves. Thus statistics is particularly well suited to testing the hypotheses of the program in the sociology of science referred to above. In this paper, in exploring some research possibilities along these lines, we will summarize various work done elsewhere (1).

Any attempt to give form to the chaos consisting of the multitude of recordings of individual events entails a use of sources and ways of coding that are always open to two challenges from the scientist: are they available, are they reliable? In the objectivist perspective, the tools of generalization are supposed to be already there, and the only questions to be asked concern the gathering of information and its, ultimately automatic, technical treatment.

However, the Durkheimian tradition, referred to above, has left as its legacy not only this imperative of objectification ("we need to treat social facts as things"). It also has a second aspect, which relates to the social and constructed nature of apparently natural classifications ("how do social facts *become* things?"). This question was first of all asked about so-called primitive societies (the "elementary forms of religious life"), whose distance rendered more visible the fact that their classifications are not natural. Then, since the 1960s, it more and more often oriented the research of those who sought to construct and use statistics about developed societies. This implied a relationship between social science and statistics very different from that which researchers as consumers of *predeveloped coding* (by themselves or by others) were accustomed to. This time they sought to *use history* to reconstitute the genesis of cognitive tools formerly considered "natural": socioprofessional categories, unemployment indicators, calculations of means or of correlations, drawing representative samples.

Towards a Social History of Statistical Coding

The focus of this work on the history of the instruments of description and of knowledge changed over time. At first, during the 1970s, it was a matter of relativizing (if not denouncing) techniques judged to be ahistorical. Next, in the canonical perspective of the "critique of sources", the emphasis was on associating historical reconstitution with information about the procedures whereby this was achieved, and thus about the genesis of the sources. But little by little these studies came to reveal the extent to which the setting up of systems of statistical recording goes hand in hand with the *construction of the State*. They led to the idea that the objects being studied were just as pertinent subjects of historical analysis as the numbers to which they were supposed to lead. Thus the succession of professional nomenclatures used by the different censuses is just as interesting as any eventual long-term comparison – which moreover it would be impossible to implement, given these changes in taxonomy. Or it is at the least interesting on other grounds, in that it encourages us to look at the evolution of the social links which make particular instances be treated as *equivalent*. We need to find an answer to this question before we can enquire *how many* cases there are in any given equivalence class.

From this point of view, classifications appear to be *conventions*, as is shown by comparisons between different countries, or between different historical periods in statistical descriptions of the social world. In order for international organizations concerned with statistical comparisons or for historians seeking to construct long series to be able to work, differences between nomenclatures are *problems* that must be *eliminated*, so that a grid can be constructed that is valid for all countries or at all times. The alternative comparative or historical attitude would, on the other hand, jealously preserve information about indigenous or contemporary taxonomies, instead of dissolving them in some ahistorical construction.

This change of viewpoint marks a clear rupture with the classical way in which quantitative social sciences use the numbers that are supposed to express things that exist independently of the conventions establishing them. But this perspective is also very different from the relativist critique of statistics, which stigmatizes "quantofrenia". This critique has been formulated often since the 1960s, for example by ethnomethodologists (Cicourel, 1964). So doing, they throw the baby out with the bathwater. Here again, we can draw inspiration from the Durkheimian tradition, which proscribes dissolving into a total relativism whereby, since nothing is ever equivalent to anything else, the social sciences are reduced to particular, incomparable, case studies. According to this tradition, social facts can be treated as things *only* if they are *hardened* in one way or another (Thévenot, 1984) – as are institutions, laws, religion, customs. This is the reason why Durkheim began his study of "society" by looking at hard facts and was wary of the subjective and of unstable facts. This suggests the second feature common to research on the history of social coding: we have to study the extent to which the "things" described by statistics are solid and "hold together" (Latour, 1987). They are solid to the extent that they are linked to hard social facts: institutions, laws, customs etc. (Héran, 1984). So doing, one defines a position as distant from the relativist viewpoint defended by the ethnomethodologists as from that of the militant positivists, for whom there are "objective facts" that you just need to count up in order to silence idle ideological polemic.

Coding, Equivalence and Equity

Over the past twenty years, various studies have been conducted in more or less the spirit just outlined. They have dealt with the nomenclatures of consumption (Boltanski, 1970), branches of industry (Guibert, Laganier, Volle 1971), socioprofessional categories (Desrosières, 1977; Desrosières and Thévenot, 1988), studies of social mobility (Thévenot, 1976), school statistics (Briand, Chapoulie and Peretz, 1979), national accounting (Fourquet, 1980), industrial statistics (Volle, 1980) and unemployment (Salais, Baverez and Reynaud, 1986). Further, two volumes on the history of statistics have been published by the French Bureau of Statistics (INSEE, 1977; INSEE, 1987).

One significant consequence of these various pieces of research has been to highlight ideas of *coding* and *equivalence*. A coding is a conventional decision to construct an equivalence class between diverse objects, the "class" being judged more "general" than any particular object. A precondition for this is the assumption that these objects can be *compared.* This is by no means apparent. Recent work on the history of probability theory (Coumet, 1970; Hacking, 1975; Daston, 1987b) can be read as posing the question: under what conditions, social and cognitive, can chance events or repeated sensations be compared? The oldest tradition dealing with this taxonomic problem no doubt goes back to *jurisprudence* (Serverin, 1985): to judge and to code both come down to classifying a *case* in a legal category, or, in legal terms, to *qualifying* it. Thus the tight link between the political and cognitive dimensions of coding becomes apparent: the legal category refers at once to the king and to knowledge. Coumet (1970), looking at how "the theory of chance was no chance development", speaks of "complicity between the judge and the geometer'.

Thus there is a link, sometimes overlooked, between *equity* and *equivalence.* It is overlooked because the social sciences came into the world in the nineteenth century through the act of cutting the umbilical cord tying them to seventeenth- and eighteenth-century political philosophy (Boltanski and Thévenot, 1987) and by progressively severing the links between the *prescriptive* and *descriptive* aspects of these disciplines – as Lorraine Daston (1987b) has shown with respect to the "end of the classical era of probability theory". At first the comparability and the equivalence between objects were less questions of knowledge than of *justice* – for example with respect to the law governing market exchange. When Adam Smith founded the discipline of economics, a precondition for the existence of a central market was not only the existence and the uniqueness of a system of *prices*, in general mentioned, but also, more often forgotten, the existence and uniqueness of a system of *goods*, subject to a common definition (Eymard-Duvernay, 1986; Boltanski and Thévenot, 1987). Before the birth of political economy as a science, the question of the definition and equivalence of goods were posed in cases where *conflict* arose, and judges had to decide if an item were of satisfactory *quality.*

Thus a social history of the creation of equivalence turns the spotlight on the figure of the judge, and behind him, the figure of the highest judge, the *king.* If he has to arbitrate conflicts between his subjects, it is in order to be able to *sum* their forces, to concentrate them on him (Latour, 1984), by raising armies or taxes. For that he has to *record* births, marriages and deaths (Edict of Villers-Cotteret of 1539) and to take a regular *census* of the population. English seventeenth-century *political arithmetic* (Graunt, Petty) drew the consequence of the administrative coding that constitutes the demographic registers and proceeded to the first regular tallies. Counts of deaths enabled them to construct *tables of mortality by age*, and these then furnished the basis for *life-insurance* rates: the distribution of chance risks between people, or between periods of the life of a single person, was the occasion of many *equivalence conventions*, and, as a result, of totals in *numbers* (Daston, 1987a).

However, the term statistics itself did not emerge from this English context of quantification, but from eighteenth-century Germany, with Conring and Achenwall's "cameral statistics", which was a science of the description of the State in its most varied aspects. The history of the successive retranslations of the word "statistics" in itself furnishes a summary of the act of separating the (political) management of people from the (scientific) management of things – this separation leading to the autonomy of the various fields of knowledge. The word's meaning has changed so profoundly between the eighteenth century and the present that it calls to mind the axe whose head and handle have frequently been changed, but which is said to still be the same axe. We can summarize these changes into three phases. In the eighteenth century, statistics was an administrative activity for describing the *State*, in *literary* terms or eventually numerically. In the nineteenth century, it was only the *numerical* part of the description of the *State*. In the twentieth century, it refers to *mathematical* techniques for *numerical* analysis of data of *whatever type* – it can be applied equally to the State, to biology or to physics.

Addition, Action, Causality: The Case of Medicine

The meaning it has ended up with thus seems to bear little relation to its initial meaning. However, it is possible to find a common thread in this history. This is the link between *addition* (rendering equivalent) and *coalition* (action). It is possible to show that, from the German mini-state of the eighteenth century up to modern science, clusters are justified if they render action possible, if they create *things* which can act and which can be acted upon (a prince, a nation, a social class, an animal species, a microbe, a physical particle, a sickness, an unemployment rate). In each case it is necessary to transcend the contingency of particular cases and circumstances and to make *things which hold together*, which display the qualities of generality and permanence.

The only way of understanding the recurrent opposition in politics, in history and in science between on the one hand contingency, singularity and circumstance and on the other hand generality, law, regularity and constancy is to ask: "for what purpose?" The question is not: "Are these objects *really* equivalent?" but: "Who decides to treat them as equivalent and to what end?" The debate is therefore endless. Some say: "I act as if these objects were equivalent, and I calculate means, I construct a time series of GNPs, etc.". Others object: "No, you are counting together things which *in fact* are not the same". They redivide the big entity into little ones, which are said to be *non-comparable*. This debate, and this "critique of the creation of equivalence classes" can be found in almost identical terms in many disciplines.

In the nineteenth century, discussion about the use of statistics, and in particular about the legitimacy of the use of *means* by Quetelet provide a good illustration of this relationship between ways of *thinking* the social world and of *acting* on it (Desrosières, 1988a). For example, we could look at the debate about the "numerical method" in medicine, between the 1830s and the 1860s (Murphy, 1981). Here we find not *two* but *three* distinct positions. Doctor *Louis* suggested the use of this method for comparing the efficiency of treatments, for example the use of bleeding or purging for treating typhoid fever. This met with two types of criticism. The first, originating in the old vitalist tradition of the eighteenth century, maintained, with *D'Amador*, that each patient was a *unique case*, not comparable with any other. He said that only a particular, personal and prolonged interview between doctor and patient enabled the former to come to an understanding of the case and how to treat it.

The second objection, in appearance close to the first in that it challenged statistical totalization, came from *Claude Bernard*. This latter, a symbol of modern science, was by no means a vitalist. But, he said, doctors cannot treat "by averages". In order to eliminate a disease completely, they have to find its *direct* causes. This hostility against statistics was linked to a determinist conception of microcausality, in terms of which probability and statistics were synonymous with *approximation* and lack of rigor. We could show that the three protagonists of this debate were right each after their own fashion, to the extent that their cognitive tools were coherent with the action that they took. These were the *hygienic movement* and preventive, *collective* social medicine for Louis (Lécuyer, 1982), *family* doctor in close, daily attendance for Amador and experimental medicine involved with the *technicization* of the clinic for Claude Bernard. Each of these positions still exists, and has its own coherence.

For its part, sociology, like Doctor Louis, embarked on a quest for macrocausality. The foundation of such a probabilistic use of statistics in social science was Quetelet's importing an interest in *normal* distributions and the calculation of *means* from astronomy and the natural sciences into social science. This was decisive for developing a response to the question: "How can we make things which hold together?" In fact, in the natural sciences, the mean appeared in the theory of *measurement errors* (the height of a star, the diameter of the earth). This theory was used to calculate the mean of imperfect, distributed measurements according to a normal distribution, in order to estimate the best approximation of the "real thing". (Accordingly, this was called the *objective mean*.)

Then, by making an analogy between the normal shape of the graph of the distribution of measurement errors around a true value and that of the heights of conscripts around a mean (called a *subjective* mean), Quetelet postulated the existence of an *average man*, more *real* and more *general* than any particular individual.

Further, although the height of individuals varies greatly, its mean is remarkable *constant* from one year to the next. This provides support for the idea that there is a reality beyond that of contingent manifestations, which are themselves analogous to chance observations of an object external to the observer. Finally, from physical statistics of height or of weight one can pass to *moral* statistics: of marriages, crimes, suicides. Although for an individual these decisions are a matter of free will, and are thus unpredictable and chance events, for society as a whole, on the other hand, the *rates* of marriage, crime or suicide are remarkably constant. The *terrifying regularity of crime rates* contributed to founding the idea of a *thing which held together*, in this case the human propensity to kill.

Debates about the Use of Statistics in Social Science

This network of connections between astronomical measurements, the heights of a large number of men and marriage or suicide rates lent great force to the idea of macrosocial causality, and formed the basis of Durkheim's arguments in his *Suicide* for the existence of *social facts* radically distinct from individual psychological facts. It is true that Durkheim later modified his point of view, judging that the average man was a sorry case, with no morality: he doesn't want to pay his taxes or to go to war (today, one would add: he is in favor of the death penalty). In this way the civic, moral man became differentiated from the average man referred to by statistics. This contradiction in Durkheim's own work is indicative of the tension between the two ways of constructing totality (Desrosières, 1988a).

But this Durkheimian challenging of the average man only appeared at the end of the century. Further, it was not in itself enough to sap the force of arguments based on macrosocial regularities. Thus the reasoning of astronomer and statistician Quetelet became very widely known throughout intellectual circles in Europe, thanks to the use made of it by English historian Henry Buckle. His monumental *History of Civilization in England* (1857) aimed to bring out underlying social tendencies, independent of individual wills, by using Quetelet's methods to transcend the sound and fury of daily contingencies. He contributed greatly to spreading Quetelet's ideas in sectors of opinion that seemed a priori impermeable to statistics or demography, by furnishing a reassuring mental tool-kit for those who feared the political upheavals resulting from the French Revolution or from the industrialization of England. But he was very severely criticized by those, particularly in Germany, who saw in the creation of equivalence classes that forms the basis of statistics a product of the abstract universalism of the Franco-English Enlightenment. These critics insisted on the incommensurability of situations defined by *local* cultures and traditions. This criticism was, for example, made by economists belonging to the German "historical school" of the end of the century, and was at the root of methodological debates that Max Weber later participated in.

From the preceding discussion, we can see that Quetelet's model could be integrated into a *holistic* model (this is what Durkheim did initially), but could also be criticized in the name of that very holism (this is what Durkheim did later, as did the German historical school). It is certain that by his insistence on the *average* features of social groups, and by the fact that he only looked at the *distribution* of the individual features analyzed, Quetelet opened himself up to this double reading, and one could find a basis for the two opposed criticisms in his work.

And so in the 1890s modern mathematical statistics was born, with the work of English eugenicists Galton and Pearson (MacKenzie, 1981). They at once inherited the formalism of the normal law, and completely altered its use, since henceforth the accent would be on *individual* features, their *distribution, correlation* and *classification* (Thévenot,

1987) – this perspective being largely absent from Quetelet's work. This opened the door to completely new ways of *making things hold together*. Variables that are correlated, or of which some are fully *explained* by others using a *regression* model, created things that were incomparably more solid than those resulting simply from a Gaussian distribution (which, moreover, little by little lost its power to fascinate). The word "explain" then took on a new meaning than that which historians were accustomed to. Henceforth these latter, however reluctant they were to use these new techniques, would have to vacillate the two meanings of this word, which could only be understood in context.

Further, we should note that Karl Pearson himself, the inventor of these techniques, only spoke of *co-occurrences* and denied any claim to causality, which he considered a metaphysical concept. Indeed, outside of his statistical work, he had published a significant work in the philosophy of science in 1891. *The Grammar of Science* does not contain any mathematical theory, but is a treatise, influenced by Ernst Mach's criticism of empiricism, on the impossibility of uncovering the ultimate nature of things. His argumentation is more subtle than Quetelet's crude realism. Like the eighteenth-century sensualists before him, he said that we cannot know anything about *real things*, we can only know impressions on the brain, which constitute *perceptual routines*. From this point of view, the regularities of correlations or regressions appear as the only possible "laws" capable of describing and measuring these "routines", which therefore constitute the *things* of the new sciences.

Pearson's book, forgotten today, was published in three editions, and had a marked influence on the founders of quantitative social science in America at the beginning of the twentieth century, such as Giddings, Ogburn and Lazarsfeld. It was published in French by Alcan in 1911, in a translation by Lucien March, director of the French Bureau of General Statistics – the forerunner of the INSEE, the current Bureau of Statistics – even though it was a purely philosophical and non-technical work. But it is striking that his very modern, relativist approach never extends to a consideration of the *socially constructed* nature of the things described and of the classification categories used – be it even in terms of *language*, as Cassirer, for example, would do a few years later. We may wonder what would have become of empirical social science if at the turn of the century Durkheim, Pearson and then Cassirer could have become acquainted with one another. And this not only because, as Selvin (1976) has maintained, Durkheim did not perceive the advent of mathematical statistics, but also because Pearson did not perceive the importance of language and of society for the construction of reality.

Within France, Durkheim's influence on the spread of the use of statistics in social science (apart from through *Suicide*, which was little read and cited by statisticians themselves) came through two of his disciples, Simiand and Halbwachs. The former's doctoral thesis concerned salaries and contained some significant statistical analyses (1908). The latter's thesis, on the living conditions of working-class families, was largely based on an examination of budgets, such as Engel and Le Play had carried out. Further, his complementary thesis was about "Quetelet and the Average Man". However, this academic activity, which used very novel methods, made little impression on official and administrative statistics – save during one period, the First World War.

Periods of war, which involve an extreme concentration and planning of the economy and of the management of people (soldiers and workers) are favorable occasions for meetings and alliances inconceivable in other times. This was the case in the cabinet of the socialist Minister of Munitions Albert Thomas, who gathered together various high-ranking scientists: mathematicians, statisticians, economists and Durkheimian sociologists (Desrosières, 1985). Thus developed an intensive collaboration between scientists and political and administrative personnel, one which disappeared after the beginning of the 1920s (Kuisel, 1981). Simiand and probability theorist Emile Borel together approached the President of the Republic Millerand, to try to convince him to create a large-scale Bureau of Statistics, thereby continuing the planning work carried out in Albert Thomas' cabinet.

However, this approach was unsuccessful, and it was only twenty-five years later in 1945 (in the second postwar period) that the INSEE (Bureau of Statistics), the Planning Commission and several scientific and administrative research institutes drawing largely on statistical methods were created. At the same time, the American Census Board began to implement three major innovations permitting the development of large-scale statistical/administrative institutes: sampling surveys, national accounting and computer science. The standardized procedure implicit in these three techniques would make a major contribution to fashioning "hard things" such as unemployment rates, the gross national product and the balance of payments (Duncan and Shelton, 1978; Anderson, 1988).

"Cadres", "Professionals", "Angestellte"

The project of producing a social history of statistical coding can be
illustrated by two examples, which are treated in more detail elsewhere:
socioprofessional classifications and *surveys* of representative samples.

The social categories described and measured by statisticians,
demographers and sociologists are constructed *things*. Nothing shows this
better than a comparison between the taxonomies used for example in
France, Great Britain, the USA and Germany. These taxonomies are very
different, and it is difficult to translate them from one language into the
other. Thus where the French speak of *cadres*, in Great Britain and in the
USA they talk about *professionals* and *managers* (which are distinct
categories), and in Germany about *Angestellte* (private-sector employees)
and *Beamte* (public servants). These groups are not the same, but they do
nevertheless intersect at various points. An examination of their current
definitions hardly helps us get a hold on the logics underlying such
diverse representations. Only a social history of statistical taxonomies
allows us to discern these logics. Here we will look only at the region of
social space corresponding to the French *cadres*. We will draw on
research involving the four countries: Boltanski (1987) for France, Szreter
(1984) for England, Freidson (1988) for the United States and Kocka
(1981) for Germany.

French *cadres* are the result of intensive mobilization and representa-
tional efforts concentrated on a kernel of engineers carried out at the end
of the 1930s, following the 1936 General Strike and the Matignon
settlements. German *Angestellte* are the outcome of similar work, carried
out fifty years earlier, at the time when Bismarck was establishing the
first great social security laws and when *non-manual* workers were
seeking to distinguish themselves from the workers (*Arbeiter*), who were
highly organized both politically and into trade unions by the social
democratic movement (Kocka, 1981). This is why they include not only
cadres but also employees (of the private sector alone, since public
servants are, for their part, covered in German bureaucracy by their own
particular statutes).

Anglo-American *professionals* are defined by a level of higher
education, and their pre-eminence in English and American
nomenclatures is inherited from the biologically based meritocratic
theories of the English eugenicists of the beginning of this century
(Szreter, 1984). These theories are based as much on an implicit denuncia-

tion of the old aristocracy as of the view of bourgeois business people that wealth is a sign of superiority. In the United States (Freidson, 1988), the central point was the moral, civic and even religious justification of the "professions" (in the English sense of the word) and the affirmation of their utility and importance for the entire nation. This importance was justified in terms of their technical competence, without there being any direct intervention from the State to guarantee it (this is the major difference with the French case). Parsons is the theorist of this conception of *professions*.

This summary comparison indicates the extent to which the social construction of equivalences is not the same from one country to another, and also that, within a given country or historical period, it is extremely difficult to *see* that construction. Thus in France before the 1930s, no one spoke in terms of *cadres* (in his *Psychology of Social Class*, published in 1938, Halbwachs never used the word), whereas today this group is completely natural, to the point that no one comments on the strangeness of the idea of *counting* it.

Sewell (1980) carried out an analogous enquiry on the group of *ouvriers* in France. He situated the moment when this group began to be thought of as such precisely in the period 1832–1834 (after the insurrections at Lyon and Paris). Before then, no one thought of counting together on the one hand the *compagnons* (craftsmen) of traditional professions and on the other hand the *manoeuvres* (laborers), workhands and vagabonds who could be found right at the bottom of nomenclatures – for example, in the 1800 prefects' statistics (Bourguet, 1988). Thus, when Marx began to write, the working class was still a *taxonomic neologism*.

Political Representation and Statistical Representativity

The few cases looked at above have demonstrated that the visibility of a group is a result of social or political mobilization, and of particular historical circumstances: the 1830 insurrections for the French *workers*, the establishment of Bismarck's social laws in 1880 for the German *Angestellte*, the debate about the inheritance of intelligence in 1900 for the English *professionals* and the organization of collective negotiations between employers and employees in 1936 for the French *cadres*. This work of representation and of construction of a common language is itself linked to the construction of the State, as demonstrated by the comparison between these four countries, wherein this construction has taken such different forms. Further, this social *reification* (the making of a thing) is also closely analogous to the work of taxonomic statisticians who create categories to which they give *titles* which represent them. We will now look more closely at the link between these diverse form of representations (political, statistical and cognitive), taking current French socioprofessional nomenclature as our empirical base. This nomenclature is caught between two quite distinct logics (Desrosières and Thévenot, 1988).

Classifications used in French censuses in the nineteenth century show the persistence of the vocabulary of guilds and crafts, despite their abolition in 1791 (Sewell, 1980). The *corps* constituted elementary social groups, and the distinction between master and craftsman did not have the same meaning as that between employer and employee. The crafts formed the first stratum of the classification, and we can still find many traces of them in the current one. Things changed towards the end of the nineteenth century, when the labor legislation emerged. This clearly defined the statute of salaried employee (*salarié*) – and, thereby, that of the unemployed – inconceivable before the statute of salaried people (Salais, Baverez and Reynaud, 1986). During this period, administrative and political measures were taken which enabled the definition of the current categories: active population, unemployment – and as a consequence productivity, and all the other measurements which macroeconomics is based on. A clear distinction between salaried employees and employers still exists in French classifications, and this distinguishes them from their English or American homologues, and from the international nomenclature of the International Labour Office.

The third stage of this history is marked by the diffusion during the 1930s and 1940s of *collective agreements* underwritten by the State and negotiated by the unions of salaried employees and employers. At this time, a new vocabulary, originating in the metallurgical industry of the 1920s, paved the way for a coding of workers' qualifications: skilled workers (P1, P2, P3), semi-skilled workers (OS1, OS2), unskilled workers and terms relating to the training period (also called *Parodi categories*). These latter served as a *partial* substitute for the old vocabulary of trades. At the same time, the group of *cadres* made its appearance, and elections into the new *comités d'entreprise* (co-determination bodies) were made in three categories: cadres; employees, technicians, supervisors (ETAM); and workers. Thus from the beginning of the 1950s any employee knew which category he or she belonged to, since this had important consequences in terms of social security, retirement and choice of profession. This indeed constitutes a *hard fact*, a thing that holds together and is the same for all. This does not, of course, imply that there are no battles at the borders of these groups. One of the difficulties of making comparisons between countries is that it is very difficult to know in each case the *relative stability* of the borders – a question rarely posed by statisticians.

Current French classification thus displays a complex admixture of these diverse historical strata, and for this reason it is sometimes denounced as a non-scientific hotchpotch, with no "single criterion" to structure it. However, like genealogical layers, these strata bear witness to the past, and at the same time they reflect the *current* situation, since all these categories and frontiers are still simultaneously operative. The reworking of the nomenclature in 1982 presented an opportunity for a systematic investigation of these historical components (comparable to the exhumation of medieval Paris during the construction of a new metro line). It ended up preserving them to the extent that they were still active, and not replacing them by a *unique criterion* as some wished.

The Body and the Institution: Two Types of Regularity

French socioprofessional nomenclature comports about thirty categories, and since the 1950s there has been a lot of research done using them. When in the 1960s French statistician Jean-Paul Benzecri's techniques for analyzing correspondences were developed, they were systematically applied to tables crossing social categories with diverse variables. This enabled the production of very stable *multi-dimensional* representations of social space. Thus, unlike Anglo-American sociology and demography, which use a classification system whose unidimensionality is written in from the start (Szreter, 1984), French social scientists employ a more complex tool for the accumulation of knowledge. The second dimension of this space, which, to put it very schematically, distinguishes cultivated people from rich ones, proves to be highly pertinent for interpreting for example voting patterns, religious practices and opinions on moral questions, etc. (Bourdieu, 1984).

The relative stability of this configuration with respect to whatever variable is being studied (consumption, leisure, votes, marriage, opinion, etc.) can make a very favorable impression, since it offers, for example, the hope of *predicting*, and thus, for once, of producing a thing which holds together. However, this sense of satisfaction is very similar to that which enchanted Quetelet and his contemporaries: there are many macrosocial regularities, knowledge of which gives one a strong feeling of power. Quetelet discerned the divine plan therein, and, in his inspired moments, Benzecri rediscovered Quetelet's voice and sung the permanence and divine order of nature, which revealed balanced and stable symmetries in clouds of points displayed by computer programs. If one does not accept God (at least in this context), then one can debate the foundations of these regularities. Here again, the Durkheimian tradition provides some help. Where Durkheim insisted on *institutionalized* social facts, like law or religion, his nephew Mauss turned his attention to *bodies* and to the incorporation of habits and of schemas organizing practice learnt unconsciously by the child in its family. This is the same as Bourdieu's *habitus* (1977) – the word's etymology goes back to the body. From this perspective, the body and its permanence are the ultimate explanations of social regularities (this again is close to Quetelet's position). The other way of interpreting these regularities is to link them to institutions that are socially and historically standardized, and thus capable of *holding things together*. Taken together, these alternatives provide a conjugation of permanence inscribed on the one hand in bodies and on the other in historical laws and institutions. Doubtless such a conjugation affords us a first explanation of statistical regularities.

It should be possible to show that there is a correspondence between these two modes of transmission of permanence (by the body in the family and by codified institutions) and the two ways of *constructing categories* described by cognitive psychology and also to be found in the definition of socioprofessional categories. The first refers to *typical cases*, which other cases *resemble*, and the second to a *criterion* (Boltanski and Thévenot, 1983). This opposition also helps us to understand what among the methods of enquiry used in social science distinguishes on the one hand *monographs* that relate cases adjudged *typical* and whose generalization is based on the idea of their exemplary nature and on the other hand studies that report the findings of *surveys* of representative samples, and whose generalization is based on probabilistic reasoning (Desrosières, 1991).

The Part for the Whole: How to Generalize?

The social history of the tools of enquiry and its implicit modes of generalization enables us to distinguish between several ways of considering the management of the social world – and in particular the management of poverty, to which the empirical social sciences have been linked since their origin. Surveys based on representative samples only appeared at the end of the nineteenth century with the Norwegian Kiaer, and even then in a form more intuitive than formalized. The first calculations of the confidence interval by Bowley in England date from 1906, and a detailed formalization of stratification techniques was only developed in 1934, by Neyman.

However, enquiries based on a small number of people were carried out very early in the nineteenth century, by engineers (Le Play, Cheysson) whose mathematical culture was more than sufficient to use the probability theory necessary for taking a sample. Laplace had already used this theory in the eighteenth century to estimate the population of France (Bru, 1988), but this pioneer work was not to bear fruit for a century.

The fact that methods of probabilistic surveys did not come into widespread use until scarcely more than fifty years ago shows that the discovery and the utilization of a technical innovation involve conditions that are inseparably social and cognitive. Before inventing the solution to the problem, one had to invent the problem itself – that is to say the constraint of *representativity*, in the sense henceforth given this word by statisticians. Now this concern, expressed in terms of a relationship of similarity, for certain well-defined elements, between the part and the whole, comes a long time after the development of censuses (Quetelet in about 1830) and of monographs (Le Play, about the same time). The history of social surveys gives the impression that we have passed directly from a period where the question of representativity was never considered to another where it is never discussed because it is so obvious.

Kiaer's new "representative method" was discussed by the International Institute of Statistics between 1895 and 1903. This debate did not focus on the constraint of representativity as such, but on the questions of deciding on the one hand if it was legitimate to "replace the whole by the part" (comparison with the census) and on the other hand if, so doing, one produced better results than Le Play-style monographs, which were then still highly valued. However, this "better" was not decided in terms of representativity as the condition of a *precise measure*, but on the possibility of describing a *diversified* population.

It seems that between 1895 and 1935 the norms presiding over legitimate descriptions of the social world were completely changed – at least with respect to the possibility of *generalizing* observations of a part of it over society as a whole. Why? We can find an initial response to this question in a comparison of the social context in which this technique appeared both in Norway and in England at the turn of the century with that surrounding the monographs of the earlier period.

All these enquiries involved looking at *poverty* and at the problems of the working class resulting from industrialization and urbanization. In the nineteenth century, these problems were treated at the town or parish level. Enquiries were *local*, as were proffered solutions to the problems of poverty, founded as they were on direct relationships between rich and poor. Le Play's monographs, which resulted from direct contacts between surveyors and families surveyed, were in tune with this type of solution. Their generalization rested on the concept of *exemplarity*, and the few cases described (a handful) were taken to be *typical*. Society was thought of as a whole, in a holistic perspective: knowledge about one case provided knowledge about them all. The typical case was taken to be representative of the whole if one had personal contact with that case.

However, at the end of the nineteenth century, purely local and municipal solutions to the problems of poverty proved insufficient. To the extent that the causes of hardship were national (the economic crisis of the period 1875–1890), they required national measures underwritten by laws and no longer based on local charity. These laws were at the root of the welfare state. English historian E.P. Hennock (1987) has described the passage from Booth and Rowntree's local enquiries in the 1880s to Bowley's national survey after 1900. He has clearly brought out how the fact that purely local solutions to poverty appeared henceforth impossible led the Poor Law Commission of the House of Commons to propose a *national* enquiry. Bowley organized this latter on the basis of a *representative sample*, and formulated the notion of the *confidence interval* for the occasion. Similarly, a few years earlier (in 1895) the Norwegian Kiaer had an inkling of the notion of representativity when, participating with his country's parliament in the preparation of new social security laws, he was asked to carry out a similar survey. In these different cases, we see the continuity between *management* and *description* of the social world, both being based on standardization and codification.

It is because people had already been coded according to a criterion and thus supposed to be *equivalent* that the probabilistic model of the *urn* from which one draws black or white balls could henceforth be evoked and applied. In the former model of knowledge, based on a holistic view of society, people were not comparable and it was not possible to imagine placing them in an urn. A significant indication of this is the fact that Le Play, who amassed a great number of *budgets* of working-class families, never had the idea of *adding them up*, in order to take averages and *compare* them in order to deduce general laws. At the same time, the German Engel carried out this type of calculation on similar types of data and deduced his famous "Engel's law" linking consumption and income. A few years later, Halbwachs himself made similar comparisons, in his thesis on "the working class and living standards".

Social Science and Statistical Forms

In the techniques of *objectification*, the social sciences and history found a powerful tool for backing up the basic insights of the Durkheimian school and the Annalists (Marc Bloch, Lucien Febvre and Fernand Braudel). The *social group* for the one and *long duration* for the other displayed *regularities*, in opposition to *particular instances* or conjunctural *events*, which were contingent and unpredictable. This use has not failed to invoke criticism and inspire debate – for example from those who look to history to find arguments for denouncing objectifying social science, which they take to attack human freedom and to be blind to crises and ruptures. This tension comes out particularly clearly in the case of social history. The latter is itself the product of a mingling of the two traditions evoked above, by way of the great names of Simiand and Labrousse, who both did a lot to introduce statistical methods into a discipline of history that no longer wanted to concern itself solely with great men, treaties and events.

In the critical mood that held sway in the 1960s and 1970s, one axis of the denunciation of statistics was the idea that, as the very etymology of the word shows, statistical activity is in league with the *State*, and that it therefore reflects the point of view of those in *power* in that it is totalizing and reductive of diversity. Looked at in this way, quantification often presents a completely ambiguous face to contemporary social science: on the one hand it constitutes an "obligatory passage point" (in Latour's (1984) sense) and is of extreme social import, but on the other hand it is implicitly considered to overlook the essential, to be impoverished, simplificatory and to explain nothing.

In this paper, I have tried to show that the only way of getting out of the quasi-magical juxtaposition of these two necessarily opposed modes of thought is to take the act of coding and the construction of equivalence classes seriously. In order to do so, the *social history of cognitive forms* becomes a pressing task. By treating statistical forms as *things which hold together*, we have indicated all the *work* which was needed in order to make them solid (Thévenot, 1984). So doing, we have not, as has sometimes been the case, sought to denounce the falsity of these things by referring to the historical context of their birth. Rather we have tried to draw attention to the fact that these cognitive schemas are linked to political categories in a much more basic way than certain single-minded criticisms of the 1970s suggest, to the extent that one can reconstitute a multiplicity of coherent cognitive and political schemas (Boltanski and Thévenot, 1987).

Thus the question of the relationship between politics and statistics cannot be reduced to an evocation of the eventual manipulation of facts by "those in power", nor to modern forms of resistance against control and computer databases as seen for example in West Germany. An example of coherence between political and statistical forms could be developed by working from the concept of *representation* in its three senses: cognitive, political and statistical. In the works on social classification that we have referred to, the authors have tried to look at these three dimensions together: (1) What spontaneous images of class are used in daily life?; (2) By what political processes do social groups acquire their historical solidarity?; and finally (3) What does an average represent? How is the representativity of a sample validated? How can we generalize?

In recent years there has been a lot of work on the history of the mathematical techniques of statistics (Benzecri, 1982; Stigler, 1986; Kruger *et al.*, 1987), and the social context of these products has also been studied (MacKenzie 1981; Porter, 1986; Hacking, 1990). However, few have looked at the way in which statistics, taken as a set of operations of *recording* and *coding* (and not only as a mathematical tool) informs social science not only in terms of its numerical data but also and above all in terms of the specific schemas which transform devices into things which hold together. For example, the passage from the problematic of the mean in Quetelet to Galton and Pearson's problematic, which combines distribution, correlation and linear regression, constituted a significant advance along this path, by allowing a number of elementary things (variables) to hold together in *probabilistic models*. Procedures of the construction of classes (taxonomies) and enquiries based on representative samples for their part provided the wherewithal for constructing things that social science can no longer do without.

In each of the four constructions just referred to (mean, correlation, social categories and sampling), equivalence conventions necessary to the development of cognitive schemas were linked, in very diverse ways, to State procedures or to attempts at mass mobilization. These schemas thus came into being as ways of holding things together. These things, in turn, allow us inextricably to think about the social world and to act on it.

Note

1. This text is a synthetic presentation of various works referred to in the references. For the concept of *things which hold together* it owes a lot to Luc Boltanski (1987) for his study of the *crystallization of the group of managers*, to Laurent Thévenot (1984) for his analysis of *investments of form* and to Michel Callon (1986) and Bruno Latour (1987) for their research on the *construction of scientific facts*. Further, the work by Boltanski and Thévenot (1987) on *economies of scale* greatly contributed to my understanding of the multiplicity of ways that there are of making things equivalent and of generalizing, and thus of *representing* things – this is particularly important for statistical work.

References

Anderson, M.J. (1988): *The American Census: a social history*, New Haven and London: Yale University Press.

Benzecri, J.P. (1982): *Histoire et préhistoire de l'analyse des données*, Paris: Dunod.

Boltanski, L. (1970): 'Taxinomies populaires, taxinomies savantes: les objets de consommation et leur classement' in *Revue Française de Sociologie*, XI, 34–44.

Boltanski, L. (1987): *The Making of a Class: "cadres" in French society*, Cambridge: Cambridge University Press.

Boltanski, L., and Thévenot, L. (1983): 'Finding one's way in social space: a study based on games' in *Social Sciences Information*, 22 (4–5), 631–680.

Boltanski, L., and Thévenot, L. (1987): *Les économies de la grandeur*, Les Cahiers du Centre d'Etudes de l'Emploi, Paris: Presses Universitaires de France.

Bourdieu, P. (1977): *Outline of a Theory of Practice*, Cambridge: Cambridge University Press.

Bourdieu, P. (1984): *Distinction: a social critique of the judgement of taste*, Cambridge, MA: Harvard University Press.

Bourguet, M.N. (1988): *Déchiffrer la France: la statistique départementale à l'époque napoléonienne*, Paris: Editions des archives contemporaines.

Briand, J.P., Chapoulie, J.M., and Peretz, H. (1979): 'Les statistiques scolaires comme représentation et comme activité' in *Revue Française de Sociologie*, **XX**, 669–702.

Bru, B. (1988): 'Estimations Laplaciennes. Un exemple: la recherche de la population d'un grand Empire, 1785–1812' in J. Mairesse (ed.), *Estimation et sondages: cinq contributions à l'histoire de la statistique*, Paris: Economica.

Bulmer, M., Bales, K., and Sklar, K.K. (forthcoming 1991): *The Social Survey in Historical Perspective*, Cambridge: Cambridge University Press.

Callon, M. (1986): 'Eléments pour une sociologie de la traduction. La domestication des coquilles Saint-Jacques et les marins-pécheurs dans la baie de Saint-Brieuc' in *L'année sociologique*, **36**, 169–208.

Cicourel, A. (1964): *Method and Measurement in Sociology*, New York: Free Press of Glencoe.

Coumet, E. (1970): 'La théorie du hasard est elle née par hasard?' in *Annales. Economie Société Civilisation*, **9** (mai-juin), 574–598.

Daston, L.J. (1987a): 'The domestication of risk: mathematical probability and insurance, 1650–1830' in L. Kruger *et al.*, *The Probabilistic Revolution: Volume 1, Ideas in History*, Cambridge MA: MIT Press.

Daston, L.J. (1987b): 'Rational individuals versus laws of society: from probability to statistics' in L. Kruger *et al.*, 1987, *The Probabilistic Revolution: Volume 1, Ideas in History*, Cambridge MA: MIT Press.

Desrosières, A. (1977): 'Eléments pour l'histoire des nomenclatures socioprofessionnelles' in *Pour une histoire de la statistique, tome 1, contributions*, Paris: INSEE, 155–231 (republished in 1987, Paris: INSEE, Economica).

Desrosières, A. (1985): 'Histoires des formes. Statistiques et sciences sociales avant 1940' in *Revue Française de Sociologie*, **2**, 277–310.

Desrosières, A. (1988): 'Masses, individus, moyennes: la statistique sociale au XIXème siècle' in *Hermes* (ex *Cahiers Sciences Technologie Société*), **2**, 41–66.

Desrosières, A. (1991): 'The part in relation to the whole: how to generalize? The prehistory of representative sampling' in Bulmer, M., Bales, K., and Sklar, K.K., *The Social Survey in Historical Perspective*, Cambridge: Cambridge University Press.

Desrosières, A., and Thévenot, L. (1988): *Les catégories socioprofessionnelles*, Paris: La Découverte.

Duncan, J.W., and Shelton, W.C. (1978): *Revolution in United States Government Statistics, 1926–1976*, Washington: U.S. Department of Commerce.

Eymard-Duvernay, F. (1986): 'La qualification des produits' in Salais, R., and Thévenot, L. (eds.), *Le travail, marchés, règles, conventions*, Paris: Economica.

Fourquet, F. (1980): *Les comptes de la puissance – Histoire de la comptabilité nationale et du Plan*, Paris: Encres (Recherches).

Freidson, E. (1988): *Professional Powers: a study of the institutionalization of formal knowledge*, Chicago and London: University of Chicago Press.

Guibert, B., Laganier, J., and Volle, M. (1971): 'Essai sur les nomenclatures industrielles' in *Economie et statistique*, **20**, 23–26.

Hacking, I. (1975): *The Emergence of Probability*, Cambridge: Cambridge University Press.

Hacking, I. (1990): *The Taming of Chance*, Cambridge: Cambridge University Press.

Hennock, E.P. (1987): 'The measurement of poverty: from the metropolis to the nation, 1880–1920' in *Economic History Review*, 2nd series, **XL**, 2, 208–227.

Héran, F. (1984): 'L'assise statistique de la sociologie' in *Economie et Statistique*, **168** (juillet-août), 23–26.

INSEE (1977): *Pour une histoire de la statistique, tome 1, contributions*, Paris: INSEE.

INSEE (1987): *Pour une histoire de la statistique, tome 2, matériaux*, Paris: INSEE, Economica.

Kocka, J. (1981): 'Class formation, interest articulation and public policy: the origins of the German white-collar class in the late nineteenth and early twentieth centuries' in Berger, S. (ed.), *Organizing Interests in Western Europe*, Cambridge: Cambridge University Press.

Kruger, L. (1987): 'The slow rise of probabilism: philosophical arguments in the nineteenth century' in L. Kruger *et al.*, *The Probabilistic Revolution: Volume 1, Ideas in History*, Cambridge MA: MIT Press, 59–89.

Kruger, L., Daston, L., and Heidelberger, H. (eds.) (1987): *The Probabilistic Revolution: Volume 1, Ideas in History*, Cambridge MA: MIT Press.

Kuisel, R.F. (1981): *Capitalism and State in France*, Cambridge: Cambridge University Press.

Latour, B. (1987): *Science in Action: how to follow scientists and engineers through society*, Cambridge, MA: Harvard University Press.

Lécuyer, B.P. (1982): 'Statistiques administratives et statistique morale au XIXème siècle' in *Actes de la journée "Sociologie et statistique"*, Paris: INSEE, Société Française de Sociologie, 155–165.

MacKenzie, D. (1981): *Statistics in Britain, 1865–1930; the social construction of scientific knowledge*, Edinburgh: Edinburgh University Press.

Mairesse, J. (ed.) (1988): *Estimation et sondages: cinq contributions à l'histoire de la statistique*, Paris: Economica.

Murphy, T.D. (1981): 'Medical knowledge and statistical methods in early nineteenth century France' in *Medical History*, **25**, 301–319.

Pollak, M. (1979): 'Paul F. Lazarsfeld, fondateur d'une multinationale scientifique' in *Actes de la recherche en sciences sociales*, **25** (janvier), 45–59.

Porter, T.M. (1986): *The Rise of Statistical Thinking, 1820–1900*, Princeton: Princeton University Press.

Salais, R., Baverez, N., and Reynaud, B. (1986): *L'invention du chômage*, Paris: Presses Universitaires de France.

Selvin, H. (1976): 'Durkheim, Booth and Yule: the non-diffusion of an intellectual innovation' in *Archives Européennes de Sociologie*, **XVII**, 39–51.

Serverin, E. (1985): *De la jurisprudence en droit privé; théorie d'une pratique*, Lyon: Presses Universitaires de Lyon.

Sewell, W.H. (1980): *Work and Revolution in France: the language of labour from the Old Regime to 1848*, Cambridge: Cambridge University Press.

Stigler, S.M. (1986): *The History of Statistics: the measurement of uncertainty before 1900*, Cambridge and London: The Belknap Press of Harvard University Press.

Szreter, S. (1984): 'The genesis of the Registrar General's classification of occupations' in *British Journal of Sociology*, **XXXV** (4), 522–546.

Thévenot, L. (1976): 'Les enquêtes Formation. Qualification professionnelle et leurs ancêtres français' in INSEE (1987), *Pour une histoire de la statistique, tome 2, matériaux*, Paris: INSEE, Economica, 117–165.

Thévenot, L. (1984): 'Rules and implements: investments in forms' in *Social Science Information*, **23** (1), 1–45.

Thévenot, L. (1987): 'Forme statistique et lien politique: éléments pour une généalogie des statistiques sociales' (note INSEE Unité de Recherche, no. 112/930 of 9 April, 1987 – forthcoming).

Turner, S. (1988): 'Giddings as the Father of American Sociology', paper presented to the Conference of the I.S.A. Research Committee for the History of Sociology, Madrid, May 1988.

Volle, M. (1982): *Histoire de la statistique industrielle*, Paris: Economica.

CHAPTER NINE

SCIENCE OF SOCIETY LOST:
ON THE FAILURE TO ESTABLISH SOCIOLOGY
IN EUROPE DURING THE "CLASSICAL" PERIOD

PETER WAGNER

Sociologists usually have a clear conception of the history of their
discipline. They may disagree on the merits of individual contributions to
the development of the subject, but they share the view that there was a
first blossoming around the turn of the century, a period which they label
the "classical era." The era is easily demarcated. While there was a wide
diffusion of sociological activity, a limited number of towering figures
emerged, often named the "founding fathers" of the discipline, whose
intellectual lifespans coincided neatly. Emile Durkheim got his first
appointment, at the University of Bordeaux, in 1887, Max Weber at the
University of Freiburg, in 1895, and Vilfredo Pareto at the University of
Lausanne, in 1893. Durkheim died in 1917, Weber in 1920 and Pareto in
1923. By that time, they had all contributed to the construction of the
intellectual field for which two of them had appropriated the name
"sociology" while the third one, Weber, was more reluctant but increasingly used this label after he had been involved in the founding of the
German Society for Sociology in 1909. It should probably be no wonder,
therefore, that sociologists look back on this period as constitutive for
their field and that even to the analytical view of an historian, the era
appears as the one of professionalization of sociology, the setting of
standards for sociological work and, consequently, the demarcation of
boundaries to other academic fields and to "lay" non-professional
activities (Torstendahl 1987).

The argument of this paper entails that such views are rather misleading. While it is true that intellectuals strove to establish a science of

P. Wagner, B. Wittrock, and R. Whitley (eds.), Discourses on Society: Volume XV, 1990, 219–245.
© 1990 Kluwer Academic Publishers. Printed in the Netherlands.

society at the academic institutions in this period, their project ultimately proved to be a failure. Sociology was not institutionalized at European universities in its "classical" era. Furthermore, no common understanding on what such a science of society should be was achieved. Standards of sociological work were developed and proposed but could not be enforced among those who considered themselves to be sociologists. During the inter-war period, the major intellectual projects of this "classical" period were almost completely abandoned. "Modern", post-World War II sociology is an intellectual enterprise essentially different from "classical" sociology. To understand this rupture (which I have discussed in more details elsewhere, cf. Wagner 1990) it is necessary to look beyond the problems of institutional and scientific legitimacy to the different ways in which politics and society were, in part implicitly, conceptualized in these approaches.

"Classical" sociology was, other than a scientific one, also a political project. All variations notwithstanding, it can be called post-liberal thinking. It started from bourgeois liberal assumptions, recognized that societal developments had superseded classical liberalism, but insisted that revisions had to be made in the continuity of that political tradition (on this argument, see Seidman 1983, for example). "Modern" sociology, however, did away with the liberal tradition from the start and rephrased the relation between the individual and society in completely different terms. A comparison of the fate of both approaches during the first half of the twentieth century cannot be undertaken without looking at the development of political institutions. "Modern" sociology proved to have greater cognitive affinity to the structures of the interventionist welfare state which emerged in this period; the political legitimacy of "classical" sociology, in contrast, decayed rapidly.

In the following I shall, first, give an impression of the intensity of the sociological debate and of the social status of which the sociological intellectuals disposed in wider society during the "classical" period, and shall point to the decline of this mood in the first decades of the twentieth century. To make these developments understood I shall, second, try to define the project of that science of society in scientific, political and institutional terms. This analysis will allow, third, to give an account of the failure of the project in exactly the same terms by relating it to the structure of academic institutions and of political institutions and to the transformation of both fields during that period. Finally, I shall give at least some indications of what happened "instead" of a continuation of those sociological projects. Attempts to study society scientifically went into different directions during the inter-war years, one of which contained the nucleus of "modern" sociology as it became dominant after the Second World War.

The Rise and Decline of Early Sociology

Between 1870 and the early 1900s, numerous attempts were made to lay the foundations of a science of society, mostly labelled sociology. Programmatic books were published, journals created, academic societies founded, and inside academic institutions moves were made to designate chairs in sociology and to introduce new types of examinations and degrees. A few examples will be given to indicate the breadth and intensity of this sociological movement in continental Europe.

In France, Durkheim's approach was only one among many. Before him Frédéric le Play had already advanced his action-oriented *science sociale* and had found followers who continued his project. Gabriel Tarde and René Worms, both contemporaries of Durkheim, competed with him for the legitimate representation of the discipline to be built. The former advocated an individualist approach based on a law of imitation as the prime mover of society, the latter reasoned in organicist terms. In Italy, the emerging sociological field was even more multifarious and pluralistic. In an attempt at clarification, Icilio Vanni listed not less than ten different conceptions of sociology in 1888 (cf. Sola 1985: 136–7). Three years earlier, Vincenzo Miceli had already complained that the field was growing very quickly and had become that fashionable that whole crowds of *letterati* had entered it:

Persons who are said to be of common sense or even ignorant speak and write continuously about this science without having at all been engaged in studying it and without, therefore, possessing the preparation which is now necessary more than ever, given the numerous difficulties which the phenomena present. (Miceli 1885)

In Austria, Ludwig Gumplowicz published his programmatic work "Foundations of Sociology" in 1885 and Gustav Ratzenhofer followed in 1898 with his treatise on "Sociological Knowledge". In all these countries, the label sociology was used without hesitation and very often with a conscious link to the positivist tradition.

In Germany, in contrast, for the very same reason, that label was untouchable for scholars who had grown up in the humanistic-philosophical tradition of the German university. The relative absence of the word, however, did not indicate the absence of attempts to establish new, or modify old, approaches to the study of society. Whereas Heinrich von Treitschke had rather defined the problem away in his "Gesellschaftswissenschaft" (Science of Society) of 1858, works by Robert von Mohl and Lorenz von Stein tried to incorporate a new understanding of society into the "state sciences" in the same period. In 1875, Albert Schäffle talked in organicist terms about the "Anatomy and Life of the Social Body", and in 1887 Ferdinand Toennies published his influential book on "Community and Society" which, however, was newly subtitled "Basic Concepts of Sociology" only in the second edition in 1912. By that time, the aversion against the word sociology had diminished and Georg Simmel and Max Weber were ready to use it, though in a different mode than their counterparts in Western Europe.

These intellectual activities found their expression also in the creation of social science journals. In Italy, the *Rassegna di scienze sociali e politiche* existed between 1883 and 1890, and the *Rivista italiana di sociologia* was founded in 1892 and continued to appear until after the First World War. In France, Durkheim's *Année sociologique* was probably the most successful, but by far not the only sociological journal. The "Le Playists" had their own journals and Worms founded the *Revue internationale de sociologie* in 1893, to give only two examples. Worms also created the *Institut international de sociologie* one year later; these were both initiatives to stimulate and enhance international sociological communication and simultaneously means to counteract the emerging dominance of the Durkheimian approach on the national scientific field by enlisting international scholars in one's support.

Besides this international academic society, national societies were established. The followers of Le Play in France, for instance, even formed two organized groups, one of a more academic nature, the other more practically oriented. For the Durkheim group, the journal provided a strong organizing focus. In the German-speaking areas, the Viennese Sociological Society was created in 1907 and the German Society for Sociology followed in 1909. In Germany, a social science association had already existed since 1872, the Association for Social Policy, which showed a broad historical orientation to social science and intended to put its work into service for the newly founded German nation-state.

Scholarly journals, academic societies and intense publication activities on theoretical and programmatic matters, all elements for the building of a discipline, seemed to exist in the early 1900s. Sociologists, however, hardly achieved recognition by academic institutions, which is an important precondition for a scientific field to be securely established.

Many contributors to the sociological debates were academics who held chairs in disciplines such as philosophy, economics, law, history or medicine. While it is obvious that "founding fathers" cannot start out from established chairs, it is important to recognize that, though many strove for it, hardly anyone of this generation of sociologists succeeded in obtaining a sociological label for their chairs. Durkheim was one of the few, and by the time of his death three more chairs at French universities carried the sociological denomination. In Germany and Austria, no chairs for sociology were created until 1919, the one at the University of Munich, which Weber had accepted shortly before his death, being among the first. For Italy, Robert Michels, who emigrated from Imperial Germany because he was not accepted in German universities at all, remarked in 1930 that sociology had "no academic citizenship, and its representatives are either outside the university itself or occupy chairs in economics or legal philosophy. ... So far as my knowledge extends, there is no course in sociology in Italy, with the possible exception of Padua" (Michels 1930: 20–21).

By the early 1900s, thus, "sociology" had experienced a boom of activities which had lasted for about three decades. It had flourished, supported by a "positive social culture" (Barbano 1985: 68), by a wide interest in new, systematic and "positive" approaches to understand social development. Inspite of this supportive context, however, it had been unable to achieve full academic institutionalization and, therefore, remained extremely vulnerable to changing circumstances. Around the turn of the century, political and intellectual tides were, in fact, changing. These changes spelled, as I will argue in some detail, the end of classical sociology because of its inability to allow for appropriate modifications of its discourse.

The last three decades of the nineteenth century were, very broadly speaking, a period of construction and consolidation in continental western Europe. Precarious and unstable socio-political constellations were overcome and the new formulae, after some critical early periods, seemed to work: the lay and socially oriented Third Republic in France, the authoritarian bureaucratic state dominating the society of Imperial Germany and the unified Italian nation-state based on the interdependence of urban and rural elite groups in the north and south. This was the constellation which bred the self-conscious and self-assuring sociological movements: while these societies surely had problems, they also disposed of the means to solve them by self-inspection through empirical analysis. Especially in Italy, but also in the other countries, one is tempted to speak of an unbound will for knowledge, to use Foucault's terminology.

By the end of the 1800s, insecurities were returning and were there to stay through the first half of the twentieth century. The rising workers' movement was about to challenge elite consensuses, industrialization and urbanization did not only change material living conditions rapidly, but also raised uncertainties about social status among many groups, including, not least, the bearers of the intellectual culture. Put in the terms of the historian Stuart Hughes (1958: 41), on all "levels of intellectual activity, doubts arose as to the reigning philosophy of the upper middle class – the self-satisfied cult of material progress which, in a vulgarized sense, could also be termed 'positivism'." All its heterogeneity notwithstanding, the thought of the early sociological movements was doubtlessly part of this reigning philosophy and went into crisis with it. While the early will for knowledge was based on rather unproblematic, mostly implicit, assumptions about the relation between social reality and the knowledge which could be generated by observing it, the new uncertainties were not least of an epistemological character; they raised the question of the very possibility of knowledge about society. The most important contributions to classical sociology reflect the culmination of these crises. Weber, Durkheim and some others doubted the easy claims made by their sociological predecessors. But in contrast to some of their "culture-critical" and relativist contemporaries they skeptically insisted on, and searched for, the possibility of a science of society.

Over time, in such a changed intellectual climate, the sociological projects were massively transformed, however. In France, Durkheimism remained strong as the basis of a quasi-official republican ideology, but in this function its moral and philosophical aspects were emphasized at the expense of its sociological ambitions. From having been considered a positivist-minded social science, it was turned into appearing to be an idealist philosophy (cf. Heilbron 1985). In Italy, sociological thinking did not survive the onslaught of idealism, as epitomized in the cultural dominance of Benedetto Croce's thinking, which has even been labelled intellectual dictatorship (Bobbio 1969; Asor Rosa 1981). As early as 1906 Croce wrote, commenting on a proposal to establish chairs in sociology, that this thinking was a "chaotic mixture of natural and moral sciences; ...

another 'new science' which as a philosophical science is unjustifiable, and as an empirical science anything else but new. It is new only as 'sociology', that is as a barbaric positivistic incursion into the domain of philosophy and history" (Croce 1942: 130). In Austria, sociology continued to flourish for a brief period in the political context of "red Vienna" but hardly influenced academic debate at the universities and the intellectual debates at large. In Germany, seemingly deviant, sociology was institutionalized at the universities after 1919 with several dozen chairs being created by 1933. As will be shown later, though, this sociology had abandoned most of its earlier ambitions, as its proponents had settled for an institutional strategy which would minimize confrontation with other, well-established academic fields.

In sum, my look at these intellectual and institutional developments between 1870 and 1930 amounts to saying that there was a strong movement for founding and establishing a sociology as the science of society, that this movement culminated intellectually in the proposals known today as classical sociology, but that by the end of that period the sociological project had failed. To substantiate this view, it is required to characterize the main features of that project first.

The Project of Classical Sociology: A Science of Society

Classical sociology was, first of all, a response to political economy. This feature has been aptly described by Göran Therborn (1976: 170–1):

In revolt against the deductive, individualist-utilitarian and laissez-faire character of orthodox (above all 'vulgar') liberal economics, new social theories developed in the last quarter of the 19th century which were inductive, social-ethical and interventionist. ... We can distinguish in this respect three critiques of political economy, each in a particular way significant for the development of the sociological project. One centred on liberal economic policies and gave rise ... to a kind of investigatory practice which is often labelled sociological, but which has increasingly become part of normal administrative routine. The other two were instrumental in ... constructing sociology as a distinct theoretical and empirical discipline. One of these started from a critical analysis of the epistemological basis of economics. The other was an across-the-board critique of the epistemology, the utilitarianism and policy recommendations of liberal economics. Max Weber may be taken to represent the second and Durkheim the third kind of critiques.

Disentangling this summarizing view, one can argue that sociology met with economics in three respects, which can be analytically separated: *scientific, political* and *institutional*.

In *scientific* terms, it was a response to the individualist methodology of economics and, in part, to its epistemological assumptions. In *political* terms, it reacted against the liberal, non-interventionalist implications of a theory, or at least vulgarizations of a theory, that postulated self-regulation and equilibration of economic interests through market forces and, thus, an automatic achievement of maximum welfare without conscious political action. In *institutional* terms, any such project would be faced with the problem that economics was already established in academia and claimed to take the place of a science of contemporary society. This threefold response shall be discussed in more detail, taking the examples of Durkheim, Weber and Pareto as the outstanding, but simultaneously typical, contributors to classical sociology.

In Durkheim's view, the economists had taken the first steps towards a science of society; they had been "the first to proclaim that social laws are necessary as physical laws, and had made this axiom the basis of a science" (Durkheim 1888: 25). They were wrong, however, in seeing in the individual the sole tangible reality that the observer can reach. The constitution of human beings was much more complex than rational-individualist theories assumed; human beings are "of a time and a place, (they have) a family, a city, a homeland, a religious and a political belief, and all these aspects and others more mix and intertwine in a thousand ways ... without it being possible to say at a first glance where the influence of the one begins and of the other ends" (*op. cit.*: 29). He replaced the economists' methodological individualism with a perspective which gave primacy to "social facts". The economists' view was not completely without value, but limited to the study of very few – for instance, demographic – phenomena. Otherwise, it is to be subordinated to a much more comprehensive social perspective, the one of sociology, as he explained immodestly at a meeting of the Society for Political Economy in 1908 (cf. Lukes 1973: 499–500).

Vilfredo Pareto, engineer and economist, had arrived at this very problem, the inexplicability of social phenomena when analyzed only with the tools of political economy: "Arrived at a certain point in my research in political economy, I found myself in an impasse. I saw the experimental reality and could not reach it. ... Driven by the desire to add an indispensable complement to the study of political economy and, above all, being inspired by the example of the natural sciences, I have been induced to compose my *Trattato di sociologia*" (quoted from: Freund 1976: 50). His judgment on political economy, however, was not that it was inappropriate to analyse social reality, but that it was incomplete. In his view, this deductive theory and its geometric and mathematical formalizations explained certain parts of society fairly well; the problem was that there were other aspects of society which were not grasped at all. His solution was a division of society, on the ontological level, into the spheres of logical actions, to be analysed by economic theory, and non-logical actions, to be analysed by sociological theory. Focusing on justifications and rationalizations of non-logical actions, his sociology was mainly an individualistically based theory of ideology. This theory limits the sphere of applicability of economic theory, but acknowledges it at the same time as one of two parts of a comprehensive social science.

The relation of sociology to economics in Durkheim was imperialist domination; in Pareto it was ontological completion of a social science; in Weber it was epistemological reconceptualization. In contrast to Pareto, Weber did not stand in the tradition of orthodox political economy, but in the one of the German Historical School. He understood, however, and appreciated attempts, like those of the Austrian Carl Menger, to put the economic and social sciences on a more solid grounding than the historical scholars provided who linked empirical studies with notions, of unclear epistemological status, from philosophy of history. While he definitely shared the concern for the fate of the German nation and people with the Historical School, he was unwilling to let notions like the spirit of the people, or the realization of the will of the state enter into his social science as foundational concepts. That is why he disagreed with Gustav Schmoller's rash dismissal of Menger's attempt at giving unequivocal foundations to theoretical sciences of society by drawing on the deductive approach of political economy. To him, the utilitarian categories of economics could well serve, in principle, as cornerstones of a social science, but only if understood as "ideal types" which render economic behaviour intelligible by naming rationalities of action.

The search for "ideal types," a key notion in Weber's methodological work, could provide a way out of the conflict between making regularities of social phenomena understandable, on the one hand, and getting at the uniqueness of every event in its historical configuration on the other and, thus, to reconcile the seemingly contradictory ambitions of political economy and the Historical School as sciences of society. The necessity of economic theory was acknowledged, but this theorizing was, at the same time, methodologically subordinated to the goal of arriving at historical knowledge. Weber, therefore, concluded that Menger was right on the impossibility "to come to 'laws' in the strict sense by adding up historical observations," but he was to be told that ideal types could never acquire "empirical *validity* in the sense of *deductibility* of reality from the 'laws'" (Weber 1973 (1904): 187 and 188). His social science, later to be called sociology, would maintain close links to history and would not abdicate the claim to come to an understanding of real society.

All main lines of sociological thinking during this period stood up against the claim of political economy to be the science of society. And all the major proponents of sociology, as shown, saw their approaches not as an addition, a further perspective on social phenomena, but as a reconsideration of the problems which society posed and as a rephrasing of the analytical requirements to study these problems adequately. The inadequacy of political economy was not only perceived on the terrain of epistemology and ontology but also with regard to the political implications which it carried.

In Continental Europe, political economy had hardly ever been received in its full intellectual sophistication, not to speak of its original philosophical groundings. The most outspoken and popular advocates of this approach in Italy and Germany, to some extent also in France, were vulgarizers who directly linked the theory to their view on the advantages of liberal, market-based societal organization and the unregulated thriving of private business. They aligned openly with economic interests and it was easy to denounce their reasoning as little more than a political ideology. Sociologists in the late 1800s often rejected this view and themselves took political standpoints in favour of a moderate socialism or conservative, state-oriented reformism. There was, thus, very often a dividing-line between economists and sociologists (or historical economists, to be precise in terminology) on matters of day-to-day policy making.

The political implications of social science theorizing, however, went even deeper and acquired the character of a major restructuration of the understanding of society, its development and coherence, in general. Classical economists, as well as the proponents of sociology in the early 1800s like August Comte and Claude-Henri de Saint-Simon, as different as their theorizing was, had shared the Enlightenment optimism about the coming of a society in which the interests of its individual members would converge to allow for the well-being of all without major force or complex organization being necessary. These theories of self-acclaimed scientific validity gave an underpinning to political liberalism, to all arguments for a liberation of the dynamic forces of society, a liberation which would lead to new social equilibria on a new social basis with everyone better off except for the holders of old, aristocratic and religious privileges. By the late 1800s, and in particular due to the experiences of nation building and reconstruction, these convictions had fallen into doubt and were being replaced not only by new ideologies, like *solidarisme* in France and *trasformismo* in Italy, but also by new analytical approaches to society.

To put it in the terms of Pietro Rossi (1982: 198–9),

after 1870 – a significant date not only because of the changes in European political equilibria, but also for the socioeconomic tissue of the continent – it appears evident ... that the development of industrial society is inadequate ... to solve the antagonisms which it itself created ... and that this society would even generate conflicts to a far larger extent than any society of the past. The change of the productive system does not deliver by itself the instauration of a new political organization; and if (the polity) changes, this occurs in a quite different sense than that of new social 'harmony'.

The classical sociologists were well aware of this constellation of a major political restructuring without a clear objective or guiding ideology. It can easily be discovered as their major political *problematique* and the basic orientation of the concepts on which they intended to found their sciences. Unable to stick to the idea of a quasi-automatic regulation of interest conflicts, but similarly unwilling to move completely away from the tenets of bourgeois liberalism, they devoted their analytical efforts to the search for those phenomena which might provide for a workable development of society. "Once the hope to construct (even, to reconstruct) an organic society has proven illusory, sociology turns its attention to the mechanisms which hold the diverse 'parts' of the 'social body' together, i.e. the groups and individuals of which it is composed and which can secure the continuity or transformation of the specific conditions of industrial society" (*loc. cit.*). In this sense, classical sociology is post-liberal political philosophy, and ideology.

The different expressions which this post-liberalism found in the works of the sociologists can broadly be related to the specificities of the national societies to the fate of which they felt committed. In Germany the national-liberal movement had failed after 1848, and when the nation-

state was built in 1871, after several wars, it was under Prussian
dominance, a creation "from above," by a strong military-bureaucratic
apparatus without the broad involvement of a societal movement (see
Schiera, in this volume). Weber had grown up in this state and with the
rapid expansion of industrial production which accompanied the early
decades of its existence. Whether wished or not, to him the bureaucratic
state and capitalist-industrial society seemed to be inevitably shaping
modern living conditions, and the guiding normative theme of his work
was the conditions for the preservation of ways of living for the individuals according to the historical and cultural specificities of their
societies. In this sense, and clearly in the tradition of German historical
thinking throughout the nineteenth century, he focused on the nation and
on the question which modes of governance might enable a nation-state to
fare best under the conditions of modern industrial society. Given the
weakness of the liberal bourgeoisie, his thoughts were often occupied
with the alternatives replacing it as the hegemonic and leading force in
society: bureaucracy, a strong individual or a responsible social
democracy.

Bureaucratic apparatuses and extended party organizations, large-scale
industry and associated rationalized forms of economic activity, these
were the phenomena which Weber identified as crucial for the "life
destiny" of individuals in modern society, reflecting the rapid political
and economic transformation of Germany during the Imperial period.
Compared to these developments east of the Rhine, the administrative and
economic transformations in France had less importance compared to the
need, under republican conditions, to find new political formulae for a
society moving again towards realization of the secular, egalitarian and
democratic claims of the French Revolution. Consequently, sociologically
based political theory set a somewhat different emphasis:

As in the writings of Max Weber, the problem, not of 'order' in a generic sense, but of
the form of authority appropriate to a modern industrial state, is the leading theme in
Durkheim's work. But whereas in Germany a different combination of political and
economic circumstances helped to establish a tradition of *Nationalökonomie* which
led liberal scholars of Weber's generation to an overwhelming concern with
'capitalism', in France the problem was posed within the context of the long-standing
confrontation between the 'individualism' embodied in the ideals of the Revolution
and the moral claims of the Catholic hierocracy. (Giddens 1986: 12)

Durkheim was always doubtful about any ideas of automatic aggregration of individual interests to a working societal whole. In his view, this was an essentially mistaken view of society. Reversing the question, he looked at existing societies as entities and identified in them social phenomena which served as binding and integrating forces. In traditional societies, this phenomenon is religion; in modern societies, some degree of interdependence is introduced through the division of social labour leading to "organic solidarity" among the functional groups. However, as these societies have tremendously increased complexity compared with traditional societies, functional interdependence alone would not lead to social integration.

> From the moment when political societies have reached a certain level of complexity, they can no longer act collectively save through the intervention of the State. ... When the State exists, the various motivations that can impel the anonymous crowd of the individuals in divergent directions are no longer adequate to determine the collective consciousness, for this process of determination is the action of the State proper. (Durkheim 1950: 45–6).

While being convinced of this moral role of the state to curb excesses of individual actions and to take account of the general needs of common life, Durkheim was also aware of possibilities for authoritarian abuses of state power, particularly likely in mass societies where direct aggregation of interests was impossible. The measures he designed against such tendencies were, first, well in the tradition of the Enlightenment, moral education towards social responsibility and, second, beyond that tradition, the concept of secondary organizations, which should stand between state and individual, based on the functional division of labour and not on the principle of territoriality.

In contrast to France and Germany, the Italian nation-state had neither socially well-rooted institutions nor was Piedmontese dominance strong enough to integrate society from above. Unification, long desired by the liberals of the *Risorgimento*, was far from leading quickly to the realization of liberal political ideas. Pareto, himself a committed liberal in political as well as in economic terms, observed how a political-intellectual elite came to power with the *Risorgimento* ideas and how when building the institutions of the new state this elite compromised its original convictions and built partial alliances with old elites to maintain its power. While in this process the liberal ideas lost persuasive power, a new social movement with a different political commitment, the workers' movement and socialism, emerged, from which a new elite was pressing into power positions.

A systematic interpretation and assessment of these alternatives was the basis for Pareto's political sociology. He drew on concepts such as, most importantly, the one of "political class" which had developed in earlier Italian political theorizing. Gaetano Mosca (1982: 206–7) had formulated in 1884: "We cannot conceive of a society, as democratic as it may be, in which government is exercised by all. Even in this case, all public functions are in fact exercised neither by one only nor by all, by a special class of persons instead. ... We shall from now on label this special class the political class." The distinction between the political class, the elite, and the masses is a universal feature of human societies according to Pareto, and the "circulation of elites" one of their important moving forces. Elites attain power through the social dynamics which their political ideologies unleash; once in power, however, they do not live up to their promises, *malcontenti* start to build an organization and ideology of their own and will, after some time, be able to succeed the ruling elite in power. "Aristocracies don't last. Whatever the reasons may be, it is uncontestable that they disappear after a certain time. History is a cemetery of aristocracies" (Pareto 1923: III, 262).

This brief exemplary characterization of sociological debates was, in sum, meant to demonstrate that around the turn of the century a new type of social theorizing existed which, all differences notwithstanding, had some basically common orientations in intellectual and political terms. It provided responses to the crisis of political economy and of classical liberalism, responses which took account of the social and political transformations during the nineteenth century, and it tried to base the empirical study of society on new foundations. As such, it faced the opposition of well-entrenched scientific approaches and political convictions.

In academic institutions, economic thinking, as political economy or as historical economics, was fairly well established all over continental Europe. Whether sociology tied in with the discourse of economics in one way or the other, like Weber and Pareto did, or whether it took the position of a fundamental alternative, like Durkheim, it was to be expected that it would not be welcomed by the representatives of the established discipline. Similarly, sociology argued for some break with, or at least rephrasing of, the concerns of philosophy and history. No smooth adaptation could be expected there either. Many, though by far not all, of the early sociologists were aware of this institutional problematique. The attempts to develop both organizational structure and institutional grounding, briefly described above, were a result of considerations to achieve institutional legitimacy for their approach, the scientific and political legitimacy of which they were convinced of and found, to a certain degree, confirmed in their own intellectual and political environment. The crucial question was the one of securing the institutional basis for intellectual reproduction. As this objective was not reached, or in the best case, the one of Durkheim, only half-way (Karady 1976), sociology was almost bound to fail once it lost political legitimacy.

The Double Dilemma of Classical Sociology and Its Loss of Legitimacy

The period of classical sociology was characterized by a remarkable conjunction of two major long-term developments in European societies: *first*, the second half of the nineteenth century was the time when the research-oriented university reached the peak of its importance, uniting the tasks of advanced scientific research, elite training for all core professions of society and general "liberal" education (Wittrock 1985; cf. also Rothblatt and Wittrock 1990). Its organizational structure had a decisive impact on the organization of knowledge in this phase. *Second*, at the same time the institutional structures of the nation states were either formed in the process of territorial consolidation as in Italy and Germany or reshaped with the advent of a republic which was born out of deep political crisis and was going to have a lasting impact on French society. This conjunction provides the background for the possibility of the sociological approaches to flourish. It gives the condition for their position as a mode of theorizing relatively detached from the day-to-day struggles in politics and oriented towards the advance of general knowledge about society. Simultaneously the sociologists were concerned about the major, long-term political restructurings which were underway and the nature and meaning of which they tried to identify through studying the contemporary situation and structure of their society in a comparative, evolutionary perspective.

The conjunction of these two institutional developments, however, also provides the clue to an understanding of the failure of sociology. From it emerged problematic constellations which proved detrimental to the future development of a science of society. They can be termed the *scientific-institutional* and the *political-institutional dilemma* of social science (cf. Wagner 1989). The two dilemmas and their impact shall be discussed each in turn in the following.

The development of the university entailed a weakening of the link to society on the one hand, and a deepening of internal structuring on the other. The first aspect is mainly responsible for the possibility of a somewhat detached scientific activity to become institutionalized; "In general, the university teacher has more and more withdrawn from practice and moved into pure sciences," to put it into the terms of a contemporary observer (Paulsen 1902: 78; cf. also Torstendahl 1987). The second aspect is in some sense the precondition of the first one. Internal structuring is motivated by the assumption that scientific approaches can be developed for different levels or spheres of reality, approaches which would develop their own object-adequate concepts and would (have to) develop according to their own logic, their standards and norms of valid scientific activity. The nineteenth century has been, in standard terms of "functionalist" sociology of science, the era of scientification of practices and of differentiation of academic disciplines. Without concurring with the idea of functionality in these terms, one can without doubt assert that a sphere, or field, of action emerged which developed partially along its own criteria, criteria which influenced the possibilities for action inside this sphere (cf. Bourdieu, e.g., 1975, 1984, for the notion of "field" of action).

To acquire full scientific status, a discourse had to dispose of unequivocal standards for the permissibility of statements and to demarcate boundaries to other discourses (cf. Foucault 1971, for related notions of discourse and discipline). Among the discourses on society, only political economy had approached such a status by the mid-1880s. Its structure, thus, marked a standard which other discourses had to strive for in order to increase their legitimacy.

In fact, one can argue that it was the crisis of classical political economy between, broadly speaking, the 1870s and 1890s which opened the space for the various sociologies and other less well-defined discourses to gain ground. The crisis was both an intellectual one, the apparently insolvable value problem, and a political one, the at that time rather undoubted need for state promotion of the economy. Many of the sociological approaches attacked political economy exactly at the points where its limits could not be overcome but which, simultaneously, were the guarantors of its cognitive coherence and, therefore, scientific standing (this observation holds in basically similar terms still today, cf.

de Villé 1990). These approaches themselves, however, can well be characterized by their neglect of the requirements of gaining institutional legitimacy. Their discourses either moved swiftly across the boundaries established by political economy, or they attempted a general redefinition of academic demarcations. The first is the case of Weber and Pareto, for instance, the second the one of Durkheim.

The strength of the logics of academic boundary setting can, in contrast, be gathered from the tendencies of formation of other discourses on society, which emerged during the same period or shortly thereafter, and proved to be of more lasting relevance. Thus many economists had opened their theorizing to historical and political considerations during the late 1800s and seemed almost ready to acknowledge the inadequacy of the classical theory. Other scholars in their field, however, attempted a modification of the theory, later termed the "marginalist revolution"; which would rid it of the value problem and restore its coherence on new foundations. Neoclassical economics did not gain institutional ground rapidly in continental Europe (except Austria and Italy; see Gioli, in this volume), where it had partly been developed by Menger and Walras. Nevertheless it proved to be a solid basis in the long run for an economic science clearly separated from other discourses on society in cognitive terms.

An analogous process of separation was undertaken by legal scholars who formalized the study of public law and the state to put it on a, as the argument went, truly scientific footing. This aim required legal theory to be rid of all impurities which the consideration of political, economic, moral or cultural phenomena might bring with it (cf. e.g., Wieacker 1952; Mozzarelli and Nespor 1981). The legal theory of the state, or legal positivism, as the approach was also called, achieved a dominant position in the faculties for law and state sciences in Italy and Germany (though not in France) towards the end of the nineteenth century and effectively pushed aside all attempts to establish a science of political institutions and administrative behaviour.

In countries which had experienced a rapid and more-or-less precarious process of state building, a theory which constructed a system of legal propositions founded on the personality and will of the state was of obvious attraction to the administrative and political elites. Furthermore, the law faculties trained for a core profession of this state, for officials who needed "to act with promptness and precision, clarify the deliberations of the law-maker, and bring unity, coherence and order into the legal system" (Dyson 1980: 111), all requirements which legal positivism fulfilled perfectly. However, it should not be overlooked that much of the dynamics in the development of this theory stemmed from the desire of legal scholars to raise their work to scientific standing. The price was to make the state a pure "fiction or abstraction" without substantial ties to society, as a critic said (Heller 1931: 610; see earlier, e.g., von Gierke 1915 (1874)), but this seemed not at all undesired for the purpose, in contrast, rather a precondition.

Marginalist economics and legal positisivm had appropriated the spheres of the economy and the polity for themselves in a radically separated and reductionist way. An open space was, however, left for a science of social interactions, if it was possible to separate them in a similar way from history, culture and ethics, as it had been done in the case of economic and public-legal behaviour. Such a science, called sociology, was exactly the project of Leopold von Wiese in Weimar Germany. His "theory of relations" (Beziehungslehre) or "formal sociology" focused on the form of the relations between human beings and not on the "substance", the knowledge of which was to come from the neighbouring disciplines (von Wiese 1920: 41). In the context of the university policy debates in Germany after the First World War, this project was the start of a, highly successful as such, strategic move to use a favourable political environment for the institutionalization of sociology. Given rather adverse attitudes in the universities towards newcomers and potential competitors in the scientific field, von Wiese found it wise to argue for a reductionist conception of sociology which would avoid all possible conflicts with other disciplines. The price, however, was a "de-historicization and de-economization" (Lukács 1954: 461–2; Käsler 1984: 252) of sociology and the abandoning of Weber's project of a comprehensive social science. This concept had some influence on sociological debates in Weimer Germany, not least due to von Wiese's strategic position as a functionary of the German Society for Sociology. It was, however, not very widespread in other countries, except in the United States, where similar debates were held and where the process of boundary setting and of discipline-based professionalization was much more pronounced than in Europe (cf. e.g., Manicas 1987 and in this volume).

The process of university restructuring during the nineteenth century pointed to this direction of formal "scientification" and disciplinary segregation. It was the *scientific-institutional dilemma* of sociology as a comprehensive social science that it relied, on the one hand, on the relative institutional autonomy of the university to develop its discourse on society without being subordinated to political needs, but that it had to insist on escaping the formalist and segregating logic of "scientific" development in these institutions, on the other hand. While the university was a necessary condition for such a sociology to develop, it also contributed to aborting these approaches.

The *political-institutional dilemma* of the social sciences stemmed from transformations of the state. The discourses of classical sociology had contributed to a reflexive understanding of state and society, and they had a part in the constitution of the state (cf. Giddens 1985; Wittrock 1988; Nowotny, in this volume). They had, however, never been the only institutionalized contributors to such a reflexive monitoring; the work of statistical offices and social research done by commissions of inquiry or administrative inspectors of various sorts were pursued parallel to the academic discourses. Throughout the twentieth century, the demand for non-academic research has considerably increased and the political institutionalization has reached such an extent that, considerable university expansion during some periods notwithstanding, non-academic researchers outnumber their academic counterparts in most societies (cf. for general arguments along this line Lutz 1975; Pollak 1976, e.g.).

Beyond quantitative reasoning, an argument can be made that the discourses of classical sociology proved increasingly inadequate for an understanding of state and society in transformation and that demands for new and different knowledge were raised. The relation between the political and the intellectual crises of the early 1900s, and in particular after the end of the First World War is, as already argued, crucial for an understanding of these developments. The outgoing nineteenth century had witnessed the shaking of the foundations of continental European societies.

After two decades of precarious equilibrium, the institutional arrangements of the major Western European states were again brought into question. The artificial, contrived character of the regimes with which unification had endowed Italy and Germany were reviewed by their malfunctioning – in the one case by the erratic changes in policy that followed the resignation of Bismarck in 1890, in the other by the social disorders and authoritarian government with which the century came to a close. In France the shock of the Dreyfus case acted as a stimulus to the reexamination of the traditional ideologies on which both the defenders and the enemies of the accused captain had rested their case. (Hughes 1958: 41)

The uncertainties and insecurities were exacerbated by the experience of the war and its aftermath. To an unprecedented degree societies had organized for this military endeavour and had thus restructured their economic and political organizations, their cleavage lines and their self-understanding, not to speak of the unforeseen, and by many unwanted, consequences of the outcome of the war.

> The 1914–1918 War was in Europe as decisive a turning point as the revolution of 1789. It perhaps marked the clear beginning of the end of pure industrial capitalism as both the apologists and Marx had described it, and yet also the beginning of institution-alized communism as virtually no-one (not even Lenin) had quite imagined it. It marked the beginning of the refutation of all the progressive social theories of the 19th century. (Hawthorn 1976: 164; see for a related argument on the USA, Manicas, in this volume)

In this perspective, the works of classical sociology can be seen as the last great attempt to save the social theory implicit in the Enlightenment tradition by rephrasing it. Durkheim, Weber and Pareto, as skeptical as they had been (increasingly, in this order), had not completely given up on finding ways to reconcile the individual's objectives of realizing her/his self with the requirement of some degree of societal cohesion, to such a degree at least as to guarantee the individual's liberties. Through historical experience they were aware of the problem that no ingenious mechanism would provide this link, still they had engaged in the empirical study of their societies in the search for specific phenomena which might enhance or endanger the objective, and had produced comprehensive theories dealing with the interrelations of all phenomena in these societies which seemed relevant for their question. In a very specific sense, this theorizing had created liberal capitalist society, it had given concepts to phenomena which had different meanings before those concepts existed. To give a shorthand example of a key nature, social theorizing after the mid-1800s had replaced "mob" or "rabble" with the notion of "proletariat;" social theorizing after the 1920s tended to replace "proletariat" with the notion of "masses" (Maier 1975: 558).

Key features of bureaucratically administered mass society and organized capitalism had been well portrayed and analysed in some contributions to turn-of-the-century sociology. What these sociologists did not recognize was that the development of this society tended to make their type of knowledge, their perspective on this very society, super-fluous. The mass worker, organization member and average citizen seemed to require different instruments than the ones they preferred to develop. The discourse of classical sociology lost its cognitive affinity to the structure of the society which it dealt with, and, therefore, the support of a positive political conjuncture on which it had been thriving for some time.

After the End of Classical Sociology: "Forward" and "Backward" Intellectual Responses

What has just been asserted as plausible against the background of political transformations in the early 1900s, the decay of the intellectual tradition of classical sociology, can be analyzed in some detail through an account of the "sociological" field in the inter-war period (beyond the descriptive remarks in an earlier section of this paper). The main tendency then was towards a bifurcation of the techniques, concerns and ways of thinking which classical sociology had been able to hold together. This bifurcation was not just a matter of empirical analysis being separated (again) from theory and philosophy of social science; what is more important is that the two diverging main lines of sociological activity entailed different understandings of the possibility of social science and different basic views on the fabric of society.

One line of thinking, the more traditionally social-philosophical one, responded to the political and intellectual crises of the early 1900s by considering the progressive elements in classical sociological and economic theory as an optimistic error. In the face of rapid social changes it was argued that the development of "mass society" itself had shown that the requirements for social integration could not be fulfilled. This reasoning was partly rooted in the bourgeois intellectuals' existential anxiety in the face of the dehumanizing aspects of the "factory system" in production and administration and of the growing strength of the workers' movement and its organizations. From such a view the turn away from previous social theories took the form of an intellectual and political movement "backwards." A moderate version was the emphasis on categories of collective morals in the idealist metamorphosis of Durkheimian thinking (Heilbron 1985), more radical ones were the expectations of an "authoritarian state" or a "strong man" (cf., e.g., Gentile 1982, Käsler 1984). Both tried to formulate the conditions under which the reestablishment of a bourgeois-liberal society and its culture along the lines of nineteenth century models would be possible. It is for this reason that we call this mode of reaction "backwards"-oriented.

This approach was clearly based in the academic institutions, among the "Mandarins" (Ringer 1969) of state-oriented European societies, and was thus rather easily identifiable as a transformation of sociological discourse, at least in settings where there was some continuity of institutionalized sociology as in France and Germany. For Italy, it can be argued that the idealist philosophies of Giovanni Gentile, Benedetto Croce and others took the place of legitimate discourse on society which sociology had tried to occupy earlier. The *second response*, however, had rather heterogeneous roots, which have impeded the seeing of links and continuities in societal and social science developments. Empirical-descriptive and neo-positivistically guided social science was strongly proposed in those intellectual contexts in which the classical sociological orientation had not developed: in the Netherlands as sociography-sociology (cf. van Doorn 1967; Heilbron 1988), in Austria in connection to the "scientific world-view" of neo-positivism (cf. Nowotny 1983). In Paul F. Lazarsfeld's project in Austria this concept was initially application-oriented research with a clear orientation to the policy needs of a Viennese social democracy in local power positions; later, in US emigration, contractor-oriented research without normative preconditions. In the Netherlands a concept which was initially purely academically oriented was later tied to a type of systematic policy intervention rooted in the social-geographical conditions of Holland. In both cases no linkages to the discourses of classical sociology existed; empirical application-oriented social research developed either in the absence of sociology in the intellectual environment or it passed by those discourses without engaging in conceptual debate. The latter was the case in Germany and, to a smaller extent, in France and Italy, where specific research institutes were set up for applied purposes with the support of interested social groups or foreign foundations and often without the academic *imprimatur*.

The barrier which was cognitively insurmountable between classical sociology and this type of empirical sociology was the conceptualization of society itself: the latter approach introduced a radical change by circumventing the problem of the relation between society and individual methodologically; mass phenomena were made sociologically accessible by treating the individual statistically and objectifying her/him in a natural science mode. The innovators, who did not share the burden of sociological-philosophical traditions of thought typical of the classical discourses, reconceptualized society as masses who reacted to a stimulus and developed regular patterns of behaviour, a reconceptualization which was impossible for classical theory.

In political terms, this discourse transformation allowed for the possibility of a planning of societal development by a scientifically informed elite. Though this idea is – in modern times – rooted in social democracy, it is obviously ambivalent. There is only a small step from the conception that a reformist elite may act as a transmission belt for the needs of the masses, needs which become known to the elites through social research, i.e. from a conception which intends to retain the emancipatory element of left-wing politics through its "modernization", to a model of will of the ruling elites organized in large-scale bureaucratic apparatuses and using knowledge about the behaviour of the mass worker and the average citizen to improve control and secure domination. In fact, given the weakness, and later the oppression, of the social democracies in inter-war Europe, the latter conception came to dominate the political context of empirical social research, thematically focused first on the factory, later on the territory. Conceptions of an empirical social science which were theoretically and politically more open remained rare and became only weakly organized. After the advent of authoritarian and totalitarian regimes, in contrast, instrumentally oriented, mostly state-owned and extra-universitarian institutes for social research consolidated and expanded; institutes which anticipated forms of knowledge which became characteristic of the full-blown interventionist state of the post-World War II period (on the notion of "intra-scientific modernization" of social science under Nazism, see Klingemann 1981: 483).

Epilogue

The fictitious sociologist, adherent to a Whiggish history of her/his discipline, who appeared in the introduction to this essay, even if s/he were convinced of my argument, might still consider these stories of the past as irrelevant for present sociology. Ultimately, did the good heritage of the founding fathers not survive in the United States, and did not sociologists all over the Western World experience a new blossoming of social theory in the 1950s and 1960s, finally bringing full academic establishment and new legitimacy to the field? These awkward dependencies on hostile institutions and adverse political climates; should they not have been overcome?

Though admittedly many features of the sociological field have changed during university expansion and reform coalitions between social scientists and policy-makers after the Second World War (cf., e.g., Wagner 1987), the problematique is, in my view, still the same and has even exacerbated. This has even been recognized by reflective representatives of the sociological mainstream, among whom James Coleman, for instance, has diagnosed a theoretical rupture in modern sociology: "Concurrently with the emerging dominance in sociology of functional theory at the level of the collectivity came a movement of empirical research that led precisely in the opposite direction ... The main body of empirical research was abandoning analysis of the functioning of collectivities to concentrate on the analysis of the behaviour of individuals" (Coleman 1986: 1313–5). At the same time, this research perspective could develop only a very limited understanding of what individuals were actually doing in society. In line with the argument presented here, Coleman remarks critically: "Empirical research ... was lacking a theory of action, replacing 'action' with 'behaviour' and eliminating any recourse to purpose or intention in its causal explanations" (*op. cit.*: 1316). Some European debates have mistakenly been taken as a revival of earlier concerns, as a return to the foundational questions of social science. The famous dispute on positivism in West Germany, for instance, which started with a debate between Karl R. Popper and Theodor W. Adorno, has been commented upon on the spot by Ralf Dahrendorf as passing by the main problems of most active social researchers who, according to Dahrendorf (1969: 148), complained that both speakers talked little about the methodological problems of empirical research and, therefore, "missed what distinguishes modern sociology from the speculative beginnings of the discipline."

Still, one might hold that the 1970s brought the (re-)emergence of essentially different approaches to social science than the instrumental objectivist, empirical ones, namely "hermeneutical and critical approaches, ... which are epistemologically oriented to *other* modes of utilization than manipulation and self-manipulation" (Habermas 1985: 321). I am not going to deny this but would argue that, when looking at the structure of the scientific field and not just at the mere existence of some mode of thinking, the picture is different. There was some revival of social theorizing in the 1960s and 1970s; the "second breakthrough of sociology," and again thriving on a positive intellectual and political climate as during the "first breakthrough" in the late 1800s (these notions have been used by Johan Heilbron). But again, and to some extent analogous to what happened in the early 1900s, this positive conjuncture has vanished and the intellectual alliances have fallen apart. We are about to experience a new bifurcation in the sociological field with narrow policy research, for which neopositivism would be a euphemistic label, but which is in high demand by political actors on the one hand, and various sorts of post-modernist thought, which has abdicated all validity criteria, but which is a media favourite, on the other. Social theorizing of the classical tradition finds itself, though not threatened in its existence, in an uncomfortably marginal position.

References

Asor Rosa, Alberto (1975), "La Cultura," in: *Storia d'Italia*, Vol. IV. 2, Turin: Einaudi.

Barbano, Filippo (1985), "Sociologia e positivismo in Italia, 1850–1910," in: Filippo Barbano and Giorgio Sola, *Sociologia e scienze sociali in Italia, 1861–1890*, Milan: Angeli.

Bobbio, Norberto (1969), "Profilo ideologico del novecento," in: *Storia della letteratura*, Vol. 9, Milan: Garzanti.

Bourdieu, Pierre (1975), "The Specificity of the Scientific Field and the Social Conditions of the Progress of Reason," in: *Social Science Information*, 14, No. 6: 19–47.

Bourdieu, Pierre (1984), *Homo Academicus*, Paris: Minuit.

Coleman, James (1986), "Social Theory, Social Research and a Theory of Action," in: *American Journal of Sociology*, 91: 1309–1335.

Croce, Benedetto (1942), *Conversazioni critiche*, Vol. I, Bari.

Dahrendorf, Ralf (1969), "Anmerkungen zur Diskussion der Referate von Karl R. Popper und Theodor W. Adorno," in: Theodor W. Adorno *et al.*, *Der Positivismusstreit in der deutschen Soziologie*, Neuwied: Luchterhand.

Durkheim, Emile (1888), "Cours de science sociale: leçon d'ouverture," in: *Revue international d'éducation*, 15, No. 1.

Durkheim, Emile (1950), *Leçons de sociologie*, Paris: Presses Universitaires Françaises.

Durkheim, Emile (1970, first 1909), "Sociologie et sciences sociales," in: Emile Durkheim, *La science sociale et l'action*, Paris: Presses Universitaires Françaises.

Dyson, Kenneth H.F. (1980), *The State Tradition in Western Europe*, Oxford: Robertson.

Foucault, Michel (1971), *L'ordre du discours*, Paris: Gallimard.

Freund, Julien (1976), *Pareto. La teoria dell'equilibrio*, Bari: Laterza (French original 1974).

Gentile, Emilio (1982), *Il mito dello stato nuovo dall'antigiolittismo al fascismo*, Rome: Laterza.

Giddens, Anthony (1985), *The Nation-State and Violence*, Cambridge: Polity Press.
Giddens, Anthony (ed.) (1986), *Durkheim on Politics and the State*, Cambridge: Polity Press.
Gierke, Otto von (1915), *Die Grundbegriffe des Staatsrechts und die neuesten Staatsrechtstheorien*, Tübingen: Mohr (first published 1874).
Habermas, Jürgen (1985), *Der philosophische Diskurs der Moderne*, Frankfurt/M.: Suhrkamp.
Hawthorn, Geoffrey (1976), *Enlightenment and Despair. A History of Sociology*, Cambridge: Cambridge University Press.
Heilbron, Johan (1985), "Les métamorphoses du durkheimisme, 1920–1940," in: *Revue française de sociologie*, **36**, No. 2.
Heilbron, Johan (1988), "Particularités et particularismes de la sociologie aux Pays-Bas," in: *Actes de la recherche en sciences sociales*, No. 74: 76–81.
Hughes, H. Stuart (1958), *Consciousness and Society. The Reorientation in European Social Thought, 1890–1920*, New York: Vintage.
Käsler, Dirk (1984), *Die frühe deutsche Soziologie und ihre Entstehungs-Milieus 1909 bis 1934*, Opladen: Westdeutscher Verlag.
Karady, Victor (1976), "Durkheim, les sciences sociales et l'Université: bilan d'un semi-échec," in: *Revue française de sociologie*, **17**, No. 2: 267–311.
Klingemann, Carsten (1981), "Heimatsoziologie oder Ordnungsinstrument? Fachgeschichtliche Aspekte der Soziologie in Deutschland zwischen 1933 und 1945," in: *Kölner Zeitschrift für Soziologie und Sozialpsychologie*, Special Issue **23**.
Lukàcs, Georg (1954), *Die Zerstörung der Vernunft*, Berlin: Aufbau.
Lukes, Steven (1973), *Emile Durkheim*, London: Allen Lane.
Lutz, Burkart (1975), "Zur Lage der soziologischen Forschung in der Bundesrepublik – Ergebnis einer Enquete der Deutschen Gesellschaft für Soziologie," in: *Soziologie*, **1**: 4–102.
Maier, Charles S. (1975), *Recasting Bourgeois Europe. Stabilization in France, Germany and Italy in the Decade after World War I*, Princeton: Princeton University Press.
Manicas, Peter T. (1987), *A History and Philosophy of the Social Sciences*, Oxford: Basil Blackwell.
Miceli, Vincenzo (1885), "La divisione nelle scienze sociali," in: *Rassegna di scienze sociali e politiche*, **3**, No. 55: 341–356.
Michels, Robert (1930), "The Status of Sociology in Italy," in: *Social Forces*, **9**, October.
Mozzarelli, Cesare, and Stefano Nespor (1981), *Giuristi e scienze sociali nell'Italia liberale*, Venice: Marsilio.
Nowotny, Helga (1983), "Marienthal and After. Local Historicity and the Road to Policy Relevance," in: *Knowledge*, **5**, No. 2: 169–192.
Pareto, Vilfredo (1923), *Trattato di sociologia generale* (2nd edition), Florence: Barbera.
Paulsen, Friedrich (1902), *Die deutschen Universitäten und das Universitätsstudium*, Berlin: Asher.
Pollak, Michael (1976), "La planification des sciences sociales," in: *Actes de la recherche en sciences sociales*, Nos. 2–3.
Ringer, Fritz K. (1969), *The Decline of the German Mandarins*, Boston: Harvard

University Press.

Rossi, Pietro (1982), "La sociologia nella seconda metà del'ottocento: dall'impiego di schemi storico-evolutivi alla formulazione di modelli analitici," in: *Il pensiero politico*, **15**, No. 1.

Rothblatt, Sheldon, and Björn Wittrock (1990), *The Three Missions: Universities in the Western World*, forthcoming.

Seidman, Steven (1983), *Liberalism and the Origins of European Social Theory*, Oxford: Blackwell.

Sola, Giorgio (1985), "Sviluppi e scenari della sociologia italiana, 1861–1890," in: Giorgo Sola and Filippo Barbano, *Sociologia e scienze sociali in Italia, 1861–1890*, Milan: Angeli.

Therborn, Göran (1976), *Science, Class and Society*, London: New Left Books.

Torstendahl, Rolf (1987), "Transformation of Professional Education in the 19th century," conference paper "Higher Education", Dalarö.

Van Doorn, J. (1965), "Die niederländische Soziologie: Geschichte, Gestalt und Wirkung," in: Joachim Matthes (ed.), *Soziologie und Gesellschaft in den Niederlanden*, Neuwied: Luchterhand.

Villé, Philippe de (forthcoming), "The General Equilibrium Tradition and Beyond," in: Björn Wittrock (ed.), *Social Theory and Human Agency*, London: Sage.

Wagner, Peter (1987), "Reform Coalitions Between Social Scientists and Policymakers," in: Stuart S. Blume, Joske Bunders, Loet Leydesdorff and Richard Whitley, *The Public Direction of the Social Sciences, Sociology of the Sciences Yearbook Vol. 11*, Dordrecht: Reidel.

Wagner, Peter (1989), "Social Science and the State in Continental Western Europe: The Political Structuration of Disciplinary Discourse," in: *International Social Science Journal*, **41**, No. 4: 509–528.

Wagner, Peter (1990), *Sozialwissenschaften und Staat*, Frankfurt/M.: Campus.

Weber, Max (1973), "Die 'Objektivität' sozialwissenschaftlicher und sozialpolitischer Erkenntnis," in: Johannes Winckelmann (ed.), *Max Weber, Gesammelte Aufsätze zur Wissenschaftslehre*, 4th edition, Tübingen: Mohr.

Wieacker, Franz (1952), *Privatrechtsgeschichte der Neuzeit unter besonderer Berücksichtigung der deutschen Entwicklung*, Göttingen: Vandenhoeck und Ruprecht.

Wiese, Leopold von (1920), "Die Soziologie als Einzelwissenschaft," in: *Jahrbuch für Gesetzgebung, Verwaltung und Volkswirtschaft (Schmollers Jahrbuch)*, Vol. 44.

Wittrock, Björn (1985), "Dinosaurs or Dolphins? Rise and Resurgence of the Research-Oriented University," in: Björn Wittrock and Aant Elzinga, *The University Research System. Public Policies for the Home of Scientists*, Stockholm: Almqvist and Wiksell.

Wittrock, Björn (1988), "Rise and Development of the Modern State: Democracy in Context," in: Diane Sainsbury (ed.), *Democracy, State and Justice, Essays in Honor of Elias Berg*, Stockholm: Almqvist and Wiksell: 113–125.

CHAPTER TEN

SOCIAL SCIENCE AND THE "SWEDISH MODEL":
SOCIOLOGY AT THE SERVICE OF THE WELFARE STATE

KATRIN FRIDJONSDOTTIR

Sometimes scholars use basic concepts that lack anything like a consistent, formal "textbook" definition, concepts which scholars themselves
may reach agreement on only temporarily and precariously and where a
process of continuous redefinition and contest is rather the normal course
of events. Society is such a concept, both within sociology and within the
social sciences as a whole. In this instance the concept denotes the basic
field of research which these sciences have in common, while each of the
social science disciplines has developed through a process of differentiation and specialization with respect to various aspects of the development
and structure of modern society. Such a process of delimitation and
differentiation, of "fencing-in" as it were, has of course been essential for
the establishment of the identity of the disciplines. It has been equally
important for their consolidation as intellectual traditions and as professional specialties entering into a range of relationships of service to
modern society and its various groupings as well as bureaucracies.
    The social sciences develop not only as ideational systems but also
within concrete social contexts to which they contribute and are expected
to contribute general analyses as well as advice and solutions in particular
cases. Such more-or-less immediate social relations of a discipline also
help shape its understanding of itself. This is probably so not only with
respect to direct uses of research results. It is also important in terms of
delimiting the very domain of research and in defining what counts and
what does not count as an acceptable solution to the research problems
within that domain. Social context should, however, be broadly conceived
so as not – to take the example of sociology – to be limited to demands
put on a discipline to contribute to a successful and enlightened social

P. Wagner, B. Wittrock, and R. Whitley (eds.), Discourses on Society: Volume XV, 1990, 247–270.
© 1990 Kluwer Academic Publishers. Printed in the Netherlands.

policy. An important part of the context is also comprised of major political and ideological currents in society.

Certainly, the discourse of a social scientific discipline may be elaborated in more-or-less conscious detachment from public and political discourse. However, even so public discourse may well exert a strong indirect influence on disciplinary developments. Normally, there is more-or-less constant interaction between these different discourses. In some periods, such interactions may well amount to a virtual invasion of the domain of the social sciences. This may be so even in the case of disciplines which have earned a far greater reputation for being "rigorous" – to use a favourite term of economists in characterizing what they perceive to be a key virtue of their own theorizing – than sociology has ever ventured to lay claim to.

The development sketched is, of course, the result of acts performed by real human beings located in time and space. Seen from such a perspective, the processes by which a discipline is formed, in a process of interaction with some larger social context, can also be described in terms of professional and intellectual projects, undertaken by actors whose interests have been in harmony with intellectual and social developments conducive to the realization, partial though it may have been, of these projects. Thus the early development of sociology has often – and with some justification – been attributed to the efforts made by its pioneers (e.g. Comte, Weber, and Durkheim) to establish a scientific foundation for the new subject. The later development of sociology, both when it has come to its taking root in different societies and to its recurring periods of reorientation, has, of course, also had its actors located within different scientific and social contexts and drawing on the rules and resources of those contexts.

The topic of this article is constituted by one small part of this greater scholarly landscape and deals with sociology in Sweden (1). However, to give a full account of the development of Swedish sociology, taking into consideration all the aspects mentioned above, is, needless to say, a task that requires far more time and space than I have at my disposal here. The aim of the article is rather to discuss in general terms the emergence and evolution of Swedish sociology since World War II in relation to three key periods in its development, namely *firstly* in the period of discipline formation during the 1940s and 1950s, *secondly* in the phase of consolidation and expansion during the 1950s and 1960s, and *thirdly* in the period of reorientation in the late 1960s and early 1970s (2). In particular, I have focussed on the development of Swedish sociology as an academic discipline. Thus the article deals first and foremost with Swedish sociology's academic history while the – by no means insignificant – development of sociological research outside the universities has been left aside.

The Scholarly and Social Sources of Swedish Sociology

The institutional history of Swedish sociology actually begins already in 1903, when Gustaf Steffen was called to a chair in economics and sociology at the University of Gothenburg. Steffen was trained as an economist but was also influenced by several European social thinkers of his day, such as the Fabians in England, the French philosopher Henri Bergson, and, not least, various German researchers and theoreticians of the times. Steffen's writings include works on a materialistic interpretation of history, on social questions, and on social policy. However, he did not create anything like a sociological "school" and his influence on the later development of Swedish sociology, although largely unexplored, seems to have been quite limited (3).

It should also be mentioned that the Swedish "sociologist" with perhaps the greatest international reputation of all time, namely Gunnar Myrdal, never belonged to the discipline in any formal sense. During the Second World War and to some extent in collaboration with a number of leading sociologists of the time (e.g. Ogburn, Shils, Stouffer, and Wirth), Myrdal carried out a study of racial problems in the United States that made him an extremely well-known name internationally among sociologists and other social scientists (4). Within Swedish social science, however, Myrdal's influence and reputation was largely based on his well-known contributions to economics in connection with the work of the so-called "Stockholm school". In passing, it might be noted that even this side of Myrdal's research, though much respected, has by and large failed to give rise to a strong research tradition or to a strong group of disciples and followers of Myrdal (5).

Besides these predecessors there were other – and every bit as trenchant – figures engaged in social research in Sweden from whom the discipline of sociology could have drawn inspiration at the time of its founding. Thus in Sweden (as to some extent in the other Scandinavian countries as well) there was a long tradition of census taking and other investigations and empirical studies into the mores and behavioural patterns of the population. For the most part, however, these studies were carried out to serve some administrative purpose and can thus be characterized as competent fact finding that has left interesting documentation to posterity. To some extent the same is true of those works which seem to have stood as sources of inspiration for sociology: Sundbärg's investigation of emigration and Thörnberg's study of social movements (6).

The gradual establishment of the discipline of sociology internationally did not go unnoticed among Swedish academics, and several university scholars had an interest in promoting the incipient discipline. This seems to have been especially true of representatives of philosophy, particularly practical philosophy, i.a. that branch of philosophy in Sweden that devotes itself to questions of moral philosophy and jurisprudence. This development is not very surprising, of course. Practical philosophy in Sweden did not – and does not – have very distinct boundaries to sociology in terms of subject area (7). The way in which sociological thinking then actually took root and became established as a separate discipline within academic life can best be described in terms of a fortuitous combination of academic and socio-political interests.

Swedish sociology became established as an independent academic discipline in 1947 when the first chair in the subject was founded at Uppsala. Torgny Segerstedt, a prominent figure in the public and academic life of the country, i.e. as future rector magnificus of Uppsala university, was the first to hold this chair. Before this, it was, however, possible to read and discuss sociological texts and problems within the subject of practical philosophy at Uppsala, Lund, and Stockholm, and the first generation of Swedish sociologists all had basic training in philosophy (8). Moreover, the first chair was created by splitting the chair in practical philosophy at Uppsala into two: the incumbent of the chair, Segerstedt, then chose the new chair in sociology (9).

The chair in sociology was also one of the outcomes of a comprehensive state inquiry into the position and organization of the social sciences in Sweden (10). As to the subject's cognitive orientation, the report of the inquiry expressed rather definite opinions concerning the desirability of following different international examples:

To give a rough characterization of this research, one might say that it has had in part a strongly speculative orientation, in part a markedly empirical one. Amongst representatives of the speculative form of sociology are to be found a number of well-known French and German scholars. The empirical form of sociology has on the other hand become most developed in the United States. There can hardly be any doubt that when the need to introduce sociology as a scientific discipline in Sweden has been put forward, what has been meant has been an empirical science with the task of investigating conditions in modern society. (SOU 1947: 74, p. 73)

Of great importance for the cognitive basis of the discipline when it was founded in Sweden was thus empirically oriented sociology such as it had become developed internationally, especially in the United States. This choice of model was naturally related to the way the task of sociology was defined:

The task of sociology is to survey the structure of the social sphere and to describe the forces that are active in this sphere. In carrying out such a survey and description it is above all quantitative methods that are used: the object is to find the quantitative units within which one can measure and compare social phenomena and events. To this end have been constructed various attitudinal scales and other instruments and tests within sociology, particularly American sociology. (*Ibid.*)

Such developments appeared in an international perspective to constitute the research frontier of empirical sociology at the end of World War II. This was true not only of the situation as seen from the Swedish horizon: sociologists in other countries were equally inspired by advances made in American sociology (11).

When the discipline was founded in Sweden it primarily came to have an empirical orientation with a theoretical bent towards socio-psychology and with its methodological roots in logical empiricism. The ideal for the proper conduct of sociology – at least as a branch of empirical research – was almost exclusively sought in the types of American sociology mentioned above, with emphasis on empirical studies for socio-political purposes. When it comes to giving a more exact picture of the direction taken by the discipline and its philosophical underpinnings during the first years of its existence, the department at Uppsala probably deserves greatest attention – not only because the first chair in the subject was founded there. A student in the early fifties, Bo Andersson, has mentioned the study of Hempel, Braithwaite, Popper, and others as being of great significance for his training in the philosophy of science.

Philosophical authors who did not belong to the tradition of analytically oriented philosophy were discarded as "metaphysicians" (if one succeeded in branding some ideas as German metaphysics, one considered oneself to have delivered the *coup de grâce*), or else as sources for "fresh ideas" or "hypotheses" (e.g. *Zur Genealogie der Moral*, or Marx's early manuscripts). Of course "hypotheses" and "fresh ideas" had to be "operationalized" within the framework of existing methods for observation and analysis before they could be taken seriously; otherwise they ran the risk of remaining "pre-scientific" (12).

Another of the first students of the Uppsala school, Georg Karlsson, has mentioned the importance of clearly distinguishing sociology from historical disciplines:

When I began at Uppsala there were two principal goals that we saw lay before the new science of sociology. It was not to be history. History was the old, general social science, and it was important to show that sociology was something new and different. Its task was instead to demonstrate causal relations in society. Sociologists were to discover the causes explaining why conditions were as they were and of the changes that take place. Sociology was a general science that could be applied to any kind of society at any time in history or of any particular culture. These goals are related, of course. If one achieves the first, the second is fulfilled almost by itself (13).

According to Karlsson, an important step in achieving this distance from history was to emphasize socio-psychological explanations. Although socio-psychological research was largely influenced by American work at this time when Swedish sociology was still young, there was a second source of inspiration, namely the early Frankfurt school (14). It should also be pointed out that several Swedish sociologists, whose contribution has mainly been to theoretical research, began their research careers as socio-psychologists (e.g. Joachim Israel, Ulf Himmelstrand, and Johan Asplund), and Segerstedt's own work is unmistakably inspired by socio-psychological theory (Mead's theories, amongst others). During the first phase of Swedish sociology, socio-psychological research was the theoretical research *par excellence* in the discipline.

Finally, the work of the American sociologist Georg Lundberg *(Foundation of Sociology*, 1939, *Social Research*, 1942, and *Can Science Save us?* 1948) probably had a considerable influence – and more so than the works of any other single American sociologist of the times – on the direction taken by Swedish sociology in its early phase. Lundberg's books reflect a liberal optimism about the future and a belief that positivist science can carry us forward in our development. Moreover, he comes down decidedly in favour of a quantitatively oriented sociology with behaviourist overtones. Lundberg's sociology was thereby not only well attuned to an interest in a sociology with a strictly empirical orientation, but also to one with a socio-psychological profile. When it came to methods, Lundberg recommended surveys and attitudinal studies as essential sociological material. Lundberg was of Swedish descent, but the first time he was invited to Uppsala he came via Norway, where sociology was also in its early stages. Of these two countries however, it was in Sweden that Lundberg came to have the greater influence.

The American influence was also secured in three other ways: through the fact that first students of sociology sought opportunities for graduate studies and further research in the United States (e.g. Hans Zetterberg, Bo Andersson, Georg Karlsson, Ulf Himmelstrand, Joachim Israel, Bengt Rundblad, Edmund Dahlström); through the role of intermediary that American sociologists came thereby to play (either directly or via neighbouring countries, such as Lundberg and Lazarsfeld in Norway); and, finally, through direct research funding from the United States (15). On the whole one might say that the American empirical tradition then predominant became the model for what was considered to be the proper way of conducting good sociological research, a fact which was naturally of significance when the discipline was later introduced at the other universities as well. Thus as sociology became accepted and expanded, further chairs in the subject were established at the other universities. Following Uppsala came Stockholm (1954), where Gunnar Boalt was the first incumbent, and then Lund (1956) with Gösta Carlsson, Gothenburg (1960) with Edmund Dahlström, and Umea (1965) with Georg Karlsson.

The subject's first professors, or for that matter the first generation of Swedish sociologists, were "in no way cast in the same mould" with respect to research (16). It did not take long before the different departments began to take on distinctive traits with regard to the areas of research they staked out and their theoretical preferences (17). Still the sociological research from this period shows many quite uniform characteristics. It is strongly empirical and empiricist, and apart from the more theoretical efforts made in the field of socio-psychology, theoretical works, particularly when it comes to macro-theoretical analysis of the development of Swedish society, are conspicuous by their absence.

Amongst the exceptions must be reckoned the nestor of Swedish sociology, Torgny Segerstedt, and his opus. Segerstedt played one of the leading roles in establishing sociology in Sweden, as professor of practical philosophy with "a certain sociological leaning" at the University of Uppsala from 1939, as representative of sociology in the state inquiry of 1946 that led to the founding of a chair in sociology at Uppsala (SOU 1947: 47), and as professor and research leader at the department at Uppsala from 1947. Segerstedt developed during the first early years of

Swedish sociology his theory of the normative integration of society. The main premises are that people are largely shaped by their environment, that their basic behaviour and motives are learned, and that this learning largely takes place through verbal influence. Thus similar behaviour within human groups can and should be explained by social norms and the way they are learned. Essentially it is thus a theory of socialization – in groups and in society (18).

For the most part, however, the normative system itself – or the "source of norms", i.e. the society and its political and economic structure and development – appears inviolable in itself. This view of society, with its appendant demarcation between science and social policy, seems however to have been shared by most Swedish sociologists of the time (and not only Swedish ones, to be sure). Segerstedt's theoretical importance for Swedish sociology is actually difficult to define with precision, for one finds little in the literature that clearly bears his mark (19). Nor was there any powerful and equally consistent alternative that was developed at this time. One might even wonder whether the theory of normative integration went hand in glove with the empirical research orientation in order to give the discipline a cohesive identity in its early years. Most likely because of the way in which Swedish sociology came to develop over the following years, no attempt was made – for the time being – to question the normative system itself.

Sociology at the Service of Harmonious Development

In Sweden, the period in which the social sciences expanded significantly and in some cases, such as sociology, were actually formally established, corresponded with the period in which the Swedish welfare state was built up. Great expectations were held for what the social sciences could achieve and what they could contribute to this development. Economists were engaged to help draw up stabilization policy, geographers for regional policy, and educationalists and psychologists came to participate in the reform of the schools. Political scientists were expected to study the new roles of organizations and the effect of political reforms, while sociologists studied the problems of working life and contributed material and proposals to implement various parts of social policy. It is from this time that one can trace the roots of the sociologists' self-image as social engineers at the service of society.

The 1950s and the first half of the 1960s can be described as the phase of consolidation and expansion for sociology. When it comes to this period parts of the history of the discipline can be found recorded in separate surveys of its specializations (such as the sociology of work, housing sociology, etc.) and attempts were also made to draw a general history of the subject and depict its foremost characteristics (20).

In an article published in the journal *Sociologisk Forskning* somewhat later than this (1973), an outside observer, Erik Allardt, contributed to this image of Swedish sociology in a discussion of the relation between research and social policy with this telling comment:

... the great majority of Swedish sociological analyses of society are written from the basic premise that social problems are something that a benevolent state can set right. The problems are more or less disturbances in interaction. There are mechanisms of rejection, barriers to higher culture, discrepancies in power, structural injustices, immigrant isolation, but when sociologists have written on these phenomena they have more or less clearly addressed themselves to the authorities. (21)

In the same issue of the journal a prominent Swedish sociologist, Göran Therborn, states that "the history of Swedish sociology is the history of its state investigations" (22).

In descriptions like these emerges perhaps at the same time the contours of a relatively "orderly" discipline in its social context: Swedish sociology, once established academically, had an agenda which seemed obvious, and the questions addressed in research oriented towards social policy seemed almost to be given by the way the authorities defined the problems. Nor did there seem to be any lack of demand for or interest in sociological analyses – or investigations.

But what was the situation like at the departments of sociology? Johan Asplund, another well-known Swedish sociologist, has described developments in the department at Uppsala during the early 1960s in the following critical terms:

It was almost unavoidable that empiricism be united with a declared willingness to carry out studies on a commission basis instead of conducting research from purely scientific considerations. All senior undergraduates as well as graduate students should have empirical data. It costs money to collect and analyse such material. The money must come from external sources. The path is thus cleared to transform a research institute into an institute for commissioned studies. At such an institute there is little opportunity to conduct a critical or inopportune brand of sociology. Nor is there any natural place for efforts at theoretical development. Everyone is busy working on their commissions. In the end they have become imperceptibly transformed into an appendage to the even pace of society. (23)

An additional factor that contributed to this development was, according to Asplund, the absence of a theory of social development (notwithstanding Segerstedt's theoretical leadership):

sociology at Uppsala, like Swedish sociology in general, missed its chance of developing a dialogue – preferably a critical one – with a "grand theory". If nothing else, such a dialogue would have provided a sustaining defence from superficiality and commercialism. (24)

In an international perspective as well as (although to a lesser extent) a Scandinavian one, the social sciences in Sweden as a whole were characterized during this period by rather decided support for the public policies carried out (25). The outward face of sociology in this respect was determined by its task of illustrating problems and finding solutions in those areas that belonged to sociology, such as work, housing, education, and social policy, and in accordance with the aspects that it chose to single out for study. This process of enclosure was in no way barren with regard to the development of the discipline as a whole. In this period were established several of the fields of research that would come to give Swedish sociology its profile. This development took place in interaction with "customers", both from the public and private sectors (26).

In the early 1960s Swedish sociologists organized themselves in the Swedish Association of Sociologists. A few years later, in 1964, its journal *Sociologisk Forskning* ("Sociological Research") began to be published. Right from the start, its task was to constitute a domestic forum for Swedish sociologists to communicate with each other and outward to the general public. The first volumes mainly contain articles and reports from on-going research projects and reflect reasonably well sociological activities during these years. Once in a while, however, it is asked where the greater correlations are to be found, and already in one of the first volumes Hans Zetterberg, just back in Sweden, expresses his displeasure at the provincialism prevailing in Scandinavian and Swedish sociology (27). Zetterberg's article was in turn the point of departure for a debate in the journal's pages about "soft data", the first serious shot fired from within the discipline at the research tradition then dominant in Sweden (28).

Zetterberg's criticism was aimed principally at what he considered to be simple-minded and provincial in Swedish (and Scandinavian) as well as in American sociology. However, it was perhaps not only the methods that an outsider could describe as unsophisticated. A few years later Erik Allardt described the society conceived of by Swedish sociologists as a "society without social forces" and as a "society without any surprises", even in comparison with the other Scandinavian countries (29).

If one takes into consideration the history of Swedish sociology (including its methods) up to then, this development (or descriptions of it) probably does not come as any great surprise. Right from the time the subject was getting started it had been limited almost exclusively to those aspects of social integration that related to norms and socialization, and had imported and developed methods for this purpose, but had left to one side other aspects of social development – such as conflict as a driving force for this development, for example – as well as the methods needed to tackle them. It seems, however, that it was this very "sociology of harmonious social development", patterned on the above lines, which was in demand amongst "customers" of sociology at that time and which was favoured in academic circles. This somewhat simplified and exaggerated image of Swedish sociology in its social (and socio-political) context contains a number of question marks and needs further elaboration, of course.

One problem concerns basic theoretical premises. The predominant theory – even if this is seldom stated clearly and openly – is structural functionalism. And even if this does not mean that the majority of sociologists would ever subscribe to some version of structural functionalism as formulated by Talcott Parsons and others, there is nevertheless more than a passing and coincidental link between key premises within that type of theorizing and the tacit theoretical premises of much sociological research in Sweden. In classical American structural functionalism, the notion of normative community and integration is also of central importance; it is particularly well developed in some of the middle-range theories, as elaborated e.g. by Robert Merton. Parsons's direct influence on Swedish sociology is however minimal. Segerstedt did not have Parsons as his source of inspiration, and of his pupils, only Bengt Rundblad and Bo Andersson – apart from Hans Zetterberg – had direct contact with the theoretical research on structural functionalism at Harvard. In textbooks written during these years, the Swedish sociologists do not profess to adhere to Parsons's basic model for social development based on equilibrium.

Instead, what characterized Swedish sociology and its view of society was that society was more or less taken for granted – and even equated with the state. In this respect the views of Swedish sociologists reveal a closer resemblance to the system of Segerstedt. The latter's own theory of normative integration terminates with the "framework system of norms" (the source of norms) and lacks a macro-theory to account for how this framework system comes into being or develops. This scientific perspective can be illustrated in part by the standard textbook referred to above, *Svensk samhällsstruktur i sociologisk belysning*, in which "structure" is defined as "a uniformity regulated by social norms", and the proper object of sociological research as "... the behaviour of individuals in comparison with other individuals seen from the perspective of uniformity or deviation from uniformity" (30). The articles in *Svensk samhällsstruktur* have moreover little to say about the concept of social structure itself and the possible factors lying behind social development. A partial exception in this regard is a discussion by Gösta Carlsson, who does not deal with the concepts of structure or society, however, but with social forces and classes in society as well as with contemporary research on these phenomena (31).

The second necessary qualification that must be made to the simple picture of Swedish sociology during its rather productive period of consolidation in the 1950s and 1960s has to do with the empirical results of research. It is probably true that Swedish sociology would have benefited in its development from a critical dialogue with a "grand theory" (cf. the quotation from Johan Asplund above). In the absence of such a dialogue, however, sociology developed perhaps more in a dialogue with empirical reality and empirical research. While large amounts of sociological research undoubtedly served a census-like function in order to gather material for political ends and planning needs, it often produced unforeseen and poorly fitting results that neither remained unknown nor could be simply reconciled to "faulty normative integration in society". I have in mind here, for example, the sociology of work and its development during the 1960s as well as the studies of living standards conducted by the state inquiry into low incomes also during the 1960s (32).

An alternative theoretical framework or a request for one thrust itself forward from below, from students and parts of the younger teaching and research staff. The alternative was certainly not always adapted to providing direct answers to the questions that can be assumed to have popped up in the research of the earlier generation. International influences also played a role here, i.e. actions taken to bring about a reorientation followed in the tracks of, or took place parallel to, similar developments abroad.

During the years that followed it was not only the predominant direction taken in sociological research in Sweden that was attacked with respect to its epistemological premises and battery of methods. The "source of norms" was also questioned, including the standard literature, the teachers, and their teaching. Interestingly enough, the attempts to renovate the discipline were facilitated by the government's policy on higher education. It was certainly not the result of any conscious planning on the government's part, but the disorder following from the various reforms of the university's sphere was often rather tumultuous – and thereby opened the door for changes from within.

Sociology of Conflict in a Society of Consensus

"During this period society disappeared from the ambit of Swedish sociology, at least for its younger generation ..."

"On the contrary! It was only then and with this generation that society was brought into Swedish sociology."

This exchange of words took place during a discussion on Swedish sociology at Lund, between the lecturer (Professor Walter Korpi) and his former pupil from the department at Stockholm in the 1960s (Professor Sune Suneson, now at Lund). The period referred to is the beginning of the 1970s, and as the quotations illustrate, there can be a difference of opinion about what happened then. It is also tempting of course to interpret this exchange as a sort of mirror of the situation as well.

Swedish sociology of an earlier time had certainly devoted itself to empirical reality. However, it had done so in such a myopic fashion that the basic functions of society had not been made clear. Those with fresh ideas helped make these things clear but they did so (at least to begin with) in such a fundamentalist fashion that the empirically given society tended to "disappear". The purely visible gave way to the purely essential – at least temporarily.

The early 1970s marked the beginning of a reorientation of sorts in sociology. It was a reorientation both with respect to attitudes to theory and method and, by extension, to attitudes to the prevailing relation between theory and social practice. The reorientation had however much to do with extra-scientific events and to these could be reckoned shifts in the ideological and political climate, including an increased consciousness

of the world beyond Sweden's borders as well as of structurally determined injustices in Sweden itself. In the international literature just prior
to this period, one particular theme in descriptions of the state of sociology was prevalent, namely that of a "crisis" of sociology. Such talk was
not least common in American sociology and what was being referred to
was the questioning of the research tradition of structural functionalism.
The view of social integration as espoused by that tradition was criticized
for being an abstract circular argument or even a purely ideological
description of society. Probably this version of the critique of sociology
was especially applicable to Swedish sociology on account of the
similarities in basic theoretical premises between Swedish and American
sociology noted above. This is not to say that the "crisis" in Swedish
sociology did not have its specially Swedish attributes owing to the
development of Swedish society and Swedish sociology's interpretation
of this development.

In the view of Ulf Himmelstrand, Segerstedt's successor at the
Uppsala chair and for many years a highly active sociologist not least
internationally, e.g. as President of the International Sociological
Association, the crisis in Swedish sociology coincides with an ever worse
fit between what was happening in the world and in Sweden and what
was printed in the sociological textbooks (33). The history of Swedish
sociology during these years is in addition closely tied to the history of
the new left in Sweden. The ideas and the social commitment that were at
the heart of the young left-wing during the years around 1970, and which
manifested themselves in Third World groups, the Vietnam movement,
etc., re-echoed in the attempts at reform that were introduced into the
social sciences. It appeared to be easier to translate these into the
language of sociology than that of the neighbouring disciplines.

Events within the various departments cannot be viewed in isolation
from the restructuring of the system of higher education that was taking
place at the same time, and which had a marked impact on the social
sciences. Thus as far as concerns the universities and in particular the
faculties of social science, the 1960s were marked by increasing conflicts.
In part they were related to the growing pains resulting from a sharp
increase in student enrollments and in part to ideological frictions. These
strains in turn were clearly brought forth by new demands put on the
universities by society and the concomitant attempts to reform higher
education and adapt it to societally and politically defined objectives, be
they directly policy-oriented or more generally related to perceived needs

on the labour market. These conflicts received their manifest expression in the so-called student revolt, which certainly affected the departments of sociology.

When it comes to factors internal to sociology, the reorientation in Sweden took place in the wake of and parallel to a couple of debates in the subject: one called the soft-data debate, and the other later christened by one Swedish observer, Anders Gullberg, the "values debate". The former debate was initiated with the article by Zetterberg referred to above and was held almost exclusively on the pages of the journal *Sociologisk Forskning*. The "values debate" was begun in the "academic underbrush" (to use Gullberg's phrase) amongst radical students and lecturers some time around 1968 (34). It took place in a much broader forum and the contributions to it were not at all addressed solely to fellow-wanderers on the academic path, even though they had a considerable effect on sociology in particular. Alongside the "values debate" as well as a part and consequence of it, critical discussions were held in the departments of sociology throughout the country concerning the sociology that was taught, and disputes occurred over required readings and institutional resources. A reform of the system of higher education that was designed amongst other things to democratize the decision-making process at the institutional level helped give the voice of the students somewhat greater weight than previously.

These reforms can in turn be seen in the light of general political and economic developments, that is, as one step in attempts to subject educational policy, both in the elementary and secondary schools and in the colleges and universities, to principles of democracy and equality as well as to the primary goals of industrial and employment policies. These efforts towards rationalization were not unique to Sweden. In the 1960s similar suggestions to streamline undergraduate education were put forward in Norway (the Ottesen Committee) and France (the Fouché Plan), for example. At the same time, higher education in Great Britain has for example remained largely unchanged at the traditional universities, while a new organization has been put into place at the new polytechnics and colleges. It is probably fair to say that the model chosen in Sweden for restructuring higher education in its expansive phase and the form in which it was implemented exacerbated the strains. It was namely decided to channel possible conflicts resulting from the combination of expansion and restructuring to the universities' own bodies. This occurred through the launching of various experimental arrangements for the direction of the departments and by giving the students somewhat greater representation (and thereby greater influence) than before.

In most cases this increase in representation did not have any significant impact on the internal development of the respective discipline. Neither mathematics, physics, nor medicine, nor for that matter the larger part of the subjects within the technical or natural sciences or even the social sciences as a whole, was significantly affected by the increase in student representation or by their demands for renewal in course literature and instruction. However, it did have such an effect on sociology, something which can be traced in a study of changes in course literature between 1967 and 1972. The study concludes that reading lists were changed such that micro-sociology (socio-psychology) yielded to macro-sociology. Moreover, the predominance of structural functionalism in the theoretical literature declined and its position was taken over by Marxist literature as well as literature dealing with questions of the theory of science and the theory of knowledge (35). Of course, one should not exaggerate the role of the students in this reorientation, not even within the departments. After all, younger members of the teaching and research staff were at least as active (36). In the state of flux that prevailed, one current pushed forward with increasing strength: Marxism.

Marxism had held a rather marginal position in sociology before 1968. Apart from the book on the Swedish social structure from a sociological perspective, as well as textbooks on method in both Swedish and English and one or two books in Swedish that surveyed special fields, the reading lists in sociology largely comprised American "readers" written in the tradition of structural functionalism. Within this tradition in the United States, Marxism was regarded as an exception. These textbooks contained one or two references to Marx and Marxism but seldom any examples or for that matter criticism that might enlighten the student of sociology about the drift of these theories.

Similarly, Marx and Marxism did not play a very significant role for the first Swedish sociologists (except as a source of fresh ideas, cf. the quotation of Bo Andersson above). References to Marxism occur extremely sporadically in Swedish textbooks and research up until the end of the 1960s. If we look beyond sociology, political scientists (e.g. Herbert Tingsten) analysed Marx and helped thus create a standard interpretation for the social sciences in Sweden (an interpretation that hardly encouraged one to look further into Marx's work). All the while, however, selected readings in Marxist literature and biographies of Marx were published, and a noticeable increase in these publications occurred in the mid-1960s. None of these books, however, constituted an immediate and important source of inspiration for Swedish sociology, and it was only later that they appear on course reading lists. The first books that can be said to be intended directly for sociologists – and written by sociologists – are Göran Therborn *et al., En ny vänster* ("A New Left") (1966), a translation of Marcuse's book *One-Dimensional Man* (1968), and Joachim Israel's book *Alienation fran Marx till modern sociologi* ("Alienation from Marx to Modern Sociology") (1968).

The book of Therborn and others is by and large a settling of accounts with the type of social science then predominant in Sweden, for although the book is mainly a declaration of the programme of a new left-wing to the left of social democracy, it contains important and influential criticism of the postulates of social science, including a criticism of the "interest model" used in research in industrial sociology and business administration. (The model presumes a harmonious development of relations within the field of working life and thus constitutes a striking example of the outlook of the social sciences.)

Marcuse's volume is, of course, too well-known to require any presentation in this context. It should be noted, however, that it contained a message clearly at odds with previous practices of Swedish sociologists, namely the (implicit) message that there is a special chance for the social scientist to bring the masses to their senses and to help inspire them to break out of the strait-jacket they have been put into through the development of industrial capitalism. Israel's book on alienation, finally, shows in theoretical respects a family resemblance to Marcuse and the tradition of the Frankfurt school. However, it is not a handbook for radical sociologists about how to transform society, but rather a theoretical survey of the theme of alienation within classical and modern social science. What distinguishes this book is that it places Marx and Marxism in relation to sociology and its theoretical problems.

When Marcuse's and Israel's books became available the period of change had already begun at the departments of sociology. Neo-Marxist thinking had already got a foot inside the door there, but it was Marxism of a sort different from that suggested and recommended by both Marcuse and Israel. Both of their books (and especially Israel's) were received by the young radical sociologists with a certain amount of criticism. Both works could nevertheless be found on course reading lists (Israel's work on alienation, in various revised editions, proved to be the longer lived of the two).

The variant of neo-Marxist thinking that came to predominate amongst Marxist-oriented academic sociologists from the beginning of the 1970s on, particularly in Lund, was a type of structuralism inspired in particular by the French "Althusser school" and with Göran Therborn as its chief exponent within Swedish sociological circles. Behind this development probably lay several factors, of which some were of random nature but others could be related to the development of the discipline in Sweden both with regard to the noted discrepancy between theory and reality and to the theoretical development of Swedish sociology in general (37).

For sociology, Marxism is not just a critical research tool. It also carries the promise of serving as an all-encompassing theory of society, a macro-theory, on which to base research. This is a feature that I believe had some significance for the reception given Marxism in Swedish social science in the late 1960s and early 1970s. Along with the establishment of Marxism in the Swedish social sciences can be noted the effects of a parallel change of position made by parts of the left-wing with relations to social democracy. From a Marxist perspective, sections of Swedish sociology – and of the social sciences in general – appeared above all as apologists for the political ideology and strategy of social democracy and for the welfare state for which this strategy must take a large share of the credit. This was indeed one of the strong points of the Althusserian school with its structural critique and its attempts to reformulate an over-arching concept of society for the social sciences.

The first rather abstract definitions made by this school – and, certainly, Althusser's style of writing contributed to the level of abstraction in presentations – were worked over at various academic centres with varying degrees of success. One of the more successful efforts to make the ideas more concrete was the work of Althusser's disciple, Nicos Poulantzas. In Sweden, Poulantzas's book on political power and social classes was translated as early as 1970 and probably came to be a more important introduction to structuralist Marxism for sociologists and other social scientists than the texts of his master. The school won adherents among social scientists interested in concrete macro-analyses of the development of Swedish society. For this task the school offered tools for an alternative analysis of the various parts of society, such as the labour market and working life, regional development, the educational system and so on. What was particularly important in this connection was that this theory, or school, provided something that had previously been conspicuous by its absence in Swedish sociology: a theory of the state and the growth of the public sector, seen in a wider perspective of the social sciences.

In sum, the path was hereby cleared for Marxism to enter into the academic study of sociology. This meant however that classical macro-oriented sociology as a whole was strengthened, for a reorientation with regard to the classical questions of sociology was unavoidable once sociologists had begun to ask questions about what it is that holds society together at all. Ulf Himmelstrand has pointed out that the introduction of Marxism helped make visible conflicts in society and in social development (38). It also helped implicitly to bring out the tradition of sociological ideas that had remained more or less hidden in the American anthologies and at all events had not been treated as problems in sociological training. This is true both of the classics of sociology and of structural functionalism, includings its Swedish variant. On the whole, the classics had been rather quiet about the epistemological foundations of their own work and had hardly touched on them except in rather sweeping terms as rules for their intellectual craft. It is likely that this state of affairs, together with the reorientation of the discipline, contributed to the great increase in interest in discussions and literature on the philosophy of science that, as many have noted, took place at this time (39).

It took a few years before this reorientation made its mark on doctoral theses in sociology. But otherwise, when it came to research, developments in Sweden followed those abroad. Marxism and its various reinterpretations all came to share a place with the problems of classical sociology. The weaknesses of structuralist Marxism would be worth mentioning in this connection. In general terms, the weak point was a lack of a theory of social action. The structuralist approach of the school had no need of a subject who acted and for that reason was branded as the very sort of mechanical positivism that it was in part intended to replace. The declining popularity of the school, at least in its pure version, in Sweden is related to this weakness but also of course to the development of Marxism in the world. As a continuation of this reorientation in Swedish sociology, a number of books then appeared in the 1970s and 1980s that offered unusual interpretations of Marxism. The integration of Marxism into the academic study of sociology and sociological research also helped facilitate and prepare the way for the inroads made, for example, by different versions of feminism in the 1970s and 1980s. That development lies outside the scope of this article, however.

A "Swedish" Sociology in the Swedish Welfare State?

But where does Swedish sociology stand in all this and how is it faring? Does there even exist a "Swedish sociology", i.e. a distinctively Swedish variant of the myriad of sociologies in the world? A peculiarly national characteristic is contingent in part upon the relation of a social science discipline to the rest of society, in part upon the openness of the discipline for impulses from outside, and in part upon what those active in developing the discipline have considered to be worth struggling for.

When it comes to the importance of social relations for the growth of the discipline, I thus partly agree with Erik Allardt when he suggests that "certain features of Swedish sociology could be accounted for in terms of the same factors and processes used to explain why social democracy has been especially strong in Sweden and why it was in Sweden that the Scandinavian welfare state achieved its greatest success" (40). Quite naturally, sociology, in part a policy science, has been shaped by its interaction with social policies and has in the process refined its theoretical outlook on society. The identity of Swedish sociology as a discipline has thus also changed in pace with – or at least in dialogue with – changes in the social policies pursued by the government. Thus one can regard developments in all the phases dealt with above as "Swedish" after a fashion.

A second Swedish trait relates to methods and methodological developments, even if this has also shifted over the years, as well as to theoretical outlook. In the recently completed appraisal of Swedish sociology, those responsible (Erik Allardt, Sverre Lysgard, and Aage Sörensen) state that Swedish sociology managed the upheavals of the late 1960s and early 1970s fairly well, at least in comparison with the other Scandinavian countries, not least because of the thorough training in method Swedish sociologists had received and their general consensus on the importance of a sound knowledge of method (41). I believe this observation to be correct as well. For various reasons, some of them historical, the development of Swedish social science has been deeply influenced by the demand for exact and reliable methods, and these demands have been looked after and further refined.

Finally, whatever the characteristically Swedish aspects and the Swedish contribution to sociology in general, these certainly owe some debt to the interplay between academic development, the influence of society, and the role of the actors within these spheres. This is as true of

Segerstedt as it is of Walter Korpi and of Göran Therborn, three representatives of the different phases in the development of Swedish sociology analyzed in this article.

Notes and References

1. Katrin Fridjonsdottir (ed.), *Om svensk sociologi. Historia, problem och perspektiv*, Stockholm: Carlssons förlag, 1987.
2. Katrin Fridjonsdottir, "Den svenska sociologin och dess samhälle", in Fridjonsdottir, *op. cit.*, pp. 250–282.
3. See however C.A. Hessler, "Att lära känna samhället", *Statsvetenskaplig tidskrift*, **3**, 1982, concerning Steffen as a teacher and a source of inspiration. See Ake Lilliestam, *Gustaf Steffen: samhällspolitiker och idépolitiker* (Gothenburg, 1960) for a biography on Steffen. (For the literary-minded it might be noted that Gustaf Steffen was August Strindberg's companion and collaborator for a while in the collection of material for Strindberg's book *Bland franska bönder* ("Among French Peasants") with its socio-anthropological character.
4. Gunnar Myrdal, *An American Dilemma*, New York: Harper and Row, 1944.
5. See e.g. G. Myrdal, *Objectivity in Social Research*. New York: Pantheon, 1969. See also Björn A. Hansson, *The Stockholm School and the Development of Dynamic Method*, London: Croom Helm, 1982, and Jan Petersson, *Erik Lindahl och Stockholmsskolans dynamiska metod*, Lund: Lund Economic Studies, No. 39, 1987.
6. Gustaf Sundbärg, *Emigrationsutredningens huvudbetänkande*, Stockholm, 1913; E.H. Thörnberg, *Folkrörelser och samhällsliv i Sverige*, Stockholm: Bonniers, 1943. See also Segerstedt's and Pfannenstil's contributions in *Om svensk sociologi (op. cit.* cf. note 1) for a discussion of "early sources of inspiration".
7. For a discussion of developments in Swedish philosophy during this period see S. Nordin, *Från Hägerström till Hadenius*, Trelleborg: Doxa, 1984.
8. Of the professors of philosophy during the 1930s and 1940s, Einar Tegen, who worked both at Lund and Stockholm, seems to have had great importance as a teacher and source of inspiration.
9. See Segerstedt's article in *Om svensk sociologi (op. cit.* cf. note 1).
10. See the report *Betänkande angånde socialvetenskapernas ställning vid universiteten och högskolerna m.m* avgivet av socialvetenskapliga forskningskommittén, Stockholm: Staten Öffentliga Utredninga 1946: 74 (in the following quoted as SOV 1946: 74).
11. For a description of a similar reorientation in German sociology see e.g. H. Kem, *Empirische Sozialforschung*, Munich: Beck Verlag, 1982.
12. B. Anderson, "Från filosof till sociolog", *Universitet i utveckling, Festskrift till Torgny Segerstedt*, Uppsala: University/Almqvist & Wicksell, 1978, pp. 7–8.
13. G. Karlsson, *Sociologi*, Umeå: Department of Sociology, 1983, p. 1. See also Karlsson's article in *Om svensk sociologi (op. cit.* cf. note 1).
14. See Joachim Israel's article in *Om svensk sociologi (op. cit.* cf. note 1).
15. T. Segerstedt, "American and Swedish Sociology" in A. Kastrup & N.W. Olsson

268   Katrin Fridjonsdottir

(eds.), *Partners in Progress*, Sumner, MD: Swedish Council of America Corp., 1977.

16. Bengt Rundblad, "Traditioner, restriktioner och möjligheter i svensk sociologi" in *Om svensk sociologi* (*op. cit.* cf. note 1), p. 72.

17. Concering this "profile" at a more recent date see E. Allardt *et al.*, *Sociologin i Sverige*, Uppsala: HSFR & UHÄ, 1988.

18. Segerstedt has presented and discussed his theory in a large number of articles, e.g. "The Uppsala School of Sociology", *Acta Sociologica*, no. 1, 1956, pp. 85–119, and "Svensk sociologi förr och nu" in *Om svensk sociologi* (*op. cit.* cf. note 1). See also Segerstedt, *The Nature of Social Reality*, Stockholm: Scandinavian University Books, 1966. The first study in industrial sociology in Sweden – T. Segerstedt & A. Lundquist, *Människan i industrisamhället*, Stockholm: Norstedts, 1952–1955 – is an early example of empirical research based on Segerstedt's normative theory.

19. This is not to say that Segerstedt did not influence his pupils! See e.g. U. Himmelstrand's thesis, *Social Pressures, Attitudes and Democratic Processes*, Stockholm: Almqvist & Wicksell, 1960, and – of course – Hans Zetterberg's "Compliant Actions", *Acta Sociologica*, 1957, pp. 179–201.

20. One of the earliest surveys of Swedish sociology is E. Tegen, "Soziologische Forschung in Schweden seit 1935", *Kölner Zeitschrift für Soziologie*, no. 3, 1948/49. Informative reading is also provided by E. Tegen & B. Rundblad, *A Survey of Teaching of Research in Sociology and Social Psychology at Swedish Universities*, Oslo: Skrivemaskinstua, 1951. Shorter surveys and presentations were published in many places in the 1950s and early 1960s. From its appearance in 1964, *Sociologisk Forskning* has constituted a source of several contributions to the debate on Swedish sociology, e.g. Hans Zetterberg, "Traditioner och möjligheter i nordisk sociologi", no. 3, 1966; Erik Allardt, "Om svensk sociologi", no. 2, 9173; Göran Therborn, "De sociologiska verksamheterna", no. 2, 1973 – to mention a few. Anders Gullberg's booklet *Till den svenska sociologins historia*, Stockholm: Unga filosofers förlag, 1974 (a revised version of an article that appeared in *Häften för kritiska studier*, 1970), is both ambitious and informative and contains moreover an appendix concerning the early period of Swedish sociology. The most up-to-date and inclusive survey is finally the report referred to above from the assessment carried out by Allardt *et al.*, *Sociologin i Sverige*, Uppsala: HSFR & UHÄ, 1988.

21. Allardt (1973), *op. cit.*

22. Therborn (1973), *op. cit.*

23. Johan Asplund, "Sociologistudier i Uppsala i början av sextiotalet" in Fridjonsdottir (ed.), *Om svensk sociologi* (*op. cit.* cf. note 1), p. 136.

24. *Ibid.*, p. 137.

25. For a discussion of this point see e.g. E. Allardt, "Svensk sociologi i ett nordiskt perspektiv" in *ibid.*, pp. 247f.

26. One example is the sociology of work, with which I have dealt in Fridjonsdottir, "Social Change, Trade Union politics, and the Sociology of Work" in Stuart S. Blume *et al.* (eds.), *The Social Direction of the Public Sciences (Yearbook Sociology of the Sciences, Vol. XI)*, Dordrecht: Reidel Publishing Co., 1987. See also E. Dahlström, "The Role of the Social Sciences in Working Life Policy: The

Case of Postwar Sweden", in H. Berglind *et al.* (eds.), *Sociology of Work in the Nordic Countries*, Oslo: The Scandinavian Sociological Association, 1978.
27. Zetterberg (1966), *op. cit.*
28. Some people, students of the present day among them, have sometimes wondered what constituted the vital difference between "hard" and "soft" data and what it was that gave so much intellectual excitement to the "soft-data debate". In other words, the debate must be set in its context and in the light of what was then predominant in Swedish sociology. Those who are keenly interested can be recommended to read the issues of the journal from these years. Some guidance is provided in Gullberg, *op. cit.* For an interesting but later observation about the use of soft methods in Swedish sociology see Göran Ahrne, "Kvalitativ svensk sociologi", *Sociologisk Forskning*, nos. 3/4, 1984.
29. Allardt, *op. cit.*
30. E. Dahlström (ed.), *Svensk samhällsstruktur i sociologisk belysning*, Stockholm: Norstedts, 1959, p. 2.
31. Gösta Carlsson: "Social stratifiering och rörlighet", *Svensk samhällsstruktur i sociologisk belysning*, Stockholm: Norstedts, 3rd ed. 1965, p. 378.
32. The increasing unrest in the labour market during the later '60s, when wild strikes broke out on a large scale, quite likely acted as an alarm clock not only for the parties active on the market but also for sociologists. For example, attempts to explain the causes of the strikes led to a certain reorientation in the sociology of work (see the works of Fridjonsdottir and Dahlström mentioned in note 26 above). The so-called "Låginkomstutredningen" (lit. Low-income inquiry) and the results of its studies of living standards (which showed amongst other things that welfare was not at all as equitably distributed in Sweden as officials had claimed) stirred up an essentially politico-ideological debate, but the researchers hardly remained unaffected – although probably not in exactly the same way events on the labour market (and the results of studies of these events) affected those engaged in the sociology of work. In connection with his work with the studies on living standards for the "Låginkomstutredning", Sten Johansson levelled the following criticism at the normative approach (and its attitudinal surveys) adopted by Swedish sociology: "To ask a person if his needs are satisfied thus does not provide any information about this person's standard of living (actual living conditions) but rather about how effective the social mechanisms in the persons' surroundings are when it comes to controlling his or her level of demand." S. Johansson, *Om levnadsnivåundersökningen*, Allmänna bokförlaget, 1970.
33. U. Himmelstrand, "Sociologikrisens efterbörd" in *Om svensk sociologi* (see note 1).
34. Gullberg, *op. cit.*
35. U. Himmelstrand *et al.*, "Ett universitetsämnes innehåll: Utvecklingstendenser inom svensk sociologi under åren 1967–1972", *Sociolognytt*, no. 6, 1974, p. 24.
36. Amongst the older generation there were also some who welcomed the "reorientation": see B. Pfannenstil, "Från praktisk filosofi till sociologi" in *Om svensk sociologi* (see note 1).
37. Concerning this development, although mainly from the perspective of Lund, see also G. Therborn, "Brytningarnas och genombrottens årtionde – den unga

vänstern och resten av 1960–talet" in L. Wikström (ed.), *Marx i Sverige*, Stockholm: Arbetarkultur, 1983.

38. See U. Himmelstrand's article in *Om svensk sociologi* (see note 1).
39. Cf. the studies of changes in course reading lists 1967–1972 (note 35).
40. E. Allardt, "Svensk sociologi i ett nordiskt perspektiv" in *Om svensk sociologi* (see note 1), p. 248.
41. See Allardt *et al.*, (1988), *op. cit.*

PART V

THE INSTITUTIONALIZATION OF ECONOMICS:
EDUCATIONAL PRACTICES, STATE POLICIES,
AND ACADEMIC RECOGNITION

CHAPTER ELEVEN

POLITICAL ECONOMY TO ECONOMICS VIA COMMERCE: THE EVOLUTION OF BRITISH ACADEMIC ECONOMICS 1860–1920

KEITH TRIBE

The Reception of Classical Political Economy

The story of the development of economics as a systematic body of theoretical knowledge is routinely held to begin with Smith's *Wealth of Nations* (1776). The work of Ricardo, so the story goes, then constitutes the first significant intellectual advance on Smith; his *Essay on Profits* (1815) and *Principles of Political Economy and Taxation* (1817) build upon Smithian foundations but develop a systematic theoretical core for economic theorising. Following a simplified linear account of the discipline, during the years from 1830 to 1870 it is thought that there is much work done that is of lasting interest; but only in the 1870s does a genuine theoretical shift take place with the so-called 'Marginal Revolution', leading on in Britain through the work of Jevons and Marshall to the elaboration of economics in its modern guise.

This picture of the course taken by the evolution of British economics is over-simplified, but it has one major practical consequence which interests us here: Britain is thereby endowed with the reputation of being the country in which economics as we understand it today first assumed recognisable form. Recent accounts of Italian, German and American economics which consider the pace and depth of the developments they describe take as read a standard which originates in later eighteenth-century Scotland and early nineteenth-century England (1). From the point of view of these national commentaries, modern economics emerges in each case towards the end of the nineteenth century. The issue thereby arises as to why the theoretical advances associated with the names of

P. Wagner, B. Wittrock, and R. Whitley (eds.), Discourses on Society: Volume XV, 1990, 273–302.
© 1990 *Kluwer Academic Publishers. Printed in the Netherlands.*

Smith and Ricardo did not have an earlier, or more decisive, impact on their respective national cultures. The problem thereby focuses on the apparently slow rate of international diffusion of a theoretical innovation originating in Britain which, while freely available through the nineteenth century in translation and popularisation, for some reason has a 'delayed start' elsewhere.

Such a perspective overlooks the fact that like is not being compared with like. When Italian, German or American writers think of the 'lead' of Britain they invariably have in mind the work of Smith, Ricardo and perhaps J.S. Mill, none of whom were 'professional economists' in the sense of living from their teaching or writing. When these modern commentators consider their own national products, they look to work produced by writers who, by the end of the century, support themselves by teaching the subject in university and college. In fact, modern economics is synonymous with the economics taught in academic institutions and this form emerges at about the same time in all in-dustrialising countries – during the closing years of the nineteenth century. Far from Britain being the undisputed originating force for economic analysis, the emergence of an academic economics in Britain conforms to the international pattern and does not in fact deviate from it in focus or timing. The need felt by many commentators to explain the slow rate of acceptance of formal economic analysis in their own countries turns out to be just as much a problem for explanation in the case of Britain.

Why then does it take so long for economic principles to become a body of knowledge diffused through British educational institutions? In part of course this takes us into problems relating to the prevailing patterns of formal education in both Scottish and English schools and colleges, such that for England at least it seems sufficient to point to the apparently backward state of most forms of formal education relative to emerging industrial competitors. Given the ostensible public relevance of the new domain of economic theorising to Britain as an industrialising nation, the acceptance of its principles and theorems as material to be systematically taught seems from this perspective unduly slow. Whether this phenomenon should be counted as a symptom or a cause of 'backwardness' then becomes in turn a matter for debate.

The mistake in posing the problem in this fashion is to assume that the relevance of economics as a component of a modern curricular structure has been eternally self-evident to those who, at one time or another, have controlled this aspect of the educational system. Put another way, it considers only the supply side of the equation and fails to take into account the existence or strength of demand – or rather, insofar as the latter is taken into account, the weakness of the demand which can be registered is treated as a problem rather than a phenomenon in its own right. We can however turn this problem-set on its head. Put baldly, we could ask the question: if there had been such a thing as a B.Sc. (Econ.) in Britain in 1870, what would it have looked like, who would have wanted one and why? And conversely, since there was no such thing in Britain or anywhere else, it should be no surprise that a modern economics with its attendant professional and institutional structure did not exist.

Accordingly, rather than document the various reasons which might contribute to an explanation of the 'failure' of the evident theoretical insights of a Smith or a Ricardo to penetrate the apparatus of formal education, attention should instead be redirected to the general nature of educational provision and the kinds of demands made upon it, and the manner in which this affected both the nature of the political economy that was propagated, as well as the pace of diffusion. In this context the question of the demand for teaching in economics assumes a more complex form, involving consideration of the media through which this discourse was directed and amplified.

As it happens, even in the case of Adam Smith this question provides interesting results: consideration of the actual contemporary reception of *Wealth of Nations* has shown that the relative success of the work as a publishing venture did not translate very rapidly into a definite intellectual impact (2). Likewise, the rate of publication in economic treatises and pamphlets of some general interest was very low in Britain right up to the end of the Napoleonic Wars and the associated debates on the Corn Laws. The decisive expansion in writing, discussion and publication of political economy takes place during the 1820s and not before.

Political Economy and Public Administration

Nonetheless, when the East India Company decided in 1804 to establish a training institution for its recruits in England, a "Professor of History, Political Oeconomy and Finance" was written into the programme of teaching, a position which Malthus accepted in July 1805 and occupied until his death in 1834 (3). While the founders of the college provided no explicit rationale for their action, it is evident that in placing political economy on the curriculum for future company civil servants they sought to provide some element of 'vocational' training. However, it should be noted that throughout Malthus' long teaching career he used as his principal textbook the *Wealth of Nations*; there was little or no discussion of Indian economic institutions, for example, such as the recruits might expect to encounter in their future employment. Political economy was taught to the cadets as a body of principles; if such principles were coloured by their British context, so much the better, since this would assist administrators in their civilising role. The teaching of law was conducted according to a similar rationale. In this way, the East India College provides a model for general administrative education of a type that subsequently did not develop in Britain.

The closure of the college during the 1850s as part of the 'nationalisation' of the company and the reform of the Civil Service put an end to this. Some training in political economy remained part of the educational requirements for the Indian Civil Service, but in the new examinations administered by the Civil Service Commissioners political economy was assigned a very minimal role. It might be supposed that the new 'science' of political economy was one admirably suited to the purposes of the reformers of the Civil Service, insofar as one of the major aspects of the reforms which began in the 1850s was the progressive rationalisation and standardisation of the educational background of recruits. In Germany the teaching of economics in the university had always been closely linked to the administrative requirements of state and principality; with the extension of central and local government activity in mid-Victorian Britain it would seem logical that some kind of vocational qualification in economics and commerce would become *de rigueur* for the aspiring state official. A closer examination of the structure of administration and the nature of reform activity in mid-century fails to bear this out, however; the pedagogical model developed by the East India Company in the first decade of the nineteenth century for the training of administrators – a training in history, political economy, law and languages – was not imitated with the reform of recruitment and qualification for the Home Civil Service.

The most famous statement of mid-century administrative reform was the "Report on the Organisation of the Permanent Civil Service" (1853), commonly known under the names of its signatories as the Northcote-Trevelyan Report. This brief document was in part a summary of recent departmental investigations and reports (beginning with Trevelyan's investigation of the Colonial Office in 1849) (4), all of which emphasised problems of corruption and inefficiency arising from the patronage system of recruitment and promotion, recommending that some form of qualifying examination be introduced, that promotion be solely on grounds of merit and that the work of the Service itself be systematically arranged in terms of a division between routine clerical work and work which involved a higher degree of responsibility.

Admission to the Civil Service, argued Trevelyan and Northcote in their report, was sought after not because it provided an opportunity to serve the state, but because it provided a haven for the indolent. Furthermore they argued that promotion was also a matter of patronage to the general detriment of the efficiency of government. The proposed solution to this problem was the introduction of a general qualifying examination coupled with the standardisation of qualifications across departments through the creation of a central board which would in effect establish general standards for recruitment and promotion within the Service:

... we need hardly allude to the important effect which would be produced upon the general education of the country, if proficiency in history, jurisprudence, political economy, modern languages, political and physical geography, and other matters, besides the staple of classics and mathematics, were made directly conducive to the success of young men desirous of entering into the public service. (5)

While the primary purpose of the report was to alter recruitment procedures and introduce general criteria into the promotion process, this subsidiary objective of exercising influence on the general content of 'secondary' education (6) became important in the marshalling of support for reform. In their crusade against appointment through a patronage system the reformers sought to develop a system based on testimonials and a written preliminary examination in writing, composition, bookkeeping and arithmetic. Successful candidates could then move on to a higher examination, the difficulty being that this meant, *de facto*, examination in classics and mathematics. As many were to point out in the ensuing months, distinction in these subjects was of little relevance in the recruitment of diligent and worthy servants of the state (7); but if the higher examination was to be introduced there was precious little else that it could examine, given the nature of English education. Jowett presumed that more specialised knowledge would be required in some departments,

viz., a knowledge of the principles of commerce, taxation and political economy in the Treasury, Board of Trade etc.; of modern languages and modern history, under which last may be included international law, in the Foreign Office. (8)

This presumption was in fact ill-founded, and pre-supposed educational resources that were in fact barely existent. Furthermore, few government departments chose to specify any qualifications for their recruits beyond bare literacy and numeracy: only the Factory Inspectors Department required "Elements of Political Economy" as the seventh of eighth areas of qualification (9). The Poor Law Board required no more than the basic qualifications, while an ordinary clerk in the Board of Trade was expected to be able to write from dictation, perform elementary arithmetical operations, write a précis, show some geographical knowledge and make a translation from one ancient or modern language (10).

These observations relate of course to the reorganisation of the 'lower reaches' of the Civil Service, an area which embraced messengers, copyists, tide-waiters and postmen among several other categories. The distinction promoted by Trevelyan between 'mechanical' and 'intellectual' labour in the Civil Service would place this heterogeneous group in the former so far as there was any clerical content to their work at all. What then of the recruitment pattern to the 'intellectual' level? With the establishment of Class I Clerkships as a high-level entry point Trevelyan's 'division of labour' was given form; and when the first competition took place in 1872 there were twenty-two candidates for ten vacancies. In 1876, thirty-eight candidates competed for four places; in 1877, sixty-one for eleven. By comparison, during the period 1876–81 1270 men and 416 boy clerks were appointed at the lower level after competition – and in fact for the whole of the later nineteenth century there were never more than an average of ten high-level appointments per year (11).

Leaving aside the merits or otherwise of the pattern of reform introduced in mid-century, the requirement of the central administrative apparatus of the state for general clerical labour was quite small, and for this kind of employment diligence and 'a good hand' (besides 'good character') were all that was required. For the overwhelming majority of civil servants the work demanded of them was routine and required no specific academic training beyond that which was already supplied by school or private tutor. At the higher level the number of places was so limited that it was not worthwhile to establish any particular course of tuition for potential recruits. While in the closing years of the century there was in fact an expanding range of subjects the aspiring Oxford or Cambridge graduate could study, this expansion was not driven by the demand for better-qualified state servants. In fact, while Oxford and

Cambridge underwent a process of reform and modernisation during this period, the dynamic of educational change, and with it the emergence of political economy as a subject to be systematically taught, lies elsewhere, with the civic universities of the provincial cities and the foundation of the London School of Economics (LSE) in 1895.

Educational Reform and Popular Education

The potential significance of the Civil Service reforms lies in the fact that they occurred at an important turning point for the English educational system. From the 1860s, discussion of elementary, secondary and technical education intensified; a series of government commissions reported on the nature and provision of education to all classes of society. Related to this, during the 1870s a number of new provincial colleges were established, aimed at improving the provision of advanced teaching in the humanities and natural sciences. These in turn both drew upon, and supported, public educational initiatives dating back to the early part of the century, initiatives that sought both to widen the educational agenda and extend the social base of formal and informal education. In this context the annual *Reports* of the Civil Service Commissioners became so many surveys of educational standards and attainment among the middle classes, laying the foundations for the critical review of vocational and commercial education that followed Britain's poor showing at the Paris Exhibition of 1868. The recent fashion of identifying a lack of 'industrial spirit' as the root cause of British industrial decline overlooks entirely the vigorous public discussion on the relation of education, science and technology which continued throughout the later part of the century and which forms the background for the emergence of political economy as a component of an adequate commercial education. This was the real driving force that placed political economy within the college curriculum (12).

In 1852 both Oxford and Cambridge universities were the subject of Commissions of Inquiry, and Oxford was over the next two decades a focus for debate on educational reform (13). Although as we shall see both of the old-established English universities did contribute indirectly to the extension of higher education, and a reformed Cambridge did eventually become one of the centres for the development of British economics, neither of the older English universities played a leading role in the processes with which we are concerned here. Indeed, the overall pattern of development within which British economics emerges is made up of a dual sequence: first there emerges in Scotland in the later eighteenth century a discourse on political economy and civilisation which 'migrates' southward in the early nineteenth century in the persons of Mill, Brougham, Horner and others who were influenced by the teaching of Dugald Stewart. The establishment of the University of London (later renamed University College) was one of the major achievements of this tendency, and J.R. McCulloch was installed in its chair of political economy in 1829. By 1830–31 his students had fallen to six, and following his resignation in 1835 teaching lapsed until 1854 (14). Although McCulloch justly enjoys a central place in accounts of early nineteenth-century economics, this is related to his more general popularising and journalistic activities and not to his role as a teacher and college professor. In this respect his contribution was relatively insignificant, compared with that of his contemporary Malthus. Moreover, the relative 'failure' of political economy to become established in the new 'godless college' at this time indicates that it was not merely the Anglican dominance of Oxford and Cambridge, and the associated requirement to submit to a religious test, which hindered the development of new subjects in the university curriculum.

While teaching in political economy did take place at Oxford and Cambridge at this time this was done by professors, i.e. was a university and not a college activity, and the lectures that were delivered in this way were more akin to annual lecture series than lectures systematically exposing a definite body of knowledge. The Drummond Chair in Political Economy, for example, was founded in Oxford in 1825; but incumbents were limited to a five-year tenure in addition to the restrictions imposed by a short series of lectures outside the regular teaching context. As was noted above, the only regular teaching in political economy that can be said to have taken place during the first half of the nineteenth century was at East India College, and this ended in the later 1850s with the termination of the patronage system for recruitment and the introduction of a more open system of examining (15).

Much of the work done at this time in political economy undoubtedly laid the foundations for its later development as an academic discipline, but there is no direct institutional line of descent that can be traced from these early disparate elements. Instead, a second sequence begins in mid-century which is rooted, not in the conventional educational structures of early Victorian England, but rather in a new and popular form of educational culture – the Mechanics' Institutions, academies and other literary and scientific associations. While related to the Dissenting Academies of the eighteenth century, which had provided at that time for the greater part of advanced education in England, the impulse for the Mechanics' Institutions also came from Scotland and was in its beginnings closely related to the emigration process referred to above. The initiator, George Birkbeck, began, on his appointment to the Professorship of Natural Philosophy at Glasgow's Anderson's Institute in 1799, to deliver three-month lecture courses on the 'mechanical properties of solid and fluid bodies' to 'mechanics' (i.e. artisans and skilled workers). When he left Glasgow in 1804 the courses were maintained by his successor, Andrew Ure; and these then formed the basis for the foundation in 1821 of the Edinburgh School of Arts by Leonard Horner. Despite the name, this School can be considered the first 'Mechanics' Institution' (16), and its initial focus on the teaching of practical sciences (chemistry, mechanics and mathematics) reflects the kind of demands placed upon these institutions. When the mechanics' class broke away from the Anderson's Institution in July 1823 to found the Glasgow Mechanics' Institution as an independent entity it too focused on natural philosophy, chemistry, mechanics and mathematics, leasing a disused chapel and hiring a lecturer to do the teaching. The enrolment exceeded 1,000 in its first year (17).

While the Edinburgh School was funded and controlled by prominent citizens, the Glasgow institute was intended to be self-supporting and self-managed (18); and these were to represent options which marked the whole of the movement. Self-management implied the prospects for a political radicalism not open to those bodies controlled by local officials and prominent philanthropists; but almost without exception such independent projects foundered upon the inability of working men to provide adequate financial support for hire of rooms and speakers. Likewise, aspirations to attract labourers and artisans to courses rather than occasional lectures rarely met with any permanent success because the majority of those who enrolled were unable to attend on a regular enough basis. With a few striking exceptions (19) the Mechanics' Movement and later the University Extension Movement were dominated by tradesmen, clerks and middle-class men and women because they were physically able to pursue a connected course of study which represented for the working man an enormous commitment of limited time, cash and energy. The durability of such foundations as genuine vehicles of popular education depended upon the existence of connected courses; occasional lectures on popular topics as the staple activity introduced an element of discontinuity fatal to part-time education, and recreational concerns then soon displaced educational ones – classes ceased, lectures became more infrequent and the reading room and library became dominated by newspapers and light fiction.

Political economy did indeed enter into popular education as a 'practical' subject; but as a 'practical science' of commerce rather than the scientific critique of capitalism conceived by early radicals. "Popular education" naturally unites a number of diverse elements, and in the context of the discussion here it is important to emphasise an emergent divergence of interest and opportunity between two educational constituencies: the first composed largely of working men, and the second composed of middle-class men and women. As will be made clear below, although it was the former constituency that at times assembled the largest audiences for lectures on political economy, it was the directly vocational aspirations of middle-class students that provided the impulse for the development of regular and systematic teaching in political economy.

Over the two decades following the foundation of the original Mechanics' Institution in London several hundred institutions were established, although over times many of them degenerated into social clubs without great educational pretensions. Nevertheless, just as the movement begun by Birkbeck led directly to the founding of the first modern university college in Britain, so too the general development of advanced educational provision built upon the patterns of courses and access established in popular adult education. The first significant provincial foundation was Owens College in Manchester (1851), which catered more for evening rather than day students during its first few years, and was thus directed towards subjects of relevance to specific occupations. Courses had been established in 1853 for teachers, and covered classics and mathematics, soon expanding however to include history and natural history "for young men of business and others"; while by 1860 classes were offered in English literature, French, logic, jurisprudence, chemistry and natural philosophy (20). Staff from Owens also took part in an initiative to found the Manchester Working Men's College, which in its first session in 1858 attracted over 200 operatives, clerks, bookkeepers and warehousemen to a variety of courses including elementary mathematics and political philosophy. Classes were in fact held in the premises of the Manchester Mechanics' Institute, the intention of the organisers however being to present a broader and less directly vocational educational programme than offered by the institute. In 1861 the Working Mens' College merged with the Owens College evening classes, contributing to the domination of evening over day classes, such that in their peak year of 1873–4 there were 900 evening-class students registered at Owens compared with 500 day students.

Extension Teaching and the Function of Political Economy

While this gives an indication of the symbiosis between local cultural and educational initiatives and the development of college institutions, this interplay is seen at work most clearly in the development of university extension teaching during the 1870s. Born out of general concern with the role of Oxford and Cambridge as educational institutions in mid-century, a number of proposals had been made for opening up these universities to a wider constituency. While opinion in Oxford tended to favour "extension" in terms of the establishment of satellite institutions, in Cambridge the model of peripatetic lecturing developed, building upon the more regular aspects of Mechanics' Institution activities. Local societies were to create the constituencies of fee-paying auditors, who would then be visited by a lecturer providing a course of study in a specified subject. This arrangement provided for complete flexibility, since the venues were hired and paid for out of the fees, as were the lecturers themselves. In this way residents of provincial towns and cities gained access to systematic teaching at a level hitherto barred to them.

The first lectures delivered under the auspices of the University of Cambridge were delivered in Derby and Leicester in October 1873. Three courses were advertised in Derby:

Political Economy – V.H. Stanton, Fellow of Trinity, "adapted to Working Men"
English Literature – E.B. Birks, Fellow of Trinity, "Mainly for Ladies"
Force and Motion – T.O. Harding, Fellow of Trinity, "Mainly for Young Men engaged in commercial and professional pursuits". (21)

This distribution of courses between 'working men, ladies and young men' was complemented by a division between daytime and evening lectures, in which women primarily attended the former and working men overwhelmingly the latter, paying for the lectures and classes on different

scales (22). By 1875–76 Cambridge had over 100 such courses functioning at various centres, the total attendance averaging 10,000. With the
addition of a programme run from London in 1876, this represented a
substantial audience for systematic teaching and examination in political
economy, such that out of 457 courses on offer in 1890–91 from Oxford,
Cambridge and London, 159 were in history or political economy, the
largest single subject category (23).

In the first term of operation of the London Society in 1876–77 there
were seven courses, two of which were in political economy and taught
by H.H. Asquith of Balliol College. The evening course at the London
Institute cost 10/6d. and had twenty-two students registered, while an
afternoon course in Wimbledon had thirty-five students paying 21s. each.
Political economy therefore attracted slightly under half the total number
of students, and contributed more than half the fee income in the first
session (24). In 1878 Henry Sidgewick reported on the papers of students
who had sat in Putney and Wimbledon, stating that

The average level of the answers is considerably higher than that of undergraduates
who pass the University Examination ... Moreover, several of the papers are distinctly
better than those of the candidates for the Fellowship [candidates presenting political
economy as a special subject]. (25)

This initial success for political economy in the London extension did not
persist, however; in the early 1880s the subject disappeared from the
courses offered, not, we might suppose, on account of a shortage of
competent lecturers – among them were Edgeworth, Bonar and Toynbee
– but because of a temporary shift in the demands of students. It does
seem likely that there was at this time a decline in the interest among
middle-class students which for a period went uncompensated by the
working-class centres of East London. In any case, when the subject re-
emerged in 1886 it had its most striking popular success in Poplar, where
Armitage-Smith enrolled 155 for the course and had an average attendance of 230 (including casual attenders), with sixty in the weekly class.

The audience, as in the case of the other East-End Centres, was drawn largely from
the working classes, and included workmen engaged in shipbuilding, boiler-makers,
coopers, sawyers, and dock-labourers. The class following the Lecture was so
thoroughly appreciated by the audience, as often to be protracted to a late hour. (26)

On the other hand, Armitage-Smith had in the same period a group of thirty-six meeting at Birkbeck College composed chiefly of clerks in banks and City houses, with a few "men of business", two or three workmen and "a few ladies probably teachers" (27).

A significant divergence between the predominantly middle-class groups which met at Birkbeck and similar centres, and the working-class groups in Poplar and Bethnal Green, was that the latter did little in the way of formal preparation and rarely sat the associated examinations, while the former group did both. In the cases noted above, the Poplar class of sixty averaged five papers handed in per week, while the Birkbeck class averaged twenty-four and produced an average of eleven papers per week. Nine of the Poplar students entered the examination, as against ten from the Birkbeck group. This indicates that the extension movement, in London at least, was serving two distinct audiences for political economy. The working-class audience was numerically significant but chiefly (and predictably) interested in the subject as a form of 'enlightenment' concerning the workings of the society they lived in. This audience wished to attend informative lectures and afterwards engage in discussion; in this respect this aspect of the demand for extension teaching was continuous with the more radical aspirations of the earlier Mechanics' Institutions. The middle-class audience – men as well as women – had on the other hand a more directly vocational interest and both worked at the subject and sat the examinations. While this group was at times numerically eclipsed, its demands were more important to the overall development of the teaching of political economy, for in London at any rate it was this grouping which went on to form the early constituency of the LSE when it was founded in 1895 (28). Likewise in the provinces, while the 'working class' demand was significant in the dissemination of economic argument, it was the more strictly vocational demands of the emergent middle class which formed the basis for the transformation of the 'peripatetic' extension movement into one supportive of the foundation of local colleges.

Extension lectures and classes required merely a local demand and sufficient finance to pay for the lecturer and the hire of rooms (often those of a local Mechanics' or Literary institute). Developing this constituency of interest in higher education, once registered, into a more permanent local institution was a large and complicated step – buildings, equipment and endowment of departments and chairs were necessary, and the simple proposition of founding a local college also implied long argument over the range of subjects to be taught. As has been noted with Owens College, the moving impetus behind its foundation was in fact the availability of a large endowment which, nonetheless, was not sufficient on its own to resolve the administrative and curricular problems of establishing a new institution. It is however significant that three of the new provincial colleges – Owens College, Mason College (Birmingham) and Firth College (Sheffield) – were named after the local industrialists who provided the initial endowments, while University College Liverpool drew on the considerable wealth and cultural connections of Liverpool merchants and shipowners. The new provincial colleges were financed by local wealth – and the complexion which they assumed as teaching institutions was thereby in turn a reflection upon local cultural and scientific concerns.

The New Civic Colleges and Political Economy

Two important foundations grew directly out of extension teaching: Firth College and University College, Nottingham. In the latter case this built on regular teaching in the Mechanics' Institute which had in 1862 gained some financial support from the Department of Science and Art, but during rebuilding of the institute after a serious fire in 1867 there was discussion of the prospects for the development of a university. An assessment made in April 1871 of the local demand for adult education suggested that an audience existed for teaching in political economy, the science of health, constitutional history and English literature; and subsequently teaching began in literature, political economy and 'force and motion' in the autumn of 1873, 1,832 students being registered for the session (29). When the question of a permanent building was raised an anonymous donor offered £10,000, and after some discussion it was decided that this donation should be used to endow extension lectureships in a building provided by the corporation. This was duly constructed, at a total cost of £70,000, and was completed in 1881. Four professors were appointed, plus six lecturers and demonstrators and also twelve teachers from the science classes transferred from the Mechanics' Institute (30). During the first session the 381 day students were, as was usual for the time, outnumbered by the 623 evening students; moreover the day students were predominantly female, there being ninety-four men to 287 women. This was a pattern common to many of these early foundations and was the outcome of all-important factors such as the availability of time to study and the means of financing it. Furthermore, the day students in such institutions were not usually pursuing a connected course of study – what was on offer was a series of lectures and classes on specific topics, to which a variety of examinations might relate but which were not focused on guiding the student towards sitting external London degrees – although the possibility existed (31).

In 1885 efforts were made to establish a commercial department in the college, based upon an endowment of £200 per annum from a group of local businessmen. A lecturer was hired to equip students with the "requirements of a merchant's office" and a course in commercial history and geography, political economy, mercantile law, bookkeeping, shorthand and modern languages was laid out over three consecutive terms (32). Little came of this, however, and a second attempt with a similar coverage was made in 1888 in collaboration with the Chamber of Commerce. This time the course survived, due perhaps to it having a definite three-year duration. As we shall see, this incorporation of regular college teaching in political economy into commerce courses is significant.

While this is on slight reflection unsurprising, what must be emphasised is the uncertain course charted by political economy in teaching at this time. As has been seen, the subject of political economy was one of the major draws for the extension movement; and yet when the movement became established in permanent institutions it played initially a very minor role. It could be that general interest in the subject waxed and waned, as we have seen in the case of the London extension movement; but it is also probably an effect of the natural and applied scientific bias of the support for such institutions among their benefactors. It was only when more directly commercial interests became involved that the subject was revived under the aegis of commercial education. This can be seen in the case of Liverpool, where MacCunn from Balliol was appointed in December 1881 to the chair of philosophy and political economy; but it was the appointment of E.C.K. Gonner in 1888 to a lectureship in political economy and commercial education which was the significant step forward, injecting a serious commercial content to the two-year old business curriculum, which was then supported by an endowment of £10,000 in 1891 for a chair in economic science (33).

The foundation of Firth College was also a direct consequence of the extension movement. In May 1874 the Sheffield School Board considered introducing university extension teaching, but decided against it on the grounds that they were not responsible for this area. Instead, the mayor and local ironmaster, Mark Firth, called a meeting in late 1874 to specifically discuss how the "extension of higher education to the great towns may best be brought before the public of Sheffield" (34). Cambridge University required that the costs of teaching should be guaranteed by a special fund, but almost as soon as money raising began the target was overshot, and this led to a meeting with James Stuart, W. Moore Ede and A.J. Mundella, MP for Sheffield, at which the prospects for directing educational developments towards the foundation of a university were discussed, Nottingham being cited as an exemplar. Extension teaching began in early 1875 with two courses, one on political economy and one on English literature – as elsewhere, the former took place in the evenings and the latter at midday, reflecting the fact that women attended primarily in daytime and men at night. Following the definite success of such teaching Firth purchased a site and at his own cost commissioned a building designed for popular lectures and extension courses; and as soon as it was available a council was established in 1879 to administer the development of a college. The intention of the foundation, as expressed in a memorandum of September 1879, was stated to be

the promotion of the moral, social and intellectual elevation of the masses, as well as of the middle and upper classes of this town, by means of Lectures and Classes, divested of the desultory character unavoidably attached to the late system of university lectures. Courses ... on subjects of historical, scientific, economic and literary interest will be given ... (35)

The first appointment made was that of the Principal, former Lecturer in Mathematics at Owens College. In November 1879 Firth offered to endow a chair in chemistry, further funds being forthcoming from his family for the equipment of a laboratory. Further appointments at this time were a Professor of Classics and Ancient History, a Lecturer in Modern History, a Lecturer in Modern Languages and a Lecturer in the Theory of Music. The doors of the college were opened to the public in January 1880, students over seventeen being admitted without any examination. Within the first few years teaching in metallurgy and mechanical engineering were also added, although the development of applied sciences such as these in Sheffield was divided between the college and the technical school.

With the transformation of Firth College into University College in 1897 a Department of Philosophy and Economics appeared; but unlike Liverpool, this did not become associated with commercial education.

Here again then we have an instance of the strong interest in political economy typical of extension teaching failing to gain an immediate hold on the established teaching which grew out of the extension; and in this case little in the way of commercial education developed either, presumably because of the predominantly industrial, rather than mercantile, local economy. What we can note is the related emergence of several new provincial institutions: Yorkshire College of Science, Leeds (1874); University College Bristol (1876); Mason College (1880); Firth College (1879); University College Nottingham (1881); University College Liverpool (1881). While teaching in political economy was in one way or another developing in the Oxford and Cambridge colleges, these provincial foundations are far more directly expressive of the actual shape that demand for new teaching took at this period. In particular, it is noteworthy that when in the 1890s teaching on a regular and systematic basis was inaugurated, the context in which these 'economic subjects' appeared was that of a broadly based commercial education. This tendency is sharply illustrated by two further cases which we can consider here, the foundation of the LSE and the development of the B.Com. degree at Birmingham.

The LSE and the Needs of Commerce

Like the provincial colleges, the London School of Economics originated in a bequest – although little of this money was actually absorbed by the institution, which was in the early years self-financing. Like the provincial colleges again, the manner in which the school was set up was makeshift: Hewins was appointed director in March 1895 with a fixed salary, a two-year lease was taken out on some rooms, fees of £3 per session agreed and a prospectus drafted. In fact, teaching began with only three full-time employees – Hewins, his secretary and a porter (36). Lecturers were brought in on a temporary basis, and in this way the first session began in October 1895 with 203 students who attended lectures from Hewins, Cunningham, A.L. Bowley, Foxwell, Cannan, Graham Wallas and others. Together the various offerings made up a training in commerce and political economy, the latter aspect being increasingly emphasised as the school expanded and a definite three-year course was worked out (37). The general objective of the LSE appears to have been to build on the interest revealed in the London extension lectures for higher education in political economy, providing a more permanent base and the possibility of systematically linked courses which then, at the turn of the century, could form the basis for a B.Sc. (Econ.) within the reformed University of London. Sidney Webb did invoke the Ecole des Sciences Politiques and MIT as examples of the kind of teaching which he and his fellow Fabians were interested in promoting. It is sufficient for the time being to note that the LSE appealed initially to those from a more strictly 'commercial' background seeking a training in economics, law and related subjects. With the development of the school it was the latter subjects that came to dominate its character, such that it increasingly moved away from a commercial bias in the first three decades of this century.

In this respect a contrast can be drawn with developments in Birmingham. It was not until 1897 that a professorship in "Mental and Moral Philosophy and Political Economy" was founded, as elsewhere emphasising the non-vocational context in which provincial college teaching in political economy in fact first appeared (38). However, in December 1898 the Chamber of Commerce proposed that a School of Commerce should be established, and in February of the following year a draft course outline was put forward including modern languages, economics, commercial history, commercial geography, elements of commercial law and mathematics with commercial arithmetic (39). £50,000 was donated from Carnegie, and Joseph Chamberlain, one of the moving spirits in the project, persuaded a friend to donate £25,000. The intention of serving the industrial and commercial needs of the Midlands was emphasised by W.J. Ashley, appointed in 1902 to head the new school:

The University of Birmingham is following the example of practical America. We want the ambitious young men of the Midlands, who have already received up to the age of 17 or 18 a secondary education, such as our Grammar Schools or even our Higher Grade Board Schools provide, to come to us for three solid years ... (40)

In a prospectus addressed to potential students of the new faculty, Ashley emphasised that the training they would give was directed to the "officers of the industrial and commercial army" (41), an emphasis made necessary by the fact that the greatest impact in commercial education had hitherto been made in technical schools running practical courses for artisans and clerical employees.

In the same prospectus Ashley outlined a syllabus which had been drafted after consultation with the Birmingham and Midland Society of Chartered Accountants, and due weight was given on the one hand to what Ashley called 'accounting', that is, accountancy for managers rather than professional accountants, while on the other the commerce element covered areas that would today be described as relating to industrial and labour organisation, marketing and finance.

This educational programme was designed for the sons of local businessmen, but it met with little success in this direction. Such sons as were destined for business careers were recruited directly into works or office as before, while those who sought a university education continued to go to Oxford or Cambridge. The overwhelming majority of the faculty's early students were in fact foreign, mostly from the Middle and Far East (42). Secondly, the educational programme was itself intended as a challenge to Marshall's activities in defining the discipline of economics *via* the institution of the Tripos in Economics at Cambridge. It is for this latter reason that Ashley's efforts with Birmingham's Faculty of Commerce have always gained attention, not for any intrinsic importance of the faculty or its organisation itself. It has however become customary to distinguish commercial education from economic science in Britain along the line that separated Ashley in Birmingham and Marshall in Cambridge. Quite apart from the actual content of the teaching in Birmingham, which quite naturally enough emphasised the more practical side of economics teaching, setting up the distinction in this manner has tended to reinforce the conception that Marshall 'succeeded' where Ashley 'failed'. Thus the subsequent development of economics in Britain is associated with the kind of economics propagated discursively by Marshall's *Principles of Economics* and institutionally through the Cambridge Tripos. Certainly the Birmingham Faculty of Commerce had an impact much less than that which had been hoped for it; but this does not mean that the general fate of commercial education in British universities is thereby written. In addition, neither is it accurate to associate Marshall so unequivocally with the route taken by British economics over the subsequent decades, for in many ways the prominence of Marshall's Cambridge is an effect of our sheer ignorance of the rest of the picture making up the development of British economics in the first half of this century (43).

Cambridge and Manchester: Economics and Commerce

Marshall's campaign for the introduction of systematic teaching in economics in Cambridge had two main phases. Returning to Cambridge in 1885, his first move was to bypass the college teaching system and the associated triposes by offering informal instruction to interested students. He then went on to offer an annual prize over five years to be awarded, not for an essay on a set subject, but for performance in an examination (44). This was a ploy to interest students taking the Moral Sciences Tripos in the political economy papers; reform of the tripos in the later 1880s increased the role of political economy within it, although it remained optional. By 1900 there were still only six honours graduates in total in Part II of the Moral Sciences Tripos, and not all of these took political economy as their field of specialisation. This is a fair indication of the general indifference of Cambridge students to the Moral Sciences Tripos; if Marshall were to lend greater prominence to the study of economics some other vehicle was called for.

Accordingly, by the turn of the century Marshall's efforts were bent to the creation of an independent Economics Tripos, through which the subject could gain a visibility denied it as an optional part of the Moral Sciences Tripos. In the course of his campaign Marshall addressed a "Plea for the Creation of a Curriculum in Economics and associated branches of Political Science" to the members of Cambridge Senate. Referring to the recent developments in London and Birmingham, Marshall complained of the relative backwardness of British economics in many areas compared with work in the United States, Germany and elsewhere (45). In particular, he emphasised the absence of systematic training of administrators and businessmen in Britain, and the need for this to be rectified. What contribution could Cambridge make to this? Not, he suggested, merely technical training; he had in view "a broad education which will bear directly on the larger management of affairs" (46). At this point the 'broad education' Marshall had in view was, in detail, not so dissimilar from aspects of the Birmingham B.Com. degree; but the symbolic sticking point turned on the place of accountancy in the training of economists. For Marshall, this was a technical aspect of the subject inappropriate to the range of courses which Cambridge should offer. As we have seen this was on the other hand a central aspect of the Birmingham degree. Moreover, the point is more than technical, for it involves the question of the purpose of training in economics in a university, and the kind of student who might be expected to wish to study the subject.

Marshall's efforts in creating an autonomous economic science were comparable with the teaching done in Birmingham, Manchester, Liverpool and elsewhere. However, there has grown up an idea that the Cambridge Tripos and Marshall's teaching represented a core of knowledge whose diffusion and acceptance was effected through a generation of his students. This perspective gives unwarranted prominence to Marshall and Cambridge. True, Marshall's students did move on elsewhere and play important roles in the development of British economics; but the assumption that they thereby disseminated a core of teaching and principles that originated in Cambridge is an assumption made out of sheer ignorance of what went on outside Cambridge and London. This can be illustrated by considering the role of Manchester University in the development of British economics, an institution noted only in the history of British economics to the extent that Jevons taught at Owens College during the later 1860s and 1870s (47).

When in 1905 Marshall became involved in a debate over the nature of business education conducted through the letters' column of *The Times*, he was responding to criticism made by Sydney Chapman, onetime student of Marshall's and at that time Professor of Political Economy at Manchester (48). Furthermore, the political economy teaching programme that Chapman had taken over and developed in Manchester was the work of A.W. Flux, winner of the Marshall Prize in 1889 and the first student of Marshall's to in fact specialise in economics within the Moral Sciences Tripos.

Flux (49) had begun teaching at Manchester in 1893, leaving in 1901 to become Professor of Political Economy at McGill. During his tenure he did much to regularise the teaching of economics, which at degree level involved an examined component of the ordinary BA degree, and the requirement for honours history students to take a political economy class for one year (50). In 1900 the political economy day classes were as follows:

I.   Descriptive Economics, 1 hr. (seven students)

II.   Economic Theory, 2 hrs. (eleven students)

III.   Industrial and Commercial History of England 1422–1803, 1 hr. (one student)

IV.   Great English Economists and Their Teaching, 1 hr. (two
        students)

V.   History of the English Poor Laws, 1 hr. (for History Honours
        Students)

Apart from the obvious historical component (51), it is important to note
that Flux had divided the theory classes off from those (I and III) attended
by Commercial Certificate students. It is also significant that it is at this
time that day students come to decisively outnumber evening students for
political economy – prior to the year 1901–2 attendances at evening
classes had always predominated, hampering the development of
systematic teaching in the subject. The systematisation of teaching that
followed during the next decade was thus in a context of rising daytime
attendance for students pursuing a course of study directed to sitting
degree-level final examinations. With the formal constitution of an
independent University of Manchester in 1903 an independent Honours
School of Economics and Political Science was formed.

There were few graduates from this school prior to 1914, the bulk of
economics teaching being directed elsewhere – to the Faculty of
Commerce that Chapman had set up soon after his arrival in 1901 and
which on its inception in 1904–5 had sixteen students, in the following
year thirty-one. In Cambridge in 1905 ten students had sat Parts I and II
of the new Economics Tripos – seven in the year following. By 1910 this
figure had risen to twenty-nine, but in this year there were forty-five
students studying in the Manchester Faculty of Commerce. The
economics element of the teaching in the Faculty of Commerce was
shared with the Honours School of Economics and Political Science,
adding to this courses on banking, industry, geography, law, accounting
and modern languages.

Note should also be made of the teachers in Manchester's Faculty of
Commerce, for many of them went on to set up and teach in similar
faculties elsewhere. The first appointments made to the Faculty of
Commerce were in 1903 with the arrival of W.G.S. Adams as a Lecturer
in Commerce and Economics, J. Macfarlane as a Lecturer in Political and
Economic Geography, R.N. Carter as a Lecturer in Accounting and
Drummond Fraser as a Lecturer in Banking. The last two were local
professionals, while Adams came from a year teaching economics in the
Graduate School of the University of Chicago and went on in 1905 to be

Superintendent of Statistics in the Irish Department of Agriculture and subsequently to Oxford to become the first Gladstone Professor of Political Theory. He was replaced in Manchester by H.O. Meredith, another Marshall student, who later was appointed Professor of Economics as Queen's University, Belfast – among his first duties, the *Economic Journal* noted at the time, being "to organise the newly established Faculty of Commerce" (52). Meredith was replaced by Douglas Knoop, the first honours graduate in Manchester who then in 1910 moved on to teach in Sheffield. This marked the beginning of a phase in which Manchester Honours Economics graduates (53) gained appointments in the Faculty of Commerce and then in many cases passed on elsewhere. Hallsworth was for example appointed in 1910, moving to Newcastle in 1911 and in 1912 being promoted to professor, with the task of setting up a Faculty of Commerce; on his promotion his lectureship was filled by another Manchester recruit. Conrad Gill was another Manchester graduate and teacher who moved on, in his case to join Meredith in Belfast.

Space is lacking here for any further detailing of developments in Manchester during the first two decades of this century, but several points deserve emphasis. Firstly, those students of Marshall who passed through Manchester taught in the Faculty of Commerce according to rubrics which Marshall himself opposed. It can be argued that in their subsequent careers it is more relevant to treat them as 'Manchester men' rather than Marshall's students. Secondly, the process of self-recruitment set in early at Manchester, so that by 1910 it was filling its junior posts with its own graduates. This is an important phase in the process of establishing a departmental style and did not develop at the LSE for example until the 1920s (54). Thirdly, from this and other data it is possible to detect a dualism in the development of economic careers up to the 1930s, whereby Oxbridge and London form one network, and the provincial universities and colleges another. In the first case students might go elsewhere, quite possibly passing through Manchester, and then return to London or Oxbridge in intermediate and senior positions; in the second case Manchester dominates the provinces, both as a teaching institution and one which is a major source of teachers for the provincial institutions.

In any case, it is evident that Manchester's Faculty of Commerce, with its associated bachelor's and master's degrees, had a far greater degree of success than did Birmingham within the developing framework for economic and commercial education in early twentieth-century Britain.

Furthermore, up until the 1920s the principal application for the teaching of economics in British universities was that provided by commercial studies. It is quite probable that this remained the case in many institutions right up until the later 1930s, and that the emergence of the teaching of economics in a recognisably modern form is a postwar phenomenon. This must remain a working hypothesis until the necessary archival work has been done.

The Institutional Dynamics of Economics

Nonetheless, underlying this essay is the implicit assumption that the role and status of economics as a public discourse is primarily an institutional, not a theoretical matter. The intrinsic theoretical interest of the development of political economy and its transformation into economic science at the end of the nineteenth century cannot be, and is not here, denied. This is the kind of historical development that is traced in the standard works of the history of economics. But this essay is based on the assumption that such a process of transformation (55) is not autonomous; rather, that it is inextricably linked to the emergence of economics as an academic discipline within modern educational institutions. Henceforth economics was an entity that was taught in lecture rooms to students who read their textbooks while following courses structured in a sequence that led them towards examinations that would in turn qualify them for employment in business or administration, or qualify them for advanced study and academic research, which then in turn would enable them to become professional teachers of economics. The construction of departments and faculties thus becomes a moment of the development of a career structure for students and teachers alike, in which the nature of economic science cannot be easily distinguished from its pedagogical and institutional function.

Not easily distinguishable, perhaps; but all the same hardly reducible the one to the other. In no sense is it argued here that we should simply replace a theoretical understanding of economic discourse with a sociological one. The argument advanced above presupposes instead that, given the current shortage, not to say absence, of knowledge concerning the institutional bases for the development of economic science in Britain, potential marginal gains in our understanding of economics as a public discourse are here at their greatest. By constructing an adequate framework within which we can observe the circulation of academics, the development of research programmes and the formation of the social fabric of economic science, it should be possible to return to the theoretical advances of this science with a fresh and productive perspective.

Notes

1. See M.M. Augello *et al.* (eds.), *Le cattedre di economia politica in Italia*, Franco Angeli, Milan, 1988; N. Waszek (ed.), *Die Institutionalisierung der Nationalökonomie an deutschen Universitäten*, Scripta Mercaturae Verlag, St. Katherinen, 1988; W.J. Barber (ed.), *Breaking the Academic Mould. Economists and American Higher Learning in the Nineteenth Century*, Wesleyan University Press, Middletown, 1988. These collections arose out of an international project on the institutionalisation of political economy jointly managed by the King's College Cambridge Research Centre and the University of Florence from 1983–1986.
2. R.F. Teichgraeber, "'Less abused than I had reason to expect': the Reception of the *Wealth of Nations* in Britain, 1776–90", *Historical Journal* **30** (1987), pp. 337–66.
3. Confinement of the appellation 'Professor' to holders of university chairs is a twentieth-century British phenomenon, and is chiefly the outcome of the development of the modern university structure on the part of the larger provincial universities. In the case of Oxford, for instance, the fact that a Drummond Chair in Political Economy existed from 1825 only meant that the incumbent gave a few lectures per year whose content was unrelated to what might loosely be thought of as the 'teaching programme' of the Oxford colleges. Likewise with Pryme in Cambridge, who in this regard is the 'first professor' of political economy in Britain. Unlike Pryme and the successive incumbents of the Drummond chair, Malthus and his successor Jones taught on a regular basis to (for the day) university-level students, and were paid substantial salaries for doing so.
4. E. Hughes, "Sir Charles Trevelyan and Civil Service Reform, 1853–5", *English Historical Review* **64** (1949), p. 53.
5. "Report on the Organisation of the Permanent Civil Service", Parliamentary Papers (P.P.), 1854, Vol. XXVII, p. 14.
6. It is not legitimate to stratify the nineteenth-century educational structure into the modern divisions of primary, secondary and higher education. Not until the Education Act of 1902 did the secondary level become well-defined, and with that the point of transition from secondary to university level unambiguously identified. Until that occurred there were constant alterations in the age limits for sitting Civil Service examinations, and also with the permitted age of entry into the Indian Civil Service. This was also a point of issue in the controversy over Scottish education, in which pupils transferred direct from parish schools to university, where they subsequently followed a general course of study. The length of time spent at university was also variable, quite apart from the issue of full- and part-time students in the case of the provincial colleges. The question of appropriate age of entry for examinations and colleges was a constant one

throughout the nineteenth century and is not simply a technical matter, but a
question of response to which implied a definite conception of the content and
level of educational organisation.

7. In the same months that Jowett wrote to Trevelyan, Trevelyan wrote to
Gladstone concerning his "Thoughts on Patronage", which he described as "...
the greatest abuse and scandal of the present age ... It is proposed to invite the
flower of our youth to the aid of the public-service; to encourage the rising
generation to diligence and good conduct by a more extensive system of rewards
than has ever been brought to bear upon popular education, and to make a nearer
approach to disinterested political action by removing one prevailing temptation
from Electors and Representatives." (letter of 17 January 1854, cited in Hughes,
"Sir Charles Trevelyan", p. 70). As the more conservative critics of the report
pointed out with justice, a conflict inhered in establishing scholastic qualification
as the criterion for entry to an occupation which demanded no scholarly talents
whatsoever. J.S. Mill, no conservative critic, recognised "... the fact that the
great majority, numerically speaking, of public employments, can be adequately
filled by a very moderate amount of ability and knowledge ..." (*Papers relating
to the Reorganisation of the Civil Service*, P.P., 1854–5, Vol. XX, p. 97); other
respondents to Trevelyan's orchestrated campaign noted that the introduction of
highly-qualified recruits into the lower reaches of the Service would promote
apathy and resignation among them when confronted with the routine nature of
the work they were to perform (P.P., 1854–5, Vol. XX, pp. 101–2, 128, 134, 315,
351, 386).

8. Letter from Jowett to Trevelyan, January 1854, P.P. 1854, Vol. XXVII, p. 27.
Jowett followed this remark with suggestions for the reorganisation of school
education in which "Political Economy, Law and Moral Philosophy" formed the
third of four groups (p. 28).

9. *First Report of Her Majesty's Civil Service Commissioners*, P.P., 1856, Vol.
XXII, Appendix I, Table B, p. 4. The qualifications for Ceylon Writerships also
made mention of political economy, but this is simply a reflection of the
continuation of the syllabus established at Haileybury.

10. *First Report*, Appendix I, Table B, p. 6. The Treasury added "1. Exercises
designed to test Handwriting and Orthography. Good Handwriting to consist in
the clear formation of the letters of the alphabet" (p. 6). The First Report also
includes all the examination papers set under its jurisdiction, from which it can
be judged what kind of abilities were being assessed. No questions in political
economy were included until the Sixth Report in 1861, where they are included
in the Irish Department (P.P., 1861, Vol. XIX).

11. W.J. Reader, *Professional Men*, Weidenfeld and Nicolson, London, 1966, p. 96.

12. M. Wiener's *English Culture and the Decline of the Industrial Spirit*, Cambridge
University Press, Cambridge, 1981, devotes a mere four pages to the general
issue of education and industry (pp. 132–5); as will be indicated below, the
reform of the educational system and the foundation of the new colleges is in fact
a product of a strong relation between provincial culture and 'industrial spirit'
which runs counter to the literary evidence assembled by Wiener. The best
outline of English educational provision at this time can be found in Ch. 3 of
Sidney Pollard's *Britain's Prime and Britain's Decline*, Edward Arnold, London,

1989, pp. 115–213. Pollard argues convincingly that, while British educational provision was more diffuse than that of our major competitors, its performance was broadly similar.

13. See for an outline of some of the issues involved M. Richter, *The Politics of Conscience. T.H. Green and His Age*, Weidenfeld and Nicolson, London, 1964, and C. Harvie, *The Lights of Liberalism*, Allen Lane, London, 1976.

14. See for the general background to this J. Maloney, "The Rise of Economics Teaching at the University of London", in I. Hont, K. Tribe (eds.), *Trade, Politics and Letters*, Routledge, London (forthcoming).

15. For an outline of the developments in the examination system for recruits to the Indian Civil Service post-Haileybury, and the elaboration of a system for the Home Civil Service, see J. Roach, *Public Examinations in England, 1850–1900*, Cambridge University Press, London, 1971, pp. 210–21.

16. T. Kelly, *A History of Adult Education in Britain*, 2nd. ed., Liverpool University Press, Liverpool, 1970, p. 119.

17. Kelly, *Adult Education*, p. 120. The Mechanics' Institution movement is import to an understanding of the development of British economics not because it was a major propagator of political economy to new audiences, but because it contributed to the establishment of a cultural and institutional basis for wider educational opportunity. This basis then, later in the century, formed the route through which political economy entered college and university syllabi. It is misleading to assume, as does for example Maxine Berg in her *Machinery Question and the Making of Political Economy 1815–1848* (Cambridge University Press, Cambridge, 1980, Ch. 7) that there was some kind of inevitable link between the demand for practical scientific education and the propagation of political economy as a 'science'.

18. It should be emphasised here that, despite the difference in organisational form of the Glasgow and Edinburgh foundations, the actual content of their courses was similar.

19. See for example Alon Kadish, "University Extension and the Working Classes: the Case of the Northumberland Miners", *Historical Research* **60** (1987), pp. 188–207.

20. T. Kelly, *Outside the Walls. Sixty Years of University Extension at Manchester, 1886–1946*, Manchester University Press, Manchester, 1950, p. 6.

21. Welch, *The Peripatetic University*, Cambridge University Press, London, 1973, p. 48. The organisational committee at Derby was chaired by the local MP and mill-owner, its secretary was the head of the local grammar school, and the committee, which numbered thirty-eight, included seven clergymen and eight members of the town council.

22. At Derby the rate for morning lectures and classes was fixed at 10/6d. per term, while the fee for evening lectures and classes for artisans was 2/6d (Welch, *Peripatetic University*, p. 48). In London during the 1880s a fee of 5s. was usual for the evening lectures on political economy.

23. Kelly, *Adult Education*, p. 224. Quite what is meant by 'political economy' in this context naturally requires consideration, although as will be seen below in the case of London the level and content of teaching was ratified by leading contemporary political economists. The discussion of London which follows is

intended primarily as an indication of the nature and context of extension teaching, and has itself to be supplemented by a treatment of the Cambridge extension movement, which is more directly relevant to the subsequent foundation of provincial colleges.

24. London Society for the Extension of University Teaching, Report of the Council (1877), "Table giving Particulars of Lectures and Classes held during the Winter of 1876–77".

25. London Society for the Extension of University Teaching, Report of the Council (1878), pp. 5–6. Foxwell and J.N. Keynes commented in similar terms in their roles as examiners, implicitly emphasising the distance between the level of extension teaching and all previous non-university courses.

26. London Society for the Extension of University Teaching, Report of the Council (1886), p. 11.

27. Report from Armitage-Smith, 23 December 1886, Birkbeck, University of London Library Mss. EM2/23/3. J.N. Keynes remarked as examiner that the students had an "even and sound grasp of the subject".

28. This division was acknowledged at the time, cf. R.G. Moulton, *The University Extension Movement*, Bemrose and Sons, London, 1887, p. 7.

29. A.C. Wood, *A History of University College, Nottingham, 1881–1948*, Basil Blackwell, Oxford, 1953, pp. 6–14.

30. Wood, *History*, p. 25. Lecturing on political economy was carried out by the Rev. J.E. Symes, Prof. of Language and Literature. The other chairs were in physics, mathematics and mechanics; chemistry and metallurgy; and natural sciences.

31. Day enrolments at Liverpool for example did not exceed 100 until the third session of 1883–84, of which over 50% were women; students enrolled term-by-term, subject-by-subject, each course carrying its own certificate. Students could sit for London matriculation or Cambridge Local Examinations; London Intermediate Arts or Science and Cambridge Higher Locals; or London BAs or BScs. T. Kelly, *For Advancement of Learning: The University of Liverpool 1881–1981*, University of Liverpool Press, Liverpool, 1981, pp. 56–8.

32. Wood, *History*, P. 31.

33. Kelly, *Advancement*, p. 74.

34. A.W. Chapman, *The Story of a Modern University. A History of the University of Sheffield*, Oxford University Press, London, 1955, p. 14.

35. Chapman, *Story*, p. 22.

36. S. Caine, *The History of the Foundation of the London School of Economics and Political Science*, G. Bell and Sons, London, 1963, pp. 40–44.

37. The 1898–99 session was composed of the following courses in economics: Year 1; Descriptive Economics, The Meaning and Use of Economic Terms, Outlines of English Economic History, Elementary Methods of Investigation, chiefly statistical. Years 2 and 3: History of Economic Theory, The Economic History of England in relation to that of Foreign Countries, Modern Currency Standards. W.A.S. Hewins, "The London School of Economics and Political Science", *Special Reports on Educational Subjects*, P.P., 1898, Vol. XXIV, pp. 88–89.

38. E.W. Vincent, P. Hinton, *The University of Birmingham: Its History and Significance*, Cornish Bros., Birmingham, 1947, pp. 61–5.

39. B.M.D. Smith, "Education for Management: Its Conception and Implementation in the Faculty of Commerce at Birmingham", Faculty of Commerce and Social Science, University of Birmingham, Occasional Paper No. 5 (1965), pp. 6–8.
40. W.J. Ashley, "The Universities and Business", *Minutes of Proceedings of the Staffordshire Iron and Steel Institute*, Dudley, 4 April 1903, p. 161.
41. W.J. Ashley, *The Faculty of Commerce in the University of Birmingham*, n.p., Birmingham, 1902, p. 1.
42. See for a detailed discussion of these and related issues Alon Kadish, "The Foundation of the Birmingham Faculty of Commerce as a Statement on the Nature of Economics", paper presented to the History of Economic Thought Conference, Manchester, 1987.
43. In the light of the argument that follows, it can be argued that the account of the development of the Moral Sciences in nineteenth-century Britain that we find in S. Collini, D. Winch, J. Burrow, *That Noble Science of Politics*, Cambridge University Press, Cambridge, 1983 – a story culminating with Sidgwick and Marshall in Cambridge – provides an intellectual thread that leads us to the wrong point.
44. The Marshall Prize for £15 to be spent on economics books; see for this and other details of Marshall's activities in Cambridge Alon Kadish, *Historians, Economists and Economic History*, Routledge, London, 1989, chs. 5, 6.
45. A. Marshall, *A Plea for the Creation of a Curriculum in Economics and associated branches of Political Science*, n.p., Cambridge, 1902, p. 4.
46. Marshall, *Plea*, p. 8.
47. Jevons began teaching on political economy, geometry and logic at Owens in 1863 and continued until 1882; most of his teaching was to evening class students.
48. Kadish, *Historians*, p. 233 and n. 53 p. 294.
49. Flux's entry in the *New Palgrave Dictionary of Economics* (Macmillan, London, 1988) gives the reader to understand that his main contribution to economics is a review written in 1894 (entry by John Whitaker, Vol. 2, pp. 395–6). No mention is made of his work during the 1920s in the Board of Trade on the census of production and estimates of national income, for which he was knighted in 1936. Chapman was subsequently Permanent Secretary of the Board of Trade 1920–26, and then Chief Economic Advisor to the Government. There is no entry for him in the *New Palgrave* at all. This underscores my view that our present estimation of the pre-eminence of Cambridge and London in the development of British economics is more the outcome of our general ignorance of anything that happens elsewhere, rather than from any informed assessment of the relation of Cambridge and London to provincial institutions.
50. In the following all information relating to teaching in Manchester is drawn from the relevant Calendars of Owens College, Victoria University (the federal body uniting Leeds, Liverpool and Manchester until 1903) and the independent Victoria University of Manchester.
51. Bear in mind here that this teaching programme is run by a Cambridge Senior Wrangler and Marshall's first successful candidate within the Moral Sciences Tripos.
52. *Economic Journal* **20** (1910), p. 669.

53. Hence, despite the limited number of economics graduates (never more than two or three a year before 1914), a great proportion of them passed into teaching at Manchester.
54. See the account of F.A. Hayek, "The London School of Economics 1895–1945", *Economica* n.s. **13** (1946), pp. 1–31.
55. A process of scientisation, to use the rather cumbersome translation of *Verwissenschaftlichung* (which has the untranslatable corollary *Disziplinierung*).

CHAPTER TWELVE

THE TEACHING OF POLITICAL ECONOMY
IN NINETEENTH-CENTURY ITALY AND THE
CHARACTERISTICS OF ITS INSTITUTIONALIZATION

GABRIELLA GIOLI

Introduction*

It isn't society as a whole or even a random collection of members that hands on the stock of scientific knowledge but a more or less definite group of professionals who teach the rising generations not only their methods and results but also their opinions about the direction and means of further advance. In a majority of cases competence in doing scientific work cannot be acquired, or can be acquired only by individuals of quite exceptional originality and force, from any source other than the teaching of recognized professionals. (1)

Such a professional corps of academics, however, did not exist for every scientific discipline in every country at every point in time. In trying to understand more precisely how the formation of a discipline of economics may have occurred in Italy and what its various phases may have been, we have chosen to stress the 'case of the academic chair' and to follow it through its phase of expansion and consolidation. This requires situating the chair within both the educational and economic systems characterizing Italian society at the end of the nineteenth century. It seems certain that the chair was also a major factor contributing towards the evolution of economics as an academic discipline with its own autonomous *status*, not only with regard to the objectives of analysis but also to the *tools* and *methods* used.

From research carried out in this field (2) the conclusion has been reached that in Italy between 1870 and 1900 many changes in the field of economics occurred, in its academic teaching and in the way it moved

P. Wagner, B. Wittrock, and R. Whitley (eds.), Discourses on Society: Volume XV, 1990, 303–328.
© 1990 *Kluwer Academic Publishers. Printed in the Netherlands.*

towards a more professionalized knowledge. These changes grouped themselves around two crucial moments in this development process. For simplicity's sake we have decided to call the first, which occurred in about 1876, 'simple institutionalization': i.e. the process by which the discipline found permanent channels of diffusion. We may consider the 'General Regulation of University Studies' (8 October 1876), which activated the teaching of economics in the second year in the faculties of jurisprudence, to be an expression of this institutionalization. On the other hand, a second phase, defined as 'extended institutionalization', took place at the end of the 1880's when economics achieved greater specialization and autonomy in research. The Coppino Royal Decree (13 December 1885), which made courses in finance and financial law and administration compulsory in the faculties of jurisprudence, is significant of this phase. This decree helped speed up the development of the universities, as well as allowing them and the teaching body greater autonomy than in the past. These two pieces of legislation may be considered as a manifestation of important changes occurring in Italian society which demonstrated a need for economic knowledge which could help resolve questions that dealt precisely with the economic development and social harmony of the country, once the problems due to unification in the 1860's had been resolved.

Having selected these two phases in the process of the institutionalization of political economy does not mean, however, that certain factors which contributed to the preparation and maturing of the aforementioned phases in the preceding years should be ignored. To this end we have presented the most important characteristics of the diffiuclt beginning of the teaching of this discipline at the beginning of this study. Following this a second section will be concerned with its 'first institutionalization', and we will finish with a discussion of the problems encountered during 'extended institutionalization'. As we shall see, the situation at the end of the 1800's still remained, in certain respects, far from the one cited by us in Schumpeter's words at the beginning of this paper.

The First Chairs in Political Economy in Italy:
General Characteristics

Historical awareness is of fundamental importance for contemporary reflection in the case discussed here. The phenomena relating to the autonomy of the discipline, scientific growth and the diffusion of scientific knowledge are strictly correlated with those related to the politics and society in which scholars of economics evolved and operated. Briefly, political economy at the end of the nineteenth century can be considered as the product of a "long winding path along which steps back, if not complete changes of direction, have not been rare, and will continue not to be" (3).

I will not speak of the primacy of the kingdom of Naples in instituting a chair in economics (or more precisely, of 'commerce and mechanics') under Ferdinand IV of Bourbon in 1754 thanks to private finance (4). This was a first step which turned out to be little more than sterile, as has been stressed by many economists in the nineteenth century. However, I feel it important to underline that the first course in economics was instituted in Naples above all due to the demands of an enlightened agricultural class which required new and improved knowledge of agricultural economics. Antonio Genovesi (1713–1769) had to teach the basics of 'commerce and mechanics' (1754–1769). In the Northern states, economics teaching had a more state-oriented origin. In Milan the Austrian government instituted a Deputation of Studies, directed by Firmian, plenipotentiary minister of Lombardy, who had a course in 'public or political economy' started up at the Palatine Schools with the aim of preparing public administrators. Cesare Beccaria (1738–1794), called upon to teach there (1768–1771), had to follow the programme of the cameral sciences adopted by Sonnenfels at the University of Vienna (5). Economics, conceived as a 'financial' science, continued to place the State at the centre of every idea (6).

At the end of the eighteenth century political economy was accepted, or rather, promoted, by governments according to their needs and the various political and economic realities of each state. However, it is necessary to point out that only a small number of chairs in economics were created in the pre-unification states (7). These shortcomings depended on many circumstances, not least those relating to the way teaching was organized. Prior to the nineteenth century universities were not considered as the main seats of research. This continued to be developed in other centres such as the academies. Moreover, there remains the fact that State control, where very strongly exercised, ended up removing vigour from university studies causing a strong growth in "private tutorials" which were authorized by the government, as happened at the University of Naples; whereas in the seats of learning where the competitive tradition of the medieval *Studia* was still preserved, as at the

University of Padua, it remained vigorous and healthy even in the nineteenth century (8).

For some time a partial agreement had been reached between the 'new' philosophical and economic ideas and the resultant institutional and economic reforms begun in the enlightened states. This agreement, however, ceased at the end of the eighteenth century. Economics was judged to be primarily a thing of the State and therefore to be subjected to censorship; interference by governments in office in the contents of courses became more authoritarian every time crises of a political nature were anticipated. Only secondarily was this discipline considered as an explanation of the causes of the accumulation of wealth and of its distribution among the greatest number of individuals.

On the other hand, given the backwardness of the pre-unification Italian states, a middle class that expressed the need to know how the economic system really functioned, and who would press – according to the realities existing in each state – for the creation of private teaching centres which would take the place of increasingly inadequate public ones, was lacking (9).

During this period, economics teachers – who were still a long way from forming a professional group in their own right – fed themselves on those principles and ideas that were at the basis of the great effort of the renewal of knowledge typical of the Enlightenment. The mercantilist and physiocratic thought of A. Genovesi and C. Beccaria, respectively, seemed to interpret the needs of Italian society even in the years following the development of their theories. Partial protectionism in manufacturing, a residue of the mercantilist era, and physiocratically based free trade in agriculture seemed to be the principles of political economy on which the development of the future economic system of a united Italy would be founded. This way of thinking about the growth of the economy tended to be disseminated also via channels of information different from those normally used in traditional teaching, as for example in the vast editorial activity undertaken by Pietro Custodi in 1803. In the collection of 'Classical Italian Writers of Political Economy' he wished to include works by scholars of economics who offered the means of economic instruction to the 'middle classes' – constituting a major factor of progress (10) – through their development of the aforementioned model of political economy.

In fact the free-market economics of Adam Smith – whose *An Inquiry into the Nature and Causes of the Wealth of Nations* was translated into

Italian in 1790 – was appreciated in Italy in a very circumstantial way (11). *Laissez-faire* was considered to be a general principle which every government should seek to implement without however excluding the means of public intervention considered necessary to support the development of private economic activity. It should be noted in this case that Smith's message was received mainly in terms of the theory of free trade: i.e. in terms of anti-authoritarian reaction against domination by foreign governors and of the promotion of a new social and political reality inspired precisely by more institutional liberty. In the period preceding unification the political element strongly conditioned both the spread of academic chairs in economics and the difficult movement of the discipline towards its own autonomy with its breaking away from other subjects such as social philosophy, history, juridical studies and administrative sciences.

The 'Simple Institutionalization' of the Teaching of Political Economy

1876 is an important date for the teaching of political economy in Italy. In that year (8 October 1876) the 'General University Regulation' was passed, abrogating the various previous dispositions and bringing about uniformity in the Italian university system. It was even more significant due to the fact that it covered the entire nation for the first time, unlike the Casati law of 1859. The regulation fixed the political economy examination in the second year of teaching of every faculty of jurisprudence. To be admitted to the examination the student had to give evidence of 'diligent presence', as well as presence at introductory courses in juridical sciences and statistics – subjects which were *not* however examined (12).

In 1876 political economy was taught in all seventeen government faculties of jurisprudence and in three of the four free universities in the kingdom; in some of the universities courses had already been divided between economics and statistics, now taught by two different teachers (Table A). By the year 1900 the number of academic chairs had increased notably (Table B). The General Regulation, passed by M. Coppino, the Minister of Public Instruction, during Depretis' first term in office (25 March 1876–25 December 1877) thus aimed to put the Italian educational system and, in the case we are interested in, the teaching of political economy in order. The latter had however retained many of the characteristics present in the university system of the pre-unity period, resulting

TABLE A
Economics Courses – 1876

Bologna	Angelo Marescotti	Political Economy
	Luigi d'Apel	Statistics
Cagliari	Giuseppe Todde	Political Economy and Statistics
Catania	Federico Marletta	Political Economy
	Mario de Mauro	Statistics
Genoa	Antonio Ponsiglioni	Political Economy
	Girolamo Boccardo	Statistics
Macerata	G. Giuliani	Political Economy
Messina	Pietro Interdonato	Political Economy and Statistics
Modena	Girolamo Galassini	Political Economy
	Giuseppe Triani	Statistics
Naples	Antonio Ciccone	Political Economy
	Giuseppe De Luca	Statistics
Padua	Angelo Messedaglia	Political Economy and Statistics
Palermo	Giovanni Bruno	Political Economy and Statistics
Parma	Ferdinando Zanzucchi	Political Economy
Pavia	Luigi Cossa	Political Economy and Statistics
Pisa	Gianquinto Giovanni De Gioannis	Political Economy
Rome	Francesco Protonotari	Political Economy
Sassari	Giovanni Pinna-Ferrà	Political Economy
	Filippo Garavetti	Statistics
Siena	C. De Stefani	Political Economy and Statistics
Turin	Giulio Emanuele Garelli della Morea	Political Economy
	Celestino Feroglio	Statistics

Free Universities

Camerino	G. Zucconi	Political Economy
Ferrara	–	–
Perugia	Filippo Perfetti	Political Economy and Statistics
Urbino	Giovan Battista Vecchiotti Antaldi	Economic Institutions and Statistics

Source: Bulletin of the Ministry of Public Instruction

in the persistence of a plurality of very diverse regulations. The process which culminated in this first substantial result was fraught with difficulties and marked by often very heated debates which dealt principally with the general rules to be imposed on the university education system in the country; a country which, it must be remembered, had only recently achieved its own national unity.

TABLE B
Economics Courses – 1900

Bologna	Tullio Martello	Political Economy and Finance[a]
	Giovanni Battista Salvioni	Statistics
Cagliari	Francesco Angioni-Contini	Statistics
	Gaetano Orrù	Finance
Catania	Giuseppe Majorana-Calatabiano	Political Economy
	Mario De Mauro	Statistics
	Federico Ciccaglione	Finance
Genoa	Antonio Ponsiglioni	Political Economy
	Giulio Salvatore Del Vecchio	Statistics
	Angelo Roncali	Finance
Macerata	Alberto Zorli	Finance
	Niccolò Lo Savio	Political Economy and Statistics
Messina	Eugenio Masé-Dari	Political Economy
	Giacomo Macrì	Statistics
	Giuseppe Oliva	Finance
Modena	Ghino Valenti	Political Economy
	Luigi Franchi	Statistics
	Carlo Conigliani	Finance
Naples	Augusto Graziano	Political Economy and Statistics
	Francesco Saverio Nitti	Finance
Padua	Achille Loria	Political Economy
	Francesco Ferraris	Statistics
Palermo	Giuseppe Ricca-Salerno	Political Economy
	Francesco Maggiore Perni	Statistics
	Vito Cusumano	Finance
Parma	Ferdinando Zanzucchi	Political Economy and Statistics
	Alessandro Malgarini	Finance
Pavia	Eteocle Lorini	Political Economy
	Rodolfo Benini	Statistics and Finance
Pisa	Giuseppe Toniolo	Statistics and Political Economy
	David Supino	Finance
Rome	Angelo Messedaglia	Political Economy and Statistics
	Antonio De Viti de Marco	Finance
Sassari	Giovanni Pinna-Ferrà	Political Economy
	Giovanni Dettori	Statistics
	Girolamo Pitzolo	Finance
Siena	Camillo Supino	Political Economy
	Filippo Virgilii	Statistics and Finance

Table B (continued)

Turin	Salvatore Cognetti de Martiis	Political Economy
	Celestino Feroglio	Statistics
	Giulio Emanuele Garelli della Morea	Finance

Free Universities

Camerino	Pericle Ricci	Statistics
Ferrara	Pietro Sitta	Political Economy, Statistics, Finance
Perugia	Amilcare Puviani	Political Economy and Finance
	Prospero Fedozzi	Statistics
Urbino	Giovan Battista Vec-chiotti Antaldi	Political Economy, Statistics, Finance

[a] The full title is Finance and Financial Law, except at Palermo and Pavia, where it is Finance.

To fully understand the significance of such a tortuous path it is necessary to spend a few lines describing what the problems which appeared unresolved in the years immediately following unification (1861) were. From a general point of view it is above all the lack of precise statistical information concerning the state of teaching in the country that is to be regretted; from this we may gather how disinterested the various Italian states were in this aspect in the years preceding unity. Furthermore, due to the heavy financial burdens demanded by the construction of the new State, the total amount of funds allocated to public instruction was rather small (scarcely 1.4% of the national budget in 1861) for many years (13).

From an institutional point of view, the Italian educational system, which had been run mainly by the state since the beginning, suffered moreover from the simultaneous presence of a plurality of old and new regulations. The Casati law, passed in 1859 in the kingdom of Sardinia, was only extended to a few provinces that were subsequently annexed, as far as universities were concerned. In 1901 it still only covered the 'ancient Sardinian states', Lombardy, Veneto, Marche and Sicily. Thus some universities in other parts of the country kept the regulations prepared by previous acting and provisional governments for a long time. The Casati law laid down regulations of a markedly authoritarian and centralized character. The number and type of subjects to be taught in each faculty was strictly fixed, as was the number of ordinary professors. Rectors were appointed by the Italian government, while the commissions dealing with competitions for academic chairs were nominated at the complete discretion of the Ministry of Public Instruction. As a whole, the law was the expression of the pre-industrial Italian society with its political elite that was limited in number and focused in its perspective on societal higher education aimed at selecting and training future members of the ruling class on the basis of a common humanistic education which has always been seen as a unifying element for the élite and as a 'social filter' for the rest (14).

Between 1861 and 1862 Carlo Matteucci tried to rationalize the university system by differentiating between "major" and "minor university seats". He did not, however, manage to carry out this plan. After the failure of the reform, the continuously problematic state of affairs could not help but incite discontent and general concern. The diagnoses of Italian intellectuals concerning the causes of such a distressing situation differed greatly; according to some the Italian university system suffered from a lack of liberty; according to others there was even too much of it. There were others who thought that the number of faculties was excessive. German universities were regarded with admiration. They represented the model of freedom of teaching united with the sound functioning and rational organization which characterized them (15).

With regard to political economy, it seems obvious that its path towards complete institutionalization derives from this general situation. Although it was provided for by the Casati law in the outline of the degree course in jurisprudence, political economy did not have a precise position in the course and continued to be transferred from one teaching year to the next until 1876. Out of nineteen faculties of jurisprudence, courses in political economy were offered in seventeen seats of learning in 1861 and put in the hands of teachers who were characterized more by their political commitment than by their scientific worth. With regard to the number of enrollments in these faculties, 4830 in 1861, it should be pointed out that they would not noticeably increase until the last twenty years of the century, coinciding with the more marked economic and social dynamism which characterized those years (16).

The history of higher education in Italy was characterized from the beginning by the dispute between two opposing concepts; one

centralizing and authoritarian, and the other aiming at reinforcing the
autonomy of the universities, the institutes and the academic bodies and
which ended up prevailing over the first only in the course of time. The
Casati law may be considered as the theoretical expression of the first
tendency since in practice it only affected a small number of universities.
The creation of business schools and institutes of higher education
belongs, rather, to the second trend. It is worth discussing these schools
not so much for their successes and practical results obtained, which were
less than expected if the truth be told, as for the ideas that were at the
basis of their conception. Their tortuous history expresses the difficulties
the social sciences faced in finding a permanent channel of institutionalization outside the already existing juridical faculties.

The 'Institute for Advanced Practical Studies and Perfection' was
created in Florence under the initiative of some members of the Tuscan
government in 1859. The intention was to create a centre for research and
specialized study. It was held that Italian universities were not capable of
carrying out the latter function. The founders wanted especially to give a
new impetus to juridical studies and social subjects. Courses in political
economy were included in the legal section of the institute, which was
soon suppressed (1867). In 1875 the School of Social Sciences was
founded in Florence, which became the 'Cesare Alfieri' Institute in 1888.
The school, which was entirely private, was funded by the 'Liberal
Education Society'. Its aim, modelled on the 'Free School of Political
Sciences' created in Paris in 1871, was to train young men to "public life
and State office" (17).

The first business school was founded in Venice in 1868, followed by
Genoa (1882) and Bari (1886). The model on which they were based was
the Institute of Commerce in Antwerp. They arose through the initiative
of local forces and, recognized immediately by the Italian State, were
placed under the tutelage of the Ministry of Agriculture, Industry and
Commerce. Their administrative and financial management was assigned
to a consortium of local boards and other small bodies. These characteristics linked the life of the schools to the interests of local economies, and
relating them to the Ministry of Agriculture made them function more
efficiently and autonomously with respect to the universities of the
kingdom, which had been placed under the jurisdiction of the Ministry of
Public Instruction. With the creation of these schools, which were warmly
supported by some of the leading Italian economists (such as F. Ferrara
and L. Luzzatti, G. Boccardo and M. Pantaleoni), attempts were made to

open a plurality of highly specialized institutes which would complement or integrate with university training. The intention was to form a genuine faculty of business (18). In Italy there was a growing demand for experts – trained qualified economists – and it was not by chance that these schools were born in three towns in the face of the new economic possibilities linked to commercial and industrial development that opened. Such training institutions were needed, noted Lacaita, "if in satisfying this growing need for scientific knowledge ... secondary and professional schools were no longer sufficient, neither were the universities, despite the development of the teaching of economics in the faculty of jurisprudence, either because the courses were simply still very limited, or because specific professional requirements remained ignored" (19). However, a degree in jurisprudence at that time still remained the preferred choice of the members of the élite graduates from the *licei*, whereas the flow to the business schools from the technical colleges remained very variable. At the beginning of the next century, the business schools turned themselves into university faculties.

To return to the mid-1870s, in which we have located the origins of the first institutionalization of economics, they may be considered the years which signal the end of an era. The most urgent problems imposed by the construction of the unified State having been overcome to a certain extent, there were demands that the political class respond more satisfactorily at the educational level to satisfy the growing demands by the economic forces in the country for economic knowledge.

The new government of the left which was formed in March 1876 (Depretis' first term in office), after the fall of the historical right, appeared particularly sensitive to such requests. It also included education, as well as the setting in motion of projects for university reform that would recognize increased autonomy of academic bodies, in its programme of expansion of public spending. The aim was to prepare and pass a general reform law aimed at conceding more financial, disciplinary and didactical autonomy to the universities. However, the law never came into operation precisely because of strong resistance from the opposition, which thus postponed the problem of the strengthening and increasing of the autonomy of courses until the end of the eighties (20).

Taking stands on the questions which the government in power intended to resolve, e.g. the finance of public works, the banking problem, customs legislation, emigration, etc., economic teachers became involved in the general discussion taking place in the country, and in particular in the dispute about which political economic measures would favour Italian industrial development. It was wondered if *laissez-faire* was better for the Italian economic system or whether moderate protectionism should be applied. The diversity of opinions on organizing economic studies, in terms of greater or lesser institutional autonomy with regard to the State, reappeared when these same social forces, scholars of economics, politicians and businessmen debated over how to make the economic system grow.

The knot to unravel which divided the Italian academic world was basically the same: i.e. what role should the State and the government be assigned with particular reference to the sphere of economics? Between 1874 and 1875 what has been defined as the 'war between the two schools' exploded in Italy. The doctrinaire dispute turned on whether or not it was necessary to go beyond the free-market dogma. The idea that, given current historical conditions, social and productive forces if left to themselves would not bring about harmonious development according to the classical model, or might even lead to disequilibrium and economic crisis, was gaining more and more ground in Italy (21). The Congress of Milan, which took place in January 1875 to discuss the subject of social legislation and political economy, started off the controversy, which had already been latent for some while, between the 'intransigent free-trader' Francesco Ferrara, and the representatives of the 'Lombardy Venice School', whose ideas were related to German historicism but radicalized into two tendencies or rather, according to Schumpeter, complete regional schools (22).

On one side there was Ferrara, who founded the 'Adam Smith Society' in Florence in 1874 and who supported the journal *L'Economista* ('The Economist'). On the other side Luzzatti, Lampertico, Messedaglia, Cusumano and Scialoja supported, during its first run (1875-1878), the *Economist's Journal* which had risen from the ashes of the Paduan *Agricultural, Industrial and Commercial Review*. If we look at the signatures on these opposing initiatives, we can state that most Italian academic economists are represented here. Although not necessarily approving of such a precise distinction, many teachers, such as Luigi Cossa (teaching at Pavia from 1858 on) and Angelo Messedaglia (teaching at Padua from 1858 on) for example, found they had to choose a group to lean towards in this climate of *referendum*.

To summarize, the latter defined themselves by the idea that it was necessary to apply experimental methods both to economic and social investigations which were more realistic than those methods that more or less excluded State activity in regulating the application of a policy of *laissez-faire*.

'Non-dogmatic' Italian economists' views derived largely from the Italian Enlightenment philosophy of P. Verri, C. Beccaria, A. Genovesi and F. Galiani, which had always been different from that that had taken root in England and France (23). Successive scholars at the beginning of the nineteenth century, such as G.D. Romagnosi, C. Cattaneo and M. Gioia, continued to reflect on the idea of progress, each according to their own particular education. They reflected on how to reconcile the growth of wealth with the development of individual liberty and with 'demands for social justice', the latter becoming explicit only at the end of the nineteenth century. In their quest for an autonomous path to follow, Italian economists tended towards solutions linked to the socio-political, economic and educational peculiarities of the Italian situation. No historical model of industrialization, at least not in its purest form, was totally applicable to it. Neither the classical English model nor the French and Prussian models seemed to respond *entirely* to the needs of the Italian economy (24).

A majority who believed in the specific nature of the Italian situation thus formed in Italy and ended up bringing together the contributions of a heterogeneous group of economists, politicians and industrialists, whose aim was the pursuit of economic growth assisted by State intervention through a policy of control of the foreign markets and a public expenditure policy (25). This was a 'new majority' whose strength did not lie – as Lanaro wrote – in theoretical homogeneity which was almost never pursued, "but in its expansive drive, and in its capacity to erode the coherence of free-market theory from within" (26). The Italian academic body, like, on the other hand, the political and social one, thus found itself divided between those who followed the general principles of free-market economics, and alternatively those who demanded temporary protectionist policies in their more detailed interpretation of the needs of Italian society.

The most prestigious theoretical economist at that time, Ferrara, who followed the methodology of the English classicists, particularly Smith, whom he compared to Galileo, maintained that the theory of free trade was a genuine 'immutable and universal' law. It was a principle that could not be departed from without eventually harming the functioning of the economic system of each nation and, more importantly, preventing the young science of economics from completely separating itself from other disciplines such as moral and juridical ones. For Ferrara, the aim of economics was incompatible with a system in which the State was "something more than a simple mental abstraction" (27). Only by respecting this postulate could political economy – defined as the study of phenomena related to the ranking of human needs – also hope to develop into a science, meaning "knowledge of the truths which result from the examination of whatever object", as distinct from the 'arts', meaning "the set of rules to obey in order to achieve whatever effect" (28).

This way of formulating the task of economic science meant strong opposition to the "broad and complex method" of analyzing the science of wealth according to the tradition of the Italian School. In the view of Ferrara's supporters, the latter's merit consisted principally "in the broad and complex method of considering questions; because they do not concern themselves with wealth from an abstract and absolute point of view, but from one of general well-being", as Adolphe Blanqui stressed, and in linking the economic question to moral and political interests as well (29). This "scientific" and "liberal" way of thinking about political economy, too, had found fertile ground in Italy at the end of the eighteenth century and the debate from 1875 onwards produced an echo in the criticism Ferrara aimed at the exponents of the Lombardian-Venetian School, who were in fact the supporters in the social sciences of the "broad and complex concepts" (30).

Extended Institutionalization of Political Economy

The place political economy occupied in the Italian educational system after its first institutionalization around 1896 was still unsatisfactory. In the programme of university studies only a single examination in economics was required, and also the process of specialization – which meant offering more economics courses – that had been considered for a while, had not yet been endorsed by government bodies. This in fact happened only in 1885 when the Minister of Public Instruction, M. Coppino, further modified the Special Regulation of the Faculty of Jurisprudence of 1876. This law established the courses to be offered in the Faculty, including statistics and finance as compulsory subjects for the first time, besides political economy. Moreover, the Coppino law of 13 December 1885 sanctioned making the royal universities of Catania, Genoa and Messina equal to the others, thus abrogating the differentiation between major and minor universities introduced by the Matteucci law in 1862.

After 1880, Italian universities experienced a period of strong development. The number of enrollments rose significantly, the number of permanent academic chairs increased, new teaching methods were introduced, and attempts were even made to improve the facilities with which the faculties were endowed. If described in figures, this growth process may appear modest compared to what was happening in other European nations, but it appears much more significant when the initial conditions of Italian universities at the time of unification are taken into account. Furthermore, if we consider that the public sector continued to be the structure that influenced the Italian educational system, the State effort in the direction of educational expansion becomes clear; this is also witnessed by the fact that the percentage of national income assigned to education grew considerably and at a steady state in the period concerned and afterwards, doubling between 1880 and 1914. It was in these years that the 'extended institutionalization' of political economy matured, reaching its conclusion at the end of the decade 1880–90. This was made possible by a profound intellectual change which affected the entire Italian world of learning in those years: the spread of positivism (31).

The increase in the specialization of economic studies also reflected the perceived necessity of educating a modern class of managers who would need a growing amount of economic, statistical and demographic data if they were to bring the Italian state up to the level of the more industrialized countries in western Europe.

Cognetti De Martiis, taking over from the teaching of the Ferraran free-trader Reymond in Turin 1880, strongly encouraged research in the field of economics, promoting the birth and growth of research centres linked to university chairs – genuine 'Research Institutes' (32). In a more relaxed educational climate the positivist method encouraged economic investigation based on the analysis of empirical data. Major initiatives started out from the academic chairs which supported new research and started up new economic reviews, as well as increasing the circulation of the older ones. The period in question opened with what we have termed the 'extended institutionalization' of political economy. Not only did free courses at the university increase, but the number of lessons doubled as well. They were often made compulsory and courses in finance and statistics were also offered, while specialized research continued to increase, attracting a growing number of students. Under the initiative of

Luigi Cossa, prizes were introduced with the aim of promoting economic study.

In 1880 the 'Juridical Circle' was created in Siena. It placed an improvement in the scientific and professional preparation of law students through exercises and seminars among its objectives. Cognetti De Martiis founded the 'Institute for Training in Juridical and Political Sciences' in Turin in 1881. The 'Political Economy Laboratory' followed in 1893. Its aim was to give an experimental orientation to the 'class of economics and social sciences' – which included courses in political economy as well as finance and statistics – without overlooking problems of a methodological nature. In other words, auxiliary structures were beginning to be created which would help the chair carry out its role and stretching the theoretical arms, so to speak, towards civil society. In conclusion, it was the political economists who tried to put their work at the service of society without, however, losing its own scientific validity (33).

The increase in studies in the field of economics underlined, among other things, the existence of serious economic and social questions, many of which have lasted ever since 1876, such as those concerning the organization of the banking system, trade policy, the construction and management of the railway and road systems, the protection of workers and social security. They were a mass of problems which the successive leaders of the country had tried to resolve through increasing interventionism. One of the most significant examples was the application of the trade tariff in 1878. This modified in a protectionist direction C. Cavour's 1864 trade legislation, which was considered to be perhaps one of the most free-market in Europe. The trade tariff became even more restrictive in 1887 (34). The Italian government's voting through of the tax on cereals and of protective measures for the national coal and steel industry rekindled the debate that had just begun to ease off.

This is not the place to discuss the differences of opinion over which development model to follow that occurred in this period. It is necessary to note, however, that the review *L'Industria* ('Industry') was created in 1886, around which a movement of ideas developed aimed at achieving a consensus of opinion regarding the actions "of that typical ideal character represented by the active economic agent, that is to say mainly by the industrialist" (35). Industrialists, landowners and also a few economists and teachers (for example V. Ellena and L. Luzzatti), the so-called experimentalists, relied on F. Lists's theory of nascent industry (rather than on J.S. Mill's). This was a crucial theory with regard to Smith's and Riccardo's long-term theories of international trade against which the more convincing arguments of a short- and medium-term model were made. Linked to the problem of rapid industrial development was also that of the social question, which was becoming more and more pressing (36).

According to the economists whose foundations were based on marginalist theory, the 1878 trade tariff went against everything the theory had tried to prove even at the economic policy level: i.e. the irrefutability of the theory of free trade. Neoclassical economics viewed the free-market system as capable of assuring the optimal allocation of available resources. It was thus a static analysis where State intervention was considered to be potentially harmful.

A section of the academic community consisting of marginalist and *laissez-faire* economists, who derived strength from permanent university positions and from the certainty of the scientific truth of their theories, formed a coalition against the government's policy. From the pages of the *Economist's Journal* – whose ownership and editorship passed, after A. Zorli's brief interregnum (1886–1890), into the hands of the marginalists Mazzola, De Viti de Marco and Pantaleoni around the middle of 1890 – sprung a political and educational conflict that ended up being the most bitter of the nineteenth century (37). In the name of the neutrality of 'pure theory', scientific economists were prepared to adopt more and more diverse positions (from those of the politician or the journalist) in order to convince the rest of the world of the errors of theory and policy in the stance adopted by the Italian government and by the economic and learned forces that supported it. The question concerning the relationship between teachers and the State – the sole provider of work – was rekindled once more, referring – in accord with the experiment in Bismarck's Germany – to the necessity of creating a tighter bond between State and society (including the world of academia and education (38).

In presenting the extremes of the debate, even if only in a synthetic way, which occurred between the economists of the period over the economic policy to adopt in order to achieve Italian industrial develop-ment, we have introduced elements that go beyond the eighties, but whose existence was announced precisely during the period in which we have located the process of 'extended institutionalization' of political economy. We refer to the fact that the community of economics teachers continued to discuss the significance of the State's role in economics, largely because of the government's ever-increasing involvement in Italian economic life which had, in certain cases such as the 'banking scandal', assumed disturbingly immoral forms. This was a problem concerning the State's functioning that contributed to the development of the study of finance, which smoothed the way for the spread of marginalism in Italy (39).

Authors such as M. Pantaleoni (1883), G. Ricca-Salerno (1888) and A. De Viti de Marco (1888), who proclaimed 'pure economics' sovereign, tended to analyze the economic behaviour of the State according to the same principles by which they explained utility-maximizing individual choice. That deeply rooted tendency in Italy to consider the fiscal activity of the State capable of resolving problems of a 'social origin' was criticized in scientific terms. It was a criticism that was even underlined in the work of Sax, *Grundlegung der theoretischen Staatswirtschaft* (1887), whose theories met with a very favourable climate in Italy (40). Along this line of thought, which made the value theory of the Marginalist School the unifying principle of all economic thought, apart from the authors already cited (Pantaleoni, De Viti de Marco and Ricca-Salerno), A. Zorli, A. Graziani and immediately afterwards (1890) A. Conigliani and U. Mazzola should be mentioned, above all for their contribution to the theory of finance.

From 1880 to the end of the century economists found themselves expressing opinions on the causes of the economic and social crises that were ravaging the country and consequently on whether the economic policy of the State, which was inclined to shift from a policy of temporary to permanent protectionism under the pressure of certain social and political groups who were trying to get industrialization going in Italy, was good or not. Under F.S. Nitti's government, a shift from a policy of protection of nascent industry to permanent forms of protection occurred which seemed to herald the era of growing Italian nationalism.

Even if the scientific, didactic and political activity carried out by teachers at the end of the century should have been more profound in Italy, it may be said that, as happened in other parts of western Europe, each of the branches of the economic sciences was recognized in the current university system and political economy had developed sufficiently to become an independent professional activity.

However, at the end of the nineteenth century, economics teachers didnot seem to have reached the stage of becoming a sociological group in their own right whose members have other things in common apart from their interest in scientific work, such as having to make a living from teaching, as explained by Schumpeter (41). The economics profession in the fullest sense of the word had not yet emerged. This situation manifested itself in a peculiar, negative way in our opinion; economists whose work was of high scientific value debarred themselves from any chance of becoming part of the Italian academic world, such as Pareto, or had themselves suspended from teaching, as in the case of Pantaleoni (42). It was all due to their "raging protest" against the violation of the "great natural laws of political economy" by an increasingly interventionist State which had caused waste, destruction of wealth, misery and corruption. They protested because, as Pantaleoni wrote in 1900, there was only one possible goal, one of "a regime which is open to all claims, and which is prepared to battle with every fighter" (43).

Conclusions

What I have tried to show in this paper may be summarized briefly in the following way: the institution of a chair in political economy – an expression that became part of everyday language only in 1876 – represented the foundation stone on which the discipline based its long and tortuous path towards the attainment of scientific and institutional autonomy.

It had been noted that the 'academic chair' has too often been attributed an excessively important role for the purpose of scientitic progress. Those who believe in such a function, wrote Schumpeter, risk not realizing that "funds and chairs are not everything; there are things that cannot be hired or bought; and if these things do not develop in step with funds and chairs, the latter may prove to have been provided in vain" (44). However, from what has emerged in this work, the institutionalization of economics in Italy appears to have been an important phenomenon linked to the changes in Italian society at the end of the nineteenth century, which made a modern managerial class that was ever more prepared for the aims of industrial development necessary. The dissemination of economic knowledge favoured, in its turn, the growth of the number of academic chairs and research centres which occurred more rapidly in the years between 1876 and 1885.

This growth derived, if in a more gradual way, from the characteristics adopted by the earlier teaching of political economy, and also from those university ordinances which regulated the subject in the respective pre-unification states. In fact, at that time the chair in economics was the vehicle through which the State directed, or rather, imposed, teaching programmes. It was the State that made demands for scientific knowledge, even selecting the teachers required to form a better-trained class of public administrators. Given the economic backwardness of the preunification states, a middle class that needed to understand how the industrial economic system functioned and who pushed for more widespread and profound knowledge was lacking in Italy.

The institutionalization process, also taken to mean a process of breaking away from neighbouring disciplines (such as social philosophy, history, jurisprudence and administration), occurred in a fragmentary way. Furthermore, the political element seemed to have the better of the scientific one in this process.

Only in 1876 can we speak of the first institutionalization of political economy. The regularization of the subject by the University Regulation was due to the far-reaching debate that had started up concerning the reformation of the Italian educational system: whether to proceed by removing autonomy from the university bodies, according to tradition; or whether to follow a policy of greater autonomy, with the recognition of the juridical value of the organization by semi-state bodies and private boards. The choice made in favour of the former solution (Matteucci law, 1862) disappointed the hopes of those social forces who viewed decentralized education as a guarantee of greater autonomy in research, a greater number of teachers, and – thanks to the introduction of the class of free teachers who would have to compete with the official teachers of the subject – a better control of the quality of teaching. The nascent industrial bourgeoisie pushed for the schools and more specialized economics courses necessary to aid Italian industrial take-off.

From these years onwards, the academic chair became an object of conquest for an academic body that aimed to make its own line or school of thought prevail. It should be noted, however, that despite the diversity of opinions regarding the way in which the State should encourage economic development, an awareness of the need to proceed towards a growing specialization of economic knowledge grew. Demands to split the faculty of jurisprudence into several departments (a genuine legal department and one of politics and administration) followed from this; as did demands for separating the teaching of economics from that of finance and statistics.

In 1885, a new phase opened for political economy, termed 'extended institutionalization', which can be characterized by the establishment of auxiliary structures linked to the academic chair which helped the teacher carry out his role, as well as by the fact that subjects such as statistics and finance were made compulsory for the degree in jurisprudence by the normatives of the Royal Decree of 22 October 1885. In other words, the importance of educating society with the principles of economics in order to reach the level of more industrialized European countries was stressed in these years. This contributed to the development of empirical research which emphasized the analysis of economic and social phenomena through statistical and demographic investigation, and subsequently caused the number of publications of an economic nature to increase.

Due to the persistence and worsening of social and economic crises, the economics world at the time confronted both the problem of Italian industrial take-off and the social question. The solution chosen to both problems lay in reinforcing protectionist policies and in repudiating free competition because it leads only to the exclusion of the weakest. These solutions led to a policy of permanent protectionism and growing nationalism. This provoked the reaction of the marginalist economists who denied the possibility of revising the theory of perfect competition with regard to either individual or public choice, both of which are dictated by the principle of cost minimization with regard to both goods and services.

In the tail-end of the century, economics divided itself into many specializations, becoming a professional activity in its own right. However, there do not appear to be any elements allowing us to view the emergence of a professional group of economists in Italy as a sociological group *per se*. In trying to reply to the question posed at the beginning of this paper, even if Schumpeter's notion about the spread of 'professionalized knowledge' could be applied to Italy at the end of the nineteenth century, it should be noted that possibilities due to the presence of a general competence in economic subjects, as existed in England, continued to be lacking. In Italy, the prestige of economics was above all due to the prestige of intellectual leaders such as Pareto, Pantaleoni, Ricca-Salerno and Mazzola, and this may explain the appearance of a discrepancy between the work of this restricted group and the great majority of the economics profession.

Notes

* I would like to thank Dr. Simonetta Bartolozzi Batignani, Prof. Piero Bini and Dr. Daniela Donnini Macciò for their valuable suggestions. Dr. Daniela Donnini Macciò has edited the part concerning Italian university regulations in the years 1861–1876 and the tables attached to the text.

1. Joseph A. Schumpeter, *History of Economic Analysis*, New York: Oxford University Press, 1954, p. 46.
2. We refer mainly to research work presented in the volume: Massimo Augello, Marco Bianchini, Gabriella Gioli and Piero Roggi (eds.), *Le cattedre di economica politica in Italia. La diffusione di una disciplina "sospetta" (1750–1900)*, Milan: Franco Angeli, 1988; and in the international version to contributions collected in the following works: 'Les problèmes de l'institutionnalisation de l'économie politique en France au XIX siècle,' *Economies et Sociétés*, no. 6, 1986; William J. Barber (ed.), *Breaking the Academic Mould. Economists and American Higher Learning in the Nineteenth Century*, Middletown: Wesleyan University Press, 1988; Chuhei Sugiuyama and Hiroshi Mizuta (eds.), *Enlightenment and Beyond. Political Economy Comes to Japan*, Tokyo: University of Tokyo Press, 1988.
3. Piero Barucci, 'La cattedra e l'autonomia della scienza economica: una riflessione,' in *Le cattedre di economia, op. cit.*, p. 27.
4. It was Bartolomeo Intieri, a Tuscan, who did his utmost in order that a chair for Antonio Genovesi be instituted with private funds. Franco Venturi, *Illuministi italiani. Riformatori Napoletani*, Vol. V, Milan-Naples: Ricciardi, 1957, p. 15 ff.
5. See the contributions of Marco Bianchini, 'Some Fundamental Aspects of Italian Eighteenth-Century Economic Thought,' in D.A. Walker (ed.), *Prospectives on the History of Economic Thought*, Vol. I., London: Edward Elgar, 1989, and the work 'Una difficile gestazione: il contrastato inserimento dell'economia politica nelle università dell'Italia nord-orientale (1769–1966). Note per un'analisi comparativa' in *Le cattedre di economia, op. cit.*, pp. 47–92.
6. Alberto Bertolino, 'Il pensiero economico italiano dal risorgimento alla ricostruzione,' in Massimo Finoia (ed.), *Il pensiero economico italiano 1850–1950*, Bologna: L. Cappelli, 1980, pp. 33–50.
7. After Naples and Milan, a chair was created in Modena in 1771. The number of chairs in political economy became more numerous around 1780 with Catania, Milan, Naples, Modena and Palermo, to which Pavia was added in 1796. Between 1800 and 1809 teaching was also started up in Turin, Bologna, Parma and Padùa. Around the 1820's an involutional phase began and at least five chairs were abolished. The situation remained unchanged up till the eve of unification, when chairs appeared at Cagliari, Genoa, Macerata, Messina and Sassari, and those at Bologna and Modena were reintroduced.
8. Antonio La Penna, 'Università e istruzione pubblica,' in *Storia d'Italia*, Vol. 5, Turin: G. Einaudi editore, 1973, pp. 1744–1745.
9. Guido Baglioni, *L'ideologia della borghesia industriale nell'Italia liberale*, Turin: G. Einaudi, 1974.
10. Daniele Rota (ed.), *Pietro Custodi tra rivoluzione e restaurazione*,' Vol. II, Lecco: Cattaneo editore, 1989. See especially the contributions by Simonetta

Bartolozzi Batignani, Marco Bianchini and Aurelio Macchioro.

11. Piero Barucci, 'Il pensiero economico "classico" nei primi decenni dell'800: un tentativo d'interpretazione d'assieme,' in *Fatti e idee di storia economica nei secoli XII-XX*, Bologna: Il Mulino, 1976, pp. 689–707; Gabriella Gioli, 'Gli albori dello smithianesimo in Italia,' *Rivista di Politica Economica*, VII, 1972, pp. 3–48.

12. This measure anticipated among other things the Special Regulation of the Faculty of Jurisprudence, according to which a 'promotion examination' was established at the end of the second year in the following subjects: Institutions of Roman Law, History of Law, Philosophy of Law and Political Economy. This regulation also confirmed the differentiation already present in the Casati law between ordinary professors and private or 'free' professors. Information regarding the regulation of Italian universities can be found in the following sources: *Il Digesto italiano, Enciclopedia metodica e alfabetica di legislazione, dottrina a giurisprudenza*, edited by Luigi Lucchini, Vol. XIII, part two, Turin: UTET, 1901–1904, p. 1035 ff; *Raccolta ufficiale delle Leggi e dei decreti del Regno d'Italia*, various years.

13. Vera Zamagni, 'Istruzione e sviluppo economico – Il caso italiano (1861–1913),' in Gianni Toniolo (ed.), *L'economia italiana (1861–1940)*, Bari: Laterza, 1978, pp. 141–144.

14. Giuseppe Ricuperati, 'La scuola nell'Italia unita,' in *Storia d'Italia*, Vol. V, Turin: G. Einaudi, p. 1700.

15. In these years there were those who proposed a return to the model of the medieval universities: these were run by free associations of students who elected the rector and the teachers, autonomously organizing their studies. The creation of the class of 'free teachers' (teachers whose salary from the public universities depended on the contributions made by those enrolled on their courses) is, to a certain extent, an expression of this tendency. It was also hoped that the presence of free teachers in competition with ordinary professors would constitute a guarantee of the quality of teaching. In reality there were very few benefits at the didactive level and many conflicts of a financial nature between free teachers and the State. On this theme, see the work by Antonio La Penna, 'Università e istruzione pubblica,' *op. cit.*; and Carlo Matteucci, *Sulle condizioni della pubblica istruzione nel regno d'Italia. Relazione generale presentata al ministro del consiglio superiore di Torino*, Milan: Stamperia reale, 1865. See also the work by Mauro Moretti and Ilaria Porciani, 'Università e Stato nell'Italia liberale: una ricerca in corso,' *Scienze e Politica*, No. 3, 1990.

16. For more information on this aspect, see Carlo G. Lacaita, *Istruzione e sviluppo industriale in Italia, 1859–1914*, Florence: Giunti, pp. 145–147.

17. On these two institutes see the work by Sandro Rogari, 'L'Istituto di Studi Superiori Pratici e di Perfezionamento e la Scuola di Scienze Sociali (1859–1924),' in *Storia dell'Ateneo Fiorentino, Contributi di Studio*, Vol. 2, Florence: Parretti, 1986, pp. 959–1030; besides the already cited *Digesto Italiano*, Volume V, *Istituti diversi d'Istruzione Superiore*, p. 1086. For a comparison with the French case see the work in this volume by Johan Heilbron.

18. On the business schools, see the work by Massimo M. Augello and Marco E.L. Guidi, 'I "Politecnici del commercio" e la formazione della classe dirigente

economica nell'Italia post-unitaria. L'origine delle Scuole Superiori di commercio e l'insegnamento dell'economia politica, 1868–1900,' in *Le Cattedre di economia, op. cit.*, pp. 335–384.

19. Carlo G. Lacaita, *Istruzione e sviluppo industriale in Italia, op. cit.*, p. 147. It was a controversial question, even when related to the problem concerned with allowing the teaching of political economy to expand to a greater or lesser extent: whether to limit it to university, para-university and technical institute studies or to extend it to the classical *licei*. Two fronts emerged in 1868 at the time of the debate taking place in the 'Italian Political Economy Society'. There were some economists (A. Scialoja, L. Luzzatti and F. Protonotari) who felt that education was necessary for the formation of the middle class, the pillar of the future modern Italian society, and others, such as F. Ferrara, who wanted to keep it in the technical institutes, denying its usefulness in the classical *licei*. A diversity of opinions continued throughout the nineteenth century. See *Nuova Antologia*, Vol. **VIII**, (20 June) 1868. see also Piero Barcucci and Pier Francesco Asso (eds.), *Francesco Ferrara e il suo tempo*, Rome: Bancaria editrice, 1990.

20. This proposal was passed by the Chamber by a few votes, but incited a strong reaction from the opposition, contributing to the crisis of the government led by Depretis. The project was abandoned by the new government, and the chance for a general reform of the universities thus faded away for more years. A system of partial reforms, passed with adjustments or specific modifications, was resorted to. Giorgio Candeloro, *Storia dell'Italia moderna*, Vol. 6, Milan: Feltrinelli, pp. 278–279.

21. Raffaele Romanelli, *L'Italia liberale (1861–1900)*, Bologna: Il Mulino, 1979, p. 180 ff.

22. Anna Pellanda, *Angelo Messedaglia, tematiche economiche e indagini storiche*, Padua: Signum edizioni, 1984, especially pp. 24–35; Cesare Mozzarelli and Stefano Nespor, *Giuristi e scienze sociali nell'Italia liberale*, Venice: Marsilio editori, 1981.

23. Franco Venturi, *Italy and the Enlightenment*, New York: New York University Press, 1972.

24. Riccardo Faucci, 'La cultura economica dopo l'unità,' in Massimo Finoia (ed.), *Il pensiero economico italiano, op. cit.*, pp. 53–65, in particular pp. 55–56; Raffaella Gherardi, 'Sul "Methodenstreit" nell'età della sinistra (1875–1885): Costituzione, amministrazione e finanza nella "Via media" di Giuseppe Ricca-Salerno,' *Materiali per una storia della cultura giuridica*, XIII, no. 1, June 1983.

25. On this subject see the works contained in the special edition 'I cento anni de "L'industria",' in *L'industria*, no. 3, 1986; and also Vera Zamagni, *Lo Stato italiano e l'economia*, Florence, Le Monnier, 1981.

26. Silvio Lanaro, *Nazione e lavoro. Saggio sulla cultura borghese in Italia, 1870–1925*, Padua, Marsilio editori, 1979, p. 169.

27. Francesco Ferrara, 'Prefazione,' in *Biblioteca dell'Economista*, first series, Vol. 3, Turin: Pomba editore, 1852, p. xxxv, now found in *Francesco Ferrara. Opere complete*, Vol. 2, *op. cit.*

28. Francesco Ferrara, *Lezioni di Economia Politica*, in Piero Barucci and Pier Francesco Asso (eds.), *Francesco Ferrara. Opere complete*, Vol. 11, Rome: Bancaria editrice, 1986, pp. 6–7.

29. The quote by Adolphe Blanqui comes from Francesco Ferrara, 'Prefazione' in *Biblioteca dell'Economista*, first series, Vol. 3, Turin: Pomba editore, 1852, p. xxxix, now found in *Francesco Ferrara. Opere complete*, Vol. 2, *op. cit.* See also Aurelio Macchioro, *Studi di storia del pensiero economico e altri saggi*, Milan: Feltrinelli, 1970.

30. These themes are discussed and outlined in Pierangelo Schiera, 'Amministrazione e costituzione: verso la nascita della scienza politica,' in *Scienza e pensiero politico nella seconda metà dell'Ottocento*, Florence: Olschki, 1982, p. 80, and in this volume. Research in Germany and Italy into "common methods for the scientific solution of social problems ..." is also discussed in Pierangelo Schiera and Friedrich Tenbruck (eds.), *Gustav Schmoller e il suo tempo: la nascita delle scienze sociali in Germania e in Italia*, Bologna: Il Mulino, 1988.

31. Emilio R. Papa (ed.), *Il positivismo e la cultura italiana*, Milan: Franco Angeli, 1985. See particularly the work by Riccardo Faucci.

32. Massimo Augello and Denis Giva, 'La definitiva istitutionalizzazione accademica dell'economia politica: le Università di Padova e di Torino (1860–1900),' in *Le cattedre di economia, op. cit.*, pp. 241–289.

33. Gabriella Gioli, 'La nascita e l'affermazione dell'insegnamento dell'economia politica in Italia: continuità e discontinuità (1750–1900),' in *Le cattedre di economia, op. cit.*, pp. 407–408. Similar works and especially legal studies may be found in Aldo Mazzacane (ed.), *L'esperienza giuridica di Emanuele Gianturco*, Naples: Liguori editori, 1987; *I giuristi e la crisi dello stato liberale in Italia fra otto e novecento*, Naples: Liguori editori, 1986, particularly the contributions by Antonio Cardini and Ilaria Porciani.

34. Piero Barucci and Piero Roggi, 'I cent'anni de "L'industria". La politica economica per l'affermazione della cultura industriale in Italia,' *L'industria*, no. 3, 1986, pp. 355–379. See also Antonio Cardini, *Stato liberale e protezionismo in Italia (1890–1900)*, Bologna: Il Mulino, 1981; Giuseppe Are, *Economia e politica nell'Italia liberale (1890–1915)*, Bologna: Il Mulino, 1974.

35. Guido Baglioni, 'L'ideologia della borghesia industriale,' *op. cit.*, p. 473.

36. Piero Bini, '"L'industria": 1887–1914. La politica economica del decollo industriale,' *L'industria*, no. 3, 1986, pp. 403–434; Giovanni Zalin, 'Protezionismo e sviluppo economico accelerato nel pensiero di Friedrich List e di Alessandro Rossi,' *Rassegna Economica*, no. 6, 1980, pp. 1363–1407.

37. Piero Bini, '"L'industria": 1887–1914,' *L'industria, op. cit.*, pp. 406–411.

38. The German university model to which Luigi Luzzatti and Vittorio Ellena tended was the same as the one which Richard T. Ely had tried, unsuccessfully, to bring to the USA in the middle of the 1880's. See the contribution to this volume by John G. Gunnell.

39. It is worth remembering that marginalist theory became known in Italy after 1883 when Maffeo Pantaleoni, following W. Stanley Jevons, developed the theory of 'the comparison of various expenditures by marginal degrees of utility' as a criterion to follow in the allocation of public expenditure. However, marginalist theory was introduced in 1876 when Gerolamo Boccardo, who succeeded Francesco Ferrara as the editor of the third series of the *Biblioteca dell'economista* included works by the aforementioned Jevons (1876) and

Walras (1878). See Piero Barucci, 'The Spread of Marginalism in Italy, 1871–1890,' *History of Political Economy, (Papers on the Marginal Revolution in Economics)*, no. 2, 1972, pp. 512–532.

40. Besides the work by James M. Buchanan 'La scuola italiana di finanza pubblica,' in Massimo Finoia (ed.), *Pensiero economico, op. cit.*, p. 207ff., see also Mauro Fasiani, 'La teoria della finanza pubblica in Italia,' (translated from the German) in Massimo Finoia (ed.), *Il pensiero economico, op. cit.*, pp. 118–202.

41. Joseph A. Schumpeter, *History of Economic Analysis, op. cit.*, p. 47.

42. Giuseppe Are, *Economia e politica nell'Italia liberale, op. cit.*, pp. 193–194.

43. Maffeo Pantaleoni, 'Il secolo ventesimo secondo un individualista,' in *Erotemi di economia*, Vol. I, Bari: Laterza, 1925, p. 280.

44. Joseph A. Schumpeter, *History of Economic Analysis, op. cit.*, p. 757.

PART VI

WESTERN SOCIAL SCIENCES IN SPACE AND TIME

CHAPTER THIRTEEN

STATES, INSTITUTIONS, AND DISCOURSES:
A COMPARATIVE PERSPECTIVE ON THE
STRUCTURATION OF THE SOCIAL SCIENCES

PETER WAGNER AND BJÖRN WITTROCK

Social Science as Organized Social Activity

One of the characteristics of modern science is its organized form in separate knowledge-producing institutions. These institutions, their internal structure and their relations to society at large, cannot be taken for granted in a sociology of the sciences but are one of its key problematiques. Even if the day-to-day activities of scientists at work were hardly distinguishable from other social activities – a claim some scholars have raised based on ethnomethodological and interactionist research – still the location of these activities in particular institutions makes for sociologically relevant differences. Thus scientists distinguish themselves and their work not least by way of their institutional position. Their claims to social relevance are based on this position. They refer socially and intellectually crucially, though of course not exclusively, to actors in similar institutions (1). The very real phenomenon of struggles over admittance of individual scholars, intellectual "approaches," or specific organizations to the realm of academic institutions could hardly be understood, if institutional difference were of little or no relevance (2). The institutional distinctiveness of science, however, varies over time and space, and across scientific fields. To disregard similarities between science and other social activities and to neglect the impact of societal institutions on science would be equally misleading as the more recent tendency towards denying all distinctiveness to science as a social activity. By implication, science would then tend to be reified, and sociological analysis precluded (3).

P. Wagner, B. Wittrock, and R. Whitley (eds.), Discourses on Society: Volume XV, 1990, 331–357.
© 1990 *Kluwer Academic Publishers. Printed in the Netherlands.*

A theoretically informed sociology of the social sciences must, as already argued, overcome the dichotomies of externalism and internalism as well as of micro- and macro-accounts, while bringing historicity back in, in a manner which is sensitive to particularities, yet does not shy away from the theoretical commitment of social science. Any such comprehensive sociology of modern social science will then have to take the development of the reformed, research-oriented, university and the development of the territorial nation-state as its points of reference. These academic and political institutions are precisely such vehicles for the mobilization of resources which underpin practices of a long duration and extension. They effectively serve to sustain – or to thwart – the intellectual projects promoted by various individuals and groupings, and form the institutional underpinning and discursive backdrop of these projects.

In this context, it is crucial to see that the historical formation of the disciplines in the social sciences was very closely linked to two other formative processes that have been fundamentally restructuring relations between the university and the state. *First*, university reformers and academics strove for a clearer separation of scientific institutions from wider society from the early nineteenth century onwards. As a consequence, sharper distinctions between academic and public discourses were introduced than had existed before: "It was less possible than before for an outsider to maintain a standpoint in scientific questions without just being dismissed as 'amateur' by the 'real' scientists, and it became more and more difficult for the outsider to go straight into the university as a teacher in scientific matters" (4).

Secondly, the education and training tasks of the academic institutions were reconsidered and widened. Training requirements were seen as having expanded, not least related to increased administrative activity of the state, and broadened beyond traditional concepts. In the field of technical education, this led to the emergence of new training institutions, alongside the university but often striving for university status. The social sciences, mainly residing at the universities, were to some extent defined via their role in training.

Neither of these developments was unilinear across time or synchronic across nations. Concepts such as "autonomatization" of scientific activities or of their "functional differentiation" – often premised on implicit macro-theories of societal development – tend to press actual historical processes into abstract logics and to grossly underestimate their variable character. Pierangelo Schiera's comparative analysis of Germany and Italy clearly reveals the limited value of such concepts, as he stresses the politically circumscribed nature of German university "autonomy" and the sheer lack of "differentiation" in the Italian setting. Similarly, it is only too obvious (see Gunnell in this volume) that an account of the development of the American academic discourse on state and politics in such terms would be pitifully unable to grasp the context-bound structuration of that discourse in its formative period.

Understood precisely as historically varying transformations, however, these two aspects of the restructuring of university-state relations can provide the background for an analysis of the emergence of organized disciplinary discourses in the social sciences. We stress the double character of this process, because it provides for two paths in social science development, which can be clearly distinguished both in organizational and in cognitive terms. If the relevant actors see the academic institutions more as research-oriented, this process encourages "scientization", the development of a closed, formal "self-referential" discourse. If they see them more as training- and education-oriented, this encourages "professionalization," here understood as the formation of a vocational group to the training of which the academic specialty is devoted. In the following, the first section will deal with the former process, the second with the latter, both, of course, only insofar as they concern the social sciences.

The outcome of the two orientations in terms of discourse, of cognitive structures, can be markedly different: this leads to the formation of various structures of organized social science which we shall try to distinguish in the fourth section in relation to the structures of political and academic institutions of Western countries, which will be briefly characterized in the third section.

Is is often held that the formation of modern social science was basically accomplished by the 1920s. The contributions by Malcolm Vout and Katrin Fridjonsdottir on political science and sociology, respectively, after the Second World War show that this assertion does not hold for large parts of Europe. Keith Tribe's analysis, furthermore, shows that not even economics in its modern form was fully established in academic institutions before 1945. It is true, however, that social science debates in Europe after 1950 were strongly influenced by "the American model," interrupting and truncating earlier intellectual developments. The hegemony of American thinking during the 1950s and 1960s demands responses to two questions. First, the nature of the "long transition" from classical to modern social science in Europe needs to be understood. And second, it has to be asked what the reopening of social science debates during the 1970s and 1980s actually meant in terms of intellectual traditions and political transformations. Concluding this chapter, we shall try to indicate directions in which answers to these questions should probably be searched.

The Separation of Academic from Public Discourse

Social science is a special form of the reflexive monitoring of societal development. As such, scientific discourse on society exists alongside other discourses. In building its categories it recurrently draws on and affects those present in public and political discourses in the society in which it evolves (5). One way of analyzing the development of social science discourse, thus, is to relate it to other discourses and identify its specifics, as Helga Nowotny does in this volume. These other discourses may be initiated by administration, such as the social research pursued by factory inspectors and statisticians, or they may be broadly public, as the ones promoted by social movements like the workers' movement. Given such relatively open boundaries as existed at that time, the discursive interaction on issues such as poverty and welfare will influence the shape of the scientific discourses.

Time and again, the social sciences have profited from such interaction in terms of institutional support. They have been able to portray themselves as contributing to the solution of social problems by scholarly means, i.e. means that only they could provide, and were honoured by policy-makers with institutional recognition and resources. The policy-makers, in turn, often belonging to broadly reformist currents of the political elites, used the recourse to scientific argument to bolster their position in political argumentation and struggle. Elsewhere we have tried to describe such interactions as discourse coalitions made possible by and drawing on a discursive affinity between scholarly programmes and policy programmes under certain circumstances (6).

In this sense, the transformation from an ameliorist-associational type of social science to an academic-disciplinary one – gradual and uneven though it was in comparative perspective – can be regarded as one major example of the workings of such discourse coalitions. Characteristically, this process was premised on a broad thematic affinity between problems perceived in intellectual and public discourse. Partly drawing on general encouragement and support, partly on more direct endorsement emanating from the participation of social scientists or would-be social scientists in *ad hoc* government, parliamentary, and local committees, the proponents of academic discourse were able to establish at least some forms of such discourse. For academic discourse this process entailed the creation of discursive boundaries and standards of acceptable solutions which from then on were difficult to violate, much less disregard.

The most familiar example of this transition is the gradual, decades-long erosion of the position of the broadly reformist American Social Science Association (ASSA) through the creation of a number of disciplinary associations (see Manicas in this volume). These developments have been studied as a master case of professionalization and as the successful claim to knowledge production to enhance social status and, in fact, political influence by other means. In contrast, English research-oriented social reformers, like the Fabian Society, have relied much more on the informal channels of influence in established elite networks and saw obviously no need to stress "scientificity" in similar ways as their American counterparts (7).

Inversely, in Italy, academic scholars have been directly engaged in political disputes around the establishment and consolidation of the nation-state, without being able to derive any particular legitimacy from this involvement which could be used to help underpin incipient social science institutions in Italy (8). In Imperial Germany, the ameliorist Association for Social Policy was able, in contrast to the ASSA, to simultaneously gain scientific and political legitimacy with its range of policy-oriented, though allegedly not partisan, activities. As a core institution of the Prussian state, the Humboldtian university was endowed with the prestige of being the centre-piece of the nation, its research and teaching, thus, an incarnation of superior reason.

The new relation of academic and public discourse can most clearly be seen where academia, or factions of it, aligned with parts only of the political opponents. In Imperial Germany, for instance, the academic institutions and the "Mandarin" caste of the professoriate were socially and politically almost perfectly closed to the working class' political representatives. As the latter exhibited a high degree of cognitive and organizational mobilization through the Social Democratic Party and its theorists, a "discourse context outside the universities" developed, not least as a reaction to the closure of the academic institutions. This extra-universitarian discourse became academically effective after the breakdown of the imperial state in 1919 (9). In the French Third Republic, Emile Durkheim's sociological project was almost from the start supported by the republican forces, not least because it centred on notions of society and solidarity as the means for social cohesion. Durkheim's own main strategic interest was in enhancing the scientific legitimacy of his approach; he was, therefore, rather adverse to political involvement. Independent of him and most of his sociological collaborators, however, a political discourse was elaborated, labelled *solidarisme*, which came to be the "inofficial ideology of the republic" and showed evident affinities to Durkheim's theory of society (10).

In analyzing the transition from ameliorist to academic social science up to this point, our reasoning has mainly stressed the strengthening of the sociopolitical position of a discourse once it was institutionally established. Equally important, however, is the fact that the transformation of the universities made it increasingly important for scholars to teach and promote their project from an institutionally acknowledged position. Indeed, this became something of a necessity for proponents who cared for securing the reproduction of their intellectual project.

Again, some examples can be given how such considerations shaped the activities of scholars. By the end of the First World War, Durkheimian sociology could pose as "the French school of sociology". The creation of just four chairs in sociology at the faculties of letters can hardly be considered full-scale institutionalization but a "halfway" success at best. However, the very fact that this had been achieved at all was remarkable in European comparison, in particular given the hierarchical structure of French academic institutions. In fact, Durkheim's school-building can be seen as a consciously developed "success strategy" to acquire scientific legitimacy in the given cognitive and organizational context (11). The Durkheimian achievements are particularly striking when counterposed to the failures of his contemporaries René Worms and Gabriel Tarde, whose sociologies, while academically debated at the time, were quickly discontinued after the death of their founders. A similar fate befell the "political sciences" of Emile Boutmy (12).

The French developments can be compared to the overwhelming concern about the academic respectability on the part of the German Society for Sociology (DGS) in the interwar period. Until the early twentieth century, the notion of sociology had rather been detested by German scholars as being scientistic, positivistic, and deterministic. As such it was seen as incompatible with the humanistic and historical heritage of the German tradition of true scholarship. On still insecure grounds in the academic milieu but with some support from the early Weimar Republic's science policy, the spokespersons of the DGS, above all Leopold von Wiese, tried to secure a place in academia by defining sociology cognitively in such a way that it would not interfere with the established disciplines. "Formal sociology" would be devoted to human relations and interactions and be devoid of any concern for historical, economic, political, or moral perspectives. This "dehistoricization" and "deeconomization", as Lukàcs had termed it, did not achieve any academic breakthrough. However, it went along with a modest in-stitutionalization of sociology in Germany until 1932, during a period, that is, when elsewhere in Europe sociology was in stagnation or decline in institutional terms (13).

It is important to see that the concern for scientific legitimacy became increasingly important in the more institutionalized context of modern research-oriented universities in the late nineteenth and early twentieth centuries. It usually entailed that intellectual discourse had to demonstrate some degree of internal coherence, often accomplished by introducing formal or deductive reasoning; that the discourse was specific and delimited with regard to other academic discourses; and that it was distinct from lay or amateur discourse. These features have often been summarized under the notion of scientization, a notion which may be useful for descriptive purposes as long as it is not used to justify claims for asymmetric relations of superiority of scientific over public discourse.

Educational Practice and Knowledge Production in Early Social Science

If Durkheim had constituted the French school of sociology, there was, as already mentioned, an equally hegemonic French school of political sciences, namely Emile Boutmy's *Ecole libre des sciences politiques*. Founded in 1871–2, its rise to virtual monopoly in the field coincided with the establishment of the Durkheimian approach. This parallel can be used to show the impact different orientations in academic projects, namely to educational practice as opposed to scientific knowledge, can have on cognitive structures.

Though some controversies of interpretation may prevail, it is quite easy to outline the basic structure of Durkheimian sociology (see, e.g., very briefly, Wagner in this volume). It is virtually impossible to do the equivalent for the intellectual programme of the *Ecole libre*. French political sciences of the 1880s as taught at the school were

> divided, splintered into courses which were not related in anything, and the teachers of which had the most diverse origins. ... They are state sciences rather than political sciences: essentially devoted to the education of high civil servants, they assemble 'political, administrative, diplomatic, economic and financial types of knowledge' needed by these practitioners, and strive for an 'openly practical and professional' teaching ... The political sciences, though they may presuppose research and reflection, in their expressions they do not always take distance anymore from the mundane discourse. (14)

This summary description implicitly contains the crucial link in the development of the school. Boutmy himself had an intellectual project for his school, a sort of political psychology, which he abandoned, however, for a long time to devote his energy to preserve the school and make it into the centre for elite training for state officials and diplomats, along the established lines of French higher education. The *grandes écoles*, the elite institutions, never really developed a research orientation. The unity of research and teaching characteristic of universities in other countries is traditionally weak in France. As a consequence, this turn to professional training forced Boutmy to sacrifice cognitive coherence and open up specific demands for knowledge.

No other case is as extreme as the counterposition of French sociology and political science (15). But quite often the cognitive development of the social sciences can hardly be understood apart from its linkages to educational and professional practices. The usual, disciplinary, histories of the social sciences have often misinterpreted the development by looking at the disciplines purely as programmes for the advancement of knowledge. In some cases, as the one just mentioned, scientific advance was not even the major objective. Even where it was, this orientation was often significantly modified by a parallel orientation to training and education purposes.

It is probably safe to state that such a professional orientation was most pronounced in the political (and administrative) sciences (16). By the time the university transformations tended to favour cognitive organization, little was left of the political philosophy of modernity to be organized to form a disciplinary core. Major themes of political theory had been appropriated by the discourses of political economy and sociology, incidentally the former rather in the liberal and the latter in the conservative tradition (17).

The attempts to set up a specific political science – i.e. one apart from traditional political philosophy, or in some instances political history, which continued to prevail in many institutions (see both Gunnell and Vout, in this volume) – in the late nineteenth century could, then, largely be seen as reactions to the formative tendencies on the part of other discourses on society. They were deeply shaped by the emergence and development of new political structures such as the political institutions of the nation-states, republican or monarchic, and the bureaucracies of the early interventionist welfare states in Europe. These were the parts of social reality which aspiring political scientists could legitimately claim as their territory, given the strong, and increasing, neglect of politics in economics and sociology, at least in their academically disciplined form.

The focus on specific institutions, however, was much less intellectually organizing than the key themes of economic and sociological discourse, on the one hand, and much closer than the latter to the description of observable reality, and to "mundane discourse", on the other. To fall in line with increasing demands for administrative training, as in the French case, therefore, was a perfectly feasible course of action. Many of the proposals to establish political or administrative sciences drew on this linkage, often in the hope to help create a scientific discipline and a modern profession at one and the same time (18).

If political science institutions were created at all in turn-of-the-century Europe under these conditions, they turned out to be shaped much more by their professional than their scholarly orientations. Apart from the *Ecole libre* in Paris, the *Istituto Cesare Alfieri* in Florence and, later, the *Hochschule für Politik* in Berlin are examples of this kind. Aspiring political scientists in the U.S.A. started under different conditions. John Gunnell, in this volume, gives an account of the attempts to combine the striving for a scientific discipline, centered on the concept of the state, with a professional orientation which would give the social and institutional basis to such a project. The main differences to the European settings are that neither was the discourse on the state set in philosophical or legal terms nor was public administration a traditionally occupied field given the lack of a fully developed state apparatus. In fact, as pointed out by Gunnell, Boutmy's *Ecole Libre* served as a model for the first real political science institution in the United States, viz. at Columbia. In that case, however, its major representative, Burgess, consciously chose to emphasize the scholarly rather than the professional component of the school's basic concept. And it also proved much easier to link scholarly work to some degree of professional education given the structure of American universities. Burgess' project gave rise to a line of development drastically different from that of its exemplar in Paris (see Gunnell in this volume).

While this professional problematique is most relevant for the emergence of political science as a discipline, the development of economics, too, would be misunderstood if it were cast purely as efforts at achieving a purely academic standing in terms of scientific standards. Thus by the late nineteenth century economics, as political economy, still had the connotation of being the "science of governance" and not an analysis of a completely separate economic sphere (19). In this tradition, the task of the economic approach to enlighten state economic policies was still widely acknowledged, and fulfilled, by the end of the nineteenth century, as Gabriella Gioli points out. On the other hand, economics was increasingly demanded for education in commercial matters, often in special schools or in newly emerging universities, not in the traditional strongholds of academia (see Tribe, and Gioli, in this volume). Both these orientations, however, were clearly at odds with the advance of neoclassical economics as a scientific programme.

In the sense we have discussed this aspect here, sociology was the least professionally oriented of the emerging social science disicplines. It developed most strongly where it could align with philosophy and define its social function in terms of moral education. Apart from providing both an intellectual and a moral rationale for the Third Republic and its self-understanding, Durkheimian sociology, for instance, was even assigned an institutionalized role down to the level of primary school teachers' education (20). While this feature of French sociology is well known, the argument has only recently been advanced that the development of American sociology might well be seen in terms of its role as a substitute for religion, or perhaps rather a correlate of it, as a secularized religion, so to say. And in Weimar Germany, social democratic science policy-makers proposed that sociology should contribute to civic education in and for the young republic (21).

These social tasks which sociology was often seen to be endowed with have to be strictly distinguished, though, from a formal professional or practical orientation, as we have, to varying extents, diagnosed them for the political sciences and economics. For this reason, sociology in its classical period can rather adequately be analyzed as a research programme. The absence of a clear professional orientation and mission explains largely its institutional difficulties. These difficulties, in turn, could most easily be overcome where sociologists succeeded in defining a professional social role early on, be it in terms of regional planning (Netherlands), analysis for local planning (U.S.), or customer-oriented research in general (Lazarsfeld; first in Austria, then in the U.S.). The United States and the Netherlands have, even today, the sociological communities which are most clearly committed to such a service-orientation even at a time when an orientation of letting sociological research serve policy objectives has become much more widespread (22).

Our account up to this point shows that there were two broad tendencies for academic discourses to develop towards the end of the nineteenth century. From the perspective of the proponents of these discourses, the one can be called the *scientific strategy*, the other the *professional strategy* to achieve legitimacy for an intellectual project. Most of the early social scientists' activities can be analyzed in terms of their striving more for the one or more for the other objective, trying to combine the two, or suffering from the dilemma to choose. As will be shown below, a third approach can be distinguished from these two, one which essentially rejected both "scientizing" and "professionalizing" of the discourses on society.

In the following, we shall try to systematically discuss the conditions under which the one or the other or the third strategy may be pursued. At the outset of such an analysis, it is necessary first to reintroduce a comparative perspective on the relation of political institutions to academic ones. We shall then give a full sketch of the discursive space for the social sciences in the period of political and institutional transformations around the turn of the century that we are mainly concerned with.

States and Social Knowledge: National Structures of Discourse-Producing Institutions

It is a common observation that national intellectual traditions exist in the social sciences. These traditions are often remarkably resistant to processes of "universalization" or "modernization" and even provide intellectual resources from which new social theorizing can continuously emerge (23). However, apart from general reflections about intellectual cultures, not many attempts have been made hitherto to systematically and comparatively relate specificities of discourses to the institutional structures of politics and academia, to root them in their national societal contexts. Given that the formation of disciplinary social science coincided with transformations of the nation states and that these latter transformations were crucially dependent on new discursive understandings of state and society, this neglect is very surprising. Some indication how such a comparative institutional perspective can be developed shall be made.

In the earlier discussion of professional strategies, it was pointed out that in the United States the social groups tried to define themselves in terms of their access to specific knowledge and to develop the universities as non-state loci of the generation and reproduction of knowledge. This phenomenon, by the way, has shaped the very understanding of the notion of "profession" in sociology, a notion which is basically (Anglo-) American and hardly transferable to other societies. In continental Europe, in contrast, most early social scientists disposed of state-endowed rank by their very position as chairholders in state universities. They could well see a need for more cognitive organization of their projects, but hardly for social organization as a special social group which they had already formed by institutional definition. In state-centered socieities the universities, in turn, had a key position as containers of state-relevant knowledge and as training institutions for political and administrative elites.

The political-institutional positions from which aspiring social scientists started out in the second half of the nineteenth century were, thus, markedly different in the U.S.A. and in Europe. In Europe, academic institutions developed parallel to political institutions and various constellations of "science and politics", to use Schiera's term, were formed from late absolutism over the liberal constitutional state to the early interventionist state taking shape at the turn of the century. In the United States, in contrast, a strong national state did not exist by the mid-nineteenth century, and the formation of modern universities was an attempt by groups in civil society to create and reform institutions of higher education and knowledge production as to be able to meet and cope with the demands of industrialization, urbanization, and the transformation of politics that went along with these phenomena. While Europeans normally had at least implicit social theories in which the state and its relations to society had a prominent place, Americans could not easily endow the state a priori with a key role in societal development (see Gunnell's analysis of the intellectual struggle around this concept, in this volume).

European structures, however, were far from homogeneous. A major distinction must be made beween England and continental Europe, a distinction which again is based on the character of the state in these societies. England and the U.S.A. have often been labelled "stateless" societies. Whereas this "relative statelessness" in the U.S.A. dates back to the community orientation and aversion against centralization of the Federalists, in the British case it rather reflected the well-entrenched position of a landed aristocracy, hostile towards efforts at formalized, central control and rule. This "statelessness" stemmed from the very strength of relatively nonformalized state institutions which had proved capable of continuous adaptation to gradual societal change. These institutions were ultimately sustained by an elite culture. To some important extent that elite culture was reproduced and modified in academic institutions, which then may be better described as seats of elite socialization rather than of formal training for particular professions.

In continental Europe, in contrast, much more formally structured bureaucratic and military apparatuses had existed in most countries since the absolutist period, and the training tasks of universities and higher education institutions were more systematically elaborated and spelled out. The centrality of the state is clearly visible in discourse terms, i.e. in the academic prominence of public law and of state-oriented philosophies. The political and institutional specificity of continental Europe and the relevance of this specificity for intellectual developments has not escaped knowledgeable observers. Three decades ago, the historian Stuart H. Hughes, for instance, remarked that "the countries on the western and central European continent shared institutions – and an intellectual heritage in philosophy, law and in the structure of higher education – that presented their leading thinkers with a similar set of problems" (24). And in his account of political restoration after World War I, Charles S. Maier emphasized in similar terms for France, Italy and Germany that "despite major differences, the three nations all had traditions of sharp ideological dispute and fragmentation, concepts of liberalism and labels for distinction that set them apart from Britain and the United States" (25).

If one is going to introduce another comparative distinction among state-centered societies, one should set France apart from "central Europe". France has often been regarded as the reference case for state developments. This is only too natural given its history of early centralization and political consolidation on a rather stable territorial basis and within clear boundaries, a development which, in fact, had a structuring impact on the political strategies of elites in neighbouring European societies. The essential features of the modernization of the French state in the post-revolutionary period have been captured by Douglas Ashford: "In hardly more than a decade, France acquired a supreme legal advisory body, the Council of State; a number of highly trained administrative bodies or *grands corps*, each with their designated duties, privileges and rules; a rigidly hierarchical educational structure ...; and a carefully designed territorial structure. Napoleon, distrustful of the common law, also set in motion the systematic codification of the rules and procedures governing every aspect of French life" (26).

Compared to other major European nations, such as Italy and Germany, France has a longer and more consolidated history of state institutions and, at the same time, a concept of the state enlarged by the revolutionary, democratic tradition. These two aspects go well hand in hand. The modern nation-state was built only in the 1860s and 1870s in Germany and Italy and this process had a more "artificial, contrived" character (Stuart Hughes), with parts of the elites imposing their conception on rather heterogeneous societies. As a consequence, legal thinking acquired a very prominent role in forging the nation and tended to preclude the development of an empirically oriented social and political science. In France, in contrast, the understanding of societal solidarity, as advanced in Durkheimian sociology, became an important element of the self-understanding of a republican state, and even tended to influence public law.

In terms of academic institutions, a major divergence of France from central Europe was introduced by the expansion of the system of elite training and scientific institutions in the wake of the Revolution. Concomitantly, the universities were weakened and their role was to be restored only towards the end of the nineteenth century. In central Europe, on the other hand, the universities were assigned the key role both in science and in elite education, starting with the Humboldtian reforms in Germany which stimulated related debates in many other countries. From this reformed and eventually ever more research-oriented university emerged the tradition of historical scholarship in the humanities as well as the disciplinary model of science which largely shaped academic debates in Europe and beyond in the course of the nineteenth century.

Varieties of Cognitive Structures: Towards the Organization of Social Science

This brief unfolding of a comparative institutional perspective will serve as the background against which the variety of social science approaches which emerged in the latter part of the nineteenth century can be analyzed. These early approaches should not be regarded as instances on the evolutionary path of scientific progress in the various disciplines as many disciplinary historians see it. On the contrary, tendencies to judge scholars basically in terms of their perceived contribution to the same present-day image of an intellectual field should be resisted as efforts at undue cognitive imposition and exercises in "whiggish" history writing. Instead, the view proposed here tries to locate an intellectual project specifically in terms of its affinity to the structures of academic and of political institutions and to an historically located constellation in discourses.

From such a perspective, three identifiably different ways of social science formation can be distinguished according to the mode in which scholars related their thinking to the two institutional transformations described above and to the resulting tendencies towards scientization and professionalization. One mode was the rejection of the institutional tendencies towards both disciplinary segmentation and professional specialization; from it resulted what we shall call *comprehensive social science*. The second mode resulted from responses to the internal organization of the university; these approaches shall be analyzed as *formalized disciplinary discourses*. Third, as reactions to orientations of higher education institutions towards codified professional training *pragmatically specializing professions* of social science emerged.

The *first* of these modes comprises a number of very different intellectual approaches. One should range under this label, for instance, continuations of political and social philosophies like idealism or social romanticism. Often enough, these are not cases of any real reaction to the challenges of cognitive-institutional transformations of the time but, given the inertia of academic institutions, rather a matter of sheer continuation of intellectual traditions which could and did persist over long periods, sometimes well into the 1950s or even the present day, though clearly declining in standing and support. More important in our context are two other strands of theorizing which emerged as a critical reaction to the advance of an increasingly coherent discourse of classical, later neoclassical economics. *One* of these critical approaches is historical, state-interventionist economics, most strongly promoted in Germany under the name of the Historical School but also in other countries such as Italy, where it was labelled "economic Germanism". The *other* one, again highly heterogeneous, has become known as "classical sociology", though its proponents – Durkheim, Weber, Pareto, and Simmel, among others – did not always see themselves as having much in common, particularly not in terms of some common project for the founding of a limited subdiscipline of the study of society (see Wagner, in this volume).

The *second* mode, i.e. what has here been termed that of *formalized disciplinary discourse*, is more easily characterized, as it in fact, though unintendedly so by the scholars, came to entail a coherent intellectual frame for a tripartite set of sciences of societal phenomena, namely neoclassical economics, the legal theory of the state, and formal sociology. Neoclassical economics emerged with the so-called marginalist revolution of Menger, Walras, Jevons, and Marshall. It was an attempt to solve theoretical problems of classical political economy and, at the same time, to restore its political legitimacy, which had been waning in a period of rising state interventionism. The legal theory of the state emerged out of the tradition of the so-called Historical School of Law. By means of abstraction from empirical laws and formal deductive reasoning, it tried to systematize a body of public law which the historical scholars had basically identified but had still seen as essentially open. There was a strong discursive affinity between this type of legal theorizing and the efforts of political elites in Germany and Italy to forge a strong modern state onto a relatively heterogeneous society by way of a powerful bureaucracy imbued with a sense of competence and commitment to the workings of a comprehensive machinery of interlocked rules and regulations.

Both neoclassical economics and legal positivism resort to a kind of ontological purification of earlier discourses by excluding extra-economic or extra-legal arguments. Theoretical difficulties of those earlier discourses were then resolved, as it were, but basically in formal terms by exclusive resort to assumptions which were internal to the discourses themselves. Thus, a self-referential system of discourse was constructed, which generated theoretical problems to be worked on with specific methods. A well-defined science – in the literal sense of boundary setting – emerged which acquired scientific, and increasingly also political, legitimacy by way of reference to its "pure" methods and its "vigour".

Not looking at the individual discipline but at their ensemble as sciences of society, the effect of this operation is the division of society into ontologically distinct realms, more specifically the market economy and the state and law. Somewhat belatedly, "formal" or "pure" sociology was proposed by Leopold von Wiese and others. This meant that the scientific study of society was complemented by identification of a third realm of discourse, that of human interactions. "Sociology" was thus rid of its historical, economic, political, and moral dimensions and could develop into a formal discipline among others.

The *third* mode of social science organization, i.e. that of *pragmatic specialization*, is most fully exemplified by the American developments where the American Social Science Association gradually split up into separate organizations for economics, history, psychology, sociology and political science (see Manicas, and Gunnell, in this volume). Some of these new associations, especially in their early years, witnessed intense and conflictual debates about their cognitive orientation. The economics association, after strong internal controversies in an initial phase, basically settled for the neoclassical approach, and the sociological association came to orient itself towards an emphasis on intra- and intergroup relations as its mark of distinction, though much less dogmatically than von Wiese argued for in Germany. So, some elements of the disciplinary structure of the second mode were clearly present. The main thrust, however, which all associations had in common, was a commitment to an empirical, often and increasingly quantitative, methodology and to some conception of the usefulness of scientific knowledge for the allegedly politically neutral solution of social problems. On this basis, the division of labour between the associations was a rather pragmatic one without any strong need for some kind of coherent theoretical rationale for this particular division or its individual disciplinary components.

Over time the first two modes of social science organization came to face serious problems of intellectual reproduction in the academic institutions. The *comprehensive social science* approaches were caught in what may be called the *scientific-institutional dilemma* (27). Some of their proponents were quite successful in advancing their thinking and in laying the basis for intellectual reproduction. Among the classical sociologists this is probably most true for Emile Durkheim, while among the historical economists Gustav Schmoller exerted a dominant influence in Germany over several decades and the neoclassical approach remained on the fringe of academia. It is clearly the case though that over the longer run this type of social thought suffered from the fact that it escaped formalizability. As argued before, the rejection to standardize skill requirements and to develop a codified set of theorems and method was exactly the characteristic feature of this thinking. The most obvious example for failed intellectual reproduction is the strong neglect of Weber's epistemological and theoretical work in German interwar sociology, in spite of wide quotation of Weber's writings, while von Wiese's severely circumscribed concept of sociology gained ground. Some of the internal debates in the American associations (see Gunnell, and Manicas, in this volume) as well as the gradual reorientation in Italian economics towards the end of the nineteenth century (see Gioli, in this volume) can be seen in a similar light.

In contrast, it was the strength of the *formalized disciplinary discourses* that they lived up to strict requirements for scientific legitimacy. The problem they faced was a different one, and can be labelled the *politico-institutional dilemma* of social science. The typical tripartite constellation of discourse can be said to have carried an implicit political theory which is the intellectual correlate to a rationalized capitalist industrial society in a normatively liberal nation-state. The economy is then seen as differentiated from political society to such an extent that it is deemed not only intellectually fruitful but also, if implicitly, reasonable and useful as a societal-political approximation to cast its workings in terms of a theory of rational utility calculations by atomistic actors. The state and its bureaucratic apparatus are then tacitly pictured as being either more or less irrelevant or, at least potentially, placed in a directly adversarian position *vis-à-vis* society and assigned little but the role of safeguarding the latter's order. The state is no longer epitomized by a princely ruler, but expresses its will through law and implements it in formal and universal bureaucratic procedures. Society is then reduced to the interactions of individuals and groups. Such a conception can well be said to have been ideologically useful for parts of the societal elites around the turn of the century. To some extent this still holds true today (28).

However, this type of theorizing hardly ever provided adequate analytical tools for an understanding of the immediate problems of contemporary society, and it soon proved unable to cover the analytical and informational needs of societal elites. The neoclassical discourse of economics underwent a new crisis in the interwar period, a crisis which became imminent with the onset of the Great Depression. It was then either superseded or transformed by Keynesian, corporative, and technocratic-interventionist economic discourses as well as by empirical studies of economic developments, most often in newly created research institutes. The legal theory of the state was largely abandoned even in its "stronghold", Germany, in the interwar period, and attempts were made to replace it by social and sociological reasonings on the state or by decisionist political philosophies. This period also witnessed the reemergence of a strong interest in the empirical study of political institutions.

Thus, by the late interwar period, the *first mode* of social science formation distinguished in this analysis, i.e. that of projects of *comprehensive social science*, had never really taken root in the American setting, while it had become increasingly clear that its future reproduction in the European context was severely undercut. The *second* mode of formation, i.e. the constellation of *formalized disciplinary discourses*, did not face the scientific-institutional problems of the first mode. However, by then key components of this second mode, notably neoclassical economics but also formal legal theory and formalistic sociology, were visibly unable to handle the political-societal dilemma of elucidating, much less solving, the major social problems of the day. Given that these first two modes were dominant in most European countries in one form or the other, and that the third mode, *pragmatic professionalization*, was comparatively weak there, this meant a deep rupture in the intellectual traditions of European social science. Indeed, with few exceptions, very little academic-institutional development of social science was experienced between 1920 and 1950. During the same period, empirical social and economic research was institutionalized mostly outside the academic institutions, while the third mode of social science formation consolidated and expanded significantly in the United States.

Modernization of the Social Sciences: The Long Transition

Two important conclusions can be directly drawn from these comparative observations on social science developments. *First*, the common notion that modern social science was basically constituted in the decades around the turn of the century and that this was a synchronic development across Western nations needs to be heavily qualified. Intellectual developments were highly dissimilar and uneven, and in a systematic analysis it can be shown that only certain intellectual and organizational projects "survived" this period, while others, among which are the works of prominent "founding fathers", were discontinued. The modernization or maturation of the social sciences is a process which meant the abandonment of most of the more ambitious proposals for a comprehensive social science and, furthermore, the neglect or simplified reformulation of many of the epistemological problems of such a science. Needless to say, the development and appropriation of a Weberian intellectual heritage is but one particularly glaring example of such a process.

Second, this modernization was a process which had a clear spatial location. It occurred almost across the board in the United States, while intellectual developments in Europe in many cases were being truncated. Insofar as "intrascientific modernization processes" (29) can be observed, they occurred outside academia. Once one tries to trace back the roots of the post-war disciplines, as Malcolm Vout does for political science in England, and Katrin Fridjonsdottir for sociology in Sweden, major intellectual transformations become visible, and no notion of smooth development can be upheld. For this reason, it seems appropriate to describe the period between 1920 and 1960 as a long transition from a classical to a modern conception of social science in Europe.

The intellectual transition is closely related to the political crises of the two world wars and the interwar years in Europe. These crises can basically be analyzed as struggles over the transformation of liberal bourgeois societies of the nineteenth century into organized, industrialized, mass societies. European societies seemed to have acquired some unstable but still workable political formulae between 1870 and 1914, like Giolitti's transformism in Italy, Radical socialist republicanism in France, and Bismarckian authoritarianism *cum* social policy in Germany. These formulae, however, broke down with the restructurings of the political field after World War I. The interwar period witnessed the strengthening of various degrees of more radical departures from the liberal tradition, such as the "people's home" of the Swedish social democracy, social-democratically oriented "organized capitalism" *à la* Rudolf Hilferding, technocratic statism of the *X-crise* type, fascism, and national socialism (30).

Of these proposals only the "Swedish model" could be continuously developed. The other "left-wing" strategies were domestically defeated before the war. The "right-wing" strategies gained power in Germany, Italy, Austria and Vichy France but were ultimately militarily defeated in the war. All these proposals were accompanied by new discursive understandings of the relationship between state and society, often drawing on national intellectual traditions and fusing them with an analysis of the contemporary crises. But as most of the political proposals failed, no strong line of direct continuity can be drawn in European social thought from the late liberal thinking of the classical period to the social science of the 1960s.

The modernization in the latter period occurred through strong borrowing in cognitive terms from American social science, which had developed much more smoothly. Rather lacking the burdens of the sociological-philosophical traditions of the classical European discourses, reconceptualizations were made more easily in a U.S. context. The main problem of classical theorizing, the relation between society and the individual, was circumvented methodologically by emphasizing statistical, quantitative methods and objectivist natural science types reasoning (see Wagner, in this volume). In the theoretically more ambitious approaches, this latter reasoning was couched in structural functionalist, structuralist, or rationalist-individualist terms. This theoretical orientation went along well with an expansion of empirical social and economic research often devoid of any explicit theoretical interest at all. One can speak of a "Mertonian synthesis" of Parsonian theorizing and Lazarsfeldian methodology and research organization as a shorthand for mainstream sociological thinking by 1960, and similar characterizations could be developed for economics and, perhaps less pronounced, for political science. The result is a social science which is basically technocratically oriented and policy permeated, the correlate of a full-blown, modern interventionist welfare state (see e.g. Manicas, and Fridjonsdottir, in this volume).

On the Future Possibility of a Science of Society

It is probably safe to state that this conception of social science is still the dominant one in the practice of social scientists at the beginning of the 1990s. But it is by no means the only one. Especially since the 1970s new, or new-old, approaches have been proposed, often linked to the political contestations of bureaucratic policymaking of the time. Some of these proposals have again decayed, such as neo-Marxist structuralism or a variety of action research concepts. Some other approaches now have a foothold in academic institutions, which it was comparatively easy to get in years of strong university expansion, and they have continued to exert influence on the theoretical and methodological debates in the social sciences. A general concern of many of these critical approaches was, in a sense, a return to key questions of classical theorizing, namely the relation of society and individual and the understanding of the potential of human beings of knowing the social world and acting on and in it.

The dominant types of theorizing were reproached for seriously neglecting the specificity of human action. Sociological theory was largely devoid of any notion of action at all. Human beings were seen as responding via social norms to functional needs of social systems, contributing to the latter's stability independent of their will, or being caught in the grip of rigid structures determining their ways to move. Economic theory, in contrast, was built on the very notion of action, but one reduced to the rational calculations of isolated individuals following their pregiven sets of preference orderings.

Though the degrees of abstraction and generality which these theories exhibit continue to attract scholars, over the last twenty years it has increasingly been recognized that such research programmes had very little to do with the realities of societies developing and transforming themselves in the real time of history. The degree of formality and formalization, regarded as a virtue of scientificity, turned out to be a barrier to the understanding of social processes, present and past. As a reaction, a return to emphasizing the specificities of historical and cultural constellations has been proposed, and realized in many studies, as has a renewal of social theorizing overcoming the limits of the grand reductionist approaches. Parts of the economics discipline are gradually moving to institutionalist approaches, including the specifics of institutional arrangements in the analysis of exchange processes, though it would be highly exaggerated to see this as a turn away from the neoclassical core. Sociology, and political science, face new ambitious proposals for conceptually more open theorizing, including the consideration of concrete space and time. These new foci in theory and research have implied a rethinking of one other problematique, the one of realism in social science.

In line with dominant strands in the philosophy of science, most social science research was long pursued with a rather unproblematic understanding of its relation to reality generally, and its modes of data generation more specifically. The basic idea was an empiricist and behaviourist one. Relevant information would be gathered directly by experience of the world and by observation of human behaviour. In the more quantitative-mathematical currents of social science, the collected data could subsequently be treated with sophisticated techniques leading to theoretical statements. While such a form of empirical realism was not really compatible with the grand approaches to sociological and economic theory, it did not seem too openly contradictory to impede a parallel development of both. Both research and theory shared the basic optimistic assumption about one existing social world and its regularities, which in principle could be unproblematically identified and analyzed.

The return to greater openness to historical and cultural uniqueness in social science has, as a by-product, shattered this assumption. First, the reemerging variety of societies, not easy to compare along identical conceptual lines, has introduced greater scepticism about the possibility of social science to ever arrive at anything like the general lawlike statements which had so often been said to constitute the essence of scientific theorizing. The complexity of an ever-changing social world appeared to constitute an insurmountable barrier even for seemingly steadily advancing research techniques to handle. Secondly, and more fundamentally, the concept of the oneness of the social world itself lost persuasive power. The variety of possible accounts different social science approaches themselves could give of phenomena often led to the conclusion that the concept of a real world was meaningless. The social world, according to such relativist positions, would be produced in the meaningful accounts given to it by social actors, and it did not exist beyond and apart from these accounts in any sensible meaning of the word existence. This relativism emerged, for instance, from sociology of science, in a sense the very reflective core of social science, but also more generally from the constructivist and interactionist tradition of social thought. It definitely shook the very foundations on which social science rested.

These two problematiques, the one of human agency and the one of realism, are really two aspects of one problem, the former one relating to social theory, the latter to philosophy of social science. Given the present state of developments, there is, on the one side, the chance that a histori-cally and culturally sensitive, but not bound, social science is emerging which remains to be generalization-oriented in the sense not of naive empirical, but of a "critical realism" (31) looking at the one historical world in all its complexity. If the tendencies towards such an orientation, however, are not strengthened and forcefully activated, then there is, on the other side, the very real danger that the project of a social science will ultimately fall apart. Among the pieces one shall find strong strands of more or less formal or imaginative theorizing which increasingly will explicitly decouple themselves from any reference to reality. The objective will be just to add another story about the world to the already existing ones. And one shall find as the quantitatively largest piece empirical research which, all methodological sophistication notwithstanding, will implicitly adhere to a naive empirical realism and will thereby foreclose its potential to significantly advance the understanding of modern society.

In the light of the analyses in this volume, the reopening of the debates about a science of society which has occurred has to be related to major political restructurings. Thus, the concept of the state as the steering centre of society, directing towards a harmonious and well-planned future, a concept which often was equally benevolent and totalitarian, has lost much, if not all, of its legitimacy both in intellectual and in societal terms. It remains to be seen whether the result will be a fragmented society in which processes of instrumentalization and rationalization assert themselves as the unconscious and unintended result of the activities of individuals even in the absence of a strong state apparatus, or whether a full concept of intentional human action will be reappropriated in the practices of knowledgeable human beings. The future possibility of a science of society will depend crucially on these social transformations. It will not be a mere reflection of them though. The future of social science – and of society – will not be determined by abstract formulae, nor by sheer contemplation. It will take shape, even if in a vulnerable and fragile form, in the actions and strivings of women and men, living in a world which is real and a society which is socially constructed but not just of talk.

Notes

1. A related position has been strongly argued for by Richard Whitley in debate with proponents of ethnomethodological and interactionist approaches in science studies, "From the Sociology of Scientific Communities to the Study of Scientists' Negotiations and Beyond", in: *Social Science Information*, **22**, No. 4/5, 1983, pp. 681–720. He has also tried to develop this viewpoint in analyses of social science fields such as economics, "The Structure and Context of Economics as a Scientific Field", in: *Research in the History of Economic Thought and Methodology*, **4**, 1986, and management studies, "The Development of Management Studies as a Fragmented Adhocracy", in: *Social Science Information*, **23**, 1984, pp. 775–818.
2. A strong emphasis on institutional distinctiveness and its relation to sociocultural

differences has been laid by Pierre Bourdieu. For his analyses of institutions of science and higher education see *Homo academicus*, Paris, Minuit, 1984 and *La noblesse d'Etat*, Paris, Minuit, 1989.

3. We have tried to develop this argument at some length in chapter one of this volume.

4. Rolf Torstendahl, "Transformation of Professional Education in the 19th Century", in: Sheldon Rothblatt and Björn Wittrock, eds., *The Three Missions: Universities in the Western World*, Cambridge, Cambridge University Press, 1990; see also Friedrich Paulsen, *Die deutschen Universitäten und das Universitätsstudium*, Berlin, Asher, 1902; Abraham Flexner, *Universities: American, English, German*, New York, Oxford University Press, 1930; McClelland, *State, Society, and University in Germany, 1700–1914*, Cambridge, Cambridge University Press, 1980.

5. For an analysis of state and society in terms of monitoring and surveillance see Anthony Giddens, *The Nation-State and Violence*, Cambridge, Polity Press, 1985, in particular pp. 172–192; Giddens draws, among others, on the works of Michel Foucault.

6. See Björn Wittrock, Peter Wagner, and Hellmut Wollmann, "Social Science and the Modern State", in: Peter Wagner, Carol H. Weiss, Björn Wittrock, and Hellmut Wollmann, eds., *Social Sciences and Modern States*, Cambridge, Cambridge University Press, 1991; Björn Wittrock and Peter Wagner, "Social Sciences and State Developments", Stephen Brooks and Alain G. Gagnon, eds., *Social Scientists, Policy, and the State*, New York, Praeger, 1990; and Peter Wagner, *Sozialwissenschaften und Staat*, Frankfurt/M., Campus, 1990.

7. See for recent analyses of these developments Libby Schweber, "Social Policymaking and the Institutionalization of Social Science in Britain and the United States, 1880–1920"; Dietrich Rueschemeyer and Ronan van Rossem, "State Structures, Social Knowledge, and Early Modern Social Policy in Britain and Germany" both in: Dietrich Rueschemeyer and Theda Skocpol, eds., *Social Knowledge and the Origins of Modern Social Policies*, in preparation; Martin Bulmer, "Mobilising Social Knowledge for Social Welfare: Intermediary Institutions in the Political Systems of the United States and Great Britain, 1900–1940", conference paper, New York, May 1989.

8. See Schiera in this volume, and Pierangelo Schiera, *Il laboratorio borhgese. Scienza e politica nella Germania dell'Ottocento*, Bologno, Il Mulino, 1987; as well as Wagner, *op. cit.*, for a comparative, continental European perspective.

9. The notion of "Mandarins" stems from Fritz K. Ringer, *The Decline of the German Mandarins*, Boston, Harvard University Press, 1969, in the meantime widely debated and criticized, e.g., by Schiera, *op. cit.*, and Sven-Eric Liedman, "Institutions and Ideas: Mandarins and Non-Mandarins in the German Academic Intelligentsia", in: *Comparative Studies of Society and History*, **28**, No. 1, 1968, pp. 119–168; the notion of extra-academic discourse context is proposed by Carsten Klingemann, "Heimatsoziologie oder Ordnungsinstrument? Fachgeschichtliche Aspekte der Soziologie in Deutschland zwischen 1933 und 1945", in: *Kölner Zeitschrift für Soziologie und Sozialpsychologie*, Sonderheft **23**, 1981; see also Helmuth Schuster, *Industrie und Sozialwissenschaften*, Opladen, Westdeutscher Verlag, 1987.

10. George Weisz, "L'idéologie républicaine et les sciences sociales", in: *Revue Française de Sociologie*, **20**, No. 1, 1979, pp. 83–112.
11. The notions of "halfway failure" and "success strategy" stem from Victor Karady's analyses, "Durkheim, les sciences sociales et l'Université: bilan d'un semi-échec", in: *Revue Française de Sociologie*, **17**, No. 2, 1976: 267–311, and "Stratégies de réussite et modes de faire-valoir de la sociologie chez les Durkheimiens", in: *Revue Française de Sociologie*, **20**, 1979, pp. 49–82; a contemporary evaluation of interwar sociology in France is Raymond Aron, "La sociologie", in: Raymond Aron et al., *Les sciences sociales en France. Enseignement et recherche*, Paris, Hartmann, 1938.
12. On Worms and Tarde see Robert L. Geiger, "Die Institutionalisierung soziologischer Paradigmen", in: Wolf Lepenies, ed., *Geschichte der Soziologie*, Frankfurt/M. Suhrkamp, 1981. We shall return to the case of Boutmy in the next section, below.
13. Georg Lukàcs, *Die Zerstörung der Vernunft*, Berlin, Aufbau, 1954; on interwar sociology in Germany see Dirk Käsler, *Die frühe deutsche Soziologie und ihre Entstehungs-Milieus 1909 bis 1934*, Opladen, Westdeutscher Verlag, 1984; and Erhard Stölting, "Kontinuitäten und Brüche in der deutschen Soziologie 1933/34", in: *Soziale Welt*, **35**, No. 1/2, 1984; for France see Johan Heilbron, "Les métamorphoses du durkheimisme, 1920–1940: in: *Revue Française de Sociologie*, **36**, No. 2, 1985; for Italy Robert Michels, "The Status of Sociology in Italy", in: *Social Forces*, **9**, October 1930.
14. Pierre Favre, "Les Sciences de l'Etat entre déterminisme et libéralisme", in: *Revue Française de Sociologie*, **22**, No. 3, 1981, pp. 461–2. The inside quotations are from a text Boutmy wrote in 1876.
15. Its very specific roots in French political and intellectual history are sketched by Heilbron, in this volume.
16. The common plural use of the term "political sciences" is indicative of an understanding of this field as uniting several perspectives rather than developing cognitive coherence.
17. See, for instance, Oskar Negt, *Die Konstituierung der Soziologie als Ordnungswissenschaft*, Frankfurt/M., EVA, 1974; Robert A. Nisbet, *The Sociological Tradition*, London, Heinemann, 1966.
18. Even the professional orientation was rather unsuccessful in Central Europe. Given the grounding of these states in legal discourse, legal training prevailed as a preparation for public administration, and even a legal theory of the state was elaborated which fulfilled the requirements of formalization and coherence much better than the, often either historicizing or flatly empirical, contributions of the political sciences. See below.
19. See the status accorded to it in S. Collini et al. *That Noble Science of Politics*, Cambridge, Cambridge University Press, 1983.
20. See Roger Geiger, "La sociologie dans les écoles normales primaires", in: *Revue Française de Sociologie*, **20**, No. 1, 1979, pp. 257–267, as well as Johan Heilbron, "Les métamorphoses du durkheimisme, 1920–1940", in: *Revue Française de Sociologie*, **36**, No. 2, 1985, and in this volume.
21. See Arthur J. Vidich and Stanford M. Lyman, *American Sociology. Worldly Rejections of Religion and Their Directions*, New Haven and London, Yale

University Press, 1985, for the U.S.; Carl Heinrich Becker, *Gedanken zur Hochschulreform*, Leipzig, 1919, for Germany; see Reba N. Soffer, *Ethics and Society in England. The Revolution in the Social Sciences 1870–1914*, Berkeley, University of California Press, 1978, for England; and for Italy, Giorgio Sola, "Sviluppi e scenari della sociologia italiana, 1861–1890", in: Giorgio Sola and Filippo Barbano, *Sociologia e scienze sociali in Italia, 1861–1890*, Milan, Angeli, 1985.

22. We shall return to an analysis of the more recent developments below.
23. A good example would be French sociology, the Durkheimian heritage of which continues to be visible in, e.g., Pierre Bourdieu's work (cf. Peter Wagner, "The Theoretical Import of Practical Sense", in: Björn Wittrock, ed., *Social Theory and Human Agency*, London, Sage, 1991). For a discussion of the antecedents to Durkheim see Heilbron, in this volume.
24. Stuart H. Hughes, *Consciousness and Society. The Reorientation in European Social Thought, 1890–1920*, New York, Vintage, 1958, p. 13f.
25. Charles S. Maier, *Recasting Bourgeois Europe. Stabilisation in France, Germany and Italy in the Decade after World War One*, Princeton, Princeton University Press, 1975, p. 5.
26. Douglas Ashford, *Policy and Politics in France*, Philadelphia, Temple University Press, 1982, p. 13.
27. Peter Wagner, "Social Science and the State in Continental Western Europe", in: *International Social Science Journal*, **36**, No. 4, 1989 pp. 509–29; *Sozialwissenschaften und Staat*, Frankfurt, Campus, 1990.
28. Obviously, neoclassical discourse in economics has an enormous power of institutional reproduction and even legal positivism experiences renewed interest (see Werner Heun, "Der staatsrechtliche Positivismus in der Weimarer Republik", in: *Der Staat*, **28**, No. 3, 1989, pp. 377–403). Furthermore, there are types of systemic and functional social theorizing, in which elements of these discourses reappear. Niklas Luhmann's theory of separate social subsystems, each working along their own formal codes, is essentially a formalized – and much elaborated – theoretical system with obvious parallels to various versions of such late nineteenth century ideology of the liberal capitalist state.
29. Carsten Klingemann, "Heimatsoziologie oder Ordnungsinstrument? Fachgeschichtliche Aspekte der Soziologie in Deutschland zwischen 1933 und 1945", in: *Kölner Zeitschrift für Soziologie und Sozialpsychologie*, Sonderheft **21**, 1979, pp. 343–357.
30. Valerio Castronovo, "Cultura e sviluppo industriale", in: *Storia d'Italia, Annali 4: Intellettuali e potere*, Turin, Einaudi, 1981, pp. 1259–1296; Björn Wittrock and Peter Wagner, "Policy Constitution through Discourse", in: Douglas E. Ashford, ed., *Comparing Public Policies* (in preparation).
31. Roy Bhaskar, *Reclaiming Reality*, London, Verso, 1989; Björn Wittrock, ed., *Social Theory and Human Agency*, London, Sage, 1991.

ABOUT THE CONTRIBUTORS

Alain Desrosières is a statistician who is a member of the research department at the *Institut national de la statistique et des études économiques* in Paris, the statistical office of the French government. He is also a member of the *Groupe de sociologie politique et morale* of the *Ecole des hautes études en sciences sociales* in Paris. He has worked on the history and social construction of social classifications. In this field he has published numerous articles and the book *Les catégories socioprofessionnelles* (with Laurent Thévenot, 1988).

Katrin Fridjonsdottir is a sociologist at the University of Lund and at the Swedish Collegium for Advanced Study in the Social Sciences in Uppsala. She has done extensive research on the organisation of the sciences and on the development of the social science disciplines. Her publications include *Vetenskap och politik* (1983), *Om Svensk sociologi* (editor, 1987), and *Svenska samhällsvetenskaper* (editor, 1990).

Gabriella Gioli is associate professor of the history of economic thought at the department of economics at the University of Pisa. She has worked on the history of economic thought in the eighteenth and nineteenth centuries; her publications in this field include *Il pensiero economico di Antonio Scialoja* (1989) and *Le cattedre di economia politica in Italia. La diffusione di une disciplina 'sospetta' (1750–1900)* (co-editor, 1988).

John G. Gunnell is professor of political science in the Graduate School of Public Affairs at the State University of New York at Albany. He specializes in the history of political theory and the philosophy and history of the social sciences. Currently he is working on an intellectual history of academic political theory in the United States. His publications include *Between Philosophy and Politics: The Alienation of Political Theory* (1986); *Political Theory: Tradition and Interpretation* (1987); *Political Philosophy and Time; Plato and the Origins of Political Vision* (1987).

P. Wagner, B. Wittrock, and R. Whitley (eds.), Discourses on Society: Volume XV, 1990, 359–361.

Johan Heilbron is a sociologist from Amsterdam who has worked in Paris, Berlin, and Uppsala. At present he is affiliated with the Erasmus University in Rotterdam. His research interests are mainly in the sociology of knowledge and culture. His publications include *Sociologie in Frankrijk* (1983); recently he completed a book on the making of sociology (1750–1850).

Peter T. Manicas is professor of philosophy and social science at Queens College, City University of New York, and at the University of Hawaii at Manoa. His research focuses on the theory and history of democracy and the state and on the philosophy and history of the social sciences. His publications include *The Death of the State* (1974), *A History and Philosophy of the Social Sciences* (1987), and *War and Democracy* (1989).

Helga Nowotny is professor of sociology in the newly founded Institute for Theory and Social Studies of Science at the University of Vienna and is its Director. She has held teaching and research positions at King's College, Cambridge, the University of Bielefeld, the *Maison des Sciences de l'Homme*, Paris, the *Wissenschaftskolleg zu Berlin*, and the *Wissenschaftszentrum Berlin*. Her main research interests and publications are in the field of social studies of science and technology, and in general sociology. Her recent publications include *Eigenzeit* (1988) and *Selforganisation – Portrait of a Scientific Revolution* (co-editor, 1990).

Pierangelo Schiera is professor of the history of political thought at the University of Trento, where he is also affiliated with the *Istituto storico italo-germanico*. As a historian his studies and publications range from an initial interest in the modern state (*Lo stato moderno*, 1972) to more recent work on science as a constitutive factor of politics (*Il laboratorio borghese*, 1987). Currently he is analyzing the binominal notion melancholy-discipline in view of the formation of modernity.

Keith Tribe is senior lecturer in economics at the University of Keele. His principal research interests are in the history of economic discourse and the histories of culture and technology. Currently he is engaged in a major research project on the history of commercial and economic education in Britain. Previous work includes a study of early German economics *(Governing Economy, The Reformation of German Economic Discourse,*

1750–1840, 1988); of Russian rural economic policy (*Marxism and the Agrarian Question*, with Athar Hussain, 1981), and of classical political economy (*Land, Labour and Economic Discourse*, 1978; *Genealogies of Capitalism*, 1981).

Malcolm Vout is senior lecturer in philosophy and history of the social sciences and head of the science, technology and culture research group at Nottingham Polytechnic, England. Present research is centered on the history of the social sciences, studying changes in political and management science education in England during the 20th century. Research interest in the past has focused on issues in social theory, particularly the work of the Frankfurt School and continental philosophy.

Peter Wagner, a political scientist, is research fellow at the *Wissenschaftszentrum Berlin für Sozialforschung*. His main research interest is in the long-term development of modern societies, focusing on the interrelations of societal discourses, technologies, economic organization, and political institutions. His publications include *Sozialwissenschaften und Staat, Frankreich, Italien und Deutschland 1870–1980* (1990), and *Social Sciences and Modern States* (co-editor, 1991).

Björn Wittrock is professor of political science at the University of Stockholm and director of the Swedish Collegium for Advanced Study in the Social Sciences in Uppsala. His main research interests are in social and political theory, the study of transformations of social knowledge, universities, and political institutions in historical and comparative perspective. His recent publications include *The University Research System* (co-editor, 1985), *Social Sciences and Modern States* (co-editor, 1991), *Social Theory and Human Agency* (1991), and *The Three Missions: Universities in the Western World* (co-editor, 1991).

NAME INDEX

MacKenzie, D. 203, 214
Mackenzie, W.J.M. 10, 164–7, 171,
    175–9, 183–7, 189–91
Madison, James 154–6
Maier, Charles S. 343, 357
Maier, Hans 19, 90, 238
Maine 176
Maitland 174, 176–7
Majone, Giandomenico 20, 40
Maloney, J. 299
Malthus, Thomas R. 29, 275–6, 280,
    297
Manca, A.G. 117
Mandeville 81
Mangoni, L. 119
Manicas, Peter T. 4–5, 7–8, 18, 22, 46,
    50–1, 66, 68, 116, 143, 236, 238,
    335, 347–8, 351, 360
Mann, Thomas 101
March, Lucien 204
Marcuse, Herbert 263
Marshall, T.H. 14, 59, 170, 273, 291–3,
    295, 301, 346
Martin, H.J. 91–2
Marwick, A. 190
Marx, Karl 96, 139, 176–7, 207, 238,
    251, 262
Matteucci, Carlo 311, 322
Matteucci, N. 118–19
Maud, John 171, 190
Mauss 210
Maxwell, James Clerk 68
Mayer, Otto 99
Mazzacane, Aldo 119, 327
Mazzola, U. 319–20, 323
Mead, G.H. 63, 252
Medawar, P. 178, 190
Menger, Carl 14, 62, 227–8, 235, 346
Meredith, H.O. 295
Merriam, Charles E. 63, 150–1, 153,
    157, 161, 186, 191
Merton, Robert K. 13, 186, 257
Messedaglia, Angelo 109, 308–9, 314
Metternich 131
Metzger, Walter P. 158
Miceli, Vincenzo 105, 221
Michels, Robert 223, 356

Mill, J.S. 49, 60, 172, 274, 280, 298,
    318
Millerand, President 205
Mills, C. Wright 47, 67
Minghetti, Marco 111–12
Miquel 118
Mitchell, John 55
Mitchell, Wesley C. 61–2
Mizuta, Hiroshi 324
Mock, W. 118
Mohl, Robert von 30, 222
Mommsen, Theodor 104, 144
Mommsen, W.J. 118
Montaigne, M.E. de 77
Montchrestien, Antoine de 87
Montesquieu 77, 82
Moore, George Edward 178
Moretti, Mauro 325
Morpurgo, Emilio 119
Mosca, Gaetano 106–7, 232
Moulton, R.G. 300
Mozzarelli, Cesare 20, 235, 326
Mulkay, Michael 17, 21
Mundella, A.J. 288
Munding, Max 117
Münsterberg, Hugo 49
Murphy, T.D. 201
Myrdal, Gunnar 249, 267

Napoleon 344
Negt, Oskar 356
Nespor, Stefano 20, 235, 326
Nettl, J.P. 20
Newcombe, Simon 49, 59–60, 68
Neyman 211
Nicholas, Herbert 186
Nicole 80–1
Niebuhr, Barthold Georg 131
Nietzsche, Friedrich 81, 91, 128, 144,
    147
Nipperday, T. 117
Nisbet, Robert A. 356
Nitti, Francesco Saverio 309, 320
Nordin, S. 267
Northcote 277
Nowotny, Helga 4, 40–1, 237, 240,
    334, 360

SUBJECT INDEX

375

Biblioteca dell'economia 108
Biblioteca di scienze politiche 108, 113
Birkbeck College 285
Birmingham and Midland Society of
    Chartered Accountants 291
Birmingham University 163, 290, 293
  B.Comm. degree 289, 292, 295
Board of Trade 278
Bologna University 324
Bonghi Act (1875) 112
Bonn University 138
Bordeaux University 219
Bristol University College 289
Britain,
    academic economics 273–97
    education 274–5
    industrial decline 279
    industrialization 274
    universities 273–97
    see also England, Scotland
British Association for the Promotion
    of Social Science 52
British Medical Association 186
British Social Science Association 143
Bryn Mawr University 140
bureaucracy 230, 343, 346
business schools 312–13

cadres 206–8
Cagliari University 324
California University 48, 55, 139
Cambridge University 10–11, 14
    Commission of Inquiry (1852) 279
    economics teaching 289, 292–6
    Economics Tripos 291–4
    extension teaching 283, 284, 288,
      299
    King's College 297, 360
    modernization 279
    Moral Sciences Tripos 292, 293, 301
    political science 163, 166, 169,
      172–4, 178, 179
    reforms 279
Cameralism 87
capitalism 23, 35, 52, 56, 143, 238, 263
Caractères (La Bruyère) 80
Carnegie Endowment for International

    Peace (CEIP) 58
Casati law (1859) 307, 310–12, 325
Catania University 316, 324
causality 200–2, 204
censuses 199, 208, 211, 249, 258
Central Europe 10, 356
certainty, loss of 27–33, 38, 40
Chamber of Commerce, Birmingham
    290
Chamber of Commerce, London 287
chance risks 200
Chicago University 47, 54, 140, 186,
    188
    Graduate School 294
    sociology department 63, 64, 66
China 58
church 76, 79, 82, 83, 95
civic colleges 286–9
Civil Liberty and Self-Government
    (Lieber) 134, 137
Civil Service 99, 117, 185, 206
    division of labour 278
    examinations 277, 297
    French 78
    patronage system 277
    promotion 277
    recruitment 276–7
    reform 276–9
Civil Service Commissioners 276, 279
Clark University 47
class war 46
Club de l'Entresol 78
coding 197–200
collective bargaining 56
collectivizing process 28, 39
Collège de France 76, 138, 145
Columbia University 48, 55, 58, 65, 66,
    68
    political science studies 129, 134,
      135, 138, 142–5, 186, 339
    School of Arts 145
    School of Law 145
    School of Political Science 145–7,
      151
commissioned studies 255
communism 134, 136, 137, 238
competition 62, 323

Knox College 144

Labor Movement (Ely) 61
labor unions *see* trade unions
laissez-faire 87, 88, 307, 314, 319
Language, Truth and Logic (Ayer) 180
Lausanne University 219
law 78, 110, 176
  teaching of 276
L'Economista 314
Leeds University 163, 179
legal positivism 235, 236, 346
legal reform 99
Leicester 283
Leicester University 163, 179
Leipzig University 138, 144
liberalism 179, 220, 229, 343
L'Industria 318
linguistic analysis 173, 174, 178, 183
linguistic philosophy 184
Liverpool University 163, 179, 180,
  181, 293
  extension teaching 289, 300
Liverpool University College 286, 287,
  289
local government 276
logic 83
Lombardian-Venetian School 314, 316
London School of Economics (LSE)
  166, 179, 181, 185, 187, 188,
  191
  commercial education 289–91
  foundation 279, 285, 289
London Society 284
London University 163, 179, 185, 280
  B.Sc. (Econ.) degree 290, 292
  extension teaching 284, 287, 289,
  299
Lund University 250, 253, 259, 267,
  269, 359

Macerata University 324
McGill University 293
management strategies 31
Manchester Liberalism 35
Manchester Mechanics' Institute 283
Manchester School 183

Manchester University 163–5, 179,
  183–9, 301
  Department of Government 187
  economics teaching 293–5
  Faculty of Commerce 294, 295
  Honours School of Economics and
    Political Science 294
Manchester Working Men's College
  282–3
'Mandarins' 335, 355
Manual of Political Ethics (Lieber) 133
marginalism 62, 235, 273, 319, 320,
  327, 346
'Marginal Revolution' 273
market economy 27, 33, 347
Marshall Prize 293, 301
Marxism 262–5
Marxist theory 34, 35, 37
Mason College, Birmingham 286, 289
Maximes (La Rochefoucauld) 80
measurement errors 202
Mechanics' Institutions 281–3, 285–6,
  299
medicine 30, 35, 200–2
mercantilism 306
Messina University 316, 324
metaphysics 251
Michigan University 54, 61, 138, 140
middle classes 38
  in America 46
  in Britain 281, 282, 284, 285
  in Italy 306, 322, 326
Milan, Congress of (1875) 314
Milan University 324
Modena University 324
moralistes 80–2, 86
moral philosophy 138, 170, 250
'Moral and Physical Condition of the
  Working Classes' (Kay) 37
moral sciences 83–6, 88
moral statistics 202
moral theory 79–82
Morrill Act (1862) 47
Munich University 223

Naples, Kingdom of 305
Naples University 305, 324

South Carolina College 133
sovereignty 128, 148
Sozialpolitik 99–100
Stanford University 47, 64, 140
state 123–43
    centrality 343
    concept of 126, 131–5
    legal theory of 10, 235
    meaning of 153–7
        as metaphysical entity 150
    moral role 231
    organic theory 129
        and politics 128–30
    Teutonic theory 139
    transformation of 149–53
        and university 138–43
    work of Francis Lieber 131–5
    see also political science
statistical societies 36, 37
statistics 5, 38, 195–215, 316
    coding 197–200, 212
    history 198, 200
    mathematical techniques 214
    representativity 207–9
    use in social science 202–5
Statistics and Economics (Smith) 65
Statistics and Sociology (Smith) 65
Stockholm school 249
Stockholm University 250, 253, 259,
        267, 361
structural functionalism 257, 260, 262,
        265, 351
structuration theory 17, 18
*Studies in Political and Historical
        Science* 139
surplus value 62
survey of social trends 66
Sweden,
    provincialism 256
    sociology 5, 247–67, 350
    welfare state 12, 247–67
Swedish Association of Sociologists
        256
Syracuse University 140

technical schools 290
theology 78, 83, 85, 129

Third World groups 260
Times, The 293
trade unions 55, 56, 148, 165, 166, 185,
        206
Traîté d' économie politique
        (Montchrestien) 87
Traîté des passions (Descartes) 84
Turin University 318, 324

uncertainty 28, 35, 40
unemployment 27, 39, 208
UNESCO 181
United Mine Workers 55
United States *see* America
universities,
    American 8, 46–67, 340
    British 273–97
    civic 165, 179, 185, 188, 279
    conflicts of 1960s 260
    curriculum 142
    detachment from society 234
    educational practices 4
    English 4
    expansion 237
    extension teaching 281–96
    French 76, 223
    funds 47
    German 99, 102, 112, 140–2, 222,
        223, 225
        organization 115, 311, 344
    Italian 303–23
    medieval 325
    reforms 3–4, 236
        in Germany 96, 115
        in Italy 311, 326, 336
        in Sweden 259
    student representation 262
    student revolt 261
    see also under names of universities
University Extension Movement
        281–96
*University Teaching of the Social
        Sciences* (UNESCO) 181
Uppsala University 250–3, 255, 361
urbanization 7, 23, 25, 27, 212
    in America 46

Sociology of the Sciences

1. E. Mendelsohn, P. Weingart and R. Whitley (eds.): *The Social Production of Scientific Knowledge.* 1977   ISBN Hb 90-277-0775-8; Pb 90-277-0776-6
2. W. Krohn, E.T. Layton, Jr. and P. Weingart (eds.): *The Dynamics of Science and Technology.* Social Values, Technical Norms and Scientific Criteria in the Development of Knowledge. 1978   ISBN Hb 90-277-0880-0; Pb 90-277-0881-9
3. H. Nowotny and H. Rose (eds.): *Counter-Movements in the Sciences.* The Sociology of the Alternatives to Big Science. 1979
ISBN Hb 90-277-0971-8; Pb 90-277-0972-6
4. K.D. Knorr, R. Krohn and R. Whitley (eds.): *The Social Process of Scientific Investigation.* 1980 (1981)   ISBN Hb 90-277-1174-7; Pb 90-277-1175-5
5. E. Mendelsohn and Y. Elkana (eds.): *Sciences and Cultures.* Anthropological and Historical Studies of the Sciences. 1981
ISBN Hb 90-277-1234-4; Pb 90-277-1235-2
6. N. Elias, H. Martins and R. Whitley (eds.): *Scientific Establishments and Hierarchies.* 1982   ISBN Hb 90-277-1322-7; Pb 90-277-1323-5
7. L. Graham, W. Lepenies and P. Weingart (eds.): *Functions and Uses of Disciplinary Histories.* 1983   ISBN Hb 90-277-1520-3; Pb 90-277-1521-1
8. E. Mendelsohn and H. Nowotny (eds.): *Nineteen Eighty Four: Science between Utopia and Dystopia.* 1984   ISBN Hb 90-277-1719-2; Pb 90-277-1721-4
9. T. Shinn and R. Whitley (eds.): *Expository Science.* Forms and Functions of Popularisation. 1985   ISBN Hb 90-277-1831-8; Pb 90-277-1832-6
10. G. Böhme and N. Stehr (eds.): *The Knowledge Society.* The Growing Impact of Scientific Knowledge on Social Relations. 1986
ISBN Hb 90-277-2305-2; Pb 90-277-2306-0
11. S. Blume, J. Bunders, L. Leydesdorff and R. Whitley (eds.): *The Social Direction of the Public Sciences.* Causes and Consequences of Co-operation between Scientists and Non-scientific Groups. 1987
ISBN Hb 90-277-2381-8; Pb 90-277-2382-6
12. E. Mendelsohn, M.R. Smith and P. Weingart (eds.): *Science, Technology and the Military.* 2 vols. 1988   ISBN Vol, 12/1 90-277-2780-5; Vol. 12/2 90-277-2783-X
13. S. Fuller, M. de Mey, T. Shinn and S. Woolgar (eds.): *The Cognitive Turn.* Sociological and Psychological Perspectives on Science. 1989
ISBN 0-7923-0306-7
14. W. Krohn, G. Küppers and H. Nowotny (eds.): *Selforganization.* Portrait of a Scientific Revolution. 1990   ISBN 0-7923-0830-1
15. P. Wagner, B. Wittrock and R. Whitley (eds.): *Discourses on Society.* The Shaping on the Social Science Disciplines. 1990   ISBN 0-7923-1001-2

KLUWER ACADEMIC PUBLISHERS – DORDRECHT / BOSTON / LONDON